THE
Old Farmer's Almanac

CALCULATED ON A NEW AND IMPROVED PLAN FOR THE YEAR OF OUR LORD

2002

BEING 2ND AFTER LEAP YEAR AND (UNTIL JULY 4) 226TH YEAR OF AMERICAN INDEPENDENCE

Fitted for Boston and the New England States, with special corrections and calculations to answer for all the United States.

Containing, besides the large number of Astronomical Calculations and the Farmer's Calendar for every month in the year, a variety of

New, Useful, and Entertaining Matter.

Established in 1792

by Robert B. Thomas

*Half our trouble's our invention
We're to blame for half our strife;
Then, if life is what we make it,
Why not make the best of life?*

–THE (OLD) FARMER'S ALMANAC, 1876

Cover T.M. registered
in U.S. Patent Office

Copyright 2001 by Yankee Publishing Incorporated
ISSN 0078-4516

Library of Congress
Card No. 56-29681

Original wood engraving by Randy Miller

Address all editorial correspondence to: THE OLD FARMER'S ALMANAC, DUBLIN, NH 03444

Contents

The Old Farmer's Almanac • 2002

(continued on page 4)

12 Great Reasons to Own a Mantis Tiller

1. Weighs just 20 pounds. Mantis is a joy to use. It starts easily, turns on a dime, lifts nimbly over plants and fences.

2. Tills like nothing else. Mantis bites down a full 10" deep, churns tough soil into crumbly loam, prepares seedbeds in no time.

3. Has patented "serpentine" tines. Our **patented** tine teeth spin at up to 240 RPM – twice as fast as others. Cuts through tough soil and vegetation like a chain saw through wood!

4. Weeds faster than hand tools. Reverse its tines and Mantis is a precision power weeder. Weeds an average garden in 20 minutes.

5. Digs planting furrows. With the optional Planter/Furrower, Mantis digs deep or shallow furrows for planting. Builds raised beds, too!

6. Cuts neat borders. Use the optional Border Edger to cut crisp edges for flower beds, walkways, around shrubs and trees.

7. Dethatches your lawn. Thatch on your lawn prevents water and nutrients from reaching the roots. The optional Dethatcher quickly removes thatch.

8. Aerates your lawn, too. For a lush, healthy carpet, the optional Aerator slices thousands of tine slits in your lawn's surface.

9. Trims bushes and hedges! Only Mantis has an optional 24" or 30" trimmer bar to prune and trim your shrubbery and small trees.

10. The Mantis Promise. Try any product that you buy directly from Mantis with **NO RISK!** If you're not completely satisfied, send it back to us within one year for a complete, no hassle refund.

11. Warranties. The entire tiller is warranted for two full years. The tines are guaranteed forever against breakage.

12. Fun to use. The Mantis Tiller/Cultivator is so much fun to use gardeners everywhere love their Mantis tillers.

For FREE details, call
TOLL FREE 1-800-366-6268

Contents

Charts, Tables, and Miscellany

Astronomical Data

CONSUMER
Tastes and Trends

Forecasts, fads, fashions, and facts • compiled by Jamie Kageleiry

A Passion for Fashion

"The American love affair with super-casual clothes is in a waning cycle. Casual Friday has been done to death, and people are hungering for something fresh. We should watch for a move toward more 'put-together' looks. That could mean going sporty, like 'preppy chic,' or more ladylike, with "50s femininity.' Also, be prepared for a return of 'The Big '80s.'"

–Aimee Marchand, fashion designer, Liz Claiborne

As the economy slows, watch for over-the-top excess to diminish. **Elegance is understated:** Put away the gold lamé, the gold-look accents (eyewear, buckles, and buttons), and the sky-high stiletto-heeled shoes.

The new **luxe look is tastefully refined.** Designers are putting pizzazz into traditional tweeds by weaving in **metallic threads.** Suede, leather, fur, and **cashmere** are in vogue this fall, though pared down.

"Fabrics for fall," reports textile trendwatcher *Bobbin Magazine,* "will be soft and colorful, with an emphasis on **natural fibers,** often treated or blended with synthetic fibers for high performance. It also will be a season of **contrasts,** playing fluid with stiff, shiny with matte, and chic with worn." Expect **more black and brown** (and camel) in the palette.

Almost **anything goes in hemlines,** from flowing maxi-floor-lengths to micro-minis up to *there*. **Avoid the midi skirt** that stops midshin; it's not even a maybe. **Mini shifts** are back, and so are shirtdresses. Also, **belts are big** again.

MAINSTREAM THEMES

■ Preppy, **country-club coordinates** will carry any day: Simply tailored **tweed riding jackets** (with an infusion of color in the tweed), fitted pants, **white cotton shirts,** and far fewer accessories work well together.

Military-inspired clothing is acceptable for men and women. Look for leather **lace-up boots, trench coats,** Eisenhower jackets, or

E.T.O. (European theater of operations) jackets made for American forces in World War II.

Disco is back, with Edwardian touches: **puffy sleeves, satiny fabrics,** blouses with **ties,** and snug-fitting, low-slung pants.

Homeward Re-Bound

"Pure techno is on its way down. The comfortable, cozy, and reassuring seem so much more interesting and appealing. Retro and vintage design themes permeate the culture: soft, used, matte, aged, worn, bleached. Watch for softly muted colors and soft fabrics, simple cotton checks, chambray, and denim—a return to naïve and charming patterns, reminiscent of our childhood."

–Ellen Sideri, CEO and founder of forecasting firm ESP, Inc.

IN
- Bell-bottom jeans
- Flower appliqués
- Plain-gray sweatshirts
- Sleek ponytails, or bobbed, cropped, and angled haircuts

OUT
- Tapered pants, including Capris
- Anything with butterflies
- Bat-wing sleeves
- Cascading curls

–SuperStock

There's no place like home; change is everywhere: We're renovating instead of "buying up," **trending toward casual** but not too quaint.

Sprawl is yielding to small. "New urbanist" is the buzzword for well-appointed, energy-efficient **cozy homes on landscaped lots** that are convenient to city services.

We're also crazy for **kit house** real estate, mail-order homes made by Sears & Roebuck and others from about 1908 to 1940. These were shipped as precut, marked pieces to be built on-site.

Driving many design decisions is our aging population.

–H. Armstrong Roberts

continued

Expect to see **wide hallways,** countertops at varying heights, **and knee spaces** beneath work areas.

Global influences abound. Look for **combos of cultural styles,** notably **Southeast Asian, Indonesian, and African. Feng Shui** guidelines dictate some floor plans and decorating schemes. **Water features,** such as fountains, are flowing indoors.

Colors are warming up. **Blue is fading** (unless it's aqua), while hues from the lilac/plum family and the spicier orange spectrum are gaining ground. (Just say no to Day-Glo.) **Think beach tones:** turquoise, pink, and salmon.

Fireplaces and wood-burning stoves are more popular than ever but not only for aesthetics; they're our backup heat sources.

GOT-TO-HAVE-IT GADGETS, FURNISHINGS, AND ACCESSORIES

■ Shake up your wake-up call with **alarm clocks that do everything but buzz.** Among the audio options are music with prayers, stand-up comedy routines, Zen gongs, crashing ocean waves, and barking dogs.

Interest in candles shows no signs of tapering off: Sales in North America could top $3 billion by 2003.

The original cleaning machine—the broom—has undergone sweeping changes. Along with brushes, dust cloths, buckets, and mops, brooms are showing up in iMac-inspired colors like blueberry, grape, tangerine, kiwi green, and cherry red.

Kids who used to play school can now pretend to be CEOs. A California manufacturer has a line of ergonomically correct and brightly colored **chairs and desks for kids who have nowhere to go but up.**

In the Garden

"Many homeowners are minimizing their lawn areas, opting instead for beds of ground cover, perennial gardens, shrub borders, or wildflower 'meadows,' which significantly slow water runoff and improve drainage."

–Alysse Einbender, landscape designer in Philadelphia

Save water! Homeowners want to **keep rain and sprinkler system water** on their property. So they are **diverting it to cisterns, water gardens, and**

WELLQUEST presents...

Vanish Unsightly Veins *Naturally!*

Stop hiding your legs and being embarrassed by unsightly spider veins. Veinish® Swedish Vein Lotion is a patented all-natural herbal formula that deeply penetrates the skin to unclog veins, to help eliminate unattractive spider veins – **even bright red ones.** Developed by a Swedish Pharmacist, Veinish® is made of an exclusive blend of herbal compounds, natural and botanical ingredients to work on spider veins. Clinical studies boast a 90% proven success rate. Safe, natural and with fast results- Veinish® virtually eliminates those spider veins in just a few weeks! 30 day money back guarantee or send back for a full product refund. *Call now and ask how to get a 30 day supply of Veinish® absolutely free!*

To order, call toll-free:

1-888-886-4478. 24 hours a day, 7 days a week

Testimonials from our many satisfied customers:
- *"It's easy to use and the spider veins disappeared in just weeks!"*   *--Suzan R.*
- *"I've had Spider Veins for years. In 2 weeks, they were lighter and after a month they were gone. Thank you Veinish!"*   *--Carol B.*
- *"I was embarrassed to wear golf shorts. After just 2 weeks of Veinish, I could see the difference and in 30 days, they were gone. No problem with shorts now."*   *--Rachel W.*
- *"I feel better about wearing shorts in the summer!"*   *--Carol K.*

Beauty & Image Essentials

Safely Fade Unsightly Stretch Marks

Developed by a noted cosmetic dermatologist, Stretch Away is a patented formula that reduces the appearance of stretch marks – even bright red ones – and restores your skin to a more natural texture. **Clinical studies** document that 100% of those considered fully compliant believed the test material was effective in reducing their stretch mark condition. Safe and effective on stomach, thighs, buttocks and more. Simply apply daily and within weeks, you will have noticeable results. 30 day money back guarantee or send back for a full product refund. *Call now and ask how to get a 30 day supply of Stretch Away absolutely free!*

To order call toll-free:

1-888-595-2156.

24 hours a day, 7 days a week

Hailed as a Best Beauty Breakthrough in a Women's Publication

©WELLQUEST INTERNATIONAL, INC.

Snore Free Nights *The Very First Night* Guaranteed!

Tired of those sleepless nights due to snoring? D-Snore is a quick, safe and proven approach to snoring and getting a great night's sleep. This amazing fast-acting, all natural formula instantly moistens the soft palate to allow free and easy breathing that lasts. Doctor approved and recommended, **clinical studies** state that "84% of the subjects showed a significant improvement while using D-Snore." Forget surgery, special pillows or all the other contraptions, D-Snore is the safe and affordable solution you've been looking for. Fast and effective, D-Snore actually works the very first night. 30 day money back guarantee or send back for a full product refund. Join the over **500,000** customers! *Call now and ask how to get a 30 day supply of D-Snore™ absolutely free!*

To order call toll-free: ## 1-888-462-8211.

24 hours a day, 7 days a week

"We put D-Snore to the test..."
"We got flooded with calls with volunteers..."
"If you have a snoring problem...give D-Snore a try"
"It works!"
--KATV-7 ABC News, Little Rock, Arkansas

WHAT'S GROWING?

■ Fruits and vegetables are out, ornamentals are in, and lurid tropical ornamentals are on top—except with native-plant enthusiasts.

Urban Canadians are growing up—creating rooftop gardens, abundant with herbs, fruits, and vegetables or with moss or hardy grasses, that offer insulation or simply a retreat from the street.

–H. Armstrong Roberts

swales (low-lying areas). "Swales can be attractively planted with wet-site-tolerant plants," says Einbender. When a swale is properly graded with **boulders and river rocks to look like a streambed,** she says, it "can direct and accommodate all the rainwater on an average home lot."

Another trend: **cutting out grass.** Lawns, she explains, are "only slightly more porous than surfaces like patios, roofs, and paved driveways or walks, and require fertilizers, polluting lawn mowers, and the like." The pollution solution? Gardens.

BUDDING INTERESTS

■ Parents are creating **garden plots with plants that are easy for their kids to maintain.** These aren't Popsicle-stick patches; some have water features. For some adults, it's as much about fashion as farming: Their kids don the latest in **gardening garb** and tote **miniature tools.** Children who want to watch their gardens grow can relax in **little lawn furniture.**

Alien Invasions

–University of California

BUG BITES

■ The latest green-space invaders are the glassy-winged sharpshooter (left) and the blue-green sharpshooter, **sap-sucking creatures that hop from leaf to leaf** around (for now) California's grape crop. They carry bacteria that cause Pierce's disease, which could wreak havoc on northern California's vineyards. A widespread spraying program may be conducted.

FIRE-ANT ALARM

■ After years of trying to get rid of those **nasty, sometimes-fatal fire ants,** scientists think they have a solution imported

–H. Armstrong Roberts

from Argentina. The pinhead-size phorid fly, also known as the **decapitating fly, injects an egg into the ant and takes off.** The egg hatches into a maggot, which slithers into the ant's head and feeds on juices there. The rest—well, you can imagine. These flies are slowly infiltrating fire-ant strongholds in seven southern states without any apparent danger to the rest of the ecosystem.

On the Farm

"There is more interest among smaller-scale farmers in raising organic crops and livestock . . . but farmer interest in raising genetically modified crops has not diminished significantly. A few are signing contracts to raise crops that are not genetically modified, specifically for the food industry. The corn and soybeans that are genetically modified continue to be used for feeding livestock."

–Dan Looker, business editor, *Successful Farming* magazine

IT TAKES A TOUGH PERSON TO BE A TENDER FARMER
■ Despite advances, farming is still considered one of the nation's most dangerous professions, according to the National Safety Council, ranking second behind mining.

Watch for an increase in "**industrial organics,**" reports Leslie Land in a *New York Times* column. "Now that there is serious money to be made," she writes, "**big players** like Dole **are buying up respected organic brands** (as well as a lot of untainted land in Latin America)." This trend is nascent, but it's clear that the production of **organic crops will not save small farms.**

Farmers are becoming less independent, Looker reports, with more and more entering into "contract production," or **franchise farming,** delivering their crops or livestock to one company for a negotiated price, or raising company-owned livestock.

Farms are getting bigger. Most in the Midwest are between 500 and 1,500 acres; some are in the 15,000- to 20,000-acre range. Farmers usually don't own all that land; they rent it from several landlords, usually retired farmers and heirs of deceased farmers.

21st-CENTURY STATE FAIRS
■ A century ago, farmers relied on state fairs to learn

about the latest crop-production techniques, machinery, seed varieties, and breeding stock. These days, many farmers are products of top agricultural schools. So **fairs have shifted their focus to youth farming** and are showcases for 4-H kids, whose **pet interests are in horses and small animals**—rabbits, sheep, and poultry.

Attendance at state and county fairs rivals that of amusement parks: about 160 million people a year. Observers say that urban **Americans want to reconnect with their rural roots** and see where their food comes from.

Livestock shows and cooking contests are perennial crowd-pleasers, but today most fairs have **technology centers** that display uses of the Internet and technology in agribusiness.

STAR SEARCH

■ **2002 marks the 200th anniversary of the publication of** *New American Practical Navigator*, **by Nathaniel Bowditch. With it, he saved countless lives and a wealth of cargo: His book of trigonometric tables (and a sextant) enabled seamen to accurately chart their course across the oceans —and it's still in use. For a story on Bowditch and modern global positioning systems, click on Article Links 2002 at www.almanac.com.**

Sky News & Views

"Decades ago, an amateur astronomer heading out to observe would take along sky charts and perhaps a guidebook of celestial targets. The advent of the personal computer offered a change to the preparation and procedures for a night out under the stars. Astronomy software on laptop computers could serve as both your charts and handbook. . . . Furthermore, computers could steer your telescope, easing the effort to locate faint galaxies and nebulae.

Now . . . you can display the sky from anywhere in the world at any date and time for thousands of years."

–Stuart Goldman, associate editor, *Sky & Telescope* magazine

FOLLOWING YONDER STAR

■ In autumn 2000, a blurry, milky orb was spotted and named C/2000 WM$_1$. It is better known as **Comet LINEAR**, for the Lincoln Laboratory Near-Earth Asteroid Research

–Stattmayer/Bavaria/H. Armstrong Roberts

program. Comet LINEAR glows feebly, about 20,000 times fainter than the dimmest stars visible without optical aid. But there's a good chance that **by the end of 2001, it will be visible to stargazers with binoculars.** "It could be a decent binocular target in the evening sky for mid-northern observers in late November," reports *Sky & Telescope* magazine, "and an even better sight for southern skygazers a few weeks later."

Keepers & Collectibles

Some say that the Internet has made regional or local collecting quaint, almost obsolete, because we can buy or sell anything electronically in an instant. But our scouts tell us that these items are increasing in interest and value:

DENIM
■ Hang on to your pants! **Vintage denim is hot.** A pair of Levis from 1927 recently sold for $41,000, and a prewar Lee cowboy jacket fetched $5,800.

GOLF GEAR: ABOVE PAR
■ Golf is a perennially popular pastime, and so is collecting **anything golf-related,** from old clubs and tees to scorecards and autographed photos.

MILITARY MEMORABILIA
■ Stash your parents' dog tags and **vintage military uniforms.** Interest surged following the release of the film *Saving Private Ryan* and continues with *Pearl Harbor*.

TWO-BIT TREASURES
■ Before you toss your loose change into a jar, fish out the **U.S. state quarters.** They may be worth more than 25 cents . . . someday.

−Camerique/H. Armstrong Roberts

continued

ON THE ROAD: A HOME AWAY, COMPLETE
■ Getting there can still be half the fun if you travel by trailer (aka RV, or recreational vehicle), thanks to Airstream,

which has created a supersleek modern edition of its timeless Bambi silver travel capsule.

Status Symbols

Want to inspire envy or admiration among friends and coworkers? You'll get their attention if you claim ownership—or even knowledge—of these:

AT THE OFFICE: THE BEST SEAT
■ **The Aeron** work chair by Herman Miller adjusts for lumbar support, seat height, and arm angle and height, as well as for hips, knees, and ankles.

AT HOME: HIGH HEAT
■ Recent renovation or new-home must-haves include a media room, a huge laundry room, and an exercise room. But if you really want to pull ahead of the Joneses, install a self-contained, freestanding **sauna.**

Food Fads

"U.S. consumers continue to spend a larger percentage of their food dollars on food prepared away from the home . . . eating more from fast-food chains and upscale takeouts (Chinese, Thai, Indian, Ameri-fusion), as well as more ready-to-eat prepared food from supermarket deli counters. More raw food is also pre-prepared: Meats are marinated, carrots are peeled, lettuce is prewashed."

–Leslie Land, contributing editor, *Food and Wine* magazine

Food fantasies and fears are spawning **a renewed interest in basic food for three reasons:** Baby boomers have **a taste for nostalgia.** Resentment is growing toward **the avalanche of nutritional advice** we are constantly fed. Then there are the increasingly **exotic menu choices.** What's a diner to do in 2002? Have it your way:

Junk food is an acceptable indulgence, but don't waste calories on ordinary filler. In Manhattan, popular party-givers offer platters of White

continued on page 24

HOT AND COLD FOOD TRENDS

IN

- Steak and steak restaurants
- Fruit- and herb-infused spirits
- Raw foods— ceviche, sushi
- Organic and soy milks
- Flavored sea salts
- Butter (try goat)
- Hot and iced tea

Castle **cheeseburgers** and Kentucky **Fried Chicken.** Other faves getting raves: Krispy Kreme **donuts** and Carvel **ice-cream cakes.** A "hostess with the mostest" might offer— what else?—Hostess **cupcakes.**

Gourmet salad-bar grazers are drifting from exotic baby greens to wedges of **iceberg lettuce dribbled with Roquefort dressing and crispy, smoked bacon.**

Evidence of the backlash against strictly healthful fare is the trend toward **full flavor:** Diners are demanding **game meats**—wild boar, venison, guinea fowl—and **"fishy" fish** like mackerel, sardines, and anchovies.

CHEESE SPREADS

- **"We predict a cheese revolution will sweep the country . . . much as wine did a decade ago."** *–Travel and Leisure* magazine

FASTER FOOD

- Long commutes, long hours, and even longer to-do lists at home mean more of us are eating on the run. So some **chefs are sticking it to us!** They're serving up **snacks on a stick.** Smoked salmon, goat cheese, and foie gras are among the sophisticated shish-kabobs available in upscale restaurants and gourmet food stores.

–H. Armstrong Roberts

High Tech

WHO SPENDS THEIR TIME ON-LINE?

- An international survey just reported that **Canadians spend the most time on-line each week** (5.1 hours), more than any other users. Also, **Canadians download more music from the Web** than any other users. Americans average 4.2 hours on-line per week, and Europeans log on for just over 3 hours, on average.

A STEP IN THE RIGHT DIRECTION

- Someday, we may put our best foot forward in **"learning shoes"** like those designed for San Francisco's Museum of Modern Art. **A chip in the sole collects information about the foot** and sends it to a shoe manufacturer, who then can create a customized new pair.

OUT

- Chicken entrées
- Cabernet and Chardonnay
- A pool of olive oil for dipping bread
- Potatoes as the starch dish
- Mild-flavored foods
- Low-fat foods
- Restaurants that don't offer "value" meals

continued

Increase Breast Size & Firmness... Naturally!

Flush Times for Crime

■ In 1994, a U.S. federal water-conservation law took effect. It decreed that from then on, Americans were to install only low-flush (1.6-gallon) toilets in their homes, not the old-style, big-flush (3.5-gallon) models. The new commodes are designed to save water, but as we've all experienced, one flush is often not enough (making us wonder how much water is really conserved). To top it off, the old-style toilets could no longer be sold in the United States (they are manufactured for export only).

Now potties from Canada are prized commodities, leading to a new form of "pot smuggling." Some Americans are going to plumbing-supply stores in the provinces, buying toilets (new and used), and bringing them back. You see, it's not illegal to bring the commodes into the United States, only to install them here.

WHAT D'YA KNOW?
■ *WomanTrends* newsletter reports that 74 percent of women tell friends about Web sites they like (not just the shopping ones), but only 58 percent of men share site preferences.

INCREDIBLE-BUT-TRUE INVENTIONS

■ Kudos to Guillermo Solomon of Santiago, Wisconsin, who invented the **"vacuum-cleaner leg-exercise device."** It consists of a tank connected by tubes to shoes and a wandlike cleaner. The shoes have springs and bellows. As you walk, air rushes into the bellows, creating suction in the wand . . . and *voilà!* You burn calories and clean the carpets all at the same time.

A big round of applause for Mariamma John from Baldwin Harbor, New York, for a compact, **waterproof stair-stepper to use while showering**—a unique blend of aerobics and aquatics.

Men vs. Women

SHOW ME THE MONEY, HONEY

■ According to the National Association of Investors Corp., a women-only investment club, **women's investment clubs get better average returns** (23.8 percent in 1999) than do men's clubs (19 percent).

THE HARDEST WORKERS

■ Considering household chores and child care, **Canadian women outwork Canadian men** by about two full weeks per year.

LOOKIN' GOOD!

■ More **men are having cosmetic surgery**—in fact, more than 25

percent of them (up from 10 percent five years ago). **Liposuction is the most common** procedure, but eyelid surgery has increased 40 percent in the last three years.

Women are having fewer cosmetic surgeries—at least, on the proboscis (that's your nose—but you knew that). Sociologists say that there is **a growing acceptance of the ethnic beauty** of that facial feature.

THE INSIDE STORY

■ **Some conditions scientists might treat with new knowledge of DNA:**

■ **Mental illnesses**
■ **Breast cancer**
■ **Cystic fibrosis**
■ **Heart disease**
■ **Skin cancer**
■ **Bowel disease**
■ **Diabetes**

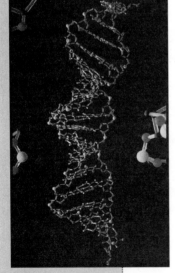

-H. Armstrong Roberts

To Your Health

"It's as if we landed on a new continent and are sending back postcards."

–Eric Lander, director, the Whitehead Institute, Cambridge, Massachusetts, as quoted in the *Boston Globe,* about the torrent of information flowing out of the Human Genome Project, which has completed its mapping of our DNA script

THE SOAP-AND-WATER CURE

■ Your mother has been telling you to do this for years; now, **'fess up: Do you wash your hands** after leaving the bathroom? Though 95 percent of Americans say they do, research indicates that the number is closer to 66 percent. The fact is, **washing your hands can do more to prevent illnesses** such as the common cold than any other single thing. A mere 15 seconds spent with warm water and soap can rid your hands of 90 percent of germs.

YOU MUST REMEMBER THIS

■ According to the *American Journal of Clinical Nutrition,* **barley and potatoes can improve your memory,** if you're old. Researchers found recently that after an overnight fast, study subjects did better on memory skills tests when they first had a bowl of cooked barley or a cup of potatoes instead of a sugary food.

QUIET, PLEASE

■ **Prayer and meditation** are good for more than just your soul. Just 20 minutes a day has been proven to **increase IQ** by nine points in four years **and may slow the aging process:** The biological age (the body's medical age, despite its years) of recent converts has been shown to be five years younger than average; that of long-term practitioners is 12 years younger.

continued

FAMILY MATTERS

■ Since 1945, the number of women aged 40 to 44 giving birth is up 23 percent.

■ More women who once ran companies

–SuperStock

are electing to stay home, and some don't easily cede financial control to the "man of the house."

■ For the first time in 25 years, families with two incomes outnumber those with one: In 51 percent of married couples, both spouses are employed at least part-time.

A BRAIN GAIN

■ We are getting smarter: Mensa membership has risen for the last three years.

Demographica

"Demographics is not destiny."

–Gail Buckner, senior vice president, Putnam Investments

Fewer of today's seniors are staying with the stereotype, playing shuffleboard or gin rummy in the Florida sun. Many of today's **seniors are going back to work** (or never leaving), going **back to school, or starting volunteer "careers."** And it's a mistake to assume that baby boomers will revert to the old ways, says Buckner.

We expect **retirement age to creep up,** not just due to the health and vitality of seniors but because couples will still have children in college or even high school. But that should come as good news to the majority of **boomers,** who **think that "old age" starts at 79.**

Our Mood

■ Collectively, as a culture, a continent, and a civilization, *we're all stressed out . . .*

■ **44 percent of Americans call themselves workaholics.**

■ Since 1995, the number of people calling in sick due to stress has tripled.

■ **Parents complain that teachers overload kids with homework.**

■ People entertain less often; they don't have time.

. . . and we aren't going to take it anymore . . .

■ Spa visits are up.

■ Architects report more requests for "meditation rooms" in office buildings.

■ A small but growing number of companies are restricting work on weekends and vacations.

■ Corporations are allowing "flex" time and granting sabbaticals.

■ Old-fashioned "hands-on" activities are back: Four million people took up knitting or crocheting in 2000.

■ Home schooling is booming, thanks in part to on-line instruction.

■ Extreme telecommuting—working from an exotic outpost—is becoming feasible and acceptable.

Ahh . . . it's enough to make you feel better already.

□□

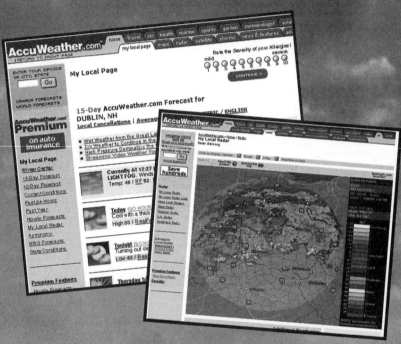

To Patrons

Why the number 13 is so lucky . . .

How many editors would you guess this publication has had in the past 210 years? Dozens? Well, actually, only 13, including the current one. And until the 11th (my uncle, Robb Sagendorph, who lived in New Hampshire), all were from Massachusetts—mostly Boston—and the majority remained at the helm for a good portion of their lives.

Our founder, Robert B. Thomas, for instance, was the editor for 54 years (from 1792 to 1846) and lived in the Massachusetts towns of Shrewsbury, Lancaster, Sterling, and West Boylston, although, as he once wrote, "I never moved from the same farm." In those days, town boundaries were constantly changing.

After Thomas's death in 1846, John H. Jenks of Boston took over (from 1847 to 1860), saying that the name of Robert B. Thomas "will always be connected with [The Old Farmer's Almanac] in the future as in past time." (And, of course, it has been.) He added a tide table "for all the New England coast" and wrote on this "To Patrons" page that he thought an apparent increase in thunderstorms was being caused by the rapid expansion of telegraph wires and railroad tracks.

Charles Louis Flint was next (from 1861 to 1869). A Harvard University man and a founder of Massachusetts Institute of Technology, Flint introduced patent-medicine advertising (for "Children Having Worms" and the like) right after the Civil War. He was followed by John B. Tileston of Dorchester, Massa-chusetts, whose tenure as editor (from 1870 to 1871) was the shortest of any before or since.

For his first edition, the fifth editor, Boston schoolteacher Loomis Joseph Campbell (from 1872 to 1876) wrote a poem I've always loved: "Among the pitfalls in our way, / The best of us walk blindly; / So, man, be wary, watch and pray, / And judge your brother kindly."

His successor, Robert Ware (from 1877 to 1899), was not so charitably inclined toward his fellow man, constantly scolding his readers for being "idle, drunk, inconsiderate, and lazy." He must have liked his brother, Horace, however, because he eventually turned the Almanac over to him. Horace Ware (from 1900 to 1918) was the first to introduce automobile rules, suggesting, for instance, that precautions be taken "against frightening horses" and recommending that cars carry brakes and bells, horns, "or other sound signals."

Equally enlightened, the eighth editor, Frank B. Newton (from 1919 to 1932), a Boston lawyer, advocated "the restorative powers of a bath," although he didn't say how *often.*

During his comparatively short tenure, Carroll Swan (1933 to 1935), a Boston advertising man and combat veteran of World War I, editorialized against airplanes flying over private property without prior permission, and then turned the Almanac over to Roger Scaife (from 1936 to 1940), a writer and editor for Little, Brown and Company of Boston. Scaife committed the one true blunder in our history: He deliberately omitted the weather forecast from the 1938 edition. Circulation plummeted to below 80,000.

It was at that point that the current owners, the Sagendorph-Trowbridge-

Kaupi-Hale family, took over. The late Robb Sagendorph (from 1941 to 1970), grandfather of our current president and CEO, Jamie Trowbridge, expanded *The Old Farmer's Almanac,* with its weather forecasts, into a bona fide North American publication, covering the entire United States and Canada. Several weeks before his death in 1970, he advised our current board chairman, Rob Trowbridge, then publisher, and me, about to take over as the 12th editor (from 1971 to 2001), "Don't grow any more, boys." Why not? we wondered. "Because," he said weakly, "the plumbing won't take it."

In the 31 years since then, we have, indeed, grown—to the point where we now have more than 18 million readers. However, as Uncle Robb predicted, the plumbing here in our Dublin, New Hampshire, offices has always been a problem.

The 13th editor? Well, she is Janice Stillman (from 2002 to, I hope, many years into the 21st century). The 210th edition, which you now hold in your hands, is her first and, of course, speaks for itself. Like all of us who preceded her, she has been guided by the words of our founder: "We must strive always to be useful," he wrote over two centuries ago, "but with a pleasant degree of humor."

J.D.H. Sr., June 2001

However, it is by our works and not our words that we would be judged. These, we hope, will sustain us in the humble though proud station we have so long held in the name of

Your obedient servant,

The 2002 Edition of

The Old Farmer's Almanac

Established in 1792 and published every year thereafter

ROBERT B. THOMAS (1766–1846), *Founder*

EDITOR IN CHIEF: Judson D. Hale Sr.
EDITOR *(13th since 1792)*: Janice Stillman
ART DIRECTOR: Margo Letourneau
SENIOR EDITOR: Mare-Anne Jarvela
COPY EDITOR: Ellen Bingham
SENIOR ASSOCIATE EDITOR: Jeff Baker
RESEARCH EDITOR: Joyce Monaco
ASTRONOMER: Dr. George Greenstein
SOLAR PROGNOSTICATOR: Dr. Richard Head
WEATHER PROGNOSTICATOR: Michael A. Steinberg
WEATHER GRAPHICS AND CONSULTATION: Accu-Weather, Inc.
CONTRIBUTING EDITORS: Bob Berman, *Astronomy;* Castle Freeman Jr., *Farmer's Calendar*
PRODUCTION DIRECTOR: Susan Gross
PRODUCTION MANAGER: David Ziarnowski
SENIOR PRODUCTION ARTISTS: Lucille Rines, Rachel Kipka, Nathaniel Stout
ADVERTISING PRODUCTION ARTIST: Janet Calhoun

GROUP PUBLISHER: John Pierce
PUBLISHER *(23rd since 1792)*: Sherin Wight
ADVERTISING SALES COORDINATOR: Melissa Van Saun
DIRECT SALES MANAGER: Cindy Schlosser
MAIL-ORDER MARKETING MANAGER: Susan Way
MAIL-ORDER/SUBSCRIPTION COORDINATOR: Beth Lorenz
MAIL-ORDER MARKETING ASSOCIATE: Priscilla Gagnon

Advertising Marketing Representatives
General and Mail-Order Advertising

Northeast & West: Robert Bernbach
Phone: 914-769-0051 • Fax: 914-769-0691

Midwest: Robert A. Rose & Associates
Phone: 312-755-1133 • Fax: 312-755-1199

South: Ray Rickles & Company
Phone: 770-664-4567 • Fax: 770-740-1399

Classified Advertising: Gallagher Group
Phone: 203-263-7171 • Fax: 203-263-7174

NEWSSTAND CIRCULATION: P.S.C.S.
DISTRIBUTION: Curtis Circulation Company

EDITORIAL, ADVERTISING, AND PUBLISHING OFFICES
P.O. Box 520, Dublin, NH 03444
Phone: 603-563-8111 • Fax: 603-563-8252

Web site: www.almanac.com
CREATIVE DIRECTOR, ON-LINE: Stephen O. Muskie
INTERNET PRODUCTION ASSISTANT: Lisa Traffie

Yankee Publishing Inc., Main St., Dublin, NH 03444

Jamie Trowbridge, *President;* Judson D. Hale Sr., John Pierce, *Senior Vice Presidents;* Jody Bugbee, Judson D. Hale Jr., Sherin Wight, *Vice Presidents;* Steve Brewer, *Treasurer.*

The Old Farmer's Almanac publications are available at special discounts for bulk purchases for sales promotions or premiums. Contact At-a-Glance Group, 800-333-1125.

The newsprint in this edition of *The Old Farmer's Almanac* consists of 23 percent recycled content. All printing inks used are soy-based. This product is recyclable. Consult local recycling regulations for the right way to do it. Printed in U.S.A.

Honey, Garlic and Vinegar Better Than Prescription Drugs?

(SPECIAL) We know from scholars that ancient civilizations relied on their healing power for a wide variety of ailments. In fact, honey was so prized by the Romans for its medicinal properties that it was sometimes used instead of gold to pay taxes. Egyptian doctors believed garlic was the ultimate cure-all. And vinegar is said to have been used for everything from arthritis to obesity for thousands of years.

Today doctors and researchers hail the healing abilities of honey, garlic and vinegar as much more than folklore. Hundreds of scientific studies have been conducted on this dream team of healers. The results are conclusive on their amazing power to help many common health problems.

These studies prove that this trio from nature's pharmacy can help **reduce blood pressure, lower cholesterol, improve circulation and lower blood sugar levels.** Scientific evidence also indicates that they may be of some value in the treatment of: **arthritis, athlete's foot, bronchitis, burns, colds and flu, cold sores, constipation, cramps, diarrhea, eczema, earaches, fatigue, fungus, heart problems, muscle aches, rheumatism, ringworm, sinus congestion, sore throat, urinary infections, virus and yeast infections and more.**

An amazing book called *Honey, Garlic & Vinegar Home Remedies* is now available to the general public. It shows you exactly how to make hundreds of remedies using honey, garlic and vinegar separately and in unique combinations. Each preparation is carefully described along with the health condition for which it is formulated .

Learn how to prepare ointments, tonics, lotions, poultices, syrups and compresses in your own kitchen. Whip up a batch to treat:

- **CORNS & CALLOUSES:** Get rid of them fast with this natural method
- **HEADACHE:** Enjoy fast relief without drugs
- **HEMORRHOIDS:** Don't suffer another day without this proven recipe
- **LEG CRAMPS:** Try this simple way to quick relief
- **MUSCLE ACHES:** Just mix up a batch of this and rub it on
- **STINGS & BITES:** Medical journals recommend this remedy to reduce pain and swelling fast
- **STOMACH PROBLEMS:** This remedy calms upset stomach and is noted in a medical journal for ulcers
- **TOOTHACHE:** This remedy can give relief until you can get to the dentist
- **WEIGHT LOSS:** Secret remedy speeds fat burn and flushes stubborn fat from hiding places

Discover all these health tips and more. You'll find: ***Dozens of easy-to-make beauty preparations for hair and skin, including a wrinkle smoother that really works. *Loads of delicious recipes using these health-giving super foods. *Tons of money-saving cleaning compounds to keep your home, car and clothing sparkling.**

Right now, as part of a special introductory offer, you can receive a special press run of the book *Honey, Garlic & Vinegar Home Remedies* for only $8.95 plus $1.00 postage and handling. Your satisfaction is <u>100% guaranteed</u>. You must be completely satisfied, or simply return it in 90 days for a <u>full refund — no questions asked.</u>

HERE'S HOW TO ORDER: Simply print your name and address and the word "Remedies" on a piece of paper and mail it along with a check or money order for only $9.95 to: THE LEADER CO., INC., Publishing Division, Dept. HG922, P.O. Box 8347, Canton, Ohio 44711. (Make checks payable to The Leader Co., Inc.) VISA or MasterCard send card number and expiration date. Act now. Orders are filled on a first-come, first-served basis.

©2001 The Leader Co., Inc.

How to Use This Almanac
Anywhere in the United States

■ The calendar pages **(64–91)** are the heart of *The Old Farmer's Almanac.* They present astronomical data and sky sightings for the entire year and are what make this book a true almanac, a "calendar of the heavens." In essence, 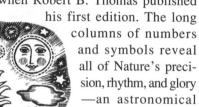 these pages are unchanged since 1792, when Robert B. Thomas published his first edition. The long columns of numbers and symbols reveal all of Nature's precision, rhythm, and glory —an astronomical look at the year 2002.

Please note: All times given in this edition of the Almanac are for Boston, Massachusetts, and are in Eastern Standard Time (EST), except from 2:00 A.M., April 7, until 2:00 A.M., October 27, when Eastern Daylight Time (EDT) is given. Key Letters (A–E) are provided so that readers can calculate times for their own localities. The following four pages provide detailed explanations.

Seasons of the Year

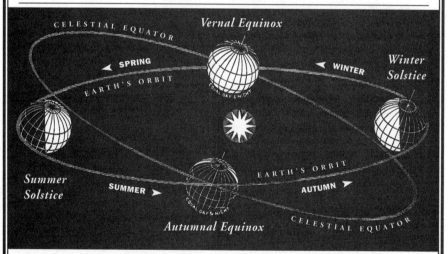

The seasons occur because Earth's axis is tilted with respect to its orbit of the Sun. Thus, the hemispheres take turns reaching their maximum tilt toward the Sun, which occurs at the solstices. The equinoxes mark the intersection of Earth's orbit with the plane of the celestial equator, when the hemispheres equally face the Sun.

■ The Web site for *The Old Farmer's Almanac,* **www.almanac.com,** has astronomical information for any location in the United States, as well as tide predictions for thousands of miles of coastline. Weather forecasts, history, advice, gardening tips, puzzles, and recipes are also available on-line. There's even a "hole" in the upper-left corner of the home page.

(c o n t i n u e d)

The Left-Hand Calendar Pages

(Pages 64–90)

2001 — NOVEMBER, The Eleventh Month

The Moon passes close to Jupiter on the 6th. Mercury displays its best morning-star [next] to Venus during the first week of November. Sat[urn]... [b]righter Jupiter rises by 10:00 P.M. EST, dominating [the] [n]ight. The Leonid meteors will keep observers awake on the night of the 17th–18th. Mars, the only bright "star" low in the south at nightfall, offers the year's best chance to locate dim Uranus when it floats just below the seventh planet on the 26th. A Moon-Saturn conjunction occurs on the 30th.

○ Full Moon	1st day	0 hour	41st minute
☽ Last Quarter	8th day	7th hour	21st minute
● New Moon	15th day	1st hour	40th minute
☽ First Quarter	22nd day	18th hour	21st minute
○ Full...	...day	1... our	...9th... ut

Times are given in Eastern Standard Time.

For an explanation of this page, see page 40; for values of Key Letters, see page 229.

Day of Year	Day of Month	Day of Week	☀ Rises h. m.	Key	☀ Sets h. m.	Key	Length of Day h. m.	Sun Fast m.	Declination of Sun ° '	High Tide Boston Light—A.M. Bold—P.M.	☽ Rises h. m.	Key	☽ Sets h. m.	Key	☽ Place	☽ Age
305	1	Th.	6 18	D	4 37	B	10 19	32	14s.36	11 11¼	5⅝12	B	6ᶰ27	E	ARI	16
306	2	Fr.	6 19	D	4 36	B	10 17	32	14 55	11¼ —	5 44	B	7 33	E	TAU	17

1 Use these two Key Letter columns to calculate the sunrise/sunset times for your locale. Each sunrise/sunset time is assigned a Key Letter whose value is given in minutes in the **Time Corrections table on page 229.** Find your city, or the city nearest you, in the table, and add or subtract those minutes to Boston's sunrise or sunset time.

E X A M P L E :

■ To find the time of sunrise in Denver, Colorado, on November 1, 2001:

Sunrise, Boston, with Key Letter D (above)	6:18 A.M. EST
Value of Key Letter D for Denver (p. 230)	+ 11 minutes
Sunrise, Denver	6:29 A.M. MST

2 This column shows how long the Sun is above the horizon in Boston. To determine your city's length of day, find the sunrise/sunset Key Letter values for your city **on page 229.** Add or subtract the sunset value to Boston's length of day. Then simply *reverse* the sunrise sign (from minus to plus, or plus to minus) and add (or subtract) this value to the result of the first step.

E X A M P L E :

■ To find the length of day in Richmond, Virginia, on November 1, 2001:

Length of day, Boston (above)	10:19
Sunset Key Letter B (p. 232)	+ 32 minutes
	10:51
Reverse sunrise Key Letter D (p. 232, +17 to –17)	– 17 minutes
Length of day, Richmond (10 hr., 34 min.)	10:34

3 The Sun Fast column is designed to change sundial time to clock time in Boston. A sundial reads natural, or Sun, time, which is neither Standard nor Daylight time except by coincidence. From a sundial reading, subtract the minutes given in the Sun Fast column to get Boston clock time, and use Key Letter C in the table **on page 229** to convert the time to your city.

on page 229

E X A M P L E :

■ To change sundial time to clock time in Boston, or Salem, Oregon, on November 1, 2001:

Sundial reading, Nov. 1 (Boston or Salem)	12:00 noon
Subtract Sun Fast (p. 40)	– 32 minutes
Clock time, Boston	11:28 A.M. EST
Use Key Letter C for Salem (p. 232)	+ 27 minutes
Clock time, Salem	11:55 A.M. PST

4 This column gives the degrees and minutes of the Sun from the celestial equator at noon EST or EDT.

5 The High Tide column gives the times of daily high tides in Boston. For example, on November 1, the first high tide occurs at 11:00 A.M. and the second occurs at 11:30 P.M. (A dash under High Tide indicates that high water occurs on or after midnight and so is recorded on the next day.) Figures for calculating high tide times and heights for localities other than Boston are given in the **Tide Corrections table on page 234.**

6 Use these two Key Letter columns to calculate the moonrise/moonset times for localities other than Boston. (A dash indicates that moonrise/moonset occurs on or after midnight and so is recorded on the next day.) Use the same procedure as explained in #1 for calculating your moonrise/moonset time, then factor in an additional correction based on longitude (see table below). For the longitude of your city, **see page 229.**

Longitude of city	Correction minutes
58° – 76°	0
77° – 89°	+1
90° – 102°	+2
103° – 115°	+3
116° – 127°	+4
128° – 141°	+5
142° – 155°	+6

E X A M P L E :

■ To determine the time of moonrise in Lansing, Michigan, on November 1, 2001:

Moonrise, Boston, with Key Letter B (p. 40)	5:12 P.M. EST
Value of Key Letter B for Lansing (p. 231)	+ 53 minutes
Correction for Lansing longitude 84° 33'	+ 1 minute
Moonrise, Lansing	6:06 P.M. EST

Use the same procedure to determine the time of moonset.

—Beth Krommes

7 The Moon's place is its *astronomical,* or *actual,* placement in the heavens. (This should not be confused with the Moon's *astrological* place in the zodiac, as explained **on page 227.**) All calculations in this Almanac are based on astronomy, not astrology, except for the information on **pages 226, 227, and 228.**

In addition to the 12 constellations of the astronomical zodiac, five other abbreviations may appear in this column: Auriga **(AUR),** a northern constellation between Perseus and Gemini; Cetus **(CET),** which lies south of the zodiac, just south of Pisces and Aries; Ophiuchus **(OPH),** a constellation primarily north of the zodiac but with a small corner between Scorpius and Sagittarius; Orion **(ORI),** a constellation whose northern limit first reaches the zodiac between Taurus and Gemini; and Sextans **(SEX),** which lies south of the zodiac except for a corner that just touches it near Leo.

8 The last column gives the Moon's age, which is the number of days since the previous new Moon. (The average length of the lunar month is 29.53 days.)

(c o n t i n u e d)

The Right-Hand Calendar Pages
(Pages 65–91)

■ Throughout the Right-Hand Calendar Pages are groups of symbols that represent notable celestial events. The symbols and names of the principal planets and aspects are:

☉	Sun	♆	Neptune
○●☾	Moon	♇	Pluto
☿	Mercury	♂	Conjunction (on
♀	Venus		the same celestial
⊕	Earth		longitude)
♂	Mars	☊	Ascending node
♃	Jupiter	☋	Descending node
♄	Saturn	☍	Opposition (180
♅	Uranus		degrees apart)

For example, ♂♄☾ next to November 3, 2001 (see opposite page), means that a conjunction (♂) of Saturn (♄) and the Moon (☾) occurs on that date, when they are aligned along the same celestial longitude and appear to be closest together in the sky.

-Beth Krommes

The Seasons of 2001–2002

Fall 2001	**Sept. 22, 7:04 P.M. EDT**
Winter 2001	**Dec. 21, 2:21 P.M. EST**
Spring 2002	**Mar. 20, 2:16 P.M. EST**
Summer 2002	**June 21, 9:24 A.M. EDT**
Fall 2002	**Sept. 23, 12:55 A.M. EDT**
Winter 2002	**Dec. 21, 8:14 P.M. EST**

Earth at Perihelion and Aphelion 2002

■ Earth will be at perihelion on January 2, 2002, when it will be 91,402,145 miles from the Sun. Earth will be at aphelion on July 6, 2002, when it will be 94,502,872 miles from the Sun.

Movable Feasts and Fasts for 2002

Septuagesima Sunday	**Jan. 27**
Shrove Tuesday	**Feb. 12**
Ash Wednesday	**Feb. 13**
Palm Sunday	**Mar. 24**
Good Friday	**Mar. 29**
Easter	**Mar. 31**
Rogation Sunday	**May 5**
Ascension Day	**May 9**
Whitsunday-Pentecost	**May 19**
Trinity Sunday	**May 26**
Corpus Christi	**May 30**
First Sunday in Advent	**Dec. 1**

Chronological Cycles for 2002

Dominical Letter	**F**
Epact	**16**
Golden Number (Lunar Cycle)	**8**
Roman Indiction	**10**
Solar Cycle	**23**
Year of Julian Period	**6715**

Era	Year	Begins
Byzantine	**7511**	. . **Sept. 14**
Jewish (A.M.)*	**5763**	. . **Sept. 16**
Chinese (Lunar)	**4700**	. . **Feb. 12**
[Year of the Horse]		
Roman (A.U.C.)	**2755**	. . . **Jan. 14**
Nabonassar	**2751**	. . . **Apr. 23**
Japanese	**2662**	. . . . **Jan. 1**
Grecian (Seleucidae)	**2314**	. . **Sept. 14**
		(or Oct. 14)
Indian (Saka)	**1924**	. . **Mar. 22**
Diocletian	**1719**	. . **Sept. 11**
Islamic (Hegira)* . . .	**1423**	. . **Mar. 14**

*Year begins at sunset.

Sample Right-Hand Calendar Page (from November 2001, page 65)

- Day of the month.
- Day of the week.
- Conjunction of Saturn and the Moon.
- The bold letter in this column is the Dominical Letter, a traditional ecclesiastical designation for Sunday. The letter for 2001 is G, because the first Sunday of the year falls on the seventh day of January. The letter for 2002 is F, the first Sunday falling on January 6.
- 22nd Sunday after Pentecost. (Sundays and special holy days generally appear in this typeface.)
- The Moon is on the celestial equator.
- St. Martin of Tours was a devout Christian born in Pannonia (now Hungary) who was forced to join the Roman army. Martin eventually became the bishop of Tours. He is known for his outstanding charity and humility, as well as several miracles. (Religious feasts and civil holidays appear in this typeface.)
- First high tide at Boston is 10.2 feet; second high tide is 11.3 feet.
- Weather prediction rhyme. **(For detailed regional forecasts, see pages 142–161.)**

When the tree bares, the music of it changes:
Hard and keen is the sound, long and mournful;
Pale are the poplar boughs in the evening light
Above my house, against a slate-cold cloud. –Conrad Aiken

D.M.	D.W.	Dates, Feasts, Fasts, Aspects, Tide Heights	Weather ↓
1	Th.	All Saints' • Full Beaver ○ • Stephen Crane born, 1871 • {10.4 / 9.7	*Damp*
2	Fr.	All Souls' • ♃ stat. • James Thurber died, 1961 • Tides {10.6 / —	*and*
3	Sa.	☌♄☾ • 96°F in Los Angeles, 1890; record high for November for 76 years •	*dismal,*
4	**G**	22nd 𝔖. af. 𝔓. • ☾ at ☊ • ☌♂♆ • {9.6 / 10.7	
5	M.	George B. Selden received first U.S. patent for automobile, 1895 • {9.4 / 10.6 •	*turning*
6	Tu.	☾ rides high • ☌♃☾ • Election Day • {9.2 / 10.5	*colder,*
7	W.	*If voting changed anything, they'd make it illegal.* • Tides {9.1 / 10.3 •	*then*
8	Th.	First U.S. college for women, Mt. Holyoke, founded, 1837 • Astronomer Edmund Halley born, 1656 •	*a*
9	Fr.	Carl Sagan born, 1934 • J. William Fulbright born, 1905 • {9.3 / 10.1 •	*warm*
10	Sa.	St. Leo the Great • Sadie Hawkins Day • {9.6 / 10.2 •	*hiatus;*
11	**G**	23rd 𝔖. af. 𝔓. • Veterans Day • ☾ at perig. •	*rain*
12	M.	St. Martin • ☾ on Eq. • 105°F, Craftonville, Calif., 1906 • {10.7 / 10.6	*and*
13	Tu.	Holland Tunnel, connecting New York City and Jersey City, N.J., opened, 1927 • {11.2 / 10.7	*snow*
14	W.	First streetcar, drawn by horses, began operating in New York City, 1832 • {11.5 / 10.7	*that's*
15	Th.	New ● • *One person with belief is equal to a force of 99 who have only interests.* • {11.7 / 10.5	*so*
16	Fr.	Arturo Toscanini made U.S. conducting debut at the Met., 1908 • {11.6 / —	*abysmal*
17	Sa.	St. Hugh of Lincoln • ☾ at ☋ • Tides {10.2 / 11.3	*comes*
18	**G**	24th 𝔖. af. 𝔓. • Margaret Atwood born, 1939 • {9.9 / 10.9 •	*to*
19	M.	☾ runs low • Roy Campanella born, 1921 • James Garfield born, 1831 •	*irritate*
20	Tu.	☌♆☾ • Hubble space telescope photographed the Eagle Nebula, 1995 •	*us!*
21	W.	☌♂☾ • ☌♅☾ • Stan Musial born, 1920 • {8.8 / 9.4	*Thanks*
22	Th.	Thanksgiving • *Gratitude is the memory of the heart.* • {8.5 / 9.1 •	*for*

For an explanation of terms used in the Almanac, see the glossaries on pages 44, 48, and 236.

Predicting Earthquakes

■ Note the dates, in the **Right-Hand Calendar Pages,** when the Moon (☾) rides high or runs low. The date of the high begins the most likely five-day period of earthquakes in the Northern Hemisphere; the date of the low indicates a similar five-day period in the Southern Hemisphere. Also noted twice each month are the days when the Moon is on the celestial equator (☾ on Eq.), indicating likely two-day earthquake periods in both hemispheres.

–Beth Krommes

More Astronomical Data for 2002

Astronomical Glossary

Aphelion (Aph.): The point in a planet's orbit that is farthest from the Sun.

Apogee (Apo.): The point in the Moon's orbit that is farthest from Earth.

Celestial Sphere: An imaginary sphere projected into space that represents the entire sky, with an observer on Earth at its center. All celestial bodies other than Earth are imagined as being on its inside surface.

Conjunction: Two celestial bodies reach the same celestial longitude, or right ascension, approximately corresponding to their closest apparent approach in the sky. (Dates for conjunction are given in the Right-Hand Calendar Pages 65–91; sky sightings of closely aligned bodies are given in the descriptive text at the top of the Left-Hand Calendar Pages 64–90.) **Inferior (Inf.):** Mercury or Venus is between the Sun and Earth. **Superior (Sup.):** The Sun is between a planet and Earth.

Declination: The celestial latitude of an object in the sky, measured in degrees north or south of the celestial equator; analogous to latitude on Earth. The Almanac gives the Sun's declination at noon EST or EDT.

Dominical Letter: Denotes the Sundays in the ecclesiastical calendar in a given year, determined by the date on which the first Sunday of that year falls. If Jan. 1 is a Sunday, the letter is A; if Jan. 2 is a Sunday, the letter is B; and so on to G. In a leap year, the letter applies through February and then takes the preceding letter.

Eclipse, Lunar: The full Moon enters the shadow of Earth, which cuts off all or part of the Moon's light. **Total:** The Moon passes completely through the umbra (central dark part) of Earth's shadow. **Partial:** Only part of the Moon passes through the umbra. **Penumbral:** The Moon passes through only the penumbra (area of partial darkness surrounding the umbra).

Eclipse, Solar: Earth enters the shadow of the new Moon, which cuts off all or part of the Sun's light. **Total:** Earth passes through the umbra (central dark part) of the Moon's shadow, resulting in totality for observers within a narrow band on Earth. **Annular:** The Moon appears silhouetted against the Sun, with a ring of sunlight showing around it. **Partial:** The Moon blocks only part of the Sun.

Ecliptic: The apparent annual path of the Sun around the celestial sphere. The plane of the ecliptic is tipped 23½° from the celestial equator.

Elongation: The difference in degrees between the celestial longitudes of a planet and the Sun. **Greatest Elongation (Gr. Elong.):** The greatest apparent distance of a planet from the Sun, as seen from Earth.

Epact: A number from 1 to 30 that indicates the Moon's age on Jan. 1 at Greenwich, England; used for determining the date of Easter.

Equator, Celestial (Eq.): The circle around the celestial sphere that is halfway between the celestial poles. It can be thought of as the plane of Earth's equator projected out onto the sphere.

Equinox, Autumnal: The Sun appears to cross the celestial equator from north to south. **Vernal:** The Sun appears to cross the celestial equator from south to north.

Evening Star: A planet that is above the western horizon at sunset and less than 180° east of the Sun in right ascension.

Golden Number: A number in the 19-year cycle of the Moon, used for determining the date of Easter. (The Moon repeats its phases approximately every 19 solar years.) Add 1 to any given year and divide the result by 19; the remainder is the Golden Number. If there is no remainder, the Golden Number is 19.

Julian Period: A period of 7,980 years beginning Jan. 1, 4713 B.C. Devised in 1583 by Joseph Scaliger, it provides a chronological basis for the study of ancient history. To find the Julian year, add 4,713 to any year. (continued on page 46)

Why wait ten months?

Now you can have rich, dark compost _in just 14 days!_

With the amazing Compos-Tumbler, you'll have bushels of crumbly, ready-to-use compost — _in just 14 days!_ (And, in the ten months it takes to make compost the old way, your ComposTumbler can produce _hundreds of pounds_ of rich food for your garden!)

Say good-bye to that messy, open compost pile (and to the flies, pests, and odors that come along with it!) Bid a happy farewell to the strain of trying to turn over heavy, wet piles with a pitchfork.

Compost the Better Way

Compost-making with the ComposTumbler is neat, quick and easy!

Gather up leaves, old weeds, kitchen scraps, lawn clippings, etc. and toss them into the roomy 18-bushel drum. Then, once each day, give the ComposTumbler's _gear-driven_ handle a few easy spins.

The ComposTumbler's Magic

Inside the ComposTumbler, carefully positioned mixing fins blend materials, pushing fresh mixture to the core where the temperatures are the hottest (up to 160°) and the composting bacteria most active.

After just 14 days, open the door, and you'll find an abundance of dark, sweet-smelling "garden gold" — ready to enrich and feed your garden!

NEW SMALLER SIZE!

Now there are 2 sizes. The 18-bushel original ComposTumbler and the NEW 9.5-bushel Compact ComposTumbler. Try either size risk-free for 1 year!

See for yourself! Try the ComposTumbler risk-free with our 1-Year Home Trial!

Call Toll-Free
1-800-880-2345

NOW ON SALE– SAVE UP TO $115!

Moon on Equator: The Moon is on the celestial equator.

Moon Rides High/Runs Low: The Moon is highest above or farthest below the celestial equator.

Moonrise/Moonset: The Moon's rising above or descending below the horizon.

Moon's Phases: The continually changing states in the Moon's appearance, caused by the different angles at which it is illuminated by the Sun. **First Quarter:** The right half of the Moon is illuminated, as seen from the Northern Hemisphere. **Full:** The Sun and the Moon are in opposition; the entire disk of the Moon is illuminated as viewed from Earth. **Last Quarter:** The left half of the Moon is illuminated, as seen from the Northern Hemisphere. **New:** The Sun and the Moon are in conjunction; the entire disk of the Moon is darkened as viewed from Earth.

Moon's Place, Astronomical: The actual position of the Moon within the constellations on the celestial sphere. **Astrological:** The position of the Moon within the astrological zodiac according to calculations made over 2,000 years ago. Because of precession of the equinoxes and other factors, this is not the Moon's actual position in the sky.

Morning Star: A planet that is above the eastern horizon at sunrise and less than 180° west of the Sun in right ascension.

Node, Ascending/Descending: Either of the two points where a body's orbit intersects the ecliptic. The body is moving from south to north of the ecliptic at the ascending node, and from north to south at the descending node. (An imaginary line through Earth that connects the Moon's nodes also aligns with an Earth-Sun line twice a year, roughly six months apart; at these times, a new or full Moon that occurs when the Moon is at or near one of its nodes will result in an eclipse.)

Occultation (Occn.): The eclipse of a star or planet by the Moon or another planet.

Opposition: The Moon or a planet appears on the opposite side of the sky from the Sun (elongation 180°).

Perigee (Perig.): The point in the Moon's orbit that is closest to Earth.

Perihelion (Perih.): The point in a planet's orbit that is closest to the Sun.

Precession: The slowly changing position of the stars and equinoxes in the sky resulting from variations in the orientation of Earth's axis.

Right Ascension (R.A.): The celestial longitude of an object in the sky, measured eastward along the celestial equator in hours of time from the vernal equinox; analogous to longitude on Earth.

Roman Indiction: A number in a 15-year cycle, established Jan. 1, A.D. 313, as a fiscal term. Add 3 to any given year in the Christian era and divide by 15; the remainder is the Roman Indiction. If there is no remainder, the Roman Indiction is 15.

Solar Cycle: A period of 28 years in the Julian calendar, at the end of which the days of the month return to the same days of the week.

Solstice, Summer: The Sun reaches its greatest declination (23½°) north of the celestial equator. **Winter:** The Sun reaches its greatest declination (23½°) south of the celestial equator.

Stationary (Stat.): The apparent halted movement, as it reaches opposition, of a planet against the background of the stars, shortly before it appears to move backward (retrograde motion).

Sun Fast/Slow: The difference between a sundial reading and clock time.

Sunrise/Sunset: The visible rising and setting of the Sun's upper limb across the unobstructed horizon of an observer whose eyes are 15 feet above ground level.

Twilight: The period of time between full darkness (when the Sun is 18° below the horizon) and either sunrise or sunset. Twilight is classified as **astronomical,** when the Sun is between 18° and 12° below the horizon; **nautical,** when the Sun is between 12° and 6° below the horizon; and **civil,** when the Sun is less than 6° below the horizon.

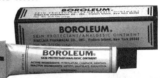

Glossary of Almanac Oddities

Many readers have expressed puzzlement over the rather obscure notations that appear on our **Right-Hand Calendar Pages (65–91).** These "oddities" have long been fixtures in the Almanac, and we are pleased to provide some definitions. (Once explained, it may seem that they are not so odd after all!)

Ember Days (Movable)

The Almanac traditionally marks the four periods formerly observed by the Roman Catholic and Anglican churches for prayer, fasting, and the ordination of clergy. These Ember Days are the Wednesdays, Fridays, and Saturdays that follow in succession after 1) the First Sunday in Lent; 2) Pentecost, or Whitsunday; 3) the Feast of the Holy Cross, September 14; and 4) the Feast of St. Lucy, December 13. The word *ember* is perhaps a corruption of the Latin *quatuor tempora,* "four times."

Folklore has it that the weather on each of the three days foretells the weather for three successive months; that is, for September's Ember Days, Wednesday forecasts weather for October, Friday for November, and Saturday for December.

Plough Monday (January)

The first Monday after Epiphany and Plough Sunday, so called because it was the end of the Christmas holidays, when men returned to their plough, or daily work. It was customary for farm laborers

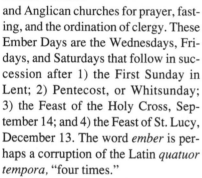

to draw a plough through the village, soliciting money for a "plough-light," which was kept burning in the parish church all year. In some areas, the custom of blessing the plough is maintained.

Three Chilly Saints (May)

Mammertius, Pancratius, and Gervatius, three early Christian saints, whose feast days occur on May 11, 12, and 13, respectively. Because these days are traditionally cold (an old French saying goes: "St. Mammertius, St. Pancras, and St. Gervais do not pass without a frost"), they have come to be known as the Three Chilly Saints.

Midsummer Day (June 24)

Although it occurs near the summer solstice, to the farmer it is the midpoint of the growing season, halfway between planting and harvest and an occasion for festivity. The English church considered it a "Quarter Day," one of the four major divisions of the liturgical year. It also marks the feast day of St. John the Baptist.

Cornscateous Air (July)

A term first used by the old almanac

"If I told you that I can end a lifetime of foot pain instantly, you probably wouldn't believe me..."

"Half a million other men and women didn't either... until they tried this revolutionary European discovery that positively killed their foot pain dead!

"Don't live with foot pain a moment longer! If you're ready to recapture the vitality and energy that healthy feet provide, I'll give you 60 days to try the remarkable foot support system I discovered in Europe. You will immediately experience relief and freedom from foot ailments. I GUARANTEE IT!

"How can I make such an unprecedented guarantee? Because I personally lived in constant, agonizing foot pain for years

Harvey Rothschild,
Founder of Featherspring Int'l.

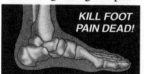

before my exciting discovery. What started out as simple aching from corns and calluses grew into full-blown, incapacitating misery only a few other foot pain sufferers could understand.

"Believe me, I tried all the so-called remedies I could get my hands on (and feet into), but none of them really worked. It wasn't until my wife and I took a trip to Europe that I discovered a remarkable invention called Flexible Featherspring® Foot Supports. Invented in Germany, these custom-formed foot supports absorb shock as they cradle your feet as if on a cushion of air.

"Imagine my complete surprise as I slipped a pair of custom-formed Feathersprings into my shoes for the first time and began the road to no more pain. The tremendous pain and pressure I used to feel every time I took a step was gone! I could scarcely believe how great a relief I felt even after walking several hours. And after just a few days of use, my pain disappeared totally - *and has never returned.*

"Whatever your problem— corns, calluses, bunions, pain in the balls of your feet, toe cramps, fallen arches, burning nerve endings, painful ankles, back aches, or just generally sore, aching feet and legs – *my Feathersprings are guaranteed to end your foot pain or you don't pay a penny.*

"But don't just take my word for it: Experience for yourself the immediate relief and renewed energy that Feathersprings provide. Send for your FREE kit today on our no risk, 60-day trial offer!"

Visit our web site at: www.featherspring.com or call us toll free at: 1-800-628-4693

© FEATHERSPRING, 712 N. 34th Street, Seattle, WA 98103-8881

makers to signify warm, damp air. Though it signals ideal climatic conditions for growing corn, it also poses a danger to those affected by asthma, pneumonia, and other respiratory problems.

Dog Days (July–August)

The hottest and most unhealthy days of the year. Also known as "Canicular Days," the name derives from the Dog Star, Sirius. The Almanac lists the traditional timing of Dog Days: The 40 days beginning July 3 and ending August 11, coinciding with the heliacal (at sunrise) rising of Sirius.

Cat Nights Begin (August)

The term harks back to the days when people believed in witches. An old Irish legend has it that a witch could turn herself into a cat eight times and then regain herself, but on the ninth time—August 17—she couldn't change back; hence, the saying: "A cat has nine lives." Because August is a "yowly" time for cats, this may have prompted the speculation about witches on the prowl in the first place.

Harvest Home (September)

In Europe and Britain, the conclusion of the harvest each autumn was once marked by great festivals of fun, feasting, and thanksgiving known as "Harvest Home." It was also a time to hold elections, pay workers, and collect rents. These festivals usually took place around the time of the autumnal equinox. Certain ethnic groups in this country, particularly the Pennsylvania Dutch, have kept the tradition alive.

St. Luke's Little Summer (October)

A spell of warm weather occurring about the time of the saint's feast day, October 18. This period is sometimes referred to as Indian summer.

Indian Summer (November)

A period of warm weather following a cold spell or a hard frost. Although there are differing dates for the time of occurrence, for more than 200 years the Almanac has adhered to the saying, "If All Saints brings out winter, St. Martin's brings out Indian summer." Accordingly, Indian summer can occur between St. Martin's Day (November 11) and November 20. As for the origin of the term, some say it comes from the early Native Americans, who believed that the condition was caused by a warm wind sent from the court of their southwestern God, Cautantowwit.

Halcyon Days (December)

A period (about 14 days) of calm weather, following the blustery winds of autumn's end. The ancient Greeks and Romans believed them to occur around the time of the winter solstice, when the halcyon, or kingfisher, was brooding. In a nest floating on the sea, the bird was said to have charmed the wind and waves so that the waters were especially calm during this period.

Beware the Pogonip (December)

The word *pogonip* is a meteorological term used to describe an uncommon occurrence—frozen fog. The word was coined by Native Americans to describe the frozen fogs of fine ice needles that occur in the mountain valleys of the western United States. According to Indian tradition, breathing the fog is injurious to the lungs. □□

Holidays and Observances, 2002

A selected list of commemorative days, with federal holidays denoted by *.

Jan. 1	New Year's Day*		**June 11**	King Kamehameha I Day *(Hawaii)*
Jan. 21	Martin Luther King Jr.'s Birthday *(observed)* *		**June 14**	Flag Day
			June 16	Father's Day
Feb. 2	Groundhog Day; Guadalupe-Hidalgo Treaty Day *(N.Mex.)*		**June 17**	Bunker Hill Day *(Suffolk Co., Mass.)*
			June 19	Emancipation Day *(Tex.)*
Feb. 12	Abraham Lincoln's Birthday; Mardi Gras *(Baldwin & Mobile Counties, Ala.; La.)*		**June 20**	West Virginia Day
			July 1	Canada Day
			July 4	Independence Day*
Feb. 14	St. Valentine's Day		**July 24**	Pioneer Day *(Utah)*
Feb. 15	Susan B. Anthony's Birthday *(Fla., Wis.)*		**Aug. 5**	Colorado Day
			Aug. 12	Victory Day *(R.I.)*
Feb. 18	George Washington's Birthday *(observed)* *		**Aug. 16**	Bennington Battle Day *(Vt.)*
			Aug. 26	Women's Equality Day
Mar. 2	Texas Independence Day		**Sept. 2**	Labor Day*
Mar. 5	Town Meeting Day *(Vt.)*		**Sept. 9**	Admission Day *(Calif.)*
Mar. 15	Andrew Jackson Day *(Tenn.)*		**Oct. 9**	Leif Eriksson Day
Mar. 17	St. Patrick's Day		**Oct. 14**	Columbus Day *(observed)* *; Thanksgiving Day *(Canada)*; Native Americans Day *(S.Dak.)*
Mar. 18	Evacuation Day *(Suffolk Co., Mass.)*			
Apr. 2	Pascua Florida Day			
Apr. 13	Thomas Jefferson's Birthday		**Oct. 18**	Alaska Day
Apr. 15	Patriots Day *(Maine, Mass.)*		**Oct. 31**	Halloween; Nevada Day
Apr. 26	National Arbor Day		**Nov. 4**	Will Rogers Day *(Okla.)*
May 1	May Day		**Nov. 5**	Election Day
May 8	Truman Day *(Mo.)*		**Nov. 11**	Veterans Day*
May 12	Mother's Day		**Nov. 19**	Discovery Day *(Puerto Rico)*
May 18	Armed Forces Day		**Nov. 22**	Acadian Day *(La.)*
May 20	Victoria Day *(Canada)*		**Nov. 28**	Thanksgiving Day*
May 27	Memorial Day *(observed)* *		**Dec. 25**	Christmas Day*
June 5	World Environment Day		**Dec. 26**	Boxing Day *(Canada)*

Religious Observances

Epiphany	**Jan. 6**	Orthodox Easter	**May 5**
Ash Wednesday	**Feb. 13**	Whitsunday–Pentecost	**May 19**
Islamic New Year	**Mar. 15**	Rosh Hashanah	**Sept. 7**
Palm Sunday	**Mar. 24**	Yom Kippur	**Sept. 16**
First day of Passover	**Mar. 28**	First day of Ramadan	**Nov. 6**
Good Friday	**Mar. 29**	First day of Chanukah	**Nov. 30**
Easter	**Mar. 31**	Christmas Day	**Dec. 25**

How the Almanac Weather Forecasts Are Made

■ We derive our weather forecasts from a secret formula devised by the founder of this Almanac in 1792, enhanced by the most-modern scientific calculations based on solar activity and current meteorological data. We believe that nothing in the universe occurs haphazardly but that there is a cause-and-effect pattern to all phenomena, thus making long-range weather forecasts possible. However, neither we nor anyone else has as yet gained sufficient insight into the mysteries of the universe to predict the weather with anything resembling total accuracy.

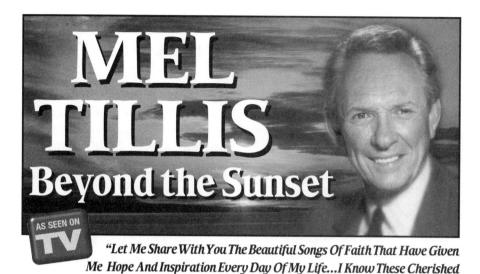

The Visible Planets, 2002

■ Listed here for Boston are the times (EST/EDT) of the visible rising and setting of the planets Venus, Mars, Jupiter, and Saturn on the 1st, 11th, and 21st of each month. The approximate times of their visible rising and setting on other days can be found by interpolation. The capital letters that appear beside the times are Key Letters and are used to convert the times to other localities **(see pages 40 and 229)**. For definitions of morning and evening stars, see the **Glossary on page 44.**

Venus is bright until late February but is never very high. This evening star dominates the spring planet gathering and comes close to dim Mars on May 10. It is low during its peak brilliance in August and September, lurking just a paltry few degrees above the southwestern horizon when achieving greatest brilliancy on September 26. Venus achieves maximum predawn brilliance on December 7, becoming 250 times brighter than nearby Mars. Look for a Venus/Moon/Mars conjunction on December 1.

Mars never reaches an opposition, nor does it attain first-magnitude status. Still, the red planet is easily seen in Aquarius from January until mid-June. Mars costars as a dim but close companion to Venus on May 10, then again throughout December, especially when it joins the lovely Venus/Moon conjunction on the 1st. The main excitement comes from anticipation, because next year, Mars will venture extraordinarily close to Earth and grow visibly brighter than it has been in thousands of years.

	Boldface—P.M.		Lightface—A.M.	
Jan. 1....... rise 7:04 E	July 1 ...... set 10:42 D	Jan. 1....... set 9:56 B	July 1 ...... set 9:15 E
Jan. 11..... rise 7:15 E	July 11 .... set 10:29 D	Jan. 11..... set 9:55 C	July 11 .... set 8:58 E
Jan. 21..... set 4:48 A	July 21 .... set 10:14 D	Jan. 21..... set 9:53 C	July 21 .... set 8:39 E
Feb. 1 ...... set 5:16 B	Aug. 1 ..... set 9:53 C	Feb. 1 ...... set 9:51 C	Aug. 1 ..... set 8:16 D
Feb. 11 .... set 5:42 B	Aug. 11 ... set 9:33 C	Feb. 11 .... set 9:49 D	Aug. 11 ... rise 5:44 A
Feb. 21 .... set 6:07 B	Aug. 21 ... set 9:11 B	Feb. 21 .... set 9:47 D	Aug. 21 ... rise 5:38 B
Mar. 1 ..... set 6:27 B	Sept. 1 ..... set 8:45 B	Mar. 1 ..... set 9:45 D	Sept. 1 ..... rise 5:32 B
Mar. 11 ... set 6:52 C	Sept. 11 ... set 8:19 B	Mar. 11 ... set 9:43 D	Sept. 11 ... rise 5:25 B
Mar. 21 ... set 7:17 D	Sept. 21 ... set 7:50 A	Mar. 21 ... set 9:40 D	Sept. 21 ... rise 5:19 B
Apr. 1 ...... set 8:44 D	Oct. 1 ...... set 7:17 A	Apr. 1 ...... set 10:37 E	Oct. 1 ...... rise 5:12 B
Apr. 11 .... set 9:10 D	Oct. 11 .... set 6:37 A	Apr. 11 .... set 10:33 E	Oct. 11 .... rise 5:06 C
Apr. 21 .... set 9:35 E	Oct. 21 .... set 5:52 A	Apr. 21 .... set 10:29 E	Oct. 21 .... rise 4:59 C
May 1 ...... set 10:00 E	Nov. 1 ...... set 4:02 A	May 1 ...... set 10:23 E	Nov. 1 ...... rise 3:51 C
May 11.... set 10:21 E	Nov. 11 .... rise 5:11 D	May 11.... set 10:17 E	Nov. 11 ... rise 3:45 C
May 21.... set 10:38 E	Nov. 21 ... rise 4:16 D	May 21.... set 10:08 E	Nov. 21 ... rise 3:38 D
June 1...... set 10:50 E	Dec. 1 ...... rise 3:43 D	June 1...... set 9:57 E	Dec. 1 ...... rise 3:32 D
June 11.... set 10:53 E	Dec. 11.... rise 3:26 D	June 11.... set 9:45 E	Dec. 11.... rise 3:26 D
June 21.... set 10:50 E	Dec. 21.... rise 3:22 D	June 21.... set 9:31 E	Dec. 21.... rise 3:20 D
	Dec. 31.... rise 3:26 D		Dec. 31.... rise 3:14 D

Mercury plays its customary hide-and-seek into the evening and morning skies. This innermost planet's optimal after-sunset appearances occur the first three weeks of the year, and then from April 16 to May 17. As a morning star, Mercury is best from October 4 to 20 and gets especially bright the final week of that period. The charbroiled world also has several fine conjunctions: It serves as "bottom man" in the fabulous string of planets seen in the west from mid-April through mid-May, then hovers alongside Mars in the predawn east during the second week of October.

DO NOT CONFUSE 1) Mercury, Mars, and Saturn when they bunch together in April and May. Mercury is always the lowest, and Mars is orange and the dimmest of the trio. 2) Jupiter with Venus when they float side by side during the first four days of June. Though both are the same yellow-white color, Venus is distinctly brighter. 3) Mars with Mercury as they hover together the second week of October. Both are yellow-orange, but Mars is much deeper in color, and Mercury is distinctly brighter.

Jupiter will be superb, often nearly attaining its highest possible position in the sky. It reaches opposition in the first hour of the year and stays brilliant through winter. In Gemini, this giant world remains conspicuous most of the night through March, after which it is seen only before midnight. Jove is the highest of the string of planets in the postsunset sky from mid-April to mid-May, then hovers next to even-brighter Venus during early June. Disappearing behind the Sun in July, it returns in August as a morning star in the east.

Saturn has its best year since 1973 (see feature on page 60). A rare combination of being high, close to Earth, and tilting its icy, highly reflective rings toward Earth keeps Saturn brighter than zero magnitude for the entire year. By midspring, its fine performances are confined to the night's first few hours; it slips into the Sun's glare late in May. Saturn returns as a morning star in late July, coming up earlier and getting higher as the summer and fall progress. It reaches its pinnacle with an opposition on December 17.

Boldface—P.M.		Lightface—A.M.	
Jan. 1....... **rise 4:10** A	July 1 ...... **set 9:13** E	Jan. 1....... set 4:53 E	July 1 ...... rise 4:00 A
Jan. 11..... set 6:36 E	July 11 .... **set 8:42** E	Jan. 11..... set 4:11 E	July 11 .... rise 3:26 A
Jan. 21..... set 5:52 E	July 21 .... rise 5:21 A	Jan. 21..... set 3:30 E	July 21 .... rise 2:51 A
Feb. 1 ...... set 5:05 E	Aug. 1 ..... rise 4:50 A	Feb. 1 ...... set 2:46 E	Aug. 1 ..... rise 2:13 A
Feb. 11 .... set 4:22 E	Aug. 11 ... rise 4:22 A	Feb. 11 .... set 2:07 E	Aug. 11 ... rise 1:38 A
Feb. 21 .... set 3:41 E	Aug. 21 ... rise 3:54 A	Feb. 21 .... set 1:28 E	Aug. 21 ... rise 1:02 A
Mar. 1 ..... set 3:09 E	Sept. 1..... rise 3:22 A	Mar. 1 ..... set 12:58 E	Sept. 1..... rise 12:22 A
Mar. 11 ... set 2:31 E	Sept. 11... rise 2:53 A	Mar. 11 ... set 12:21 E	Sept. 11... **rise 11:46** A
Mar. 21 ... set 1:54 E	Sept. 21... rise 2:24 A	Mar. 21 ... **set 11:42** E	Sept. 21... **rise 11:08** A
Apr. 1 ...... set 2:14 E	Oct. 1 ...... rise 1:53 A	Apr. 1 ...... set 12:03 E	Oct. 1 ...... **rise 10:26** A
Apr. 11 .... set 1:39 E	Oct. 11 .... rise 1:22 A	Apr. 11 .... **set 11:28** E	Oct. 11 .... **rise 9:47** A
Apr. 21 .... set 1:05 E	Oct. 21 .... rise 12:46 A	Apr. 21 .... **set 10:54** E	Oct. 21 .... **rise 9:08** A
May 1 ...... set 12:28 E	Nov. 1 ..... **rise 11:10** A	May 1 ...... **set 10:20** E	Nov. 1 ..... **rise 7:23** A
May 11.... **set 11:56** E	Nov. 11 ... **rise 10:34** A	May 11.... **set 9:47** E	Nov. 11 ... **rise 6:42** A
May 21.... **set 11:23** E	Nov. 21 ... **rise 9:58** A	May 21.... **set 9:13** E	Nov. 21 ... **rise 6:00** A
June 1 ...... set 10:48 E	Dec. 1...... **rise 9:20** A	June 1 ...... **set 8:37** E	Dec. 1...... **rise 5:18** A
June 11.... **set 10:17** E	Dec. 11.... **rise 8:40** A	June 11.... **set 8:04** E	Dec. 11.... **rise 4:35** A
June 21.... **set 9:45** E	Dec. 21.... **rise 7:58** A	June 21.... rise 4:34 A	Dec. 21.... set 6:54 E
	Dec. 31.... **rise 7:15** A		Dec. 31.... set 6:12 E

Eclipses, 2002

■ There will be five eclipses in 2002, two of the Sun and three of the Moon. Solar eclipses are visible only in certain areas and require eye protection to be viewed safely. Lunar eclipses are technically visible from the entire night side of Earth, but during a penumbral eclipse, the dimming of the Moon's illumination is slight.

1 Penumbral eclipse of the Moon, May 26. This eclipse will be visible in most of North America except the northeastern part and the Pacific Ocean; the end will be visible in southwestern Alaska and the Pacific Ocean. The Moon enters penumbra at 6:13 A.M. EDT (3:13 A.M. PDT) and leaves at 9:54 A.M. EDT (6:54 A.M. PDT).

2 Annular eclipse of the Sun, June 10. This partial eclipse will be visible throughout North America and Hawaii. In eastern North America, it will begin at about sunset. In western North America, it will begin at about 5:00 P.M. PDT and will last for about two hours.

3 Penumbral eclipse of the Moon, June 24. This eclipse will not be visible in the United States or Canada.

4 Penumbral eclipse of the Moon, November 19. The beginning of the penumbral phase will be visible in North America except the western part; the end will be visible in North America. The Moon enters penumbra at 6:32 P.M. EST (not visible PST) and leaves penumbra at 11:01 P.M. EST (8:01 P.M. PST).

5 Total eclipse of the Sun, December 3–4. This eclipse will not be visible in the United States or Canada.

Full-Moon Dates

	2002	2003	2004	2005	2006
Jan.	28	18	7	25	14
Feb.	27	16	6	23	12
Mar.	28	18	6	25	14
Apr.	26	16	5	24	13
May	26	15	4	23	13
June	24	14	3	22	11
July	24	13	2 & 31	21	10
Aug.	22	12	29	19	9
Sept.	21	10	28	17	7
Oct.	21	10	27	17	6
Nov.	19	8	26	15	5
Dec.	19	8	26	15	4

Principal Meteor Showers

Shower	Best Viewing	Point of Origin	Date of Maximum*	Peak Rate (/hr.)**	Associated Comet
Quadrantid	Predawn	N	Jan. 4	80	—
Lyrid	Predawn	S	Apr. 22	12	Thatcher
Eta Aquarid	Predawn	SE	May 4	20	Halley
Delta Aquarid	Predawn	S	July 30	10	—
Perseid	Predawn	NE	Aug. 11–13	75	Swift-Tuttle
Draconid	Late evening	NW	Oct. 9	6	Giacobini-Zinner
Orionid	Predawn	S	Oct. 21–22	25	Halley
Taurid	Midnight	S	Nov. 9	6	Encke
Leonid	Predawn	S	Nov. 18	20	Tempel-Tuttle
Andromedid	Late evening	S	Nov. 25–27	5	Biela
Geminid	All night	NE	Dec. 13–14	65	—
Ursid	Predawn	N	Dec. 22	12	Tuttle

*Date of actual maximum occurrence may vary by one or two days in either direction.
**Approximate.

Bright Stars, 2002

Transit Times

■ This table shows the time (EST or EDT) and altitude of a star as it transits the meridian (i.e., reaches its highest elevation while passing over the horizon's south point) at Boston on the dates shown. The transit time on any other date differs from that of the nearest date listed by approximately four minutes per day. To find the time of a star's transit for your location, convert its time at Boston using Key Letter C.*

| Star | Constellation | Magnitude | Time of Transit (EST/EDT) Boldface–P.M. Lightface–A.M. | | | | | | Altitude (degrees) |
			Jan. 1	Mar. 1	May 1	July 1	Sept. 1	Nov. 1	
Altair	Aquila	0.8	**12:49**	8:57	5:58	**1:58**	**9:50**	**4:50**	56.3
Deneb	Cygnus	1.3	**1:40**	9:48	6:48	2:49	**10:41**	**5:41**	92.8
Fomalhaut	Psc. Aus.	1.2	**3:55**	**12:03**	9:03	5:03	12:56	**7:56**	17.8
Algol	Perseus	2.2	**8:06**	**4:14**	**1:14**	9:14	5:10	12:10	88.5
Aldebaran	Taurus	0.9	**9:33**	**5:41**	**2:41**	10:41	6:37	1:38	64.1
Rigel	Orion	0.1	**10:11**	**6:19**	**3:19**	11:20	7:16	2:16	39.4
Capella	Auriga	0.1	**10:13**	**6:21**	**3:21**	11:21	7:18	2:18	93.6
Bellatrix	Orion	1.6	**10:22**	**6:30**	**3:30**	11:30	7:27	2:27	54.0
Betelgeuse	Orion	var. 0.4	**10:52**	**7:00**	**4:00**	**12:00**	7:56	2:57	55.0
Sirius	Can. Maj.	−1.4	**11:42**	**7:50**	**4:50**	**12:50**	8:46	3:46	31.0
Procyon	Can. Min.	0.4	12:39	**8:43**	**5:44**	**1:44**	9:40	4:40	52.9
Pollux	Gemini	1.2	12:45	**8:49**	**5:50**	**1:50**	9:46	4:46	75.7
Regulus	Leo	1.4	3:08	**11:12**	**8:13**	**4:13**	**12:09**	7:09	59.7
Spica	Virgo	var. 1.0	6:25	2:33	**11:29**	**7:29**	**3:25**	10:25	36.6
Arcturus	Bootes	−0.1	7:16	3:24	12:20	**8:20**	**4:16**	11:16	66.9
Antares	Scorpius	var. 0.9	9:28	5:36	2:37	**10:33**	**6:29**	**1:29**	21.3
Vega	Lyra	0	11:36	7:44	4:44	**12:40**	**8:36**	**3:37**	86.4

Risings and Settings

■ To find the time of a star's rising at Boston on any date, subtract the interval shown at right from the star's transit time on that date; add the interval to find the star's setting time. To find the rising and setting times for your city, convert the Boston transit times above using the Key Letter shown at right before applying the interval.* The directions in which the stars rise and set, shown for Boston, are generally useful throughout the United States. Deneb, Algol, Capella, and Vega are cir- cumpolar stars—they never set but appear to circle the celestial north pole.

Star	Interval (h. m.)	Rising Key	Rising Dir.	Setting Key	Setting Dir.
Altair	6:36	B	EbN	E	WbN
Fomalhaut	3:59	E	SE	D	SW
Aldebaran	7:06	B	ENE	D	WNW
Rigel	5:33	D	EbS	B	WbS
Bellatrix	6:27	B	EbN	D	WbN
Betelgeuse	6:31	B	EbN	D	WbN
Sirius	5:00	D	ESE	B	WSW
Procyon	6:23	B	EbN	D	WbN
Pollux	8:01	A	NE	E	NW
Regulus	6:49	B	EbN	D	WbN
Spica	5:23	D	EbS	B	WbS
Arcturus	7:19	A	ENE	E	WNW
Antares	4:17	E	SEbE	A	SWbW

*The values of Key Letters are given in the Time Corrections table (page 229).

Visit www.almanac.com *for more wit, wisdom, and weather.*

Long-term care coverage
Who needs it; how to find the right policy

Americans are living longer than ever and are now facing the important decision of whether to purchase long-term care insurance. Most people buy this coverage to protect assets, preserve independence and provide quality care. A growing number of younger people are buying it to help their aging parents.

Shop Smart

In general, long-term care protection makes sense for those with assets of at least $75,000 (excluding your home and car) and an annual income of at least $25,000 to $35,000.

With over 100 policies on the market—each with different benefits, premiums, exclusions and application requirements—it pays to comparison shop. According to respected *Money Magazine* financial editor, Jean Chatzky, "Your best bet is to get quotes from at least three companies."[1] In addition, you should consider a policy with at least a three-year term—the average time people need care.

Look for a daily benefit that would cover the average daily nursing-facility cost in your area. The national average is $125 ($46,000 per year), but in some areas it can run twice as much.[2]

Look for an elimination period (the time before your benefits begin) of 90 days. Remember, this is catastrophic coverage. Most people who need the insurance can afford the cost of care for three months. Plus, this approach lowers your cost—in some cases, by as much as 30% per year. Equally important, insist on insurers rated "A" or better by A.M. Best and "strong" by Standard & Poor's and Moody's.

If you'd like to receive three quotes with just one call, Long-Term Care Quote will provide them—free of charge. The company—which has been recommended in *Consumers Digest, Kiplinger's* and on NBC's *The Early Today Show*—will ask for basic information on your age, health and location, then shop up to 17 top-rated carriers on your behalf. You'll get details and quotes on the three most suitable policies for you, plus a copy of *The Consumer's Guide to Long-Term Care Insurance.*

To request your free Information Kit and personalized quotes, either write to Long-Term Care Quote, 600 W. Ray Road, Bldg. D4, Chandler, AZ 85225, visit www.LongTermCareQuote.com or call 1-800-587-3279.

[1] *USA Weekend*, June 15, 1998; [2] The Health Insurance Association of America, 2000; Writing agent Robert W. Davis, CA License #0875084. All inquiries will be kept strictly confidential.

BEHOLD
the Lord of the Rings

Celestial

coincidences

make this a

spectacular

year for Saturn.

by Bob Berman

id you catch Saturn in 1973? That was the last time the solar system's most beautiful planet appeared in its full glory. It has taken until now—this year—for the ringed world's near-mystical geometry to repeat. Backyard observers have waited a quarter-century to once again see Saturn this high, this big, and this brilliant.

Man's fascination with Saturn started in 1610, when Galileo pointed his crude telescope toward the most distant of the known planets. His actual expression wasn't recorded, but his jaw must have dropped. What was this thing before him? His meager 20× instrument had just enough power to tease him with a truly strange apparition, but the telescope's optical defects didn't give him an image sharp enough to let him clearly figure out the nature of the strange planet.

He never did. Decades later, his best drawings depicted a sphere with handles, something like a sugar bowl. Galileo's problem?

Saturn's form lies totally outside human experience. There simply is no earthly example of a globe surrounded by unattached rings.

Today, the most inexpensive department-store telescopes easily reveal Saturn's glorious rings; even 100× does the job nicely. Aside from the changing faces of Saturn, the only image-spoiling interference is the frequent turbulence of Earth's atmosphere. If you encounter common jittery air, or "poor seeing," wait for a night when stars aren't twinkling and planetary images are rock-steady. As for Saturn, the giant planet helps us out this year with optimum conditions, patiently posing for Earth's curious onlookers.

The ringed planet's meandering is predictable and simple. Each year, as Earth revolves around the Sun, we spend a month or two close to Saturn—always at a time when the three bodies form a straight line, with our world sandwiched in the middle, in a configuration

OUT OF THIS WORLD. *Saturn (opposite), as photographed by the NASA Hubble Space Telescope on December 1, 1994. Here, the rings are almost edge-on, or in a middling-tilt position. This year, we'll see them face-on, completely encircling the globe of the planet.*

61

This year,

the rings are

face-on

and nothing

short of

magnificent.

☆
☆

called opposition. Then we move on, whirl around the Sun once more, and again approach Saturn. But Saturn, in its own slow 29½-year orbit, has inched forward ever so slightly, so that our rendezvous occurs about two weeks later each year. For example, in 2000, we met Saturn on November 19, and in 2001, we pass by on December 3. Our close encounter in 2002 will take place on December 17, and in 2003, it will be on New Year's Eve.

But all Saturn meetings are not created equal. Far from it. Due to the tilt of Earth, people in the Northern Hemisphere are angled in Saturn's direction only half the time. When we tilt away from Saturn during the other half of those oppositions, we see the ringed planet low in the sky, its features blurred by thick horizon air. Unfavorable oppositions for U.S. and Canadian observers kept recurring like a bad dream from 1985 to 1996, and only slowly improved. Now, this year and next, we will enjoy a maximal tilt toward Saturn. Finally, it hovers high in the sky, clear of buildings and trees, with a near-vertical light path that whisks Saturn's image through the least amount of distorting air. The viewing experience is, in a word, perfect.

Then there's the issue of its fabled rings. Saturn's tilt is similar to ours, so its rings can be angled edge-on and seem to disappear, as they did in 1995 and will again in 2010. At other stages of its orbit, they slant face-on (or facing in our direction), revealing their wondrous ring-within-ring structure; the widest and brightest rings are separated by a dramatic inky gap called the Cassini division, named for the first astronomer to discern it, in 1676.

This year, the rings are face-on and nothing short of magnificent. Composed mostly of ice particles (ranging in size from pebbles to boulders), the rings are more reflective than the planet itself. When they're facing us this way, in a wide-open orientation, Saturn's brightness is tripled. So even naked-eye observers get a treat: The planet now shines as the night's fourth-brightest "star," bested only by Venus, Jupiter, and the Dog Star, Sirius.

There's more. Like every other celestial body, Saturn has an oval, rather than a round, orbit: Earth meets it at varying distances at each opposition. This variation is not small; the gap between the orbits can range up to a whopping 90 million miles, making Saturn appear dimmer whenever it's that far from Earth and from the Sun that illuminates it. Here again, we are in luck in 2002 and 2003, when Saturn's oppositions will be the closest since 1975. As a result, Saturn will appear larger (20.7 arc-seconds) than it has in more than a quarter-century.

What's remarkable is that the convergence happens all at once. With Saturn, it's all or nothing. Imagine: The various geometries could be different. The rings could be poor and edge-on just as the planet comes closest to us. Or both those parameters could be favorable just as our hemisphere is facing the wrong way, keeping

Saturn low and blurry. Instead, every possible variable that can make Saturn optimally big, bright, and glorious meshes, by incredible coincidence, this year and next. It's reason enough to run, not walk, to that telescope gathering dust in the attic.

When this present Saturn season passes, everything goes kaput. The rings close down (that is, face away), the planet moves away, Earth's axis tilts away from it, and Saturn starts creeping into the lower portions of the zodiac. Circumstances for similarly good views don't come around again until the year 2030.

Saturn will be big news long before then, however. The fabulous *Cassini* spacecraft, the last of the glitzy, billion-dollar probes of the Voyager and Galileo class, is now finishing its long journey and will arrive at the ringed world in 2004. This first-ever spacecraft to orbit Saturn will spend years examining its many moons and beaming back astounding close-up photos of the planet and the rings. New discoveries will make headlines; you can count on it. And everyone, even casual stargazers, will want to experience for themselves the planet's unique impact.

But when that news breaks, Saturn won't be quite so large and dramatic. To catch the ringed wonder at its best, the time is now.

CLOSER ENCOUNTERS

Go to **www.almanac.com** and click on **Article Links 2002** for Web sites related to this article.

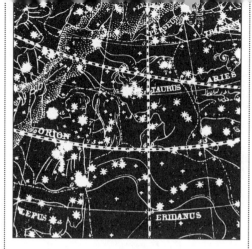

Desperately Seeking Saturn

ow do you find Saturn in the night sky? One way is fairly simple: The ringed world spends the year in Taurus, near the well-known Pleiades Seven Sisters star cluster. Or you can try this: Look for the night's brightest star anytime after 9 P.M. That's dazzling Jupiter. The brightest star closest to Jupiter is Saturn. Also, throughout 2002, Saturn hovers quite near orange Aldebaran, the eye of Taurus the Bull, and it distinctly outshines that famous star. If further help is needed, remember the ancient and accurate advice that stars often twinkle, but planets usually do not.

Saturn has two optimum viewing periods in 2002: from January 1 to March 1 and from October 1 to December 31. These are the times that it ascends high and hovers nearby, within a few months of its opposition. Nonpurists can see Saturn for the entire year except during its brief period behind the Sun from late May to late June, but it will be low and blurry during the spring and most of the summer. Even for a slow-moving planet, timing is everything. □□

The Moon passes close to Jupiter on the 6th. Mercury displays its best morning-star appearance of the year as it hovers next to Venus during the first week of November. Saturn now rises at nightfall, and much brighter Jupiter rises by 10:00 P.M. EST, dominating the heavens for the remainder of the night. The Leonid meteors will keep observers awake on the night of the 17th–18th. Mars, the only bright "star" low in the south at nightfall, offers the year's best chance to locate dim Uranus when it floats just below the seventh planet on the 26th. A Moon-Saturn conjunction occurs on the 30th.

○	Full Moon	1st day	0 hour	41st minute
☾	Last Quarter	8th day	7th hour	21st minute
●	New Moon	15th day	1st hour	40th minute
☽	First Quarter	22nd day	18th hour	21st minute
○	Full Moon	30th day	15th hour	49th minute

Times are given in Eastern Standard Time.

For an explanation of this page, see page 40; for values of Key Letters, see page 229.

Day of Year	Day of Month	Day of Week	☼ Rises h. m.	Key	☼ Sets h. m.	Key	Length of Day h. m.	Sun Fast m.	Declination of Sun ° '	High Tide Boston Light—A.M. Bold—P.M.		☽ Rises h. m.	Key	☽ Sets h. m.	Key	☽ Place	☽ Age
305	1	Th.	6 18	D	4 37	B	10 19	32	14s.36	11	11½	5PM12	B	6♈27	E	ARI	16
306	2	Fr.	6 19	D	4 36	B	10 17	32	14 55	11½	—	5 44	B	7 33	E	TAU	17
307	3	Sa.	6 20	D	4 35	B	10 15	32	15 13	12¼	12¼	6 21	A	8 40	E	TAU	18
308	4	**G**	6 21	D	4 34	B	10 13	32	15 32	12¾	1	7 06	A	9 47	E	TAU	19
309	5	M.	6 23	D	4 32	B	10 09	32	15 50	1½	1¾	8 00	B	10 49	E	GEM	20
310	6	Tu.	6 24	D	4 31	B	10 07	32	16 08	2½	2½	9 02	B	11♈46	E	GEM	21
311	7	W.	6 25	D	4 30	B	10 05	32	16 26	3¼	3½	10 11	B	12PM35	E	CAN	22
312	8	Th.	6 26	D	4 29	A	10 03	32	16 43	4¼	4½	11♈M24	B	1 17	E	CAN	23
313	9	Fr.	6 28	D	4 28	A	10 00	32	17 01	5¼	5½	—	–	1 53	E	LEO	24
314	10	Sa.	6 29	D	4 27	A	9 58	32	17 18	6¼	6¾	12♈38	C	2 24	D	LEO	25
315	11	**G**	6 30	D	4 26	A	9 56	32	17 34	7¼	7¾	1 52	D	2 53	D	VIR	26
316	12	M.	6 31	D	4 25	A	9 54	31	17 50	8¼	8¾	3 06	D	3 20	C	VIR	27
317	13	Tu.	6 33	D	4 24	A	9 51	31	18 06	9	9½	4 20	E	3 49	C	VIR	28
318	14	W.	6 34	D	4 23	A	9 49	31	18 22	10	10½	5 34	E	4 19	B	LIB	29
319	15	Th.	6 35	D	4 22	A	9 47	31	18 37	10¾	11¼	6 47	E	4 53	B	LIB	0
320	16	Fr.	6 36	D	4 21	A	9 45	31	18 52	11½	—	7 58	E	5 33	B	OPH	1
321	17	Sa.	6 38	D	4 20	A	9 42	31	19 06	12	12¼	9 04	E	6 18	A	OPH	2
322	18	**G**	6 39	D	4 20	A	9 41	30	19 20	1	1	10 05	E	7 09	A	SAG	3
323	19	M.	6 40	D	4 19	A	9 39	30	19 34	1¾	1¾	10 56	E	8 06	A	SAG	4
324	20	Tu.	6 41	D	4 18	A	9 37	30	19 48	2½	2¾	11♈M40	E	9 05	B	SAG	5
325	21	W.	6 43	D	4 17	A	9 34	30	20 02	3½	3½	12PM17	E	10 06	B	CAP	6
326	22	Th.	6 44	D	4 17	A	9 33	30	20 15	4¼	4½	12 47	E	11PM06	B	CAP	7
327	23	Fr.	6 45	D	4 16	A	9 31	29	20 27	5¼	5¼	1 14	D	—	–	AQU	8
328	24	Sa.	6 46	D	4 16	A	9 30	29	20 39	6	6¼	1 38	D	12♈07	C	AQU	9
329	25	**G**	6 47	D	4 15	A	9 28	29	20 51	7	7¼	2 01	D	1 07	D	PSC	10
330	26	M.	6 48	D	4 15	A	9 27	28	21 02	7¾	8	2 23	C	2 07	D	CET	11
331	27	Tu.	6 50	E	4 14	A	9 24	28	21 13	8½	8¾	2 47	B	3 09	D	PSC	12
332	28	W.	6 51	E	4 14	A	9 23	28	21 24	9	9½	3 13	B	4 12	E	CET	13
333	29	Th.	6 52	E	4 13	A	9 21	27	21 34	9¾	10¼	3 42	B	5 18	E	ARI	14
334	30	Fr.	6 53	E	4 13	A	9 20	27	21s.44	10½	11	4PM18	B	6♈26	E	TAU	15

NOVEMBER hath 30 days. 2001

When the tree bares, the music of it changes:
Hard and keen is the sound, long and mournful;
Pale are the poplar boughs in the evening light
Above my house, against a slate-cold cloud. –Conrad Aiken

D. M.	D. W.	Dates, Feasts, Fasts, Aspects, Tide Heights	Weather ↓
1	Th.	All Saints' • Full Beaver ○ • Stephen Crane born, 1871 • {10.4 9.7	*Damp*
2	Fr.	All Souls' • ♃ stat. • James Thurber died, 1961 • Tides {10.6 —	*and*
3	Sa.	☌♄☾ • 96°F in Los Angeles, 1890; record high for November for 76 years •	*dismal,*
4	G	22nd S. af. P. • ☾ at ☊ • ☌♂♆ • {9.6 10.7	
5	M.	George B. Selden received first U.S. patent for automobile, 1895 • {9.4 10.6 •	*turning*
6	Tu.	☾ rides high • ☌♃☾ • Election Day • {9.2 10.5	*colder,*
7	W.	*If voting changed anything, they'd make it illegal.* • Tides {9.1 10.3 •	*then*
8	Th.	First U.S. college for women, Mt. Holyoke, founded, 1837 • Astronomer Edmund Halley born, 1656 •	*a*
9	Fr.	Carl Sagan born, 1934 • J. William Fulbright born, 1905 • {9.3 10.1 •	*warm*
10	Sa.	St. Leo the Great • Sadie Hawkins Day • {9.6 10.2 •	*hiatus;*
11	G	23rd S. af. P. • Veterans Day • ☾ at perig. •	*rain*
12	M.	St. Martin • ☾ on Eq. • 105°F, Craftonville, Calif., 1906 • {10.7 10.6	*and*
13	Tu.	Holland Tunnel, connecting New York City and Jersey City, N.J., opened, 1927 • {11.2 10.7	*snow*
14	W.	First streetcar, drawn by horses, began operating in New York City, 1832 • {11.5 10.7	*that's*
15	Th.	New ● • *One person with belief is equal to a force of 99 who have only interests.* • {11.7 10.5	*so*
16	Fr.	Arturo Toscanini made U.S. conducting debut at the Met., 1908 • {11.6 —	*abysmal*
17	Sa.	St. Hugh of Lincoln • ☾ at ☋ • Tides {10.2 11.3	*comes*
18	G	24th S. af. P. • Margaret Atwood born, 1939 • {9.9 10.9 •	*to*
19	M.	☾ runs low • Roy Campanella born, 1921 • James Garfield born, 1831 •	*irritate*
20	Tu.	☌♆☾ • Hubble space telescope photographed the Eagle Nebula, 1995 •	*us!*
21	W.	☌♂☾ • ☌♅☾ • Stan Musial born, 1920 • {8.8 9.4	*Thanks*
22	Th.	Thanksgiving • *Gratitude is the memory of the heart.* • {8.5 9.1 •	*for*
23	Fr.	St. Clement • ☾ at apo. • Franklin Pierce born, 1804 • {8.5 8.8 •	*our*
24	Sa.	Congress passed Brady handgun-control bill, 1993 • {8.6 8.80	*abundant*
25	G	25th S. af. P. • Carry Nation born, 1846 • {8.8 8.8	*blessings!*
26	M.	☾ on Eq. • ☌♂♅ • Sojourner Truth died, 1883 • {9.2 8.9	*Sunny*
27	Tu.	Savings and loan bailout: Congress authorized additional $70 billion for FDIC, 1991 •	*days*
28	W.	20°F, Tallahassee, Fla., 1950, matched previous November record • Tides {9.9 9.3	*and*
29	Th.	Louisa May Alcott born, 1832 • Busby Berkeley born, 1895 • {10.3 9.4	*onion*
30	Fr.	St. Andrew • Full Frost ○ • Occn. ♄☾ •	*dressing!*

Do not condemn the judgment of another because it differs from your own. You may both be wrong. –Dandemis

Farmer's Calendar

■ Some years ago in a little town in Maine, the kids arrived at their school one Monday morning around this time of year to find a bear sleeping in the playground. The playground had one of those tunnels made of a half-buried steel culvert. The children at play were meant to creep through it. None did so that morning, you may be sure, for the bear had chosen their tunnel as its winter den. I don't recall exactly how the episode ended; one of the teachers told the bear to hibernate someplace else, I guess. Teachers put up with a lot these days.

All over the North, the bears are going into their dens. The sexes den differently, it seems. Male bears flop down about anywhere—hence, no doubt, the playground bear above. Females prepare a proper den, a protected hole, a hollow log, or a tree cavity that they improve with leaves and other insulation. A female bear may give birth in her den, so she's more deliberate than her mate in choosing a place for hibernation.

In fact, *hibernation* is a misnomer in the bear. Unlike woodchucks, bats, and some mice, bears don't exhibit true hibernation. Their essential physical processes don't slow down as much, or as uniformly, as the real hibernators do. Still, bears *do* sleep, deeply, in the den. And whatever you call their wintering, it sounds like a good deal. There is something comforting about the idea of hibernation, a kind of vicarious solace for us all. When the days get short, dark, and cold, and the snow begins to fly—you check out. Maybe scientists don't call that hibernation, but the bears do.

Saturn, close to the nearly full Moon as December opens (and again on the 27th), reaches opposition on the 3rd, rising at sunset. At magnitude -0.4, it is outshone only by the Dog Star, Sirius, and dazzling Jupiter. With Mars fading and sinking lower in the southwest, and Mercury and Venus low and unimpressive, Jupiter and Saturn are the year-end celebrities. Look for the splendid Geminid meteors on the 13th and 14th. A partial solar eclipse can be seen from the central United States and Canada on the 14th. The winter solstice occurs on the 21st, at 2:21 P.M. EST. Jupiter is closest to Earth on the 30th and brightest on New Year's Eve, rising brilliantly in the northeast at nightfall.

☾ Last Quarter	7th day	14th hour	52nd minute
● New Moon	14th day	15th hour	47th minute
☽ First Quarter	22nd day	15th hour	56th minute
○ Full Moon	30th day	5th hour	40th minute

Times are given in Eastern Standard Time.

For an explanation of this page, see page 40; for values of Key Letters, see page 229.

Day of Year	Day of Month	Day of Week	☀ Rises h. m.	Key	☀ Sets h. m.	Key	Length of Day h. m.	Sun Fast m.	Declination of Sun ° '	High Tide Boston Light—A.M. Bold—P.M.		☽ Rises h. m.	Key	☽ Sets h. m.	Key	Place	☽ Age
335	1	Sa.	6 54	E	4 13	A	9 19	27	21s.53	11	11¾	5ᴹ00	B	7ᴹ34	E	TAU	16
336	2	G	6 55	E	4 12	A	9 17	26	22 02	11¾	—	5 52	B	8 41	E	TAU	17
337	3	M.	6 56	E	4 12	A	9 16	26	22 10	12½	12½	6 53	B	9 41	E	GEM	18
338	4	Tu.	6 57	E	4 12	A	9 15	26	22 18	1¼	1½	8 02	B	10 34	E	GEM	19
339	5	W.	6 58	E	4 12	A	9 14	25	22 25	2	2¼	9 14	B	11 19	E	CAN	20
340	6	Th.	6 59	E	4 12	A	9 13	25	22 32	3	3¼	10 28	C	11ᴹ56	E	LEO	21
341	7	Fr.	7 00	E	4 12	A	9 12	24	22 39	4	4¼	11ᴹ41	C	12ᴹ28	D	LEO	22
342	8	Sa.	7 00	E	4 11	A	9 11	24	22 46	5	5¼	—	–	12 57	D	VIR	23
343	9	G	7 01	E	4 11	A	9 10	23	22 52	6	6½	12ᴬ54	D	1 24	C	VIR	24
344	10	M.	7 03	E	4 12	A	9 09	23	22 57	7	7½	2 05	D	1 51	C	VIR	25
345	11	Tu.	7 03	E	4 12	A	9 09	23	23 02	8	8½	3 17	E	2 19	B	VIR	26
346	12	W.	7 04	E	4 12	A	9 08	22	23 06	8¾	9½	4 28	E	2 51	B	LIB	27
347	13	Th.	7 05	E	4 12	A	9 07	22	23 10	9¾	10¼	5 39	E	3 27	A	LIB	28
348	14	Fr.	7 06	E	4 12	A	9 06	21	23 14	10½	11	6 47	E	4 09	A	OPH	0
349	15	Sa.	7 07	E	4 12	A	9 05	21	23 17	11¼	11¾	7 50	E	4 57	A	SAG	1
350	16	G	7 08	E	4 13	A	9 05	20	23 20	12	—	8 46	E	5 52	A	SAG	2
351	17	M.	7 08	E	4 13	A	9 05	20	23 22	12½	12¾	9 34	E	6 51	B	SAG	3
352	18	Tu.	7 09	E	4 13	A	9 04	19	23 23	1¼	1¼	10 14	E	7 51	B	CAP	4
353	19	W.	7 10	E	4 14	A	9 04	19	23 25	2	2	10 47	E	8 53	B	CAP	5
354	20	Th.	7 10	E	4 14	A	9 04	18	23 26	2¾	3	11 16	E	9 53	C	AQU	6
355	21	Fr.	7 11	E	4 15	A	9 04	18	23 26	3½	3¾	11ᴬ41	D	10 53	C	AQU	7
356	22	Sa.	7 11	E	4 15	A	9 04	17	23 26	4¼	4½	12ᴹ04	D	11ᴹ53	C	AQU	8
357	23	G	7 12	E	4 16	A	9 04	17	23 25	5¼	5½	12 26	C	—	–	CET	9
358	24	M.	7 12	E	4 16	A	9 04	16	23 24	6	6½	12 49	C	12ᴬ53	D	PSC	10
359	25	Tu.	7 12	E	4 17	A	9 05	16	23 22	6¾	7¼	1 13	B	1 55	D	PSC	11
360	26	W.	7 12	E	4 18	A	9 06	15	23 20	7¾	8¼	1 40	B	2 59	E	ARI	12
361	27	Th.	7 12	E	4 18	A	9 06	15	23 17	8½	9	2 12	B	4 05	E	TAU	13
362	28	Fr.	7 13	E	4 19	A	9 06	14	23 14	9¼	9¾	2 51	B	5 14	E	TAU	14
363	29	Sa.	7 13	E	4 20	A	9 07	14	23 11	10	10½	3 40	A	6 22	E	TAU	15
364	30	G	7 13	E	4 21	A	9 08	13	23 07	10¾	11¼	4 38	A	7 27	E	GEM	16
365	31	M.	7 13	E	4 21	A	9 08	13	23s.03	11½	—	5ᴹ46	A	8ᴬ25	E	GEM	17

DECEMBER hath 31 days. 2001

Ring out false pride in place and blood,
The civic slander and the spite;
Ring in the love of truth and right,
Ring in the common love of good. –Alfred, Lord Tennyson

D. M.	D. W.	Dates, Feasts, Fasts, Aspects, Tide Heights	*Weather* ↓
1	Sa.	Marilyn Monroe appeared in first issue of *Playboy*, 1953 • Tides {10.9 / 9.6 •	*Bright*
2	G	**1st S. in Advent** • ☾ at ☊ • Monroe Doctrine, 1823 •	*out,*
3	M.	☾ rides high • ☌ ♃ ☾ • ♄ at ☍ • Tides {9.6 / 11.1	*then*
4	Tu.	☿ in sup. ☌ • Record highs in the Northeast: 70°F, Boston; 65°F, Burlington, Vt., 1982 •	*a*
5	W.	The AFL and the CIO labor groups merged, 1955 • Tides {9.5 / 10.8	*whiteout!*
6	Th.	St. Nicholas • ☾ at perig. • ☌ ♇ ☉ • {9.5 / 10.5	*Cloudy*
7	Fr.	St. Ambrose • **National Pearl Harbor Remembrance Day** • Tides {9.6 / 10.2	*with*
8	Sa.	*Using your imagination is the one time in life you can really go anywhere.* • {9.7 / 10.0	*a*
9	G	**2nd S. in Advent** • ☾ on Eq. • {10.0 / 9.8 •	*chance*
10	M.	First day of Chanukah • First recorded sighting of Aurora Borealis in New England, 1719 •	*of*
11	Tu.	Nitrous oxide (laughing gas) first used in dentistry, Hartford, Conn., 1844 • {10.7 / 9.8 •	*glop;*
12	W.	Beethoven paid Haydn 19¢ for his first music lesson, Vienna, 1792 • Tides {11.0 / 9.9	*shop*
13	Th.	St. Lucy • Abel Tasman discovered New Zealand, 1642 • Grandma Moses died, 1961 •	*'til*
14	Fr.	☾ at ☋ • **New** ● • Eclipse ☉ • Tides {11.2 / 9.8	*you*
15	Sa.	Halcyon Days • *Visits always give pleasure—if not the arrival, the departure.* • {11.1 / 9.6	*drop.*
16	G	**3rd S. in Advent** • ☾ runs low • {10.9 / —	*Season's*
17	M.	Aztec calendar stone discovered in Mexico City, 1790 • {9.4 / 10.6 •	*greetings*
18	Tu.	☌ ♆ ☾ • Antonio Stradivari died, 1737 • Tides {9.2 / 10.3	*might*
19	W.	☌ ⛢ ☾ • Ember Day • Albert L. Jones patented corrugated paper, 1871 •	*bring*
20	Th.	☌ ♂ ☾ • Branch Rickey born, 1881 • Tides {8.8 / 9.5	*sleetings.*
21	Fr.	St. Thomas • ☾ at apo. • **Winter Solstice** • Ember Day •	*Here's*
22	Sa.	Ember Day • First gorilla born in captivity, Columbus, Ohio, 1956 • Tides {8.6 / 8.8	*a*
23	G	**4th S. in Advent** • ☾ on Eq. • Beware the Pogonip. •	*year*
24	M.	For the first time since Lenin's death, the bells of St. Basil's Cathedral, Moscow, rang, 1990 • {8.8 / 8.4	*you*
25	Tu.	**Christmas Day** • *Music is well said to be the speech of angels.* •	*might*
26	W.	St. Stephen • **Boxing Day (Canada)** • Henry Miller born, 1891 • {9.5 / 8.6 •	*find*
27	Th.	St. John • Johannes Kepler, the "father of modern astronomy" born, 1571 •	*comic—*
28	Fr.	Holy Innocents • Occn. ♄ ☾ • Tides {10.3 / 9.1 •	*2002*
29	Sa.	☾ at ☊ • American Meteorological Society founded, St. Louis, Mo., 1919 • {10.7 / 9.4	*is*
30	G	**1st S. af. Ch.** • ☾ rides high • Eclipse ☾ • **Full Long Nights** ○	
31	M.	*Happiness is a form of courage.* • Tides {11.4 / — •	*palindromic!*

Farmer's Calendar

■ It occurs to me that I have seen snow, in greater or lesser quantities, in every winter of my life except possibly the first. I happened to be born well to the south of snow country and so must have missed out at the very beginning. Since then, though, I have never lived through a winter in which no snow at all fell on my head—or if I have, such winters have been no more than one or two.

I am 55. You would think that anyone who has shoveled, scraped, and waded his way through that many winters' snow might be getting the hang of the stuff at last. Snow ought to hold nothing new for one who has served it for more than half a century. Alas, it's not so. Snow can still surprise me, not by its depth, certainly not by its sublime intractability, but, even now, by its stealth.

Each year in this season, for a moment, snow puzzles me. Spring, summer, and autumn have taken away my memory. I'll be outdoors, tending to some task of doubtful necessity, when I become aware of . . . *stuff* . . . *matter* that seems to be falling from the sky. Not much of it, a piece here, another there. It's solid but slight, it settles softly, almost like ash. Is it ash? Is the chimney on fire? Are the neighbors burning brush? Is it a kind of out-of-season bud- or flower-fall that's coming from the trees? Is it manna from heaven, as in the Bible? Is it flying gnats? A little more falls. It's pale in color, and when it lands, it disappears. Not manna, then. Oddly cold to the touch, too, almost wet. Hold on! I know this stuff. It was here last winter.

The year begins brilliantly, as Jupiter reaches opposition and attains its greatest brightness of 2002 just one hour into the new year. Saturn (see feature on page 60), too, is exceptionally bright and high this month, its rings optimally presented to those viewing through telescopes. Both giant planets—Jupiter in Gemini and Saturn in Taurus—are visible all night. In the opposite part of the heavens, Mercury is easily seen in evening twilight the first three weeks of the new year. An inconspicuous Mars stands halfway up the western sky at nightfall, and sets around 10:00 P.M. EST. Earth is at perihelion (closest to the Sun) on the 2nd.

☾	Last Quarter	5th day	22nd hour	55th minute
●	New Moon	13th day	8th hour	29th minute
☽	First Quarter	21st day	12th hour	46th minute
○	Full Moon	28th day	17th hour	50th minute

Times are given in Eastern Standard Time.

For an explanation of this page, see page 40; for values of Key Letters, see page 229.

Day of Year	Day of Month	Day of Week	☼ Rises h. m.	Key	☼ Sets h. m.	Key	Length of Day h. m.	Sun Fast m.	Declination of Sun ° '	High Tide Boston Light—A.M. Bold—P.M.		☽ Rises h. m.	Key	☽ Sets h. m.	Key	Place	☽ Age
1	1	Tu.	7 14	E	4 22	A	9 08	12	22s.58	12¼	**12¼**	7ᴹ00	B	9ᴹ15	E	CAN	18
2	2	W.	7 14	E	4 23	A	9 09	12	22 53	1	**1¼**	8 16	C	9 56	E	LEO	19
3	3	Th.	7 14	E	4 24	A	9 10	11	22 48	1¾	**2**	9 31	C	10 31	D	LEO	20
4	4	Fr.	7 14	E	4 25	A	9 11	11	22 41	2¾	**3**	10 45	D	11 01	D	LEO	21
5	5	Sa.	7 14	E	4 26	A	9 12	10	22 34	3¾	**4**	11ᴹ57	D	11 28	D	VIR	22
6	6	**F**	7 13	E	4 27	A	9 14	10	22 27	4½	**5**	—	–	11ᴹ55	C	VIR	23
7	7	M.	7 13	E	4 28	A	9 15	10	22 20	5½	**6**	1ᴬ08	D	12ᴹ22	C	VIR	24
8	8	Tu.	7 13	E	4 29	A	9 16	9	22 12	6½	**7¼**	2 18	E	12 52	B	LIB	25
9	9	W.	7 13	E	4 30	A	9 17	9	22 03	7½	**8¼**	3 27	E	1 26	B	LIB	26
10	10	Th.	7 13	E	4 31	A	9 18	8	21 55	8½	**9¼**	4 35	E	2 05	B	OPH	27
11	11	Fr.	7 12	E	4 32	A	9 20	8	21 45	9¼	**10**	5 39	E	2 50	A	OPH	28
12	12	Sa.	7 12	E	4 33	A	9 21	8	21 36	10¼	**10¾**	6 37	E	3 42	A	SAG	29
13	13	**F**	7 11	E	4 34	A	9 23	7	21 25	11	**11½**	7 28	E	4 39	B	SAG	0
14	14	M.	7 11	E	4 36	A	9 25	7	21 15	11½	—	8 11	E	5 39	B	CAP	1
15	15	Tu.	7 11	E	4 37	A	9 26	6	21 04	12¼	**12¼**	8 46	E	6 40	B	CAP	2
16	16	W.	7 10	E	4 38	A	9 28	6	20 53	1	**1**	9 17	E	7 42	B	CAP	3
17	17	Th.	7 10	E	4 39	A	9 29	6	20 41	1½	**1¾**	9 43	D	8 42	C	AQU	4
18	18	Fr.	7 09	E	4 40	A	9 31	5	20 29	2¼	**2¼**	10 07	D	9 42	D	AQU	5
19	19	Sa.	7 09	E	4 42	A	9 33	5	20 16	3	**3**	10 29	D	10 41	D	PSC	6
20	20	**F**	7 08	E	4 43	A	9 35	5	20 03	3½	**4**	10 51	C	11ᴹ41	D	CET	7
21	21	M.	7 07	E	4 44	A	9 37	4	19 50	4¼	**4¾**	11 14	C	—		PSC	8
22	22	Tu.	7 07	E	4 45	A	9 38	4	19 36	5¼	**5¾**	11ᴹ39	B	12ᴹ42	E	CET	9
23	23	W.	7 06	D	4 47	A	9 41	4	19 22	6	**6½**	12ᴹ08	B	1 46	E	ARI	10
24	24	Th.	7 05	D	4 48	A	9 43	4	19 07	7	**7½**	12 42	B	2 52	E	TAU	11
25	25	Fr.	7 04	D	4 49	A	9 45	3	18 53	7¾	**8½**	1 25	A	4 00	E	TAU	12
26	26	Sa.	7 04	D	4 50	A	9 46	3	18 38	8¾	**9¼**	2 18	A	5 06	E	LEO	13
27	27	**F**	7 03	D	4 52	A	9 49	3	18 22	9½	**10¼**	3 22	B	6 08	E	GEM	14
28	28	M.	7 02	D	4 53	A	9 51	3	18 07	10¼	**11**	4 35	B	7 03	E	LEO	15
29	29	Tu.	7 01	D	4 54	A	9 53	3	17 51	11¼	**11¾**	5 52	B	7 49	E	CAN	16
30	30	W.	7 00	D	4 56	A	9 56	2	17 34	**12**	—	7 11	C	8 27	E	LEO	17
31	31	Th.	6 59	D	4 57	A	9 58	2	17s.18	12¾	**1**	8ᴹ29	D	9ᴹ00	D	LEO	18

JANUARY hath 31 days. 2002

No time for self-pity or rankling despair
But bless the power that rules the changing year:
Assured...though horrors round his cottage reign
That Spring will come, and Nature smile again. –R. Bloomfield

D. M.	D. W.	Dates, Feasts, Fasts, Aspects, Tide Heights	*Weather* ↓
1	Tu.	New Year's Day • **Circumcision** • ♃ at ☍ •	*Skiers*
2	W.	☾ at perig. • ⊕ at perihelion • First photograph of the Moon, 1839 •	*strike*
3	Th.	Sarcophagus of King Tut-ankhamen discovered, 1924 • Stars and Stripes adopted as official flag, 1777	*gold*
4	Fr.	St. Elizabeth Seton • *Deliberate slowly, execute promptly.* • {10.1 / 10.8 •	*but*
5	Sa.	☾ on Eq. • First divorce granted in the Colonies, 1643 • Twelfth Night • {10.1 / 10.3	*mighty*
6	**F**	**Epiphany** • Tom Mix born, 1880 • Joan of Arc born, 1412 • {10.1 / 9.8	*cold.*
7	M.	Plough Monday • St. Distaff's Day • Hirohito died, 1989 Tides {10.2 / 9.4	*Only*
8	Tu.	☌ ☿ ♆ • *'Tis better to wear out than to rust out.* • Loch Ness monster photographed, 1974 •	*an*
9	W.	New York outlawed public flirting, 1902 • Ocean liner *Queen Elizabeth* destroyed by fire, 1972 •	*Inuit*
10	Th.	Dashiell Hammett died, 1961 • First major oil strike in Texas, (near Beaumont), 1901	*would*
11	Fr.	☿ Gr. Elong. (19° E.) • ☾ at ☋ • Caesar crossed the Rubicon River, 49 B.C. •	*go*
12	Sa.	☾ runs low • First museum in United States established, Charleston, S.C., 1773 • {10.6 / 9.1	*out*
13	**F**	**1st S. af. Ep.** • New ● • Sophie Tucker born, 1884 •	*into it.*
14	M.	St. Hilary • ☌ ☿ ☾ • ♀ in sup. ☌ • Tides {10.4 / —	*A*
15	Tu.	☌ ♅ ☾ • Pentagon completed, 1943 • Matthew Brady died, 1896 •	*thaw'll*
16	W.	Prohibition took effect, 1920 • *Never mistake endurance for hospitality.* • {9.0 / 10.1	*turn*
17	Th.	Benjamin Franklin born, 1706 • Gary Gilmore executed by firing squad, 1977 • {9.0 / 9.8 •	*to*
18	Fr.	☾ at apo. • ☌ ♂ ☾ • ☿ stat. • Tides {8.9 / 9.4 •	*squall,*
19	Sa.	☾ on Eq. • Hudson River froze, 1810 • Tin can patented, 1825 •	*recalling*
20	**F**	**2nd S. af. Ep.** • First basketball game played, Springfield, Mass., 1892	*storms*
21	M.	Martin Luther King Jr.'s Birthday (observed) •	*appalling!*
22	Tu.	St. Vincent • George Foreman k.o.'d Joe Frazier, 1973 {8.9 / 8.1	*Flurrying—*
23	W.	*No one is entirely useless; even the worst of us can serve as horrible examples.* • {9.0 / 8.1 •	*even*
24	Th.	☌ ♄ ☾ • Canned beer first sold, Richmond, Va., 1935 • Gold found in Calif., 1848	*brass*
25	Fr.	Conversion of Paul • ☾ at ☊ • Raccoons mate now. •	*monkeys*
26	Sa.	Sts. Timothy & Titus • ☌ ♃ ☾ • {10.3 / 8.9	*are worrying.*
27	**F**	**3rd S. af. Ep.** • ☾ rides high • **Septuagesima** •	
28	M.	St. Thomas Aquinas • Full Old ○ • ☌ ♆ ☉ • {11.3 / 9.8	*Still*
29	Tu.	W.C. Fields born, 1880 • Robert Frost died, 1963 • Thomas Paine born, 1737 {11.7 / 10.3	*wilder;*
30	W.	☾ at perig. • Anton Chekhov born, 1860 • *As the day lengthens, the cold strengthens.* •	*then*
31	Th.	"The Green Hornet" first heard on Detroit radio station WXYZ, 1936 • Tides {10.6 / 11.8	*milder.*

Farmer's Calendar

■ It was mid-January last year when people in these parts became aware that the thickets and roadsides were full of robins. In the depth of winter arrived the harbinger of spring, full of beer and business and at least two months early, as though the singer had begun "The Star Spangled Banner" while the teams were still in the locker room. What was going on? Was this yet another ominous sign of global warming? Why were the robins back so early?

Fortunately, the truth was not far to seek. People who know a lot about birds (a class of citizens of whom every country town has at least four) were quick to explain that the robins were back early because they had never left. In the latitudes of northern New England, it seems, robins are always present. Some live here year-round, others arrive for the winter from farther north. They live on seeds and berries in the woods and not on earthworms under your lawn, and so you don't see them. But they're here. The beloved harbinger of spring is in reality the harbinger of nothing at all.

The only honest response would seem to be for us to fire the robin as harbinger of spring and hire a new one, a real migrant who packs up in the fall and decamps. There are plenty of candidates; the trouble is, they're more or less unplentiful. The robin's advantage as harbinger of spring was that he was a common bird. He was there when you needed him. He was reliable. Who wants to wait around through the gray end of winter to be harbingered-to by, say, the yellow-bellied flycatcher?

2002 FEBRUARY, The Second Month

Jupiter and Saturn continue their dominance, already up nicely at nightfall and remaining brilliantly visible most of the night. Their most-striking Moon meetings of the year occur this month for North American observers, as Saturn virtually touches the gibbous Moon on the 20th and Jupiter passes extremely close to the nearly full Moon on the 22nd. By contrast, Mars, though easily located, keeps fading in the west, and Mercury pays a low, horizon-hugging visit to the predawn eastern sky, where it is drowned in bright twilight and can't be seen. The Moon makes its closest approach of the year to Earth on the 27th, the same day that it is full.

☾ Last Quarter	4th day	8th hour	33rd minute
● New Moon	12th day	2nd hour	41st minute
☽ First Quarter	20th day	7th hour	2nd minute
○ Full Moon	27th day	4th hour	17th minute

Times are given in Eastern Standard Time.

For an explanation of this page, see page 40; for values of Key Letters, see page 229.

Day of Year	Day of Month	Day of Week	☼ Rises h. m.	Key	☼ Sets h. m.	Key	Length of Day h. m.	Sun Fast m.	Declination of Sun ° '	High Tide Boston Light—A.M. Bold—P.M.	☽ Rises h. m.	Key	☽ Sets h. m.	Key	☽ Place	☽ Age
32	1	Fr.	6 58	D	4 58	A	10 00	2	17 s.01	1½ **1¾**	9ᴹ44	D	9ᴹ30	D	VIR	19
33	2	Sa.	6 57	D	4 59	A	10 02	2	16 43	2¼ **2¾**	10ᴹ57	E	9 58	C	VIR	20
34	3	**F**	6 56	D	5 01	A	10 05	2	16 25	3¼ **3¾**	—	–	10 25	B	VIR	21
35	4	M.	6 55	D	5 02	A	10 07	2	16 07	4¼ **4¾**	12ᴬ09	E	10 55	B	LIB	22
36	5	Tu.	6 54	D	5 03	A	10 09	2	15 49	5 **5¾**	1 20	E	11ᴬ27	B	LIB	23
37	6	W.	6 52	D	5 05	A	10 13	2	15 31	6¼ **6¾**	2 28	E	12ᴾ04	A	OPH	24
38	7	Th.	6 51	D	5 06	A	10 15	2	15 13	7¼ **8**	3 33	E	12 47	A	OPH	25
39	8	Fr.	6 50	D	5 07	B	10 17	1	14 54	8¼ **9**	4 32	E	1 36	A	SAG	26
40	9	Sa.	6 49	D	5 09	B	10 20	1	14 35	9 **9¾**	5 24	E	2 31	A	SAG	27
41	10	**F**	6 47	D	5 10	B	10 23	1	14 15	10 **10½**	6 09	E	3 30	B	SAG	28
42	11	M.	6 46	D	5 11	B	10 25	1	13 55	10¾ **11¼**	6 47	E	4 31	B	CAP	29
43	12	Tu.	6 45	D	5 13	B	10 28	1	13 35	11¼ **11¾**	7 18	E	5 32	C	CAP	0
44	13	W.	6 44	D	5 14	B	10 30	1	13 15	**12** —	7 46	D	6 33	C	AQU	1
45	14	Th.	6 42	D	5 15	B	10 33	1	12 55	12½ **12½**	8 10	D	7 33	D	AQU	2
46	15	Fr.	6 41	D	5 16	B	10 35	1	12 34	1 **1¼**	8 32	D	8 32	D	PSC	3
47	16	Sa.	6 39	D	5 18	B	10 39	1	12 13	1½ **1¾**	8 54	C	9 32	D	CET	4
48	17	**F**	6 38	D	5 19	B	10 41	2	11 52	2¼ **2½**	9 16	C	10 32	E	PSC	5
49	18	M.	6 37	D	5 20	B	10 43	2	11 31	3 **3¼**	9 40	B	11ᴹ34	E	CET	6
50	19	Tu.	6 35	D	5 22	B	10 47	2	11 10	3½ **4**	10 06	B	—	–	ARI	7
51	20	W.	6 34	D	5 23	B	10 49	2	10 48	4½ **5**	10 37	B	12ᴬ37	E	TAU	8
52	21	Th.	6 32	D	5 24	B	10 52	2	10 26	5¼ **6**	11ᴬ15	A	1 42	E	TAU	9
53	22	Fr.	6 31	D	5 25	B	10 54	2	10 04	6¼ **7**	12ᴾ02	A	2 48	E	TAU	10
54	23	Sa.	6 29	D	5 27	B	10 58	2	9 42	7¼ **8**	12 59	A	3 50	E	GEM	11
55	24	**F**	6 28	D	5 28	B	11 00	2	9 20	8¼ **9**	2 06	B	4 47	E	GEM	12
56	25	M.	6 26	D	5 29	B	11 03	2	8 58	9¼ **9¾**	3 21	B	5 37	E	CAN	13
57	26	Tu.	6 25	D	5 30	B	11 05	3	8 36	10 **10¾**	4 41	C	6 19	E	LEO	14
58	27	W.	6 23	D	5 31	B	11 08	3	8 13	11 **11½**	6 01	D	6 55	D	LEO	15
59	28	Th.	6 21	D	5 33	B	11 12	3	7 s.51	11¾ —	7ᴾ20	D	7ᴹ27	D	LEO	16

FEBRUARY hath 28 days. 2002

Deep down within the frozen brook
I hear a murmur faint and sweet,
And lo! The ice breaks as I look,
And living waters touch my feet. –Jane Goodwin Austin

D. M.	D. W.	Dates, Feasts, Fasts, Aspects, Tide Heights	*Weather* ↓
1	Fr.	St. Brigid • ☾ on Eq. • First U.S. Supreme Court session, 1790 •	*Groundhog*
2	Sa.	Candlemas • Groundhog Day • *Laziness is a weary load.* { 10.8 / 10.9	*flees—*
3	**F**	**4th S. af. Ep. • Sexagesima** • James Michener born, 1907	*it*
4	M.	USO founded, 1941 • Popular Reference Bureau estimated 77 billion people had lived, 1962	*starts*
5	Tu.	St. Agatha • United States issued first "greenback" bills, 1862 • *Year of snow, fruit will grow.* •	*to*
6	W.	Tom Brokaw born, 1940 • Mamie Van Doren born, 1933 • Tides { 10.0 / 8.7	*freeze.*
7	Th.	☾ at ☋ • Shoe rationing began, 1943 • Dead Sea Scrolls found, 1947 • { 9.9 / 8.6	*It's*
8	Fr.	☿ stat. • First sundial in Rome, 293 B.C. • Boy Scouts of America incorporated, 1910	*snowing*
9	Sa.	☾ runs low • 73 million watched The Beatles on the *Ed Sullivan Show,* 1964 •	*up north,*
10	**F**	**5th S. af. Ep. • Quinquagesima** • ☌ ☿ ☾ •	
11	M.	*Some rain, some rest, fine weather isn't always best.* • Thomas Edison born, 1847 { 10.2 / 9.0	*raining*
12	Tu.	Shrove Tuesday • Chinese New Year • New ● •	*southerly;*
13	W.	**Ash Wednesday** • ☌ ♅ ☉ • { 10.1 / —	*warmth*
14	Th.	St. Valentine • **Sts. Cyril & Methodius** • ☾ at apo. • { 9.2 / 10.0 •	*that's*
15	Fr.	Susan B. Anthony born, 1820 • Winter's back breaks. • { 9.3 / 9.8 •	*motherly.*
16	Sa.	☌ ♂ ☾ • ☾ on Eq. • DuPont patented nylon, 1937 • Tides { 9.3 / 9.5	*Hit*
17	**F**	**1st S. in Lent** • Geronimo died, 1909 • First sardine canned, 1876 •	*the*
18	M.	George Washington's Birthday (observed) • { 9.2 / 8.7 •	*slopes—*
19	Tu.	U.S. Marines landed on Iwo Jima, 1945 • Swarm of 60 tornadoes killed 800 in Southeast, 1884 •	*up*
20	W.	Ember Day • Occn. ♄ ☾ • Paper made from rags, 1417 •	*periscopes!*
21	Th.	☿ Gr. Elong. (27° W.) • *Buried hatchets are easily found.* • Battle of Verdun, 1916 •	*We're*
22	Fr.	☌ ♃ ☾ • ☾ at ☊ • G. Washington born, 1732 • Ember Day	*dying*
23	Sa.	☾ rides high • Ember Day • First mammal cloned ("Dolly"), 1997	*by inches:*
24	**F**	**2nd S. in Lent** • ☌ ☿ ♆ • Wilhelm Grimm born, 1786 { 10.3 / 9.1	
25	M.	St. Matthias • Tennessee Williams died, 1983 • Marathon dancing craze, 1928	*Feed*
26	Tu.	Adolph Hitler launched the Volkswagon to compete with Ford Model T and boost German economy, 1936	*those*
27	W.	**Full Snow** ○ • ☾ at perig. • John Steinbeck born, 1902 • { 11.9 / 10.9 •	*gold-*
28	Th.	*Talent is born in silence, but character is born in the struggles of life.* • { 12.0 / —	*finches!*

The Sun, with all those planets revolving around it and dependent upon it, can still ripen a bunch of grapes as if it had nothing else in the universe to do. –Galileo Galilei

Farmer's Calendar

■ Bad ice. Temperatures in the teens or lower; a big wind that blows the snow off the roads and walkways, exposing the ice beneath; bright sun that melts the surface of the ice at midday, so it can freeze anew overnight; then more wind that whirls dust and snow around to polish the ice 'til it glints like diamond.

This is fracture weather. You can't walk, you can't drive—all you can do is slip and hope. At this house, the driveway is maybe 75 feet long. It isn't steep, really—not *really*—but it *does* have a pitch from the road to the house. In bad ice conditions, the driveway turns into the kind of facility they spend thousands to construct at the Winter Olympics. The only thing more dangerous than trying to walk up it is trying to walk down it. Therefore I own a set of those little steel cleats that you strap onto the bottoms of your shoes: ice creepers. With them securely fastened, I can get up and down, perilously. Coming up the driveway from the mailbox in my creepers, I feel like I'm involved in some self-imposed ordeal-by-nature such as an ascent of the south col of Annapurna: an ordeal extreme, dreadful, and finally absurd.

There are people who make their living putting sand on driveways like mine. In a bad-ice winter you'll see those people looking good, driving new cars. The sandmen are about the only ones who love bad ice—the sandmen and the orthopedic surgeons. This weather can break your ankle, it can wreck your car, and it has done more to populate the state of Florida than Disney.

Venus returns to the evening sky after a year's absence. Showing up progressively higher each day but still low in the west at dusk, it usurps Jupiter's status as the night's brightest "star" until it sets at the end of twilight. Jupiter and Saturn remain the planets of interest, extremely high at nightfall and visible until midnight. Saturn floats just to the right of Aldebaran, the "eye" of Taurus the bull. Dim Mars sinks further in the west at nightfall, small and unimpressive through a telescope. Spring begins with the vernal equinox on the 20th at 2:16 P.M. EST, when the Sun rises and sets precisely due east and west. Contrary to popular belief, days and nights are equal a few days earlier.

☾	Last Quarter	5th day	20th hour	24th minute
●	New Moon	13th day	21st hour	2nd minute
☽	First Quarter	21st day	21st hour	28th minute
○	Full Moon	28th day	13th hour	25th minute

Times are given in Eastern Standard Time.

For an explanation of this page, see page 40; for values of Key Letters, see page 229.

Day of Year	Day of Month	Day of Week	☼ Rises h. m.	Key	☼ Sets h. m.	Key	Length of Day h. m.	Sun Fast m.	Declination of Sun ° ′	High Tide Boston Light—A.M. Bold—P.M.		☽ Rises h. m.	Key	☽ Sets h. m.	Key	☽ Place	☽ Age
60	1	Fr.	6 20	D	5 34	B	11 14	3	7 s.28	12¼	12½	8ᴮ37	E	7ᴹ56	C	VIR	17
61	2	Sa.	6 18	D	5 35	B	11 17	3	7 05	1	1½	9 53	E	8 24	C	VIR	18
62	3	F	6 17	D	5 36	B	11 19	4	6 42	2	2½	11ᴮ07	E	8 54	B	VIR	19
63	4	M.	6 15	D	5 38	B	11 23	4	6 19	2¾	3¼	—	–	9 26	B	LIB	20
64	5	Tu.	6 13	D	5 39	B	11 26	4	5 56	3¾	4¼	12ᴬ19	E	10 02	B	SCO	21
65	6	W.	6 12	D	5 40	B	11 28	4	5 33	4¾	5½	1 26	E	10 44	A	OPH	22
66	7	Th.	6 10	D	5 41	B	11 31	4	5 10	5¾	6½	2 28	E	11ᴹ32	A	SAG	23
67	8	Fr.	6 08	D	5 42	B	11 34	5	4 46	6¾	7½	3 23	E	12ᴮ25	A	SAG	24
68	9	Sa.	6 07	D	5 44	B	11 37	5	4 23	7¾	8½	4 10	E	1 23	B	SAG	25
69	10	F	6 05	D	5 45	B	11 40	5	3 59	8¾	9½	4 49	E	2 24	B	CAP	26
70	11	M.	6 03	D	5 46	B	11 43	5	3 36	9½	10¼	5 22	E	3 25	C	CAP	27
71	12	Tu.	6 02	C	5 47	B	11 45	6	3 12	10¼	10¾	5 50	E	4 26	C	AQU	28
72	13	W.	6 00	C	5 48	B	11 48	6	2 48	11	11¼	6 15	D	5 26	C	AQU	0
73	14	Th.	5 58	C	5 49	B	11 51	6	2 25	11½	12	6 37	D	6 25	D	AQU	1
74	15	Fr.	5 56	C	5 51	B	11 55	7	2 01	12¼	—	6 59	C	7 25	D	CET	2
75	16	Sa.	5 55	C	5 52	B	11 57	7	1 37	12½	12¾	7 21	C	8 25	E	PSC	3
76	17	F	5 53	C	5 53	B	12 00	7	1 13	1	1½	7 43	B	9 26	E	PSC	4
77	18	M.	5 51	C	5 54	B	12 03	7	0 50	1¾	2	8 08	B	10 29	E	ARI	5
78	19	Tu.	5 49	C	5 55	B	12 06	8	0 26	2¼	2¾	8 37	B	11ᴮ33	E	TAU	6
79	20	W.	5 48	C	5 56	C	12 08	8	0 s.02	3	3½	9 11	B	—	–	TAU	7
80	21	Th.	5 46	C	5 57	C	12 11	8	0 N.21	3¾	4½	9 53	A	12ᴬ37	E	TAU	8
81	22	Fr.	5 44	C	5 59	C	12 15	9	0 45	4¾	5½	10 44	A	1 39	E	GEM	9
82	23	Sa.	5 43	C	6 00	C	12 17	9	1 09	5¾	6½	11ᴹ45	B	2 36	E	GEM	10
83	24	F	5 41	C	6 01	C	12 20	9	1 32	6¾	7½	12ᴹ55	B	3 27	E	CAN	11
84	25	M.	5 39	C	6 02	C	12 23	9	1 56	7¾	8½	2 10	B	4 11	E	CAN	12
85	26	Tu.	5 37	C	6 03	C	12 26	10	2 19	8¾	9½	3 29	C	4 49	E	LEO	13
86	27	W.	5 36	C	6 04	C	12 28	10	2 43	9¾	10¼	4 49	D	5 22	D	LEO	14
87	28	Th.	5 34	C	6 05	C	12 31	10	3 06	10½	11	6 08	D	5 52	D	VIR	15
88	29	Fr.	5 32	C	6 07	C	12 35	11	3 30	11½	11¾	7 26	E	6 20	C	VIR	16
89	30	Sa.	5 30	C	6 08	C	12 38	11	3 53	12¼	—	8 44	E	6 50	B	VIR	17
90	31	F	5 29	C	6 09	C	12 40	11	4 N.16	12¾	1¼	10ᴮ00	E	7ᴹ21	B	LIB	18

MARCH hath 31 days. 2002

Black boughs against a pale, clear sky,
Slight mists of cloud-wreaths floating by;
Soft sunlight, gray-blue smoky air,
Wet thawing snows on hillsides bare. –Emma Lazarus

D. M.	D. W.	Dates, Feasts, Fasts, Aspects, Tide Heights	Weather ↓
1	Fr.	St. David • ♃ stat. • ☾ on Eq. • Lindbergh baby kidnapped, 1932 • {11.3 11.9	*In*
2	Sa.	St. Chad • World premiere of *King Kong,* 1933 • Theodore Geisel (Dr. Seuss) born, 1904	*like*
3	F	3rd S. in Lent • "Candlestick" tornado killed 57 in central Mississippi, 1966 •	*a*
4	M.	P.T. Barnum purchased "Jumbo," 1882 • *Thunder in March betokens a fruitful year.* •	*sea*
5	Tu.	St. Piran • Madame Tussaud began making wax figures, 1770 • Tides {10.6 9.4	*lion:*
6	W.	☾ at ☋ • Davy Crockett killed at the Alamo, 1836 • Aspirin patented, 1899 •	*rainy*
7	Th.	St. Perpetua • Total eclipse of Sun, 1970 • Alexander Graham Bell patented telephone, 1876	*and*
8	Fr.	☾ runs low • ☌ ☿ ♅ • N.Y. first state to license dogs, 1894 {9.5 8.4	*warmish.*
9	Sa.	False teeth patented, 1822 • Marriage of Napoleon and Josephine, 1796 • Tides {9.5 8.5	*The*
10	F	4th S. in Lent • ☌ ♆ ☾ • *Well begun is half done.* {9.6 8.7	*Sun*
11	M.	☌ ♅ ☾ • ☌ ☿ ☾ • Jennifer Capriati, age 13, youngest finalist in pro tennis, 1990	*is*
12	Tu.	St. Gregory • The American Girl Guides (renamed Girl Scouts) est., 1912 •	*tryin',*
13	W.	New ● • ☾ at apo. • First bloodshed of the American Revolution, Westminster, Vt., 1775	*but*
14	Th.	Red snow and hail fell on Tuscany, 1813 • Albert Einstein born, 1879 • {10.0 9.6 •	*still*
15	Fr.	☾ on Eq. • Beware the Ides of March. • Buzzards return to Hinckley, Ohio. • {9.9 —	*it's*
16	Sa.	Skunks mate now. • *Plough deep, while sluggards sleep, and you shall have corn to sell or keep.*	*stormish.*
17	F	5th S. in Lent • St. Patrick • ☌ ♂ ☾ •	*Luck*
18	M.	Pure Monday • Schick, Inc. introduced first electric shaver, 1931 • Tides {9.7 9.2	*o' the*
19	Tu.	St. Joseph • Swallows return to San Juan Capistrano. • Wyatt Earp born, 1848 •	*Irish*
20	W.	☌ ♄ ☾ • Vernal Equinox • Ovid born, 43 B.C. • {9.5 8.5 •	*doesn't*
21	Th.	♇ stat. • ☾ at ☊ • Pocahontas died, Kent, England, 1617 {9.4 8.3	*last—*
22	Fr.	☌ ♃ ☾ • Earliest possible Easter date. • Tides {9.4 8.3 •	*wintry*
23	Sa.	☾ rides high • *Keep a thing for seven years and you'll find a use for it.* • {9.6 8.5 •	*blast!*
24	F	Palm Sunday • Sunday of Orthodoxy {9.9 8.9	*Aren't*
25	M.	Annunciation • ☾ on Eq. • Howard Cosell born, 1920 • {10.4 9.5 •	*we*
26	Tu.	56-foot whale swam up the Thames River, England, 1699 • Tides {10.9 10.3	*supposed*
27	W.	Lithographer Nathaniel Currier, of "Currier and Ives" fame, born, 1813 • {11.4 11.0	*to go out*
28	Th.	First day of Passover • Full Worm ○ • ☾ on Eq. • ☾ at perig.	
29	Fr.	Good Friday • Ice jam stopped Niagara Falls, 1848 • {11.8 11.9	*like a*
30	Sa.	U.S. bought Alaska from Russia for $7.2 million, 1867 • Incubator patented, 1843 •	*lamb?*
31	F	Easter • *There are forty kinds of lunacy but only one kind of common sense.* •	*Wham!*

Farmer's Calendar

■ *A Field Guide to the Birds,* not a book given to overstatement, calls the pileated woodpecker "spectacular." Except for the game birds and the crow, this woodpecker is the biggest nonpredatory bird in our territory, standing a foot and a half tall and having broad, strong wings whose span can approach two feet. It has vivid black and white plumage; a high, bright-red crest; and an odd, dipping way of flight that carries it off through the trees as though the bird were riding a flying pogo stick. The pileated is the bird responsible for the deep piles of rough-cut chips you find at the base of trees where no axman has been at work.

Indeed, those tailings are all of the pileated you're likely to see. If it's one of the biggest deep-woods birds, it's also one of the shiest. It doesn't want you to come near it or even see it. I once spent a half-hour trying to get a good look at a pileated that was up in a locust tree. It wouldn't let me get on its side of the tree. I moved around, and it moved around, keeping the trunk between us. At last we both got bored and gave it up. A wary, secretive bird—mostly—and a solitary bird—mostly. But this woodpecker has another side. The pileated has a kind of mob psychology. I've seen five and six of them racketing around the trees near the house here, fighting, roughhousing, and squawking away at the top of their lungs. Exactly like boys in middle school, the pileated is a shy and silent customer taken alone, but in a group of its fellows, it's boisterous, disorderly, silly, and loud.

Starting at midmonth, an extraordinary lineup of all the naked-eye planets forms a highly visible string of pearls after sunset. Upward from the western horizon as bright twilight fades stands bright Mercury, brilliant Venus, dim Mars, radiant Saturn, and brilliant Jupiter. The crescent Moon meets each in turn, floating just above Mercury on the 13th, Venus on the 14th, Mars on the 15th, Saturn on the 16th, and Jupiter on the 18th. This latter, highest-up conjunction is particularly close and striking. Meanwhile, daylight increases at the rate of two to four minutes a day, and Daylight Saving Time begins at 2:00 A.M. on the 7th.

☾	Last Quarter	4th day	10th hour	29th minute
●	New Moon	12th day	15th hour	21st minute
☽	First Quarter	20th day	8th hour	48th minute
○	Full Moon	26th day	23rd hour	0 minute

After 2:00 A.M. on April 7, Eastern Daylight Time (EDT) is given.

For an explanation of this page, see page 40; for values of Key Letters, see page 229.

Day of Year	Day of Month	Day of Week	☀ Rises h. m.	Key	☀ Sets h. m.	Key	Length of Day h. m.	Sun Fast m.	Declination of Sun ° '	High Tide Boston Light—A.M. **Bold—P.M.**		☽ Rises h. m.	Key	☽ Sets h. m.	Key	☽ Place	☽ Age
91	1	M.	5 27	B	6 10	C	12 43	12	4 N.39	1½	2	11ᴾ12	E	7ᴬ57	B	LIB	19
92	2	Tu.	5 25	B	6 11	C	12 46	12	5 02	2¼	3	—	–	8 38	A	OPH	20
93	3	W.	5 23	B	6 12	C	12 49	12	5 25	3¼	4	12ᴬ19	E	9 24	A	OPH	21
94	4	Th.	5 22	B	6 13	C	12 51	12	5 48	4¼	5	1 18	E	10 17	A	SAG	22
95	5	Fr.	5 20	B	6 14	D	12 54	13	6 11	5¼	6	2 09	E	11ᴬ15	A	SAG	23
96	6	Sa.	5 18	B	6 16	D	12 58	13	6 34	6¼	7¼	2 50	E	12ᴾ16	B	CAP	24
97	7	**F**	6 17	B	7 17	D	13 00	13	6 57	8¼	9	4 25	E	2 17	B	CAP	25
98	8	M.	6 15	B	7 18	D	13 03	14	7 19	9¼	10	4 54	E	3 18	C	AQU	26
99	9	Tu.	6 13	B	7 19	D	13 06	14	7 42	10¼	10½	5 20	D	4 19	C	AQU	27
100	10	W.	6 12	B	7 20	D	13 08	14	8 04	10¾	11¼	5 43	D	5 18	D	AQU	28
101	11	Th.	6 10	B	7 21	D	13 11	14	8 26	11½	11¾	6 04	D	6 18	D	PSC	29
102	12	Fr.	6 08	B	7 22	D	13 14	15	8 48	**12¼**	—	6 26	C	7 18	D	CET	0
103	13	Sa.	6 07	B	7 23	D	13 16	15	9 10	12¼	12¾	6 48	B	8 20	E	PSC	1
104	14	**F**	6 05	B	7 25	D	13 20	15	9 31	1	1¼	7 12	B	9 22	E	ARI	2
105	15	M.	6 03	B	7 26	D	13 23	15	9 53	1½	2	7 40	B	10 26	E	ARI	3
106	16	Tu.	6 02	B	7 27	D	13 25	16	10 14	2	2¾	8 12	B	11ᴹ31	E	TAU	4
107	17	W.	6 00	B	7 28	D	13 28	16	10 35	2¾	3½	8 51	A	—	–	TAU	5
108	18	Th.	5 59	B	7 29	D	13 30	16	10 56	3½	4¼	9 38	A	12ᴬ33	E	LEO	6
109	19	Fr.	5 57	B	7 30	D	13 33	16	11 17	4¼	5	10 34	A	1 31	E	GEM	7
110	20	Sa.	5 56	B	7 31	D	13 35	17	11 37	5¼	6	11ᴬ39	B	2 23	E	GEM	8
111	21	**F**	5 54	B	7 32	D	13 38	17	11 58	6¼	7	12ᴹ50	B	3 08	E	CAN	9
112	22	M.	5 53	B	7 34	D	13 41	17	12 18	7¼	8	2 05	C	3 46	E	LEO	10
113	23	Tu.	5 51	B	7 35	D	13 44	17	12 38	8½	9	3 22	C	4 20	D	LEO	11
114	24	W.	5 50	B	7 36	D	13 46	17	12 58	9½	10	4 39	D	4 49	D	VIR	12
115	25	Th.	5 48	B	7 37	D	13 49	18	13 17	10¼	10¾	5 57	D	5 18	C	VIR	13
116	26	Fr.	5 47	B	7 38	D	13 51	18	13 36	11¼	11¾	7 15	E	5 46	C	VIR	14
117	27	Sa.	5 45	B	7 39	D	13 54	18	13 56	**12¼**	—	8 33	E	6 16	B	LIB	15
118	28	**F**	5 44	B	7 40	D	13 56	18	14 15	12½	1	9 49	E	6 49	B	LIB	16
119	29	M.	5 42	B	7 41	D	13 59	18	14 33	1¼	1¾	11ᴾ01	E	7 28	A	SCO	17
120	30	Tu.	5 41	B	7 43	D	14 02	18	14 N.52	2	2¾	—	–	8ᴹ13	A	OPH	18

APRIL hath 30 days. 2002

Buds are bursting in the hedges,
Leaves are stirring in the lane,
Everywhere the sap is stirring,
Love returns to life again. –John Dennis

D. M.	D. W.	Dates, Feasts, Fasts, Aspects, Tide Heights	Weather ↓
1	M.	**All Fools'** • U.S. troops invaded Okinawa, 1945 • Lon Chaney born, 1883 • {11.7 10.6	No
2	Tu.	☾ at ☋ • *As the World Turns* debuted on CBS, 1956 • Tides {11.2 9.9 •	joke:
3	W.	**St. Richard of Chichester** • Jesse James shot and killed, 1882 •	Spring's
4	Th.	☾ runs low • NATO formed, 1949 • Hank Aaron hit 714th home run, 1974 • {10.0 8.7	a
5	Fr.	Indian maize first planted by Colonists, 1609 • *Today is yesterday's pupil.*	slowpoke.
6	Sa.	☌ ♆ ☾ • Raphael born, 1483; died, 1520 • "Richard the Lion-Hearted" died, 1199	Stoke
7	F	**1st S. af. Easter** • **Daylight Saving Time begins, 2:00 A.M.** • ☌ ⛢ ☾	
8	M.	Pablo Picasso died, 1973 • Works Progress Administration approved by Congress, 1935	the fire
9	Tu.	*Concorde* made first test flight, 1969 • Frank Lloyd Wright died, 1959 • {9.4 9.2	before
10	W.	☾ at apo. • Bataan Death March began, 1942 • Omar Sharif born, 1932 • {9.6 9.5 •	you
11	Th.	☾ on Eq. • *A forest is in an acorn.* • Erskine Caldwell died, 1987 • {9.7 9.7	retire.
12	Fr.	**New ●** • Civil War began, Ft. Sumter, S.C., 1861 • Tides {9.7 — •	The
13	Sa.	Thomas Jefferson born, 1743 • *Plant pears for your heirs.* • Tides {9.9 9.7 •	Sun
14	F	**2nd S. af. Easter** • ☌ ♀ ☾ • {10.0 9.6	is warm,
15	M.	☌ ♂ ☾ • Bessie Smith born, 1898 • Abraham Lincoln died, 1865 • {10.1 9.4	the
16	Tu.	☌ ♄ ☾ • FCC warns "shock jocks," 1987 • Charlie Chaplin born, 1889	breeze
17	W.	☾ at ☊ • 500-year-old oak toppled, Sudbury, Mass., 1959 • Tides {10.0 8.9 •	is
18	Th.	☌ ♃ ☾ • First laundromat in U.S. opened, 1934 • Revere's midnight ride, 1775	wet;
19	Fr.	☾ rides high • Oklahoma City bombing, 1995 • Charles Darwin died, 1882 • {9.9 8.6	have
20	Sa.	Pierre Trudeau became prime minister of Canada, 1969 • Bram Stoker died, 1912 • {9.8 8.7	you
21	F	**3rd S. af. Easter** • Manfred von Richtofen (the "Red Baron") died, 1918	got
22	M.	*"If" and "when" were planted, and "nothing" grew.* • Tides {10.1 9.5 •	your
23	Tu.	**St. George** • Shakespeare born, 1564; died, 1616 • Tides {10.4 10.1 •	peas
24	W.	Robert B. Thomas born, 1766 • Library of Congress created, 1800 • Tides {10.8 10.8	in
25	Th.	**St. Mark** • ☾ on Eq. • ☾ at perig. • Ella Fitzgerald born, 1918 {11.1 11.4	yet?
26	Fr.	**Full Pink ○** • John James Audubon born, 1785 • Civil War ended, 1865 {11.3 11.9	A
27	Sa.	S.S. *Sultana* exploded on Miss. River near Memphis, 1,450 killed, 1865 • {11.3 —	daffodil
28	F	**4th S. af. Easter** • Mutiny on the H.M.S. *Bounty,* 1789 {12.1 11.1	will
29	M.	☾ at ☋ • Gideon Sundback patented the zipper, 1913 • {12.0 10.7	laugh at
30	Tu.	*A man with a fixed idea is like an old goose that tries to hatch out a cobblestone.* • {11.6 10.2	chill.

People talk about the dead past. The past isn't dead. It isn't even past. –William Faulkner

Farmer's Calendar

■ Holidays, festivals, annual celebrations of whatever kind would seem to be a defining part of our humanity; other creatures, as far as we know, take one day pretty much as they take another. Only men have found a need to endow certain days with special meaning. These meanings are various, and some of them are obscure. Most holidays derive more or less directly from religious observances or from a people's wish to commemorate important dates in their nation's history. But some holidays have origins less clear, and of these, the most curious is April Fools' Day.

If you look it up, you discover that nobody really knows how April Fools' Day got started. It may be related to the ancient Roman spring festival known as Hilaria (March 25). More recently, the custom of devoting April 1 to practical jokes of all kinds seems to come from France. Around 1560, the French king Charles IX (Valois) announced that, thenceforth, New Year's Day, which from time immemorial had been celebrated on April 1, would take place on January 1. Those who stuck to the old dispensation and continued to keep New Year's in April, became the butt of jokes. They were the original April fools—or, to the French, *April fish.*

Since then, all over Europe and the New World, April Fools' Day has been observed by people setting out to gull, mislead, betray, and otherwise deceive their fellows. A cynic would remark that, therefore, apart from its formality, it's no holiday at all but a day like every other.

MAY, The Fifth Month

A true spectacle of the planets, the year's best, adorns the western sky in fading twilight from the 1st to the 16th. Dazzling Venus floats very close to dim, orange Mars and medium-bright Saturn, with bright Mercury just below and brilliant Jupiter much higher up. Within this impressive bunching in Taurus, Venus and Mars are extremely close on the 10th, a superb treat for the naked eye but a dud telescopically. The slender crescent Moon—the icing on the cake—hovers between Mercury and Saturn on the 13th and very near Venus and Mars on the 14th. The Moon undergoes a penumbral eclipse on the 26th, but sunlight on its surface will scarcely be diminished—a nonevent.

☾	Last Quarter	4th day	3rd hour	16th minute
●	New Moon	12th day	6th hour	45th minute
☽	First Quarter	19th day	15th hour	42nd minute
○	Full Moon	26th day	7th hour	51st minute

Times are given in Eastern Daylight Time.

For an explanation of this page, see page 40; for values of Key Letters, see page 229.

Day of Year	Day of Month	Day of Week	☼ Rises h. m.	Key	☼ Sets h. m.	Key	Length of Day h. m.	Sun Fast m.	Declination of Sun ° '	High Tide Boston Light—A.M.	Bold—P.M.	☽ Rises h. m.	Key	☽ Sets h. m.	Key	☽ Place	☽ Age
121	1	W.	5 40	B	7 44	D	14 04	18	15N.10	3	**3½**	12 A.M. 06	E	9 A.M. 05	A	SAG	19
122	2	Th.	5 38	B	7 45	D	14 07	19	15 28	3¾	**4½**	1 02	E	10 03	A	SAG	20
123	3	Fr.	5 37	B	7 46	D	14 09	19	15 46	4¾	**5½**	1 49	E	11 A.M. 04	B	CAP	21
124	4	Sa.	5 36	A	7 47	D	14 11	19	16 03	5¾	**6½**	2 27	E	12 P.M. 06	B	CAP	22
125	5	**F**	5 34	A	7 48	D	14 14	19	16 20	6¾	**7½**	2 58	E	1 08	B	CAP	23
126	6	M.	5 33	A	7 49	D	14 16	19	16 37	7¾	**8¼**	3 25	D	2 09	C	AQU	24
127	7	Tu.	5 32	A	7 50	D	14 18	19	16 54	8¾	**9¼**	3 48	D	3 09	D	AQU	25
128	8	W.	5 31	A	7 51	D	14 20	19	17 10	9½	**10**	4 10	D	4 09	D	PSC	26
129	9	Th.	5 29	A	7 52	D	14 23	19	17 26	10¼	**10½**	4 31	C	5 09	D	CET	27
130	10	Fr.	5 28	A	7 54	D	14 26	19	17 42	11	**11¼**	4 53	B	6 10	E	PSC	28
131	11	Sa.	5 27	A	7 55	D	14 28	19	17 58	11¾	**11¾**	5 16	B	7 13	E	CET	29
132	12	**F**	5 26	A	7 56	D	14 30	19	18 13	**12¼**	—	5 42	B	8 18	E	ARI	0
133	13	M.	5 25	A	7 57	D	14 32	19	18 28	12½	**1**	6 13	B	9 23	E	TAU	1
134	14	Tu.	5 24	A	7 58	D	14 34	19	18 42	1	**1¾**	6 50	A	10 27	E	TAU	2
135	15	W.	5 23	A	7 59	E	14 36	19	18 56	1¾	**2¼**	7 35	A	11 P.M. 28	E	TAU	3
136	16	Th.	5 22	A	8 00	E	14 38	19	19 10	2½	**3**	8 28	A	—	–	GEM	4
137	17	Fr.	5 21	A	8 01	E	14 40	19	19 24	3¼	**4**	9 31	A	12 A.M. 22	E	GEM	5
138	18	Sa.	5 20	A	8 02	E	14 42	19	19 37	4	**4¾**	10 39	B	1 08	E	CAN	6
139	19	**F**	5 19	A	8 03	E	14 44	19	19 50	5	**5¾**	11 A.M. 52	B	1 48	E	LEO	7
140	20	M.	5 18	A	8 04	E	14 46	19	20 02	6	**6¾**	1 P.M. 06	C	2 22	D	LEO	8
141	21	Tu.	5 17	A	8 05	E	14 48	19	20 15	7	**7¾**	2 21	C	2 51	D	LEO	9
142	22	W.	5 16	A	8 06	E	14 50	19	20 26	8	**8¾**	3 35	D	3 19	C	VIR	10
143	23	Th.	5 16	A	8 07	E	14 51	19	20 38	9	**9½**	4 51	E	3 46	C	VIR	11
144	24	Fr.	5 15	A	8 08	E	14 53	19	20 50	10	**10½**	6 07	E	4 14	B	VIR	12
145	25	Sa.	5 14	A	8 09	E	14 55	19	21 00	11	**11¼**	7 23	E	4 44	B	LIB	13
146	26	**F**	5 13	A	8 09	E	14 56	19	21 11	11¾	—	8 38	E	5 20	B	LIB	14
147	27	M.	5 13	A	8 10	E	14 57	19	21 21	12	**12¾**	9 48	E	6 01	A	OPH	15
148	28	Tu.	5 12	A	8 11	E	14 59	18	21 30	1	**1½**	10 49	E	6 51	A	SAG	16
149	29	W.	5 12	A	8 12	E	15 00	18	21 40	1¾	**2½**	11 P.M. 41	E	7 47	A	SAG	17
150	30	Th.	5 11	A	8 13	E	15 02	18	21 49	2½	**3¼**	—	–	8 48	A	SAG	18
151	31	Fr.	5 11	A	8 14	E	15 03	18	21N.57	3¼	**4**	12 A.M. 24	E	9 A.M. 52	B	CAP	19

MAY hath 31 days. 2002

Come ramble awhile through this exquisite weather
Of days that are fleet to pass,
When the stem of the willow shoots out a green feather,
And buttercups burn in the grass! –Edgar Fawcett

D. M.	D. W.	Dates, Feasts, Fasts, Aspects, Tide Heights	*Weather* ↓
1	W.	**Sts. Philip & James** • **May Day** • ☾ runs low {11.1 9.7	*Brilliant—*
2	Th.	**St. Athanasius** • *A wet May will fill a byre full of hay.* • Tides {10.5 9.2 •	*but*
3	Fr.	**Invention of the Cross** • ☌ ♆ ☾ • First U.S. medical school opened, 1765 •	*you'd*
4	Sa.	☿ Gr. Elong. (21° E.) • ☌ ♂ ♄ • Kent State riot killed four, 1970 {9.4 8.6	*better*
5	**F**	**Rogation S.** • **Orthodox Easter** • ☌ ♅ ☾ •	*be*
6	M.	*Live so that you would not mind giving the family parrot to the town gossip.* •	*resilient—*
7	Tu.	☌ ♀ ♄ • ☾ at apog. • Great Natchez (Miss.) tornado, 317 killed, 1840 {9.0 9.0	*and*
8	W.	**St. Julian of Norwich** • ☾ on Eq. • Tides {9.1 9.4 •	*water-*
9	Th.	**St. Gregory of Nazianzus** • **Ascension** • {9.2 9.7	*repillient!*
10	Fr.	☌ ♂ ♀ • Stonewall Jackson died, 1863 • First transcontinental railroad link, 1869	*Cool*
11	Sa.	Original Siamese twins, Chang and Eng Bunker, born, 1811 • Pharoah drowned, 1461 B.C. **Three**	*and*
12	**F**	New ● • Alcoholics Anonymous founded, 1935 • {9.4 — **Chilly**	*dour,*
13	M.	♆ stat. • Man killed by hailstorm near Lubbock, Tex., 1930 • {10.3 9.4 • **Saints**	*but*
14	Tu.	☌ ☾ ♄ • ☌ ♀ ☾ • ☌ ♂ ☾ • ☾ at ☊ •	*each*
15	W.	Gov. George Wallace shot, 1972 • *Never stop a running horse to give it sugar.* •	*shower*
16	Th.	☿ stat. • ☾ rides high • ☌ ♃ ☾ • Studs Terkel born, 1912 {10.4 9.1	*brings*
17	Fr.	**Shavuot** • U.S. Supreme Court declared segregation unconstitutional, 1954 •	*a flower.*
18	Sa.	Earth passed through the tail of Halley's Comet, 1910 • Washington's Mount St. Helens erupted, 1980 •	*I*
19	**F**	**Whit S.** • **Pentecost** • Dark at noon in New England, 1780	*don't*
20	M.	**St. Dunstan** • **Victoria Day (Canada)** • Columbus died, 1506 • {10.1 9.6 •	*want*
21	Tu.	Conn. enacted first speed limit (12 mph), 1901 • Eisenhower broke ground for Lincoln Center, 1959 •	*to*
22	W.	☾ on Eq. • Ember Day • Canned rattlesnake meat went on sale, Arcadia, Fla., 1931 •	*jinx*
23	Th.	☾ at perig. • Benjamin Franklin invented bifocals, 1785 • Bonnie and Clyde ambushed, 1934	*it;*
24	Fr.	Ember Day • *Morning showers and an old woman's dancing do not last long.* • {10.5 11.6 •	*but*
25	Sa.	**St. Bede** • Ralph Waldo Emerson born, 1803 • Ember Day	*methinks it's*
26	**F**	**Trinity** • **Full Flower** ○ • Penumbral Eclipse ☾ • {10.5 —	*now*
27	M.	**Memorial Day** • ☾ at ☋ • ☿ in inf. ☌ • {11.9 10.4 •	*safe*
28	Tu.	de Soto landed in Fla., 1539 • Jim Thorpe born, 1888 • Noah Webster died, 1843 • {11.7 10.1 •	*to*
29	W.	☾ runs low • Hillary and Norgay reached summit of Mt. Everest, 1953 • *Wishes won't wash dishes.*	*park*
30	Th.	**Corpus Christi** • *A burden one chooses is not felt.* • Tides {10.9 9.5 •	*the*
31	Fr.	**Visit. of Mary** • ☌ ♆ ☾ • 2,300 perished in Johnstown flood, 1889	*plow!*

Farmer's Calendar

■ *May 20.* A good day to begin cutting the grass. By now, the spring growth makes it absolutely necessary to open the annual event. There are shoal waters here, however. Brought mower up from cellar, dusted it off, filled the tank, set the spark, seized the starter cord, and gave it a lusty yank. Nothing. Another yank. Nothing. A third. Zero. I wasn't even eliciting the faint echo from the motor's interior that signals intent to start at some point in the future. Bad luck, I thought, but there are other mowers.

I called my neighbor. He's a better householder than I. He would have had his mower out of its stall and into the traces for at least a week. I'd borrow his machine. He agreed, assured me it was running fine. I got it up here, rolled it around back, made sure the tank was full, set the spark, seized the cord, and gave it a lusty yank. Nothing. And again. Zero. Now a problem appears—not only a problem of unmown grass but a moral problem. My friend's mower worked perfectly. Now it doesn't. If his horse goes lame in my corral, I pay for the vet, right? It's the law of the West, including western New England.

Had to think things over. Went indoors, had a cup of coffee. Looked out the window. Read the paper. A half-hour passed. Thought I'd give the mower one last shot. Went to it, set the spark, yanked the cord—*Bingo!* She started up as easy as turning on the radio, and I was off. But as I mowed, I knew I had proved a dangerous theorem. Ignore a problem, do nothing, and it will in time solve itself: a fatal lesson for a lazy man.

JUNE, The Sixth Month

The night's two brightest "stars," Venus and Jupiter, meet beautifully in the west from the 1st to the 4th, while the rest of the planets descend into the dusk and vanish. The crescent Moon meets Venus on the 13th, as the evening star brightens and shifts more to the left each night. Twilight reaches its longest length, and daylight its maximum amount, when the solstice arrives at 9:24 A.M. EDT to usher in the summer on the 21st. As luck would have it, an annular solar eclipse on the 10th and a penumbral lunar eclipse on the 24th are both invisible from North America. True night (full darkness) is now less than five hours long for everyone north of Philadelphia or Denver.

☾	Last Quarter	2nd day	20th hour	5th minute
●	New Moon	10th day	19th hour	46th minute
☽	First Quarter	17th day	20th hour	29th minute
○	Full Moon	24th day	17th hour	42nd minute

Times are given in Eastern Daylight Time.

For an explanation of this page, see page 40; for values of Key Letters, see page 229.

Day of Year	Day of Month	Day of Week	☼ Rises h. m.	Key	☼ Sets h. m.	Key	Length of Day h. m.	Sun Fast m.	Declination of Sun ° '	High Tide Boston Light—A.M.	Bold—P.M.	☽ Rises h. m.	Key	☽ Sets h. m.	Key	☽ Place	☽ Age
152	1	Sa.	5 10	A	8 14	E	15 04	18	22N.06	4¼	**5**	12 A.M. 58	E	10 A.M. 55	B	CAP	20
153	2	**F**	5 10	A	8 15	E	15 05	18	22 14	5	**5¾**	1 27	E	11 A.M. 57	C	AQU	21
154	3	M.	5 09	A	8 16	E	15 07	18	22 21	6	**6¾**	1 52	D	12 P.M. 58	C	AQU	22
155	4	Tu.	5 09	A	8 17	E	15 08	17	22 28	7	**7½**	2 14	D	1 58	D	AQU	23
156	5	W.	5 08	A	8 17	E	15 09	17	22 35	7¾	**8¼**	2 36	C	2 58	D	CET	24
157	6	Th.	5 08	A	8 18	E	15 10	17	22 41	8¾	**9**	2 57	C	3 59	D	PSC	25
158	7	Fr.	5 08	A	8 19	E	15 11	17	22 47	9½	**9¾**	3 19	B	5 01	E	PSC	26
159	8	Sa.	5 07	A	8 19	E	15 12	17	22 53	10¼	**10½**	3 44	B	6 05	E	ARI	27
160	9	**F**	5 07	A	8 20	E	15 13	17	22 58	11	**11¼**	4 13	B	7 11	E	TAU	28
161	10	M.	5 07	A	8 20	E	15 13	16	23 02	11¾	**11¾**	4 47	B	8 16	E	TAU	0
162	11	Tu.	5 07	A	8 21	E	15 14	16	23 07	**12½**	—	5 30	A	9 20	E	TAU	1
163	12	W.	5 07	A	8 21	E	15 14	16	23 10	12½	**1¼**	6 21	A	10 17	E	GEM	2
164	13	Th.	5 07	A	8 22	E	15 15	16	23 14	1¼	**2**	7 22	A	11 07	E	GEM	3
165	14	Fr.	5 07	A	8 22	E	15 15	16	23 16	2	**2¾**	8 30	B	11 P.M. 49	E	CAN	4
166	15	Sa.	5 07	A	8 23	E	15 16	15	23 19	3	**3¾**	9 43	B	—	–	LEO	5
167	16	**F**	5 07	A	8 23	E	15 16	15	23 21	3¾	**4½**	10 A.M. 56	C	12 A.M. 25	D	LEO	6
168	17	M.	5 07	A	8 23	E	15 16	15	23 23	4¾	**5½**	12 P.M. 10	D	12 55	D	LEO	7
169	18	Tu.	5 07	A	8 24	E	15 17	15	23 25	5¾	**6¼**	1 23	D	1 23	C	VIR	8
170	19	W.	5 07	A	8 24	E	15 17	14	23 26	6¾	**7¼**	2 36	D	1 49	C	VIR	9
171	20	Th.	5 07	A	8 24	E	15 17	14	23 26	7¾	**8¼**	3 50	E	2 16	B	VIR	10
172	21	Fr.	5 07	A	8 25	E	15 18	14	23 26	8¾	**9¼**	5 04	E	2 44	B	LIB	11
173	22	Sa.	5 08	A	8 25	E	15 17	14	23 26	9¾	**10**	6 18	E	3 16	B	LIB	12
174	23	**F**	5 08	A	8 25	E	15 17	14	23 25	10¾	**11**	7 29	E	3 54	B	OPH	13
175	24	M.	5 08	A	8 25	E	15 17	13	23 24	11¾	**11¾**	8 34	E	4 39	A	OPH	14
176	25	Tu.	5 08	A	8 25	E	15 17	13	23 23	**12½**	—	9 31	E	5 32	A	SAG	15
177	26	W.	5 09	A	8 25	E	15 16	13	23 21	12½	**1¼**	10 18	E	6 32	A	SAG	16
178	27	Th.	5 09	A	8 25	E	15 16	13	23 19	1¼	**2**	10 56	E	7 35	B	CAP	17
179	28	Fr.	5 10	A	8 25	E	15 15	13	23 16	2¼	**2¾**	11 27	E	8 40	B	CAP	18
180	29	Sa.	5 10	A	8 25	E	15 15	12	23 13	3	**3½**	11 P.M. 54	D	9 44	B	AQU	19
181	30	**F**	5 11	A	8 25	E	15 14	12	23N.09	3¾	**4¼**	—	–	10 A.M. 46	C	AQU	20

JUNE hath 30 days. 2002

The earliest breath of June
Blows the white tassels from the cherry boughs,
And in the deepest shadow of the noon
The mild-eyed oxen browse. –Elizabeth Ann Allen

D. M.	D. W.	Dates, Feasts, Fasts, Aspects, Tide Heights	Weather ↓
1	Sa.	☌ ♅ ☾ • *If thine enemy wrongs thee, buy each of his children a drum.* • {9.9 8.9	*Moist*
2	F	2nd S. af. P. • Native Americans granted citizenship, 1924 • {9.4 8.8 •	*at*
3	M.	♅ stat. • ☌ ♀ ♃ • Jefferson Davis born, 1808 • Tides {9.1 8.8	*foist,*
4	Tu.	☾ at apog. • Casanova died, 1798 • Stephen Foster born, 1826 • Tides {8.8 8.9	*then*
5	W.	St. Boniface • ☾ on Eq. • Socrates born, 470 B.C. • {8.8 9.2	*wondrous*
6	Th.	D day, 1944 • First drive-in movie theater opened, N.J., 1933 • J. Paul Getty died, 1976	*warm.*
7	Fr.	♇ at ☍ • Famous New England snow; drifts of 20" in Danville, Vt., 1816 {8.8 9.7	*Muggy*
8	Sa.	☿ stat. • 3,000 letters sent from sub U.S.S. *Barbero* to Jacksonville, Fla., via Regulus 1 missile, 1959 •	*and*
9	F	3rd S. af. P. • ☌ ♄ ☉ • ☌ ☿ ☾ • {9.0 10.3	*buggy,*
10	M.	New ● • Eclipse ☉ • ☾ at ☊ • *Every shut eye ain't asleep.* •	*with*
11	Tu.	St. Barnabas • John Wayne died, 1979 • Jacques Cousteau born, 1910	*thundrous*
12	W.	☌ ♂ ☾ • ☾ rides high • *Before honor is humility.* • {10.7 9.3 •	*storms.*
13	Th.	☌ ♃ ☾ • ☌ ♀ ☾ • **Orthodox Ascension** •	*"Sunny skies"*
14	Fr.	St. Basil • U.S. Army founded, 1775 • Tides {10.9 9.5 •	*is outlook*
15	Sa.	☾ on Eq. • Fast day held with prayers for rain, Salem, Mass., 1662 • Tides {10.8 9.6 •	*for*
16	F	4th S. af. P. • Stan Laurel born, 1890 •	*commencement*
17	M.	☌ ♀ ☾ • Five Branch Davidian cult members sentenced to jail, 1994	*exercises.*
18	Tu.	☾ on Eq. • *If there were wisdom in beards, all goats would be prophets.* • {10.2 10.2	*Toast*
19	W.	☾ at perig. • The French and Indian War began, 1754 • *Rain before seven, clear before eleven.*	*the*
20	Th.	Errol Flynn born, 1909 • U.S. Great Seal adopted, 1782 • Tides {9.9 10.9 •	*grooms,*
21	Fr.	**Summer Solstice** • ☿ Gr. Elong. (23° W.) • LP record first demonstrated, 1948 {9.9 11.1	*toast*
22	Sa.	St. Alban • Circus train crashed in Ivanhoe, Ind., 68 killed, 1918 • Machiavelli died, 1527	*the*
23	F	5th S. af. P. • ☾ at ☋ • **Orthodox Pentecost** •	*brides;*
24	M.	Nativ. John the Baptist • **Full Strawberry** ○ • **Midsummer Day** •	
25	Tu.	☾ runs low • Custer's Last Stand, 1876 • Romulus conceived, 772 B.C. {9.8 —	*toast*
26	W.	*Better a diamond with a flaw than a pebble without one.* • Col. Tom Parker born, 1919 •	*yourself*
27	Th.	☌ ♆ ☾ • Helen Keller born, 1880 • "Rain of fish" from sky at Tiller's Ferry, S.C., 1901 •	*on*
28	Fr.	St. Irenaeus • ☌ ♅ ☾ • Archduke Ferdinand assassinated, 1914 •	*both*
29	Sa.	Sts. Peter & Paul • Mysterious lake appeared in Colorado desert, 1891 •	*sides!*
30	F	6th S. af. P. • **Orthodox All Saints'** • Montezuma died, 1520 • Tides {9.8 9.0	

If you're going to be thinking anyway, you might as well think big. –Donald Trump

Farmer's Calendar

■ If the antique New England spirit has a sovereign flower, it must be the rhodora, a wild shrub, akin to the laurel, that blooms at this time beside the bogs and beaver ponds. *Rhododendron canadense* produces profuse, extravagant flowers that spill down off of branches which as yet show no leaves. The flowers are pink, red, purple—the colors of a tropical garden. You're a little startled to come upon that kind of show in the waste, remote environs where the rhodora briefly blows. It's that surprise, that contrast of display and diffidence that expresses a characteristic New England mind.

For, at least traditionally, the best of that mind is hidden. Wit, fun, joy, love, emotion are there, all right, but you have to look for them, and you have to look in the right places. The right places are not always—they are not ever—the expected places. You find wit in plain tales of the shop or farm, and you find it on tombstones. You find deep feeling in the spare lines of village churches. You find this warm, bright flower growing out of a sour acid bog on the cold side of a gray mountain, and the contrast, perhaps, moves you to make some expression of what is in your mind. Being moved in that way is also a New England trait, hence the strange eloquence of Ralph Waldo Emerson's short poem on this same flower, with its famous flourish: *Rhodora! if the sages ask thee why / This charm is wasted on the earth and sky, / Tell them, dear, that if eyes were made for seeing, / Then Beauty is its own excuse for being.*

2002　JULY, The Seventh Month

Earth arrives at its annual aphelion (point farthest from the Sun) at midnight, on the night of July 5–6. Though now 7 percent dimmer than in January, the Sun's overhead position makes this the warmest month in most locations in the mid-Northern Hemisphere. Venus, steadily brightening in the western sky at dusk, meets Leo's blue star, Regulus, on the 10th. Jupiter is behind the Sun, where it crosses unseen into Cancer, its home for the rest of the year. Saturn returns, still in Taurus, rising in the east just ahead of morning twilight. At midmonth, Vega, the brightest star that ever reaches zenith from most of the United States, hovers overhead at midnight.

◖ Last Quarter	2nd day	13th hour	19th minute
● New Moon	10th day	6th hour	26th minute
◗ First Quarter	17th day	0 hour	47th minute
○ Full Moon	24th day	5th hour	7th minute

Times are given in Eastern Daylight Time.

For an explanation of this page, see page 40; for values of Key Letters, see page 229.

Day of Year	Day of Month	Day of Week	☼ Rises h. m.	Key	☼ Sets h. m.	Key	Length of Day h. m.	Sun Fast m.	Declination of Sun ° '	High Tide Boston Light—A.M. **Bold**—P.M.		☽ Rises h. m.	Key	☽ Sets h. m.	Key	☽ Place	☽ Age
182	1	M.	5 11	A	8 25	E	15 14	12	23n.05	4½	5	12♒17	D	11♍46	D	AQU	21
183	2	Tu.	5 12	A	8 25	E	15 13	12	23 00	5¼	6	12 39	D	12♎46	D	PSC	22
184	3	W.	5 12	A	8 24	E	15 12	12	22 56	6¼	6¾	1 00	C	1 46	D	CET	23
185	4	Th.	5 13	A	8 24	E	15 11	11	22 51	7	7½	1 22	B	2 47	E	PSC	24
186	5	Fr.	5 13	A	8 24	E	15 11	11	22 45	8	8¼	1 45	B	3 50	E	ARI	25
187	6	Sa.	5 14	A	8 24	E	15 10	11	22 40	8¾	9	2 12	B	4 54	E	ARI	26
188	7	**F**	5 14	A	8 23	E	15 09	11	22 33	9¾	9¾	2 44	B	6 00	E	TAU	27
189	8	M.	5 15	A	8 23	E	15 08	11	22 26	10½	10¾	3 23	A	7 06	E	TAU	28
190	9	Tu.	5 16	A	8 22	E	15 06	10	22 19	11¼	11½	4 11	A	8 07	E	GEM	29
191	10	W.	5 17	A	8 22	E	15 05	10	22 11	**12**	—	5 09	A	9 01	E	GEM	0
192	11	Th.	5 18	A	8 22	E	15 04	10	22 03	12¼	1	6 16	B	9 47	E	LEO	1
193	12	Fr.	5 18	A	8 21	E	15 03	10	21 55	1	1¾	7 29	B	10 25	E	CAN	2
194	13	Sa.	5 19	A	8 20	E	15 01	10	21 47	1¾	2½	8 44	C	10 58	D	LEO	3
195	14	**F**	5 20	A	8 20	E	15 00	10	21 38	2¾	3¼	10 00	C	11 27	D	LEO	4
196	15	M.	5 21	A	8 19	E	14 58	10	21 29	3½	4¼	11♍14	D	11♎53	D	VIR	5
197	16	Tu.	5 22	A	8 19	E	14 57	10	21 19	4½	5	12♎27	D	—	–	VIR	6
198	17	W.	5 22	A	8 18	E	14 56	10	21 09	5½	6	1 40	E	12♏20	C	VIR	7
199	18	Th.	5 23	A	8 17	E	14 54	9	20 58	6½	7	2 53	E	12 47	C	LIB	8
200	19	Fr.	5 24	A	8 16	E	14 52	9	20 47	7½	8	4 06	E	1 17	B	LIB	9
201	20	Sa.	5 25	A	8 16	E	14 51	9	20 36	8½	8¾	5 17	E	1 53	B	SCO	10
202	21	**F**	5 26	A	8 15	E	14 49	9	20 24	9½	9¾	6 23	E	2 34	A	OPH	11
203	22	M.	5 27	A	8 14	E	14 47	9	20 13	10½	10¾	7 22	E	3 23	A	SAG	12
204	23	Tu.	5 28	A	8 13	E	14 45	9	20 00	11½	11½	8 12	E	4 19	B	SAG	13
205	24	W.	5 29	A	8 12	E	14 43	9	19 48	12¼	—	8 53	E	5 21	B	CET	14
206	25	Th.	5 30	A	8 11	E	14 41	9	19 35	12¼	1	9 27	E	6 26	B	CAP	15
207	26	Fr.	5 31	A	8 10	D	14 39	9	19 22	1	1¾	9 55	E	7 30	B	CAP	16
208	27	Sa.	5 32	A	8 09	D	14 37	9	19 08	1¾	2¼	10 20	D	8 33	C	AQU	17
209	28	**F**	5 33	A	8 08	D	14 35	9	18 54	2½	3	10 42	D	9 35	C	AQU	18
210	29	M.	5 34	A	8 07	D	14 33	9	18 40	3¼	3¾	11 03	C	10 35	D	PSC	19
211	30	Tu.	5 35	A	8 06	D	14 31	9	18 26	4	4½	11 24	C	11♍34	D	CET	20
212	31	W.	5 36	A	8 05	D	14 29	9	18n.11	4¾	5	11♏47	B	12♎34	E	PSC	21

JULY hath 31 days. 2002

O to lie in the ripening grass
That gracefully bends to the winds that pass,
And to look aloft the oakleaves through
Into the sky so deep, so blue! –William Roscoe Thayer

D. M.	D. W.	Dates, Feasts, Fasts, Aspects, Tide Heights	*Weather* ↓
1	M.	**Canada Day** • "Rough Riders" captured San Juan Hill, 1898 • Medicare went into effect, 1966	*Of*
2	Tu.	☾ at apo. • ☌☿♄ • ☾ on Eq. • Nostradamus died, 1566	*Founding*
3	W.	Dog Days begin. • ☌♂♃ • *To be safe on the 4th, don't buy a 5th on the 3rd.*	*Fathers*
4	Th.	**Independence Day** • "America" first sung publicly, Boston, 1832 • {8.5 9.2 •	*let's*
5	Fr.	Bikini swimsuit intro. in Paris, 1946 • *If ant hills are high in July, the coming winter will be hard.* •	*be*
6	Sa.	⊕ at aphelion • Louis Pasteur perfected rabies vaccine, 1885 • {8.5 9.7 •	*proud*
7	**F**	**7th S. af. P.** • ☾ at ☊ • Marc Chagall born, 1887 {8.6 10.0	*(and*
8	M.	☌♄☾ • John L. Sullivan won last bare-knuckle prizefight in U.S., 1889	*Founding*
9	Tu.	Mayor La Guardia read comic strips to public on WNYC during newspaper strike, 1945 •	*Mothers,*
10	W.	New ● • Ford Motor Co. had $223.65 in the bank, 1903 • Kissing illegal, France, 1439	*too);*
11	Th.	Vice Pres. Aaron Burr mortally wounded Alexander Hamilton, 1804 • Yul Brynner born, 1915 •	*In*
12	Fr.	Last Checker Cab produced, 1982 • *He that digs a pit for another may fall into it himself.*	*summer's*
13	Sa.	☌♀☾ • 24-hr. blackout in N.Y.C.; looting caused $1 billion loss, 1977 • {11.3 10.0	*sky*
14	**F**	**8th S. af. P.** • ☾ at perig. • Bastille Day • {11.2 10.2	*there's*
15	M.	**St. Swithin** • Duck-billed platypus first exhibited to the public, 1922 • {11.0 10.4	*scarce*
16	Tu.	☾ on Eq. • Wash., D.C., became U.S. capital, 1790 • Jack the Ripper's 8th victim, 1889 •	*a*
17	W.	Cornscateous air is everywhere. • British Royals adopted name of "Windsor," 1917 {10.2 10.6	*cloud,*
18	Th.	Nero fiddled while Rome burned, A.D. 64 • First women's rights convention, Seneca Falls, N.Y., 1848	*so if*
19	Fr.	**St. Vincent de Paul** • ☌♃☉ • Samuel Colt born, 1814 {9.5 10.8	*you*
20	Sa.	☿ in sup. ☌ • ☾ at ☋ • Neil Armstrong's "small step" on Moon, 1969	*start*
21	**F**	**9th S. af. P.** • Robert Burns died, 1796 • *Ne'er trust a July sky.* • {9.3 10.9	*to*
22	M.	**St. Mary Magdalene** • "Public Enemy #1" John Dillinger gunned down by G-men, 1933	*stew*
23	Tu.	☾ runs low • Ice-cream cone invented, 1904 • *Fear not the day you have not seen.* •	*about*
24	W.	**Full Buck** ○ • ☌♆☾ • Brigham Young and followers arrived at Salt Lake, Utah, 1847	*the*
25	Th.	**Sts. James & Christopher** • First "test tube baby" born, 1978 • {10.7 9.4	*heat,*
26	Fr.	**St. Ann** • ☌♅☾ • Eva Perón died, 1952 • {10.6 9.4	*remember—*
27	Sa.	Grasshopper scourge in Iowa, Neb., S.D., 1931 • *Wonder is the beginning of wisdom.* {10.4 9.3	*how*
28	**F**	**10th S. af. P.** • Noah sent forth a dove and a raven, 2348 B.C. {10.1 9.3	*you'll*
29	M.	**Sts. Mary & Martha** • ☾ at apo. • ☾ on Eq. • {9.7 9.3 •	*crave*
30	Tu.	MGM lion roared to introduce first "talkie," 1928 • Emily Brontë born, 1818 • {9.4 9.2 •	*it in*
31	W.	**St. Ignatius of Loyola** • Hunt medicinal herbs now. • {9.0 9.2	*December!*

Farmer's Calendar

■ A medical news report not long ago described laboratory tests that have shown that eating blueberries helps you to be smarter, more agile, and longer-lived. In experiments at Tufts University, researchers found that rats who were fed blueberries were more intelligent, showed more agility, and aged more slowly than others. Brains, grace, long life. Who knew the humble blueberry to have such prowess?

I knew. Over the years, I have come to believe that in the blueberry we have the perfect fruit. It was more than 20 years back that we put in blueberries on this place, where the thin hillside soil grows reluctantly the few crops it grows at all. Sixteen highbush plants we set out. Two of them promptly expired, but the survivors settled in for the long haul and have since produced abundantly, unfailingly. The bushes are now taller than I by at least a foot. Deer browse them up as far as they can rear. Birds take the highest berries. Bears haul down the branches to reach them. And still they thrive, and still they make more than enough berries for their human owners' use. This they do with no care from us at all. Like the fruit that grew in the Garden of Eden, the blueberry brings forth without the gardener's having to labor. You put it in and forget about it—and it goes. Here is gardening as it ought to be, and, I have learned, as it very, very seldom is.

So when Tufts tells me that a diet of blueberries may give me life, intellect, and good moves, I'm glad to hear it, for I can use all three. But I am unsurprised.

2002 AUGUST, The Eighth Month

The Moon (near Venus) sets early on the 11th, leaving the sky dark for the famous Perseid meteor shower, which peaks after midnight under ideal conditions for the first time in three years. Lesser events include a meeting of Venus and Virgo's blue star Spica, on the 31st, and the reemergence of Jupiter in the predawn east. Neptune, visible only through telescopes, reaches opposition on the 1st. Uranus, a green "star" easily seen with binoculars, can be dimly glimpsed by the naked eye in dry, rural, moonless conditions as it attains its greatest brightness at its opposition on the 19th.

☾	Last Quarter	1st day	6th hour	22nd minute
●	New Moon	8th day	15th hour	15th minute
☽	First Quarter	15th day	6th hour	12th minute
○	Full Moon	22nd day	18th hour	29th minute
☾	Last Quarter	30th day	22nd hour	31st minute

Times are given in Eastern Daylight Time.

For an explanation of this page, see page 40; for values of Key Letters, see page 229.

Day of Year	Day of Month	Day of Week	☼ Rises h. m.	Key	☼ Sets h. m.	Key	Length of Day h. m.	Sun Fast m.	Declination of Sun ° '	High Tide Boston Light—A.M.	Bold—P.M.	☽ Rises h. m.	Key	☽ Sets h. m.	Key	☽ Place	☽ Age
213	1	Th.	5 37	A	8 04	D	14 27	9	17N.56	5½	**6**	—	–	1 P.M. 36	E	ARI	22
214	2	Fr.	5 38	A	8 03	D	14 25	9	17 41	6½	**6¾**	12 A.M. 11	B	2 39	E	ARI	23
215	3	Sa.	5 39	A	8 01	D	14 22	9	17 25	7¼	**7½**	12 40	B	3 43	E	TAU	24
216	4	**F**	5 40	A	8 00	D	14 20	9	17 10	8¼	**8½**	1 15	B	4 48	E	TAU	25
217	5	M.	5 41	A	7 59	D	14 18	10	16 53	9	**9¼**	1 59	A	5 51	E	TAU	26
218	6	Tu.	5 42	A	7 58	D	14 16	10	16 37	10	**10¼**	2 52	A	6 49	E	GEM	27
219	7	W.	5 43	A	7 56	D	14 13	10	16 20	10¾	**11**	3 56	B	7 39	E	GEM	28
220	8	Th.	5 44	A	7 55	D	14 11	10	16 03	11¾	**11¾**	5 08	B	8 21	E	CAN	0
221	9	Fr.	5 45	A	7 54	D	14 09	10	15 46	**12½**	—	6 24	B	8 57	D	LEO	1
222	10	Sa.	5 46	A	7 52	D	14 06	10	15 28	12¾	**1¼**	7 42	C	9 28	D	LEO	2
223	11	**F**	5 47	A	7 51	D	14 04	10	15 10	1½	**2**	8 59	D	9 56	D	LEO	3
224	12	M.	5 48	A	7 50	D	14 02	10	14 52	2¼	**3**	10 15	D	10 22	C	VIR	4
225	13	Tu.	5 49	A	7 48	D	13 59	11	14 34	3¼	**3¾**	11 A.M. 30	E	10 50	B	VIR	5
226	14	W.	5 50	A	7 47	D	13 57	11	14 16	4¼	**4¾**	12 P.M. 44	E	11 19	B	VIR	6
227	15	Th.	5 51	B	7 45	D	13 54	11	13 57	5¼	**5½**	1 58	E	11 P.M. 53	B	LIB	7
228	16	Fr.	5 52	B	7 44	D	13 52	11	13 39	6¼	**6½**	3 09	E	—	–	SCO	8
229	17	Sa.	5 53	B	7 42	D	13 49	11	13 19	7¼	**7½**	4 16	E	12 A.M. 32	B	OPH	9
230	18	**F**	5 54	B	7 41	D	13 47	12	13 00	8¼	**8½**	5 17	E	1 19	A	SAG	10
231	19	M.	5 55	B	7 39	D	13 44	12	12 40	9½	**9½**	6 09	E	2 12	A	SAG	11
232	20	Tu.	5 57	B	7 38	D	13 41	12	12 21	10¼	**10½**	6 52	E	3 12	B	SAG	12
233	21	W.	5 58	B	7 36	D	13 38	12	12 01	11¼	**11¼**	7 28	E	4 15	B	CAP	13
234	22	Th.	5 59	B	7 35	D	13 36	13	11 40	**12**	—	7 57	E	5 19	B	CAP	14
235	23	Fr.	6 00	B	7 33	D	13 33	13	11 20	12	**12½**	8 23	D	6 22	C	AQU	15
236	24	Sa.	6 01	B	7 32	D	13 31	13	11 00	12¾	**1¼**	8 46	D	7 24	C	AQU	16
237	25	**F**	6 02	B	7 30	D	13 28	13	10 39	1¼	**1¾**	9 07	D	8 25	D	AQU	17
238	26	M.	6 03	B	7 28	D	13 25	14	10 18	2	**2¼**	9 28	C	9 25	D	CET	18
239	27	Tu.	6 04	B	7 27	D	13 23	14	9 57	2¾	**3**	9 49	B	10 25	D	PSC	19
240	28	W.	6 05	B	7 25	D	13 20	14	9 36	3¼	**3¾**	10 12	B	11 A.M. 25	E	PSC	20
241	29	Th.	6 06	B	7 23	D	13 17	14	9 14	4	**4¼**	10 39	B	12 P.M. 27	E	ARI	21
242	30	Fr.	6 07	B	7 22	D	13 15	15	8 53	4¾	**5¼**	11 11	B	1 30	E	TAU	22
243	31	Sa.	6 08	B	7 20	D	13 12	15	8N.31	5¾	**6**	11 P.M. 49	A	2 P.M. 33	E	TAU	23

AUGUST hath 31 days. 2002

When high the sun in noonday glory rides,
Where willows keep the lake's green margin cool,
The speckled trout amid their shadow hides,
And dragonflies haunt every shaded pool. –Thomas S. Collier

D. M.	D. W.	Dates, Feasts, Fasts, Aspects, Tide Heights	Weather ↓
1	Th.	**Lammas Day** • ♆ at ☍ • Diamonds found in Arkansas, 1906 • { 8.6 / 9.2	*What*
2	Fr.	*When an old person dies, a library burns to the ground.* • Jesse Owens set world record for 100 meters, 1935	*a*
3	Sa.	☌ ♆ ☾ • Columbus set sail from Spain for New World, 1492 •	*sensation!*
4	F	**11th S. af. P.** • ☾ at ☊ • "Lizzie Borden took an ax," 1892	*Beware*
5	M.	☌ ♄ ☾ • *The sharper the blast, the sooner it's past.* { 8.5 / 10.0	*precipitation.*
6	Tu.	**Transfiguration** • ☾ rides high • Alfred, Lord Tennyson born, 1809 •	*In*
7	W.	**Name of Jesus** • Hatfield-McCoy "blood feud" began, 1882 • { 9.2 / 11.0 •	*mid-*
8	Th.	**St. Dominic** • **New** ● • Tides { 9.6 / 11.4 •	*rustication,*
9	Fr.	☌ ☿ ☾ • Izaak Walton born, 1593 • *"They say" is half a lie.* •	*produce*
10	Sa.	**St. Laurence** • ☌ ♂ ☉ • ☾ at perig. •	*perspiration*
11	F	**12th S. af. P.** • ☌ ♀ ☾ • Dog Days end. • { 11.7 / 10.8	*by*
12	M.	**St. Clare** • ☾ on Eq. • World's last quagga died at Amsterdam Zoo, 1883	*eradication*
13	Tu.	Blue Sun observed throughout South, 1831 • Gunpowder invented, 1330 • Annie Oakley born, 1860	*of*
14	W.	Last stone placed on Cologne Cathedral after 632 years of construction, 1880 • { 10.6 / 10.9 •	*weed*
15	Th.	**Assumption** • Walter Scott born, 1771 • *Mackerel sky, not 24 hours dry.*	*infestation.*
16	Fr.	☾ at ☋ • Last stage performance at Hippodrome vaudeville hall, N.Y.C., 1939	• *Invite*
17	Sa.	Cat Nights begin. • *A man convinced against his will is of the same opinion still.* • { 9.1 / 10.4	*your*
18	F	**13th S. af. P.** • Lincoln's birthplace made national shrine, 1916	*relations*
19	M.	♅ at ☍ • ☾ runs low • Daguerreotype process divulged, 1839 • { 9.0 / 10.4	*to*
20	Tu.	3,000,000 acres burned by wildfire in Idaho, 1910 • Jellyfish invaded beaches in Conn. and R.I., 1978	*share*
21	W.	☌ ♆ ☾ • "Mona Lisa" stolen from the Louvre, 1911 •	*recreation—*
22	Th.	**Full Sturgeon** ○ • ♂ Gr. Elong. (46° E.) • ☌ ♅ ☾ • { 9.3 / —	*and*
23	Fr.	*If you give a pig and a boy everything they want, you'll get a good pig and a bad boy.* • { 10.4 / 9.4 •	*with*
24	Sa.	**St. Bartholomew** • Vesuvius destroyed Pompeii, A.D. 79 •	*consternation,*
25	F	**14th S. af. P.** • Law providing pensions for former presidents, 1958 •	*await*
26	M.	☾ at apo. • ☾ on Eq. • First successful typewriter patented, 1843	*termination*
27	Tu.	♇ stat. • Confucius born, 551 B.C. • *Tarzan of the Apes* published, 1912 • { 9.6 / 9.5 •	*of*
28	W.	**St. Augustine of Hippo** • Leo Tolstoy born, 1828 • "I have a dream," 1963	*your*
29	Th.	**St. John the Baptist** • Strange noises heard in the sky over London, 1607	*summer*
30	Fr.	Cleopatra committed suicide by permitting an asp to bite her, 30 B.C. • { 8.6 / 9.2 •	*vacation.*
31	Sa.	☾ at ☊ • John Ford died, 1973 • U.S.S.R. shot down South Korean airliner, 269 killed, 1983 •	

Farmer's Calendar

■ A big red truck with a long, long boom rolled into town here one summer afternoon a couple of years ago. A crew came with it. They got set up and proceeded to dismantle the two old pine trees that grew at the north end of the village. It took the crew most of two days to do the job, but they finished at last. After them came another truck with a grabber, which presently drove away loaded with the biggest logs anybody around here had ever seen or would see again in our time, or our children's, or their children's.

They were white pines, among the biggest trees in the state. The bigger of the two was 146 feet tall, and each of them must have been close to 20 feet around the base. Neither of the two pines had branches less than, say, 80 feet up. Every so often one of them would let go of a branch that would fall into somebody's yard, a branch bigger than many trees. That was why the pines were cut. Neither was sound at its center, and beneath them, the nearby buildings looked like dollhouses. No house, no householder would have survived the fall of one of those trees, and every tree falls sooner or later. They had to go.

Nobody knows exactly how old they were. The best guess was 200 years. When those pines were the kind of green, sticky whips you try to keep cut down in the pasture, the president was Thomas Jefferson and the newest state was Ohio. That they should end in our time is not sad, exactly—but solemn, at least, and worth recording.

Jupiter and Saturn are both up in the east as morning twilight begins; the ringed planet finally leaves Taurus and passes into Orion's upraised arm for the next two months. Venus is near the blue star Spica on the 1st and attains its greatest brilliancy on the 26th. This truly dazzling autumn display always occurs when the cloud-covered evening star is low in the sky. On the 9th, Venus lurks less than 10 degrees above the southwestern horizon in the fading dusk. The Moon rises at nearly the same time for several nights before and after the full Harvest Moon on the 21st. During the first hour of the 23rd, fall arrives with the equinox.

●	New Moon	6th day	23rd hour	10th minute
☽	First Quarter	13th day	14th hour	8th minute
○	Full Moon	21st day	9th hour	59th minute
☾	Last Quarter	29th day	13th hour	3rd minute

Times are given in Eastern Daylight Time.

For an explanation of this page, see page 40; for values of Key Letters, see page 229.

Day of Year	Day of Month	Day of Week	Rises h. m.	Key	Sets h. m.	Key	Length of Day h. m.	Sun Fast m.	Declination of Sun ° '	High Tide Boston Light—A.M. Bold—P.M.		Rises h. m.	Key	Sets h. m.	Key	Place	Age
244	1	F	6 09	B	7 18	D	13 09	15	8 N.10	6¾	7	—	A	3ᴾₘ36	E	TAU	24
245	2	M.	6 10	B	7 17	D	13 07	16	7 48	7½	7¾	12ᴬₘ37	A	4 35	E	GEM	25
246	3	Tu.	6 11	B	7 15	D	13 04	16	7 26	8½	8¾	1 35	A	5 28	E	GEM	26
247	4	W.	6 12	B	7 13	D	13 01	16	7 04	9½	9¾	2 42	B	6 13	E	CAN	27
248	5	Th.	6 13	B	7 12	D	12 59	17	6 41	10¼	10½	3 57	B	6 51	E	CAN	28
249	6	Fr.	6 15	B	7 10	D	12 55	17	6 19	11¼	11½	5 15	C	7 25	D	LEO	0
250	7	Sa.	6 16	B	7 08	D	12 52	17	5 57	**12**	—	6 34	D	7 54	D	LEO	1
251	8	F	6 17	B	7 06	D	12 49	18	5 34	12¼	12¾	7 53	D	8 22	C	VIR	2
252	9	M.	6 18	B	7 05	C	12 47	18	5 12	1¼	1½	9 11	D	8 50	C	VIR	3
253	10	Tu.	6 19	B	7 03	C	12 44	18	4 49	2	2½	10 29	E	9 19	B	VIR	4
254	11	W.	6 20	B	7 01	C	12 41	19	4 26	3	3¼	11ᴬₘ45	E	9 52	B	LIB	5
255	12	Th.	6 21	B	6 59	C	12 38	19	4 04	3¾	4¼	12ᴾₘ59	E	10 30	B	LIB	6
256	13	Fr.	6 22	B	6 58	C	12 36	19	3 41	4¾	5¼	2 10	E	11ᴾₘ15	A	OPH	7
257	14	Sa.	6 23	B	6 56	C	12 33	20	3 18	6	6¼	3 13	E	—	–	SAG	8
258	15	F	6 24	B	6 54	C	12 30	20	2 55	7	7¼	4 08	E	12ᴬₘ07	A	SAG	9
259	16	M.	6 25	B	6 52	C	12 27	21	2 31	8	8¼	4 53	E	1 05	A	SAG	10
260	17	Tu.	6 26	B	6 51	C	12 25	21	2 08	9¼	9¼	5 30	E	2 07	B	CAP	11
261	18	W.	6 27	B	6 49	C	12 22	21	1 45	10	10¼	6 01	E	3 11	B	CAP	12
262	19	Th.	6 28	B	6 47	C	12 19	22	1 22	10¾	11	6 27	D	4 14	B	AQU	13
263	20	Fr.	6 29	C	6 45	C	12 16	22	0 58	11½	11¾	6 50	D	5 16	C	AQU	14
264	21	Sa.	6 30	C	6 43	C	12 13	22	0 35	**12**	—	7 12	D	6 17	D	AQU	15
265	22	F	6 31	C	6 42	C	12 11	23	0 N.12	12¼	12½	7 32	C	7 17	D	CET	16
266	23	M.	6 32	C	6 40	C	12 08	23	0 s.12	1	1¼	7 53	B	8 17	D	PSC	17
267	24	Tu.	6 34	C	6 38	C	12 04	23	0 35	1½	1¾	8 16	B	9 17	E	PSC	18
268	25	W.	6 35	C	6 36	C	12 01	24	0 58	2¼	2¼	8 41	B	10 18	E	ARI	19
269	26	Th.	6 36	C	6 35	C	11 59	24	1 22	2¾	3	9 10	B	11ᴬₘ21	E	TAU	20
270	27	Fr.	6 37	C	6 33	C	11 56	24	1 45	3½	3¾	9 45	A	12ᴾₘ23	E	TAU	21
271	28	Sa.	6 38	C	6 31	B	11 53	25	2 08	4¼	4½	10 28	A	1 26	E	TAU	22
272	29	F	6 39	C	6 29	B	11 50	25	2 32	5¼	5¼	11ᴾₘ20	A	2 25	E	LEO	23
273	30	M.	6 40	C	6 28	B	11 48	25	2 s.55	6	6¼	—	–	3ᴾₘ18	E	GEM	24

SEPTEMBER hath 30 days. 2002

September strews the woodlot o'er
With many a brilliant color;
The world is brighter than before,
Why should our hearts be duller? –Thomas W. Parsons

D. M.	D. W.	Dates, Feasts, Fasts, Aspects, Tide Heights	Weather ↓
1	F	15th S. af. P. • ☌ ♄ ☾ • ☿ Gr. Elong. (27° E.) • {8.2 9.4	
2	M.	Labor Day • Great fire of London, 13,000 houses lost, 1666 • *Compete, don't envy.*	*School*
3	Tu.	St. Gregory the Great • Revolutionary War ended, 1783 • Tides {8.5 10.1	*bells*
4	W.	☌ ♃ ☾ • Crazy Horse slain, 1877 • Cranberry harvest begins, Cape Cod. •	*summon*
5	Th.	*Patience and a mulberry leaf will make a silk gown.* • First Labor Day parade, 1882 •	*reluctant*
6	Fr.	New ● • ☾ on Eq. • Pres. McKinley shot, 1901 • {10.2 11.6	*scholars;*
7	Sa.	Rosh Hashanah • ☾ at perig. • Grandma Moses born, 1860 •	*heat*
8	F	16th S. af. P. • ☌ ☿ ☾ • Galveston hurricane, 6,000 killed, 1900	*wave*
9	M.	St. Omer • ☌ ♀ ☾ • Congress decided on "United States," 1776 •	*makes*
10	Tu.	Fay Wray born, 1907 • Huey Long assassinated, 1935 • *A bad workman blames his tools.* {11.5 11.6	*us*
11	W.	Sts. Protus & Hyacinth • Paul "Bear" Bryant born, 1913 • {11.1 11.5	*loosen*
12	Th.	☾ at ☋ • Hot, dry winds caused leaves to wither, Kansas, 1882 • {10.4 11.1	*collars.*
13	Fr.	World-record temp. of 136° F, Libya, 1922 • Attica prison riot, 1971 • "Uncle Sam" born, 1766	*Apple*
14	Sa.	Holy Cross • ☿ stat. • *The Waltons* premiered on CBS, 1972	*branches*
15	F	17th S. af. P. • ☾ runs low • James Fenimore Cooper born, 1789 •	*sag*
16	M.	Yom Kippur • The settlement of Shawmut was renamed Boston, 1630 • {8.8 9.9 •	*with*
17	Tu.	☌ ♆ ☾ • *A sunshiny shower never lasts half an hour.* • {8.9 9.9 •	*riches:*
18	W.	☌ ♅ ☾ • Ember Day • First issue of the *New York Times,* 1851	*Cortlands,*
19	Th.	Johann Gutenburg died, 1468 • Mickey Mouse made his debut, 1928 •	*Greenings,*
20	Fr.	St. Eustace • Ferdinand Magellan's flotilla set sail, 1519 • Ember Day • {9.5 10.1	*Red*
21	Sa.	Succoth • Full Harvest ○ • Ember Day • {9.6 — •	*Delicious.*
22	F	18th S. af. P. • ☾ on Eq. • ☾ at apo. • Tides {10.0 9.8	*The*
23	M.	Harvest Home • **Autumnal Equinox** • Neptune discovered, 1846 • {9.9 9.8	*rain,*
24	Tu.	Woodchucks hibernate. • Little Rock, Ark., integration crisis, 1957 • *It's not a fish 'til it's on the bank.*	*we*
25	W.	☾ runs low • Publication of *Publick Occurrences,* first newspaper in U.S., 1690	*maintain,*
26	Th.	♀ Gr. Bril. • John Chapman ("Johnny Appleseed") born, 1774 • Tides {9.1 9.6 •	*is*
27	Fr.	☿ in inf. ☌ • ☾ at ☊ • First passenger rail service (10 mph), 1826	*plainly*
28	Sa.	☌ ♄ ☾ • Jerry Clower born, 1926 • *Bad weather always looks worse through a window.* •	*on*
29	F	19th S. af. P. • Cervantes born, 1547 • Jerry Lee Lewis born, 1935 {8.3 9.4	*the*
30	M.	St. Sophia • ☾ rides high • Ether first used in tooth extraction, 1846 {8.3 9.5	*wane.*

A lie gets halfway around the world before the truth even has a chance to get its pants on. –Winston Churchill

Farmer's Calendar

■ "If the clouds be full of rain, they empty themselves upon the earth: and if the tree fall toward the south, or toward the north, in the place where the tree falleth, there it shall be." So writes Ecclesiastes, in an early instance of skepticism directed against the claims of weather forecasters. Plainly, the writer hasn't much use for such predictions or those who make them. But observe the subtlety of his doubt: He's not saying that weather forecasts are always, or even often, inaccurate. He's saying they're *irrelevant.* They tell us that if it's going to rain, it probably will; but they don't tell us what we want to know.

Ecclesiastes, it is well known, takes a pretty dim view of things in general where human affairs are concerned. This short book of the Old Testament must be the most eloquent, most authoritative statement in any language of the limits on our ability to know and to act. It's a statement supremely rigorous and bleak, but it is also full of consolation. For, at least in this part of his argument, the writer seems to say that we do best to accept the experience of our days—including the weather—with a light heart and without much analysis. Reasoning about the weather—about anything—can't tell us what to do or how to meet our own lives. Only principle can do that—or, say, conviction, or faith. Ecclesiastes is operating on the middle ground where knowledge meets morals, ground the Weather Bureau doesn't own.

So keep your umbrella loaded, and don't worry too much about the weather.

2002   OCTOBER, The Tenth Month

Venus quickly falls further into the glare of the setting Sun each evening. It is performing its swan song as an evening star; bright twilight is the best time to see its enormous slender crescent shape through binoculars or a telescope. By 7:30 P.M., Venus has set and no bright planets remain, so the action shifts to the predawn east. There, the crescent Moon meets brilliant Jupiter on the 2nd, and Mercury and Mars are easily seen as they float side by side from the 9th to the 13th. Saturn is high in the south at dawn and starts rising before 10:00 P.M. by month's end. The bright full Hunter's Moon on the 21st will spoil the Orionid meteor shower, normally the year's fourth best.

●	New Moon	6th day	7th hour	18th minute
☽	First Quarter	13th day	1st hour	33rd minute
○	Full Moon	21st day	3rd hour	20th minute
☾	Last Quarter	29th day	0 hour	28th minute

After 2:00 A.M. on October 27, Eastern Standard Time (EST) is given.

For an explanation of this page, see page 40; for values of Key Letters, see page 229.

Day of Year	Day of Month	Day of Week	☀ Rises h. m.	Key	☀ Sets h. m.	Key	Length of Day h. m.	Sun Fast m.	Declina- tion of Sun ° '	High Tide Boston Light—A.M. **Bold—P.M.**	☽ Rises h. m.	Key	☽ Sets h. m.	Key	☽ Place	☽ Age
274	1	Tu.	6 41	C	6 26	B	11 45	26	3 s.18	7 7¼	12ᴬM21	A	4ᴹ05	E	LEO	25
275	2	W.	6 42	C	6 24	B	11 42	26	3 41	8 8¼	1 31	B	4 46	E	CAN	26
276	3	Th.	6 43	C	6 22	B	11 39	26	4 05	9 9¼	2 46	B	5 20	E	LEO	27
277	4	Fr.	6 44	C	6 21	B	11 37	27	4 28	10 10¼	4 04	C	5 51	D	LEO	28
278	5	Sa.	6 46	C	6 19	B	11 33	27	4 51	10¾ **11**	5 23	D	6 19	D	VIR	29
279	6	**F**	6 47	C	6 17	B	11 30	27	5 14	11½ **12**	6 43	D	6 47	C	VIR	0
280	7	M.	6 48	C	6 16	B	11 28	28	5 37	12¼ —	8 02	E	7 16	C	VIR	1
281	8	Tu.	6 49	C	6 14	B	11 25	28	6 00	12¾ **1¼**	9 22	E	7 48	B	LIB	2
282	9	W.	6 50	C	6 12	B	11 22	28	6 23	1¾ **2**	10 41	E	8 25	B	LIB	3
283	10	Th.	6 51	C	6 11	B	11 20	28	6 46	2½ **2¾**	11ᴬM56	E	9 08	A	OPH	4
284	11	Fr.	6 52	C	6 09	B	11 17	29	7 08	3½ **3¾**	1ᴹ04	E	9 59	A	OPH	5
285	12	Sa.	6 53	C	6 07	B	11 14	29	7 31	4½ **4¾**	2 04	E	10 56	A	SAG	6
286	13	**F**	6 55	C	6 06	B	11 11	29	7 53	5½ **5¾**	2 53	E	11ᴾM58	B	SAG	7
287	14	M.	6 56	D	6 04	B	11 08	29	8 16	6¾ **7**	3 33	E	—	–	CAP	8
288	15	Tu.	6 57	D	6 02	B	11 05	30	8 38	7¾ **8**	4 06	E	1ᴹ02	B	CAP	9
289	16	W.	6 58	D	6 01	B	11 03	30	9 00	8¾ **9**	4 33	D	2 06	B	AQU	10
290	17	Th.	6 59	D	5 59	B	11 00	30	9 22	9½ **9¾**	4 56	D	3 09	C	AQU	11
291	18	Fr.	7 00	D	5 58	B	10 58	30	9 44	10¼ **10½**	5 18	D	4 10	C	AQU	12
292	19	Sa.	7 02	D	5 56	B	10 54	30	10 06	11 **11¼**	5 38	C	5 10	D	PSC	13
293	20	**F**	7 03	D	5 55	B	10 52	31	10 27	11½ **11¾**	5 59	C	6 10	D	CET	14
294	21	M.	7 04	D	5 53	B	10 49	31	10 49	12 —	6 20	B	7 10	E	PSC	15
295	22	Tu.	7 05	D	5 52	B	10 47	31	11 10	12½ **12¾**	6 44	B	8 11	E	ARI	16
296	23	W.	7 06	D	5 50	B	10 44	31	11 31	1 **1¼**	7 12	B	9 14	E	ARI	17
297	24	Th.	7 08	D	5 49	B	10 41	31	11 52	1¾ **1¾**	7 45	A	10 17	E	TAU	18
298	25	Fr.	7 09	D	5 47	B	10 38	31	12 12	2½ **2½**	8 24	A	11ᴬM19	E	TAU	19
299	26	Sa.	7 10	D	5 46	B	10 36	32	12 33	3 **3¼**	9 12	A	12ᴹ19	E	TAU	20
300	27	**F**	6 11	D	4 44	B	10 33	32	12 53	3 **3**	9 10	A	12 14	E	GEM	21
301	28	M.	6 12	D	4 43	B	10 31	32	13 13	3¾ **4**	10 15	B	1 02	E	GEM	22
302	29	Tu.	6 14	D	4 42	B	10 28	32	13 33	4¾ **4¾**	11ᴹ25	B	1 43	E	CAN	23
303	30	W.	6 15	D	4 40	B	10 25	32	13 53	5¾ **6**	—	–	2 18	E	LEO	24
304	31	Th.	6 16	D	4 39	B	10 23	32	14 s.12	6½ **7**	12ᴬM40	C	2ᴹ49	D	LEO	25

OCTOBER hath 31 days. 2002

Bright yellow, red and orange,
The leaves come down in hosts;
The trees are Indian princes,
But soon they'll turn to ghosts. –William Allingham

D. M.	D. W.	Dates, Feasts, Fasts, Aspects, Tide Heights	Weather ↓
1	Tu.	St. Gregory • First Model T, $850, 1908 • J. Carson first hosted *The Tonight Show,* 1962	*Now*
2	W.	☌ ♃ ☾ • Mahatma Ghandi born, 1869 • Telescope first demonstrated, 1608 •	*the*
3	Th.	Thanksgiving made national holiday, 1863 • James Herriott born, 1916 • { 9.5 / 10.7	*tourists*
4	Fr.	St. Francis of Assisi • ☌ ♂ ☾ • Cattle stampede in N.Y.C., 1874	*clog*
5	Sa.	☿ stat. • Former slave Charlie Smith, said to be age 137, died, 1979 •	*the Notches,*
6	F	**20th S. af. P.** • New ● • ☾ on Eq. • ☾ at perig.	
7	M.	Georgia Tech beat Cumberland Univ. in football 222–0, 1916 • Oliver Wendell Holmes died, 1894 •	*gape*
8	Tu.	☌ ♀ ☾ • Sgt. York single-handedly captured 132 Germans, 1918 • Tides { 11.6 / 12.1	*at*
9	W.	4" snow, Boston, 1703 • *Hunger is the best cook.* • Tides { 11.3 / 12.0 •	*maple's*
10	Th.	♀ stat. • ☾ at ☋ • Tuxedo first worn, 1886 • Hippocrates died, 370 B.C.	*orange*
11	Fr.	♄ stat. • 300,000 died in Calcutta earthquake, 1737 • { 10.2 / 11.1	*splotches,*
12	Sa.	☾ runs low • *For a happy marriage, never shout at one another unless the house is on fire.*	*yellow*
13	F	**21st S. af. P.** • ☿ Gr. Elong. (18° W.) • Paul Simon born, 1941	*bursts*
14	M.	Columbus Day • **Thanksgiving Day (Canada)** • ☌ ♆ ☾ • { 8.8 / 9.7 •	*of*
15	Tu.	☌ ♅ ☾ • Gregorian calendar adopted; this day in 1582 was Oct. 5 • { 8.8 / 9.5	*birch*
16	W.	"Cardiff giant" found near Syracuse, N.Y., 1869 • Marie Antoinette died, 1793 • { 8.9 / 9.5	*and*
17	Th.	St. Ignatius of Antioch • Mountain gorillas discovered, 1902 • { 9.2 / 9.6 •	*ash,*
18	Fr.	St. Luke • Walt Kelly died, 1973 • *Many irons in the fire, some will cool.* •	*sumac's*
19	Sa.	☾ on Eq. • Child's letter convinced Lincoln to grow beard, 1860 • { 9.7 / 9.7 •	*scarlet*
20	F	**22nd S. af. P.** • ☾ at apo. • ♆ stat. •	*cymbal*
21	M.	**Full Hunter's** ○ • Battle of Cherokee, Ala., 1863 • Alfred Nobel born, 1833	*clash!*
22	Tu.	☾ runs low • So. California heatwave; San Diego, 104°F, 1965 • Great influenza epidemic, 1918	*Till,*
23	W.	☌ ♂ ☾ • World created (according to Bishop Ussher) at 9 A.M., 4004 B.C. • { 9.5 / 10.1	*by*
24	Th.	☾ at ☊ • Alarm clock patented, 1876 • *Onion skins very thin, mild winter coming in.*	*rain*
25	Fr.	Pablo Picasso born, 1881 • -10°F at Bismarck, N.D., 1919 • Minnie Pearl born, 1912 •	*and*
26	Sa.	☌ ♄ ☾ • *Are the gaps in your walls mended?* • Coffee shortage in United States, 1949	*wind*
27	F	**23rd S. af. P.** • **Daylight Saving Time ends, 2:00 A.M.** • ☾ rides high	
28	M.	Sts. Simon & Jude • First baby born in an airplane, 1929 •	*diminished,*
29	Tu.	☌ ♃ ☾ • "Black Tuesday" stock market crash, 1929 • { 8.5 / 9.6	*autumn's*
30	W.	Orson Welles's radio dramatization of "The War of the Worlds" caused nationwide panic, 1938	*symphony*
31	Th.	All Hallows Eve • St. Wolfgang • ♀ in inf. ☌	*is finished.*

Farmer's Calendar

■ A friend of mine, who probably doesn't know what he's talking about any more than I do, has told me that those hardwood trees that are especially slow to turn color in the fall are species originating in the tropics. In the north, they relinquish their green late, just because they have a kind of ancestral, vegetable memory of the south, where their forerunners didn't have to relinquish it at all.

I'd like to believe that. It's pleasant to think that trees are no smarter than people and that they too can delude themselves with a mythology, a vision of ease and plenty in a distant past. Perhaps the hypothesis accounts for the beech trees' reluctance to turn color and drop their leaves. Three quarters of the way through October, when the maples, ashes, and birches are bare and the oaks hang onto dry, leathery mummies of leaves, many of the smaller beeches in the forest understory may be mostly green. The beeches seem to turn color from the top down—though it's hard to say for sure. You'll see a tree whose top has turned to chestnut color while the lowest branches are still green-going-yellow. They seem to yield to the season fighting all the way, leaf by leaf: On close inspection, a beech leaf will show light lemon color at the margins, green at the center.

Into November, though, even the die-hard beeches bow. Overnight, their last green gives up and their brown and yellow leaves begin to drop. No apocryphal tradition of warmer, better ages can help them when the serious frosts arrive. They get in line and go down with the rest.

NOVEMBER, The Eleventh Month

The combination of the clocks having "fallen back" to end Daylight Saving Time and the planets rising two hours earlier each month suddenly brings Saturn out right after nightfall and brilliant Jupiter up by 11:00 P.M. in midmonth. Saturn's rings are now wide open, giving the planet a rare brilliance as it retrogrades back into Taurus. Meanwhile, Venus charges into the morning sky, rapidly rising ahead of the Sun and displaying its final lovely crescent profile (through binoculars) until the year 2004. On the 17th, the East Coast could experience a fantastic Leonid meteor shower. Predictions suggest that more than 25,000 meteors per hour will be visible.

●	New Moon	4th day	15th hour	34th minute
☽	First Quarter	11th day	15th hour	52nd minute
○	Full Moon	19th day	20th hour	34th minute
☾	Last Quarter	27th day	10th hour	46th minute

Times are given in Eastern Standard Time.

For an explanation of this page, see page 40; for values of Key Letters, see page 229.

Day of Year	Day of Month	Day of Week	☼ Rises h. m.	Key	☼ Sets h. m.	Key	Length of Day h. m.	Sun Fast m.	Declination of Sun ° '	High Tide Boston Light—A.M.	Bold—P.M.	☽ Rises h. m.	Key	☽ Sets h. m.	Key	☽ Place	☽ Age
305	1	Fr.	6 17	D	4 38	B	10 21	32	14s.31	7½	**8**	1 A.M. 56	C	3 P.M. 17	D	LEO	26
306	2	Sa.	6 19	D	4 36	B	10 17	32	14 50	8½	**8¾**	3 13	D	3 44	C	VIR	27
307	3	**F**	6 20	D	4 35	B	10 15	32	15 09	9¼	**9¾**	4 31	D	4 11	C	VIR	28
308	4	M.	6 21	D	4 34	B	10 13	32	15 28	10¼	**10¾**	5 51	E	4 41	B	VIR	0
309	5	Tu.	6 22	D	4 33	B	10 11	32	15 46	11	**11½**	7 11	E	5 16	B	LIB	1
310	6	W.	6 24	D	4 32	B	10 08	32	16 05	11¾	—	8 31	E	5 57	A	LIB	2
311	7	Th.	6 25	D	4 30	B	10 05	32	16 22	12½	**12½**	9 45	E	6 45	A	OPH	3
312	8	Fr.	6 26	D	4 29	A	10 03	32	16 40	1¼	**1½**	10 52	E	7 42	A	SAG	4
313	9	Sa.	6 27	D	4 28	A	10 01	32	16 57	2¼	**2¼**	11 A.M. 47	E	8 45	B	SAG	5
314	10	**F**	6 29	D	4 27	A	9 58	32	17 14	3¼	**3¼**	12 P.M. 32	E	9 50	B	SAG	6
315	11	M.	6 30	D	4 26	A	9 56	32	17 30	4¼	**4¼**	1 08	E	10 56	B	CAP	7
316	12	Tu.	6 31	D	4 25	A	9 54	32	17 46	5¼	**5¼**	1 37	E	11 P.M. 59	C	CAP	8
317	13	W.	6 32	D	4 24	A	9 52	31	18 02	6¼	**6½**	2 02	D	—	–	AQU	9
318	14	Th.	6 34	D	4 23	A	9 49	31	18 18	7	**7¼**	2 24	D	1 A.M. 01	C	AQU	10
319	15	Fr.	6 35	D	4 22	A	9 47	31	18 34	8	**8¼**	2 44	D	2 02	D	PSC	11
320	16	Sa.	6 36	D	4 21	A	9 45	31	18 49	8¾	**9**	3 04	C	3 02	D	CET	12
321	17	**F**	6 37	D	4 21	A	9 44	31	19 04	9¼	**9¾**	3 25	C	4 02	D	PSC	13
322	18	M.	6 39	D	4 20	A	9 41	31	19 18	10	**10½**	3 48	B	5 03	E	ARI	14
323	19	Tu.	6 40	D	4 19	A	9 39	30	19 32	10½	**11**	4 15	B	6 05	E	ARI	15
324	20	W.	6 41	D	4 18	A	9 37	30	19 45	11	**11¾**	4 46	A	7 09	E	TAU	16
325	21	Th.	6 42	D	4 18	A	9 36	30	19 59	11¾	—	5 23	A	8 12	E	TAU	17
326	22	Fr.	6 43	D	4 17	A	9 34	30	20 11	12¼	**12¼**	6 09	A	9 14	E	TAU	18
327	23	Sa.	6 45	D	4 16	A	9 31	29	20 24	1	**1**	7 03	A	10 11	E	GEM	19
328	24	**F**	6 46	D	4 16	A	9 30	29	20 37	1¾	**1¾**	8 06	A	11 01	E	GEM	20
329	25	M.	6 47	D	4 15	A	9 28	29	20 48	2½	**2½**	9 14	B	11 A.M. 44	E	CAN	21
330	26	Tu.	6 48	D	4 15	A	9 27	29	21 00	3¼	**3½**	10 26	B	12 P.M. 20	E	CAN	22
331	27	W.	6 49	E	4 14	A	9 25	28	21 11	4¼	**4½**	11 P.M. 38	C	12 51	D	LEO	23
332	28	Th.	6 50	E	4 14	A	9 24	28	21 21	5¼	**5½**	—	–	1 19	D	LEO	24
333	29	Fr.	6 51	E	4 13	A	9 22	28	21 32	6¼	**6½**	12 A.M. 52	D	1 45	D	VIR	25
334	30	Sa.	6 53	E	4 13	A	9 20	27	21s.41	7	**7½**	2 A.M. 07	D	2 P.M. 10	C	VIR	26

Dry leaves upon the wall,
Which flap like rustling wings and seek escape,
A single frosted cluster on the grape
Still hangs,—and that is all. –Sarah Chauncey Woolsey

Farmer's Calendar

■ One of the less satisfactory points about owning cats is their insatiable and sadistic predation. Any cat worth its hire will catch, kill, and tear to pieces a toll of victims to make Genghis Khan look like a summer afternoon. Now, for the owner of one of these engines of destruction, finding the hindquarters of a mouse on the kitchen counter, a little more in the hall, the rest in the parlor, is a lousy way to start the day. It's enough to make you take up dogs. Fortunately, with cats, as with much else, age seems to change things.

In the middle of the night, I'm awakened by the unmistakable sound of our middle cat's having caught a mouse: a long, penetrating *meeee-oww-wow-wow,* having an oddly guttural or muffled timbre, as though you tried to sing with your mouth full of peas; then a scurrying and a patter of footfalls, followed by the same cry—announcing the near approach of one mouse's hideous demise.

And yet, in the morning, peace and calm. There's the cat, asleep in her chair. There's the mouse, her last night's prey, very much alive, watching her from under the stove. On my coming into the kitchen, he exits under the pantry door, fit as a flea.

What's here? What else but *catch-and-release mousing,* a kind of feline dry-fly refinement, in which all the joy is in the style and rigor of the pursuit. It's a mature sport, reflective and quite bloodless. This cat is 12 years old, after all. In her slashing salad days, she'd have made that rodent smart, but now she's a philosopher.

D.M.	D.W.	Dates, Feasts, Fasts, Aspects, Tide Heights	Weather ↓
1	Fr.	**All Saints'** • Osceola led Seminoles in resisting removal from Fla. homeland, 1836 • { 10.0 / 10.5 }	*It's*
2	Sa.	**All Souls'** • ☾ on Eq. • ♂♂☾ • Daniel Boone born, 1734 •	*waiting*
3	F	**24th S. af. P.** • ☾ at perig. • Tides { 11.4 / 11.1 }	*season.*
4	M.	**New** ● • ☿ stat. • Nothing is easy to the unwilling. • Will Rogers born, 1879 •	*In*
5	Tu.	Rudolph Valentino's marriage to Jean Acker lasted 6 hours, 1919 • { 12.2 / 11.1 }	*pickups,*
6	W.	☾ at ☍ • Noah born, 2948 B.C. • 6,000 U.S. Defense Dept. computers hit with virus, 1988	*on*
7	Th.	Suspension bridge known as "Galloping Gertie" collapsed in high winds in Tacoma, Wash., 1940 •	*cold*
8	Fr.	Pigeons darkened sky over Boston, 1630 • Louvre opened in Paris, 1793 { 10.4 / 11.5 }	*mornings,*
9	Sa.	☾ runs low • X-15 rocket went 4,093 mph, 1961 • Power failure in Northeast, 1965 •	*hunters*
10	F	**25th S. af. P.** • ♂☿☾ • "Dr. Livingstone, I presume?"–1871	*wait*
11	M.	**St. Martin** • **Veterans Day** • "Unknown Soldier" dedication, 1921 { 9.0 / 9.7 }	*for*
12	Tu.	♂☾☾ • Indian Summer • Skunks hibernate { 10.0 / 10.5 }	*dawn.*
13	W.	First "Dust Bowl" storm, 1933 • It takes about ten years to get used to how old you are.	*Crows*
14	Th.	☿ in sup. ♂ • Second successful landing of space shuttle Columbia, 1981	*assemble*
15	Fr.	☾ on Eq. • William Lyon Mackenzie King retired as Prime Minister of Canada, 1948 • { 9.1 / 9.1 }	*in*
16	Sa.	☾ at apo. • Missouri earthquake caused Mississippi River to flow backward, 1811 •	*trees,*
17	F	**26th S. af. P.** • Elizabethan Age began, 1558 { 9.7 / 9.2 }	*waiting.*
18	M.	**St. Hugh of Lincoln** • ♀ stat. • First ticker-tape parade, N.Y.C., 1919	*Orion*
19	Tu.	Penumbral Eclipse ☾ **Full** **Beaver** ○ • Clear Moon, frost soon. { 10.1 / 9.2 }	*rises.*
20	W.	☾ at ☍ as I write," N.Y.C., 1720 • Diarist: "My ink freezes End of Pony Express, 1861 •	*The*
21	Th.	"Piltdown Man" skull revealed as hoax, 1953 • Voltaire born, 1694 • Socrates born, 470 B.C. •	*hills*
22	Fr.	♂♄☾ • Everyone is crazy but me and thee, and sometimes I suspect thee a little. { 9.1 / 10.2 }	*wait*
23	Sa.	**St. Clement** • ☾ rides high • Doctors banned from prescribing beer, 1921 •	*for*
24	F	**27th S. af. P.** • "Battle above the Clouds" Lookout Mt., Tenn., 1863 •	*snow.*
25	M.	Prune grape-vines now. • A meal of soup, steak, coffee, and half a pie cost 12¢, 1834 •	*We*
26	Tu.	♂♃☾ • Queen Elizabeth II announced she would pay taxes, 1992 •	*gather*
27	W.	James Agee born, 1909 • Meteor hit Lake Michigan, 1919 • Shakespeare married, 1582	*around*
28	Th.	**Thanksgiving** • Washington Irving died, 1859 • William Blake born, 1757 •	*a*
29	Fr.	☾ on Eq. • Mules make a great fuss of their ancestors having been horses. { 9.7 / 9.9 }	*table,*
30	Sa.	**First day of Chanukah** • Mark Twain born, 1835 • { 10.3 / 10.1 }	*waiting.*

Do your duty in all things. You cannot do more.
You should never wish to do less. –Gen. Robert E. Lee

DECEMBER, The Twelfth Month

The year ends with uncommon splendor. Venus has a superb, don't-miss conjunction with the crescent Moon and Mars on the 1st, an awesome predawn coming-together of our three nearest cosmic neighbors. Simply dazzling, Venus achieves its greatest brilliancy on the 6th and floats near dim Mars all month. The Geminid meteor shower, this year's richest, peaks on the 13th and 14th. A gibbous Moon will diminish the show for those unwilling to wait until the Moon sets around 2:00 A.M. Saturn is out all night and reaches an extraordinary opposition on the 17th, high up and at its brightest since 1973. Winter arrives with the solstice on the 21st. Jupiter is brilliant and rises by 8:00 P.M. on the 23rd.

●	New Moon	4th day	2nd hour	34th minute
☽	First Quarter	11th day	10th hour	49th minute
○	Full Moon	19th day	14th hour	10th minute
☾	Last Quarter	26th day	19th hour	31st minute

Times are given in Eastern Standard Time.

For an explanation of this page, see page 40; for values of Key Letters, see page 229.

Day of Year	Day of Month	Day of Week	☀ Rises h. m.	Key	☀ Sets h. m.	Key	Length of Day h. m.	Sun Fast m.	Declination of Sun ° '	High Tide Boston Light—A.M. Bold—P.M.		☽ Rises h. m.	Key	☽ Sets h. m.	Key	Place	☽ Age
335	1	F	6 54	E	4 13	A	9 19	27	21s.51	8	8½	3ᴍ23	E	2ᴘ38	B	VIR	27
336	2	M.	6 55	E	4 12	A	9 17	26	22 00	9	9½	4 41	E	3 09	B	LIB	28
337	3	Tu.	6 56	E	4 12	A	9 16	26	22 08	9¾	10½	6 00	E	3 46	B	LIB	29
338	4	W.	6 57	E	4 12	A	9 15	26	22 17	10½	11¼	7 18	E	4 30	A	OPH	0
339	5	Th.	6 58	E	4 12	A	9 14	25	22 25	11½	—	8 31	E	5 24	A	OPH	1
340	6	Fr.	6 59	E	4 12	A	9 13	25	22 32	12¼	12¼	9 33	E	6 25	B	SAG	2
341	7	Sa.	7 00	E	4 12	A	9 12	24	22 38	1	1	10 24	E	7 32	B	SAG	3
342	8	F	7 01	E	4 11	A	9 10	24	22 45	1¾	2	11 05	E	8 39	B	CAP	4
343	9	M.	7 02	E	4 11	A	9 09	24	22 51	2¾	2¾	11ᴍ38	E	9 46	B	CAP	5
344	10	Tu.	7 03	E	4 12	A	9 09	23	22 56	3½	3¾	12ᴍ05	D	10 49	C	AQU	6
345	11	W.	7 03	E	4 12	A	9 09	23	23 02	4½	4¾	12 28	D	11ᴿ51	C	AQU	7
346	12	Th.	7 04	E	4 12	A	9 08	22	23 06	5½	5¾	12 49	D	—	—	AQU	8
347	13	Fr.	7 05	E	4 12	A	9 07	22	23 10	6¼	6½	1 09	C	12ᴀ51	D	CET	9
348	14	Sa.	7 06	E	4 12	A	9 06	21	23 14	7	7½	1 30	C	1 51	D	PSC	10
349	15	F	7 06	E	4 12	A	9 06	21	23 17	8	8¼	1 52	B	2 52	D	PSC	11
350	16	M.	7 07	E	4 13	A	9 06	20	23 19	8½	9¼	2 16	B	3 53	E	ARI	12
351	17	Tu.	7 08	E	4 13	A	9 05	20	23 22	9¼	10	2 46	A	4 57	E	TAU	13
352	18	W.	7 08	E	4 13	A	9 05	19	23 24	10	10½	3 21	A	6 01	E	TAU	14
353	19	Th.	7 09	E	4 14	A	9 05	19	23 25	10¾	11¼	4 04	A	7 04	E	TAU	15
354	20	Fr.	7 10	E	4 14	A	9 04	18	23 26	11¼	12	4 57	A	8 04	E	GEM	16
355	21	Sa.	7 11	E	4 15	A	9 04	18	23 26	12	—	5 58	A	8 58	E	GEM	17
356	22	F	7 11	E	4 15	A	9 04	17	23 26	12¾	12¾	7 05	B	9 44	E	LEO	18
357	23	M.	7 11	E	4 16	A	9 05	17	23 25	1½	1½	8 17	B	10 22	E	LEO	19
358	24	Tu.	7 11	E	4 16	A	9 05	16	23 24	2¼	2¼	9 29	C	10 55	D	LEO	20
359	25	W.	7 12	E	4 17	A	9 05	16	23 23	3	3¼	10 42	D	11 23	D	LEO	21
360	26	Th.	7 12	E	4 17	A	9 05	15	23 22	3¾	4¼	11ᴍ54	D	11ᴿ49	D	VIR	22
361	27	Fr.	7 12	E	4 18	A	9 06	15	23 19	4¾	5¼	—	—	12ᴀ13	C	VIR	23
362	28	Sa.	7 13	E	4 19	A	9 06	14	23 16	5¾	6¼	1ᴀ07	D	12 39	C	VIR	24
363	29	F	7 13	E	4 20	A	9 07	14	23 13	6¾	7¼	2 22	E	1 08	B	LIB	25
364	30	M.	7 13	E	4 20	A	9 07	13	23 09	7¾	8¼	3 38	E	1 40	B	LIB	26
365	31	Tu.	7 13	E	4 21	A	9 08	13	23s.04	8½	9¼	4ᴍ54	E	2ᴘ20	B	SCO	27

DECEMBER hath 31 days. 2002

The hills look gaunt in russet garb:
Against the sky the leafless woods
Are dark, and in their solitudes
The chill wind pierces like a barb. –Clinton Scollard

D. M.	D. W.	Dates, Feasts, Fasts, Aspects, Tide Heights	*Weather* ↓
1	**F**	1st S. in Advent • ☌ ♂ ☾ • ☌ ♀ ☾ •	*Deck*
2	M.	St. Viviana • ☾ at perig. • Charles Dickens gave first American reading, Boston, 1867	*the*
3	Tu.	☾ at ☋ • Heavy fog enveloped London, causing 106 deaths, 1962 • { 11.9 / 10.5	*halls*
4	W.	New ● • Eclipse ☉ • ♃ stat. • National Grange founded, 1867	*with*
5	Th.	Gypsies banned, England, 1537 • Ty Cobb died, 1951 • Strom Thurmond born, 1902	*plastic*
6	Fr.	St. Nicholas • ☾ runs low • ♀ Gr. Bril. • { 10.3 / 11.7	*sheeting:*
7	Sa.	St. Ambrose • **National Pearl Harbor Remembrance Day** • Willa Cather born, 1873	*First*
8	**F**	2nd S. in Advent • ☌ ♆ ☾ • Eli Whitney born, 1765 •	*it*
9	M.	☌ ♅ ☾ • ☌ ♇ ☉ • Marco Polo died, 1324 • { 9.3 / 10.1 •	*rains*
10	Tu.	St. Eulalia • *You cannot open a book without learning something.* • Tides { 9.0 / 9.5	*and*
11	W.	A monument to the boll weevil, which had forced farmers to diversify, erected in Enterprise, Ala., 1919	*now*
12	Th.	"The Katzenjammer Kids" first appeared, 1897 • *Depend not on fortune but on conduct.* •	*it's*
13	Fr.	St. Lucy • ☾ at apo. • ☾ on Eq. • 35°F at Miami, Fla., 1962 •	*sleeting.*
14	Sa.	Prince Albert died, 1861 • Charlie Rich born, 1932 • South Pole discovered, 1911	*Southern*
15	**F**	3rd S. in Advent • Gustave Eiffel born, 1832 { 9.2 / 8.6	*breezes,*
16	M.	30-ft.-high ice jam backed up Ohio River for 100 miles, 1917 • Beethoven born, 1770 • { 9.5 / 8.6	*warm*
17	Tu.	♄ at ☍ • Wrights in flight, 1903 • Lazarus died for the second time, A.D. 63 • { 9.8 / 8.8	*but*
18	W.	☾ at ☊ • Ember Day • N.H. passed act to mark horse thieves' faces with ink, 1792	*fleeting;*
19	Th.	St. Timothy • **Full Long Nights** ○ • ☌ ♄ ☾ •	*showers*
20	Fr.	Ember Day • Cold front caused quick drop from 40° to 0°F in central Illinois, 1836 • Halcyon Days	*soak*
21	Sa.	St. Thomas • **Winter Solstice** • ☾ rides high • Ember Day • { 10.5 / —	*our*
22	**F**	4th S. in Adv. • Bluebeard the pirate strangled, 1440 •	*season's*
23	M.	☌ ♃ ☾ • Van Gogh cut off part of his ear, 1888 • { 9.1 / 10.5 •	*greetings.*
24	Tu.	"Silent Night" composed, 1818 • *There are no miracles to the man who does not believe in them.*	*Santa*
25	W.	Christmas Day • 62°F Burlington, Vt., 1964 • { 9.3 / 10.2 •	*has*
26	Th.	St. Stephen • **Boxing Day (Canada)** • ☿ Gr. Elong. (20° E.) • Tides { 9.5 / 9.9	*to*
27	Fr.	St. John • ☾ on Eq. • Beware the Pogonip. • Tides { 9.8 / 9.7 •	*water-*
28	Sa.	Holy Innocents • Creosote bush in Mojave Desert reported to be 11,700 years old, 1984 •	*ski,*
29	**F**	1st S. af. Ch. • ☾ at perig. • ☌ ♂ ☾ •	*splashing*
30	M.	☌ ♀ ☾ • Albatrosses nest now. • Union of Soviet Socialist Republics formed, 1922	*into*
31	Tu.	St. Sylvester • ☾ at ☋ • *A closed mouth gathers no foot.* • { 11.2 / 9.7	*'003!*

Farmer's Calendar

■ There is really only one weather story in the news these days. It runs on the obituary page. Winter has died. Whether by the hand of man or from natural causes, winter has met with its end at last; it will be seen no more. Melting polar ice, receding glaciers, softening permafrost, thinning mountain snowpack, warmer seas here, colder seas there, southern species wandering north, northern species moving farther north, hotter summers, shorter winters—the vital signs are flat. It's time to give winter a shave, fold his hands on his breast, lay him out in the black wagon, and haul him up to Boot Hill. The old boy has croaked.

And the odd thing is, we mourn. You'd think we'd be dancing in the streets. In the north, unless you happen to live by winter tourism, you've spent your life either dreading winter, enduring it, or recovering from it. Now it's gone. Are we glad? We are not. We're full of foreboding, regret, and a kind of vague guilt. Nobody takes the news of the death of winter to be good news. It's as though we were subjects of a cruel king who has died without a visible successor. We don't know what comes next.

Well, let us not worry ourselves too much. Recall the famous line of Mark Twain: "Reports of my death are greatly exaggerated." As I write this, it is snowing so hard that the big maple trees beside the road, 50 feet off, are only fitfully visible. The forecast is for ten below tomorrow, when the usual big freeze follows the passing storm. It looks like winter may be around for a while yet.

AMERICA'S
UNLIKELY
EXPLORER

12 things you probably don't know about the first man to navigate the Colorado River.

John Wesley Powell seemed an unlikely candidate to become one of our nation's greatest adventurers. The son of English immigrants—a deeply religious Methodist minister and his wife—Powell grew up to be a restless, ambitious man. A Civil War injury had cost him his right arm, and when the war ended in 1865, the 31-year-old had no idea what to do with his life.

For several years, he drifted from job to job, working as a university science professor and as a curator of a natural history museum that he established in Illinois. But the West lured him, and by 1867, this 5-foot 6-inch adventurer had decided to explore the mysterious canyon beyond the Rocky Mountains, the only unmapped territory remaining in the continental United States.

He convinced friends, relatives, and acquaintances to risk their lives and follow him into uncharted wilderness for two expeditions down the Colorado River. "He had ambition, scope,

BY ALICE CARY

Major John Wesley Powell (above) and his wife, Emma Dean Powell (below), in 1862.

Dangerous rapids on the Green River (right).

determination, and a willingness to risk all for the sake of science," writes biographer Donald Worster, author of *A River Running West: The Life of John Wesley Powell* (Oxford University Press, 2001). For that and more, he's been called one of the great trailblazers of American history.

Powell's feats were nothing short of miraculous. He and the men who joined him had little idea where they were going or what they would encounter. By today's standards, their gear and boats were pitiful, if not irresponsible. Nonetheless, their journeys were a success. Upon Powell's return, he became a hero, giving lectures and interviews that helped introduce the Grand Canyon to the American public.

The first expedition began on May 24, 1869, when Powell and a crew of nine launched four wooden boats down the Green River in Wyoming, with the Grand Canyon as their goal. Day after day, Powell and his men came close to drowning, starving, or being attacked by Native Americans. Newspapers, in fact, repeatedly reported them missing or drowned.

The group expected to be gone for at least ten months, but just 69 days later, all but three had completed the trip, having covered more than 900 miles.

Two years later, in May 1871, Powell returned with a new crew and three new boats to survey and map the area, collect specimens, and learn more about the Native Americans. After an extensive winter layover in Kanab, Utah, and many unscheduled stops and excursions, the group ended its journey on September 8, 1872. Powell had become the first non-native expert on one of the wildest and most scenic areas of our country.

But John Wesley Powell was more than an explorer—he was a surveyor, a geologist, an anthropologist, an early conservationist, an authority on Native Americans, and a prophet of the West. Here are 12 intriguing facts about his life and voyages that aren't included in most history books.

1 **Powell was "officially" disabled.** He lost his right arm during the Battle of Shiloh, although he managed to return to the battlefields after re-

Members of the second expedition meet up at Green River City, Wyoming (left); their first campsite (right); Powell with Taugu, a Paiute chief (far right).

cuperating for several months. His 1865 application for a disability pension stated that as a result of his injury, the Yankee major was "totally disabled . . . from manual labor." The nerve endings at the amputation site pained him for the rest of his life. One tribe of Native Americans that he later encountered—the Paiutes—called him *Kapurats,* meaning "he who is missing an arm."

2   Although they were exploring one of the driest areas of our country, Powell and his men were plagued with rain on both trips. As soon as the second day of the first trip, rain became a problem. Between rain and rapids, the explorers and their supplies were constantly wet. Everyone was so miserable that they began to regard the canyon walls that surrounded them as a prison. A member of the first crew dismissed the natural beauty of the Grand Canyon, saying: "I never want to see it again anywhere." He added that the area would "probably remain unvisited for many years again, as it has nothing to recommend it."

3   Within his boat, Powell ruled the roost from a makeshift throne, a "captain's chair" that he bought for the second expedition. His clumsy wooden boat—called the *Emma Dean,* after his wife—had a covered compartment in the middle, where he secured the chair. There he rode, even through rapids, with a life preserver at his side. At the end of the trip, the boats were abandoned at the bottom of the canyon. Years later, one crew member returned and retrieved Powell's special chair, taking it to Salt Lake City, where he presented it to another crew member as a memento.

4   When Powell was nervous about river conditions, he sang. Crew members could tell he was worried about rapids and other hazards if he sang a boisterous song. Over more peaceful sections of the river, however, he led his men in soothing tunes. Some of his favorites were hymns and operas such as *Figaro.* A few of the men accompanied him on the mouth organ and flute.

(C O N T I N U E D)

John F. Steward (above left), assistant geologist on the second trip, played the mouth organ when Powell sang; repairing a boat at First Granite Gorge along the Colorado River (above right).

5 **At times, the explorers were** at each other's throats. Danger and disasters hardly fazed Powell, who was engrossed with his scientific mission. Early on, he noted: "Never before did I live in such ecstasy." His crews were much less enthralled. At one point during the first trip, mutiny was narrowly avoided. On the second trip, the men bickered over everything from manners to cooking.

Powell alienated several crew members by refusing to let them observe the Sabbath. Even his brother-in-law was so incensed that he fumed in his diary: "I do not care a cuss whether [Powell] comes with us or not on the river."

Powell tried to separate himself from the barrage of complaints, often sitting alone at meals. He didn't mention the tiffs in his writings.

Later, Powell dedicated his account of the journeys to his first crew (thus irritating his second crew, who weren't mentioned), writing: "I was a maimed man; my right arm was gone; and these brave men, these good men, never forgot it. In every danger, my safety was their first care, and in every waking hour, some kind service was rendered me, and they transfigured my misfortune into a boon."

6 **The first expedition nearly** failed. At one point, the explorers faced two sets of seemingly impassable rapids followed by a large, dangerous rock jutting across the current. Sharply rising cliffs made portaging impossible, and they did not have enough rope to lower the boats downstream, as they had done with previous rapids. Some of the crew decided that they should forget the river, climb to the rim of the canyon, and head home.

After a night of worrying, Powell concluded, "For years I have

Powell's boat, the *Emma Dean,* with its makeshift throne, a captain's chair.

been contemplating this trip . . . and I determine to go on."

Three men decided to leave anyway; the rest continued with Powell. Each group was sure the other was crazy. As it turned out, Powell and the remainder of his crew navigated the rapids safely and ended

Crew member Frederick S. Dellenbaugh enjoying a quiet moment near the Canyon of Lodore, in Utah, 1871.

their journey a few days later as they found their way back to civilization.

The three men who climbed out to go home never made it. They were mistaken for miners who had raped and killed a Native American woman, and they were killed by Native Americans seeking revenge.

7 **Powell had a strange competitor,** a man who called himself "Captain Samuel Adams." He appeared at the beginning of the first expedition and tried to convince Powell's crew that he was in charge—until Powell arrived and sent the impostor on his way. Undaunted, Adams gathered his own crew, and two months behind Powell, they attempted to float down Colorado's Blue River. The trip was a disaster. On the second day, their boats crashed, losing all maps and instruments, and before long, most of the crew deserted.

8 **Powell wasn't happy during the** second expedition. Although science had drawn him back to the

landscape he loved, "he was no outdoor recreationist lusting for thrills," Worster notes. Instead, he was interested in observing and surveying the land and learning about the Native Americans. Recalling many harrowing moments during the first trip, Powell fretted about providing enough food for his crew and safely navigating the dangerous parts of the river.

Powell left his crew more than once: For a week in July, he left for Salt Lake City supposedly to get mail and supplies but really to check on his wife, Emma, who was pregnant. Soon after returning, he left again to arrange provisions for the rest of the journey. In October, the crew stopped the trip for the winter and stayed in primitive areas of Utah, while Powell left for nearly two months to see Emma and his new daughter, who was born in September. Later, Powell traveled to Washington, D.C., to seek additional funding for his survey work. One crew member wrote in his diary: "The whole party is disgusted with the way the expedition is run."

9 **Powell nearly drowned on the sec-** ond trip. A wave capsized his boat, tossing him and another man into a whirlpool. Crew member Frederick S. Dellenbaugh remembered how the two men reappeared: "[They] shot up alongside

us as if from a gun." The crew righted the boat, bailed with their hats, and made it to safety. The crew member added: "We joked [with Powell] a good deal about his zeal in going to examine the geology at the bottom of the river, but as a matter of fact, he came near departing."

 Powell wrote his own report about exploring the Colorado, but it isn't entirely accurate. He kept a journal during his trips but never intended to write a public narrative. However, Congressman James Garfield advised him to produce a history of his expedition or risk losing funding for future survey work out west. In 1874, Powell produced *Exploration of the Colorado River of the West and Its Tributaries, Explored in 1869, 1870, 1871, and 1872,* which exaggerates some details and combines events and scenery from various trips.

 Powell had a sizable ego, and late in his life, he made a bet with a colleague about whose brain was bigger. Autopsies eventually showed that Powell was the "winner."

 During his later years, Powell served as director of the U.S. Geological Survey and the U.S. Bureau of Ethnology. He died at age 68 after a cerebral hemorrhage at his summer home in Maine on September 23, 1902. He is buried at Arlington National Cemetery.

In his account of the second expedition, crewman Dellenbaugh celebrated the achievements of Powell and another member of their group by concluding: "Strew their graves with roses and forget them not. They did a great work in solving the last geographical problem of the United States."

RUNNING THE RIVER TODAY

hen John Wesley Powell guided his first crew down the Colorado River in 1869, he had no notion of the tourist industry he would launch. Today, more than 5 million people visit the Grand Canyon each year—and about 20,000 of them take a trip on the river.

What's more, if Powell were alive today, he couldn't go off on his own—not without a commercial guide or plenty of patience. The National Park Service does not allow unescorted trips without a permit, and the waiting list for those is currently 12 years.

Here are a few comparisons between Powell's trips and today's river runs that would no doubt surprise its first "tour guide":

- Number in Powell's crew: 10
- Number in today's commercial trips: 36

- Powell's boats: heavy, clumsy wooden boats
- Today's vessels: motorized neoprene rafts

- Length of Powell's first trip: 69 days
- Length of today's tour: 6 to 8 days

- What Powell provided for his crew: food for 10 months, ammunition, animal traps, tools, and the promise of $25 per month for labor
- What today's adventurers need: plenty of cash—$1,500 to $1,800 per person for a 7-day trip

- What Powell longed for: painkillers to assuage the nerve damage to his amputated arm
- What today's travelers lust for: great weather, scenery, and cappuccino

□□

A RIVER OF WORDS
Want to know more about John Wesley Powell? For suggested readings, click on **Article Links 2002** at www.almanac.com.

The Best Ways to Avoid the Worst Kind of Cold

ACCORDING TO THE NATIONAL Institute of Allergy and Infectious Diseases, people in the United States suffer an estimated 1 billion colds every year. Since the dawn of modern medicine, researchers have tried to find a cure—but with little luck, largely because there are about 200 different viruses that cause the all-too-common cold.

Though many people turn to their drugstores and pharmacies for a quick fix, cold sufferers might do better to look around the kitchen for some tried-and-true—and inexpensive—folk, or home, remedies. "Because there is no cure for the common cold, over-the-counter drugs can only relieve the symp-

toms," says Kyle Waugh, M.D., of Weatherford, Oklahoma. "In a lot of cases, folk remedies do that better, with fewer side effects." In fact, he says, the number of pharmaceuticals that were discovered through home remedies is "amazing."

Next time you feel a cold coming on, consider trying one or more of these home remedies, which have stood up to medical research and the test of time. Of course, we don't promise a cure; see a doctor if your symptoms persist or indicate a more serious illness. But these remedies have been used to prevent colds and relieve symptoms for years—and just may do the trick in a healthful way.

by Staci Kusterbeck

EAT MORE GARLIC AND ONIONS

■ GARLIC AND ONIONS, MEMBERS of the *Allium* genus (which includes chives, shallots, scallions, and leeks), have long been valued for their healing powers. They were used in Europe in the Middle Ages and in China for centuries. The ancient Greek historian Herodotus referred to Egyptians as "the stinking ones," because they loved these foul-smelling bulbs. In fact, six cloves of garlic were found in King Tut's tomb.

Early American settlers ate onions for good health. "The old pioneer meal of bread, milk, and onions probably prevented a lot of colds," says James North, chief of microbiology at Brigham Young University (BYU) in Provo, Utah.

Garlic's role in preventing sickness was confirmed in 1858, when Legion of Honor–winning chemist Louis Pasteur discovered that it killed bacteria. More recently, a flurry of studies has confirmed garlic's immune-enhancing powers. North's own BYU study showed that garlic killed a variety of cold viruses in test tubes.

The distinctive flavor of garlic comes from allicin, which is similar to Mucodyne, a popular medication that helps expel mucus. Similarly, quercetin, an antioxidant in onions, has been found to destroy viruses and bacteria.

To use garlic to treat a cold, cut up fresh cloves and add them to chicken soup or other recipes, or swallow small chunks of raw garlic like pills. The effectiveness of processed garlic—powders, oils, and pills—varies. When you really need help, fresh is best.

SIP ON ECHINACEA TEA

■ AMERICAN PLAINS INDIANS used *Echinacea purpurea,* or purple coneflower, as their primary medicine. They introduced European settlers to this daisylike perennial, which they drank as tea to treat colds.

In 1870, H.C.F. Meyer, M.D., of Pawnee City, Nebraska, patented a formula containing the plant for use in his Meyer's Blood Purifier, promoted as "an absolute cure" for a host of illnesses. Soon after, echinacea was recommended by John

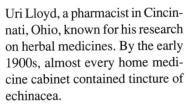

Uri Lloyd, a pharmacist in Cincinnati, Ohio, known for his research on herbal medicines. By the early 1900s, almost every home medicine cabinet contained tincture of echinacea.

With the discovery of antibiotic drugs in the 1930s, the use of echinacea faded—until recently. Today, this immune-enhancing herb is one of the best-selling herbal medicines in North America and Europe. Numerous studies have shown the pretty wildflower to be a potent cold preventive. Echinacea is believed to act like interferon, the body's own virus-fighting chemical, which is released by infected cells so that other cells can fight invading viruses.

Echinacea can be taken as tablets, tincture, powder, or tea. Dosage varies depending on the potency, so follow label instructions carefully. If taken as tea, expect a tingling sensation on the tongue. Experts agree that the herb works best in cycles: Take it for no more than a couple of weeks at a time, with about a week's break in between. Constant use may weaken the body's natural immune response.

$\mathcal{P}$ICK A PEPPER

■ TO CURE RESPIRATORY INFECTIONS, the ancient Greek physician Hippocrates prescribed vinegar and peppers. "They've treated colds with peppers in India, in Greek-Roman cultures, and in Asia for centuries," says Irwin Ziment, M.D., professor and chief of medicine at Olive View–University of California at Los Angeles Medical Center and UCLA School of Medicine.

Now science has given its seal of approval. The mouth-burning ingredient in hot peppers and chilies is capsaicin, which chemically resembles the drug guaifenesin, an expectorant found in 75 percent of over-the-counter and prescription cold and cough remedies. The active agents in hot and spicy foods such as hot mustard, spicy salsa, and horseradish act as expectorants, loosening up the lungs' secretions and unclogging air passages. Coughing and sneezing then expel cold viruses from the body. In this way, hot and spicy foods break up congestion, flush out sinuses, and wash away irritants.

"Most over-the-counter drugs for colds and coughs do exactly the same thing as peppers, but I think peppers are more effective, and they don't cause any side effects," says Ziment.

So gargling with a few drops of Tabasco sauce in a glass of water, putting hot mustard on your sandwich, or chewing on a chili may do more for a cold than any pharmaceutical.

G~ET~ C~ULTURE~

◼ IF YOU LIKE YOGURT, GOBBLE it up; it may keep you healthy next winter. In a 1991 UCLA study of this age-old immune booster's powers, adults ate a pound, or about one pint, of plain yogurt with active cultures every day for four months.

Researchers got unexpected results. "To our surprise, in every single individual, there was a dramatic increase of gamma interferon, which fights off infection, after only a few weeks," says Georges M. Halpern, M.D., professor emeritus of medicine at UCLA-Davis and the study's principle investigator. The study revealed that the yogurt eaters had five times the normal amount of gamma interferon in their blood. A subsequent study in 1993 involving 120 people discovered that this phenomenon also affects the number of colds caught by yogurt eaters. When 40 people consumed a cup of yogurt with active cultures every day for a year, they stayed much healthier than the 40 who ate yogurt without active cultures and the 40 who ate no yogurt. "We found a dramatic reduction of colds, hay fever, upper respiratory infections, and allergies," says Halpern.

If you're thinking about joining this culture club, you should know that it takes at least a few weeks for gamma interferon to build up in your body, so plan ahead. "If you're expecting to cure your cold overnight by eating yogurt, it won't work," says Halpern. "Cold season starts in the fall, so start eating yogurt in the spring." ☐ ☐

Reader Remedies: See Almanac readers' recommendations for treating the common cold by clicking on **Article Links 2002** at **www.almanac.com.**

We're looking for people to—

Write Children's Books

IF YOU WANT TO WRITE AND SEE YOUR WORK PUBLISHED, there's no better way to do it than writing books and stories for children and teenagers. Ideas flow naturally, right out of your own life. And while it's still a challenge, the odds of getting that first, unforgettable check from a children's publisher are better than they are from any other kind of publisher.

Your words will never sound as sweet as they do from the lips of a child reading your books and stories. And the joy of creating books and stories that truly reach young people is an experience you won't find anywhere else.

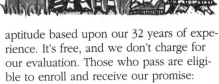

A surprisingly big market

But, that's not all. The financial rewards go far beyond most people's expectations, because there's a surprisingly big market out there for writers who are trained to tap it. More than $2 *billion* worth of children's books are purchased annually, and more than 500 publishers of books and 600 publishers of magazines related to children and teenagers buy freelance writing. That means that *there are thousands of manuscripts being purchased every month of the year!*

Yet two big questions bedevil nearly every would-be writer…"Am I really qualified?" and "How can I get started?"

"Am I really qualified?"

At the Institute of Children's Literature®, this is our definition of a "qualified person": someone with an aptitude for writing who can take constructive criticism, learn from it, and turn it into a professional performance.

To help us spot potential authors, we've developed a reliable test for writing

aptitude based upon our 32 years of experience. It's free, and we don't charge for our evaluation. Those who pass are eligible to enroll and receive our promise:

You will complete at least one manuscript suitable for submission to an editor or publisher by the time you finish the course.

You learn by corresponding with your own personal instructor—a nationally published writer or professional editor—in the privacy and comfort of your own home.

One-on-one training with your own instructor

Each relationship is tailored to the individual student's needs, yet every instructor works more or less the same way:

• When you're ready—at your own time and your own pace—you mail back each completed assignment.

• Your instructor reads it and rereads

 Writing for Children and Teenagers is recommended for college credits by the Connecticut Board for State Academic Awards and approved by the Connecticut Commissioner of Higher Education.

The students' statements in this ad were provided voluntarily by them, without remuneration, from 1994 to 2000.

it to get everything out of it that you've put into it.

• Then he or she edits your assignment just the way a publishing house editor might—if he or she had the time.

• Your instructor mails it back to you with a detailed letter explaining his or her edits and tells you what your strong points and weaknesses are, and what you can do to improve.

It's a matter of push and pull. You push and your instructor pulls, and between you both, you learn how to write and how to market your writing.

"I hit pay dirt"

This method really works. The proof of the pudding is offered by our students.

"My first two attempts met with rejection, and on the third, I hit pay dirt with *Listen Magazine,*" says Marjorie Kashdin, East Northport, NY. "My instructor was invaluable…It's not everyone who has his own 'guardian editor!'"

"I was attracted by the fact that you require an aptitude test," says Nikki Arko, Raton, NM. "Other schools sign you up as long as you have the money to pay, regardless of talent or potential."

"…a little bird…has just been given…freedom"

"The course has helped me more than I can say," writes Jody Drueding, Boston, MA. "It's as if a little bird that was locked up inside of me has just been given the freedom of the garden."

Romy Squeri, Havertown, PA, says, "I met two of your students in my critique group and realized that they were the best writers there."

"I'd take the course again in a heartbeat!"

"I'd take the course again in a heartbeat!" says Tonya Tingey, Woodruff, UT. "It made my dream a reality."

"It is comforting to know that there are still people out there who deliver what they promise," writes Meline Knago, Midland, TX. "The Institute is everything it says it is—and maybe even more."

Of course, not everyone gets published; we simply promise you the best training available.

FREE—Writing Aptitude Test and illustrated brochure

We offer a free Writing Aptitude Test to people who are interested in writing for children and teenagers, and we don't charge for our professional evaluation of it.

We also offer a free, illustrated brochure describing our course, *Writing for Children and Teenagers,* and introducing you to 64 of our instructors.

If your test reveals a true aptitude for writing, you'll be eligible to enroll. But that's up to you.

There is no obligation.

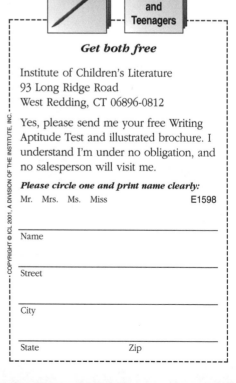

Writing Aptitude Test

Writing for Children and Teenagers

Get both free

Institute of Children's Literature
93 Long Ridge Road
West Redding, CT 06896-0812

Yes, please send me your free Writing Aptitude Test and illustrated brochure. I understand I'm under no obligation, and no salesperson will visit me.

Please circle one and print name clearly:

Mr.   Mrs.   Ms.   Miss   E1598

Name

Street

City

State   Zip

COPYRIGHT © ICL 2001, A DIVISION OF THE INSTITUTE, INC.

HOCUS-POCUS FOCUS

Join the not-so-secret society where magicians have met for 100 years to learn, practice, and perform tricks.

George Schindler first fell in love with magic in grammar school when a magician came to the school to entertain the class. For one trick, he cast a fishing line into the audience and kept reeling in goldfish, placing each into a fishbowl on stage, proving that the catch was alive. Schindler was captivated by the mystique of the performance as well as the awe it struck in the audience. But he did not figure out how the trick was done for decades.

Schindler grew up to be a full-time magician, the author of seven books on magic, and the owner of a magic-supply business. (You didn't think for a second, did you, that hats with rabbits in them came from a department store?) Yet the 72-year-old only recently discovered how the goldfish trick is done. He saw it in a book that was published in 1902—the year the Society of American Magicians, commonly known as S.A.M., was founded. Schindler, a longtime member of the society and one of its historians, recalls: "I was doing research, and I was surprised to find the trick. But it proves that good tricks keep going around."

S.A.M. was the brainchild of William Golden Mortimer, a doctor, who also developed an interest in magic at a young age. As a teenager in the late 1860s, before

A MAGICIAN WITH A MISSION. The legendary Harry Houdini (left) sought to expose people who used magic to deceive the public.

by Alan Behr

"To give away secrets to people who are merely curious about what magicians do spoils the fun."

he went to medical school, Mortimer performed magic throughout the western United States. In 1874, when he was 20 years old, he brought his show, "Mortimer Brothers"—later changed to "Mortimer's Mysteries"—to New York City and stayed there to study and later practice medicine. Over the years, Mortimer never lost his enthusiasm for magic and the camaraderie of other magicians. So after much planning, on May 10, 1902, he gathered about two dozen fellow magicians in Martinka's Magical Palace in New York City and formally founded the Society of American Magicians. Mortimer was elected the first president, a post he held for three consecutive yearlong terms. During that time, he wrote the first constitution, bylaws, and initiation ritual; designed the official seal; and organized the first annual dinner. He also initiated the awarding of the presidential medal, a custom followed to this day.

Membership in S.A.M. grew rapidly. By September 1903, nearly 150 magicians had joined, including the first female magician, Madame

MAGIC MAKERS. (From left to right) Francis J. Martinka, founder of Martinka & Co. and a cofounder of S.A.M.; Doc A. M. Wilson, editor of *Sphinx,* a magician's journal; The Great Dunninger, a famous mentalist; and Dr. Saram Ellison, a cofounder and the first member of S.A.M.

Redan of Boston, Massachusetts, and Ehrich Weiss, a magician specializing in escape and better known by his stage name, Harry Houdini.

The society's original membership had three main reasons for banding together: to expose frauds, who use the techniques of magic to deceive the public; to keep the secrets of magic tricks secret, and therefore fun for audiences as well as magicians; and to enable magicians to meet and learn from each other. For a century, those three goals have united the members.

Houdini, who became S.A.M.'s president in 1917 and held the post until his death in 1926, perhaps more than any other member, turned the first mission of the society into a personal and public crusade: He sought to expose people who he felt fraudulently claimed to have abilities to communicate with the dead and who used magic to dupe believers. Even today, the society is on the lookout for tricksters who use magic to deceive people. Recently, according to Schindler, a member claimed that he could manufacture money and even sold people a machine to do it. When his trickery was exposed, S.A.M. expelled him.

The second mission of the society—keeping secrets secret—may be the most challenging. If asked, most of us would probably say we want to know how a trick is done; but once we know its secret, it loses its fascination. "To give away secrets to people who are merely curious about what we do hurts everybody because it spoils the fun," Schindler says. "We want [aspiring magicians], especially young people, to perfect their craft and to succeed."

The third mission of S.A.M, to create a community of magicians, may be its greatest success. Over the years, the society has had nearly 40,000 members—professionals, amateurs, collectors, and historians among them. Today, S.A.M. is a worldwide organization

ABRACADABRA!
A Trick to Try

Here's a magic trick of simple suspension that you can perform for family and friends, using a long, thin object such as a pencil, a dinner knife, or a wand.

Discreetly place the object into your left hand so that it lies across the pads of your palm, just below your fingers. Hold the object in place with your thumb, as you display the back of your hand to your audience.

Then, curl your right hand around your left wrist and extend your right index finger across your left palm (see illustration 1). Hold the object in place with that finger, as you release and straighten out your left thumb (see illustration 2). While doing this, you can embellish your performance (and distract your audience) by saying a few magic words, blowing on your hand, or wiggling your fingers.

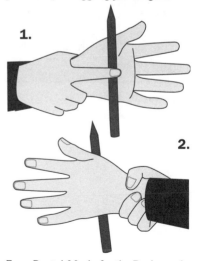

1.

2.

From Presto! Magic for the Beginner, *by George Schindler (Barnes & Noble, 1977).*

"Most tricks aren't hard to learn. What's hard is performing them in front of an audience."

A TREASURE TROVE. The cover of a Martinka & Co. catalog. The breadth of its contents was no illusion.

with about 8,000 members in more than 270 active assemblies. Most assemblies hold regularly scheduled meetings, often in churches, community centers, restaurants, or libraries.

Members are drawn together by the quirky allure of conjuring (another word for magic), a craft that is difficult to define. For example, Schindler says that magic happens when magicians make the impossible seem possible. Bruce Lish, another member of the society, likes the definition offered by Robert Houdin (the magician on whom Houdini based his pseudonym): "He said that a magician is really an actor playing the part of a magician."

Lish, like many S.A.M. members, is a part-time magician. By day, he's a practicing dentist, but on weekends—presto change-o—he's Dr. Molar Magic, using the craft to teach children about dental health. For example, he makes teeth multiply in a child's hand, causes toothbrushes to change color, and pulls giant X-rays from apparently empty boxes.

"The art of magic is about performance," he says. "You entertain with tools such as surprise and misdirection. Most people like it when the magician fools them. You talk to them afterward and they don't remember individual tricks, only that they had a really good time."

As in all crafts, the skill of magic comes from practice, but accidents *do* happen; magicians can make mistakes. "Most of the tricks themselves aren't hard to learn," says Lish. "What's hard is performing the tricks in front of an audience. You need to know how to juggle the routine, how to talk to an audience—unless silence is part of your act—and you need technical skill, of course. The great magicians have mastered all three elements."

According to Lish, "A good magician also has to know his audience. Some people go to magic shows because they want to be fooled. Others want to figure out how the tricks are done. A good audience is one that signs an unspoken agreement with the magician that says, 'We know these are tricks. Let's enjoy them.'"

Often magicians select people from the audience to assist them—leaving the rest of the audience to wonder if that person has really been randomly selected or is in on the act. "Most people you call up to the stage aren't in on the trick," says Lish. "Ideally, that person serves as the representative of the audience, to witness the trick close up. He or she should be the most entertained. You have to be careful about whom you select and how you treat him. You don't want to embarrass a guy who's out on a first date."

Although magicians tend to be tight-lipped about new tricks, some told us that Mylar and other materials, and laser and other technologies, are opening the door to ever more captivating illusions, as in "Now you see it; now you don't." Audiences can look forward to more close-up magic (the kind done within a few feet of an audience, such as card and coin tricks) and ever-grander illusions like those found on Las Vegas stages.

"One thing that won't change," predicts Schindler, "is the fun that comes from illusion. Even professional magicians regularly see tricks that stump them. That's OK with us. We like to be fooled, too."

A CLASS ACT. George Schindler has been captivated by magic since grammar school.

–photo courtesy George Schindler

THE MAGIC TOUCH. Martinka & Co., Inc., established in 1877, was acquired in 2000 by Ted Bogusta, who provided photos for this story and has created a virtual magic memorabilia shop at www.martinka.com.

GETTING STARTED

A passion for magic often starts at an early age; after all, many magic shows are designed to entertain children. In recognition of that, the Society of American Magicians (S.A.M.) started the Society of Young Magicians (S.Y.M.) in 1984 for aspiring magicians aged 7 to 17. Today, there are more than 100 S.Y.M. assemblies, and many members later join S.A.M.

Every year, S.A.M. holds a convention, with magic shows open to the public. The 100th anniversary convention will be held in New York City for four days over the weekend of July 4, 2002.

To find a S.A.M. or S.Y.M. assembly near you, contact S.A.M., P.O. Box 510260, St. Louis, MO 63151-0260; or call 314-846-5659. For information about the convention or the society, visit the Web site: www.magicsam.com.

□□

A SPECIAL
REPORT

Once upon a time, love and marriage went together like a horse and carriage. These days, the vehicle of choice is not all that's changed. With weddings on the rise, we decided to look at the customs, traditions, and etiquette of wedding rituals, from "way back when" until today.

A HAPPY-MARRIAGE ADAGE

"Keep your eyes wide open before marriage, and half shut afterwards."

—Benjamin Franklin, American statesman (1706–1790)

Wonderful

Popping the Question

"The young man who asks a father for the hand of his daughter in marriage is a rare and endangered species," writes 1990s manners expert Letitia Baldrige. Though that custom has died off, the tradition of a man planning a special occasion to propose marriage has made a comeback. The latest trend, according to *Smithsonian* magazine, is to pop the question in public: in flashing colored lights, in skywriting, or even on a television show. One Philadelphia Eagles football fan told *Cosmopolitan* magazine that the faces of her and her boyfriend appeared on the huge stadium screen at halftime, and, in front of the entire stadium audience, he asked her to marry him. With the team mascot egging her on, she said there was only one answer she could give: "Absolutely!"

BY

CHRISTINE
SCHULTZ

–photos above:
www.comstock.com

(continued)

114

–photo opposite: Library of Congress

Weddings

THEN AND NOW

Nikki,
WILL YOU MARRY ME?
YES ❤ Ed

WORDS TO THE WISE

LADIES . . .

A man in the house is worth two in the street.

–Mae West, American actress (1893–1980)

GENTS . . .

By all means marry; if you get a good wife, you'll become happy; if you get a bad one, you'll become a philosopher.

–Socrates, Greek philosopher (c. 470–399 B.C.)

Rules of Engagement

Although engagement rings have been popular through the ages, it wasn't until Archduke Maximilian of Austria presented a diamond to Mary of Burgundy in 1477 that the tradition of offering the most enduring gem on Earth took hold.

These days, 85 percent of all Canadian brides receive a diamond engagement ring, notes Canada's popular *Weddingbells* magazine, giving that country the highest diamond-engagement-ring acquisition rate in the world. In the United States, 74 percent of brides received diamond engagement rings in 2000, according to the Diamond Information Center.

Ties That Bind

Prenuptial agreements used to be considered relevant only for billionaires, movie stars, and highly paid athletes," writes Baldrige. "Today, they are prevalent enough to inspire many states to adopt the 'Uniform Premarital Agreement Act'—the benchmark legislation for marital contracts."

The editors of *Bride's* magazine have likewise noted a rising trend toward prenuptial agreements among not-necessarily-so-wealthy brides and grooms. Couples are using prenuptial contracts to seal the deal on such matters as having children, the use of surnames, and even who will feed the dog or diaper the baby.

–Library of Congress

Wedding-Day Dreaming

Ancient Greeks used pig entrails to determine the luckiest day to marry; the Japanese traditionally looked to an ancient astrological calendar for propitious days. In New England, Wednesday was the luckiest day for weddings, and Friday (hangman's day) was considered the unluckiest, notes historian and folklorist Duncan Emrich.

Today, *Bride's* magazine reports, couples tend to marry on weekends or on symbolically romantic days, such as the anniversary of their meeting or their grandparents' anniversary. June is still the most popular month to marry, followed by August, July, May, and September.

(continued)

New York City wedding planner JoAnn Gregoli, of Elegant Occasions, says that she and her brides always check *The Old Farmer's Almanac* for weather predictions. Folklore holds that if a ray of sun shines on the bride as she steps from the church, good luck will shine on her thereafter.

Brought to You By . . .

Tradition suggests that the bride's parents pay all wedding expenses. "The responsibilities and expenses of the parents of the groom are light and pleasant," noted etiquette expert Emily Post nearly four decades ago.

Not so today, when couples tend to be older and more advanced in their careers, and thus have more money. The majority of couples share

the wedding expenses with their parents, according to *Weddingbells* magazine; one-third pay for everything themselves. Only 8 percent still rely on their parents to fully fund their big event.

With guests coming from all over, more couples are hiring wedding consultants to troubleshoot their event— for a fee of $3,000 to $10,000, or 10 to 15 percent of the wedding budget. About 5 percent of engaged couples hire wedding consultants, says Gerard J. Monaghan, president of the Association of Bridal Consultants. "Who's going to be the one to tell the stepmother where she has to sit?" he asks. "A wedding consultant can act as an impartial outsider."

WHAT PRICE LOVE?

The average cost of an American wedding is

just under $19,000.

–*Bride's* magazine

The Criminal Cost of a Wedding

The high cost of weddings these days might help explain the radical action taken by a prospective bride and groom in 2000. According to Chuck Sheperd's "News of the Weird" syndicated newspaper column, the two "were arrested in Brooklyn, N.Y., and charged with attempting to rob a Chase Manhattan bank (a robbery that they had to abort when a teller delayed getting the money) on June 7. The couple had scheduled a huge wedding for

–photos on these pages: H. Armstrong Roberts

June 10 with out-of-town guests, intending to pay for it with a tax refund. But when the IRS denied the refund, the bank robbery was the best way the couple knew, according to police, to pay the caterers and avoid disappointing their relatives."

I Hope, I Wish, I Want . . .

Once, a bride prepared for marriage by filling a hope chest with hand-sewn linens and other household furnishings," note the editors of *Bride's*. "Today, gifts are as likely to include cross-country skis and scuba gear as lasagna pans and lingerie." The tradition of couples registering at local department stores for china, glassware, and silver has now mushroomed into computerized registry wish lists that are updated daily. Gift requests range from hardware to home mortgage contributions, from sports gear to stock investments.

One rule of etiquette that hasn't changed is that the couple should never mention gifts on their wedding invitations.

(continued)

How Much Does the Thought Count?

We asked readers of *The Old Farmer's Almanac* to share stories of wacky wedding gifts they received. Here are a few. You can find more at our Web site, www.almanac.com.

A bottle of Jim Beam whiskey and two glasses. I wondered if the guests thought that we were alcoholics or that my husband would need a stiff drink after the wedding!

A yard ornament that reeked of mothballs, from an older couple who are friends of our parents. It must have been a "re-gift" from their own wedding.

A life-size statue of a seagull. Where do you display such an item? In a dark space in the closet where no one can find it!

Prewedding Whirls

HERS: Wedding "showers" started in the 1890s, when a hostess filled a paper parasol with small presents from the guests and turned it over the head of the bride-to-be. "When word of this hit the fashion pages,"

-H. Armstrong Roberts

writes author and poet Diane Ackerman, "everyone wanted to have a 'shower' of their own." But over the years, with brides needing every household gadget from tea sets to toasters to electric blenders, gifts became too big to drop on the heads of even the bravest recipients, so other practices evolved. According to etiquette experts such as Miss Manners, one rule still stands: The mother or a relative of the bride-to-be should not host the shower.

HIS: The stag party, initiated by the soldiers of ancient Sparta as a bonding feast among the groom's male friends, was called "the men's mess." In 1904, the term *stag,* referring to a male deer, was used to describe a bachelor's party at which a female stripper was hired to entertain. Such rowdy gatherings have now evolved into more civilized golf outings or cigar dinners.

THEIRS: These days, coed wedding showers, bachelorette bashes, and even "his and hers" lingerie fashion shows are common. "Expect the unexpected," note the editors of *Bride's.*

(continued)

Maids of Honor, Best Men, and Dogs

According to tradition, only an unmarried woman could be a maid of honor, and only the brother, best friend, or father of the groom could be the best man. Today, anyone from the bride's best male friend to her beloved dog can be a "maid" of honor. Likewise, a groom's female friend or sister can stand as the best "man" (no tux needed).

The original purpose of bridesmen and the best man was to aid in the capture of the bride, get her to the church on time, and keep any hostile family members away. Now the bridesmen, more commonly known as ushers, show the family and guests to their seats, and rather than wield a sword, the best man carries the ring and offers a toast to the happy couple.

Once, the flower girl's role was not simply to spread petals down the aisle but, with her shield of virginity, to protect the bride from the Devil. Today, children in attendance can trade roles. Etiquette writer Martha A. Woodham notes, "There is no law . . . that says the ring bearer can't be a girl and the flower girl can't be a boy." Or a dog—the latest trend, according to the editors of *Bride's:* "Some couples are decking their dog in flowers and slipping a small sacheted ring pillow around his or her neck."

Formal Wear and Flair

The white wedding dress, now traditional in the western world, was first worn in 1499 by Anne of Brittany on the occasion of her marriage to Louis XII of France, but it wasn't until 1840, when Queen Victoria married Prince Albert (shown at right), that

–Library of Congress

the white dress became a classic. Prior to this, a bride wore her best dress in a fashionable color.

White still reigns, but the latest fashion in wedding dresses, according to wedding-gown designer Priscilla of Boston, is toward glamorous gowns with beaded bodices, puffy bustles, and full, lacy skirts. Strapless gowns with matching jackets are in—but the wraps come off at the reception. Mixing old and new, a Priscilla bride will often borrow her mother's long wedding veil and fasten it with Velcro to her headpiece.

Despite that traditional tie, sentimental attachment to the wedding dress is fading. Unlike her grandmother, who stored her gown with tissue paper in a cool place, today's bride might rent a dress or find one in a secondhand shop and then sell it after the ceremony.

To cut a dashing figure, the groom should match the bride, writes manners expert Baldrige. For a formal afternoon wedding, he should don a cutaway, she notes; after six, a black tie. There is no symbolism in his clothes, as there is in the bride's. But there can, in fact, be symbolism in the boutonniere he chooses, note the editors of *Bride's:* A red chrysanthemum means "I love you"; a white rose means "I am worthy of you"; a sweet William represents gallantry.

–photos: Mare-Anne Jarvela (top);
H. Armstrong Roberts (right)

124

Western wear, including string ties and cowboy boots, has become common

wedding attire for grooms in the Southwest.

–*Bride's* magazine

Bridal Wows

B eing given away is a tradition that evolved from the days when men bought brides from fathers or, even worse, captured them," writes Woodham. "Today, more and more brides are asking their moms to make the stroll down the aisle instead of benchwarming the first pew."

The traditional wedding vows have given way to more-creative and more-personal expressions of love, says planner Gregoli. She notes that most couples have dropped the pledge to "honor and obey" in favor of promising to be each other's best friend.

Another changing trend in wedding tradition is that the bride no longer walks down the aisle to "Here Comes the Bride." That song, says Gregoli, comes from a funeral procession and is not allowed for weddings in some churches. The more popular choice these days for the wedding march is Pachelbel's "Canon in D" or the "Trumpet Voluntary," she says.

CRYIN' TIME

Forty-five percent of women cry at

their own weddings. Only 25 percent of men

admit to shedding tears.

–Barry Sinrod and Marlo Grey, *Just Married*

(Andrews McMeel, 1998)

www.comstock.com

(continued)

Let Them Eat Cakes

I n Elizabethan times, small spiced cakes were given to wedding guests to toss over the bride's head as she left the church. The remaining cakes were piled high on a table at the reception, and the couple kissed over the top of the stack and tried not to knock it down. In the 1660s, King Charles II's French pastry cooks iced the pile of cakes. The tiers on today's wedding cakes evolved from that early custom.

The most popular cakes among brides, Baldrige notes, are airy, egg-white-based silver cakes or gold or yellow pound cakes. Grooms traditionally favor dark, rich fruitcakes. But men's tastes are changing. According to the editors of *Bride's,* grooms are requesting cakes made in their favorite flavors (banana or chocolate, for example) and cleverly shaped and decorated to display their interests, with, say, a golf course or a top hat.

Some couples today would even top that. In place of plastic wedding figures on the highest tier, they are more likely to adorn cakes with personalized ornaments, such as an antique car or tennis racquets. Others are borrowing a family heirloom, such as a grandmother's sterling-silver cake knife, for cutting the lower layers. Another new trend, although labor-intensive for the baker and cost-prohibitive for all but the most affluent, is to make individual wedding cakes for the guests.

The custom of saving the top layer of the cake for the newlyweds to share on their first anniversary remains in vogue.

Food Fight!

The current custom of feeding wedding cake to the new spouse can sometimes, regrettably, get out of hand, as was the case a few years ago in Westport, Connecticut. According to a *Chicago Tribune* report, the groom fed the bride her cake too roughly after she had told him to take it easy. "Fighting ensued when she responded in kind," according to the *Tribune.* "The newlyweds were arrested at their reception for disturbing the peace."

We can only guess where the marriage went from there.

For a Smooth Send-Off

R̲ice is the latest in a long list of fertility symbols that have been thrown at newlyweds. Over the centuries, guests have tossed cakes, grain, fruit, sweetmeats, and biscuits. Nowadays, it's common for

bridesmaids to fill small sacks with rice or the more environmentally friendly birdseed. "Guests are supposed to open the bags before tossing," notes Woodham, "but folks at one Mississippi wedding skipped the intermediate step and threw the bags at the couple. The bride went on her honeymoon with a black eye." To prevent such disasters, including slipping on rice or seeds, planner Gregoli recommends tossing dried rose petals instead.

Final Words of Wisdom

We asked married readers of *The Old Farmer's Almanac* to share their advice for making a marriage work. Here's what some said. You'll find more words of wisdom at www.almanac.com.

❧ Be prepared to give more than you think you are receiving, and you will receive more than you know.

❧ The secret is Communication, Compromise, Cooperation, and Compassion.

❧ Listen, listen, listen.

☐☐

HAPPILY EVER AFTER
Go to **www.almanac.com** and click on **Article Links 2002** for Web sites related to this article.

-H. Armstrong Roberts

-www.comstock.com

-H. Armstrong Roberts

How to Get Out of Doing Wha

Let's face it: There are moments in each person's life when what you need is a polite way to say no. You may have heard about the best-selling book called *Getting to Yes: Negotiating Agreement Without Giving In* (by Roger Fisher and William Ury), but what if you're on the other side and really don't want to say yes?

All it takes

is a lively

imagination

and a healthy

disregard for

the truth.

I once got out of a civic obligation by telling the chairman of that particular group that I was having suicidal thoughts. I'm not proud of that. But it was a superb excuse; who's going to try to talk you into staying? It had the additional advantage of being true: Only that afternoon, I had stood by the roadside and mused, "If I step in front of this oncoming truck, I won't have to go to that meeting tonight."

It's not an excuse you can use very often. If word gets around (and it will), you'll spend more time fending off well-meaning friends urging you to "talk about it" than you would have wasted going to the meetings. Reserve it for truly desperate situations.

Still, there are a host of other options you can choose when you don't feel like going somewhere or doing something. All it takes is a lively imagination and a healthy disregard for the truth.

OPTION A

**Three Things on
a Plate**

■ A wise friend introduced me to the "three things on a plate" excuse. When asked to serve on a board, for example, he would say, "I never have more than three things on my plate at once. If I accept any more obligations, I won't have time to fulfill them adequately." Then he'd list the three things currently on his plate. The beauty of it is that you can list three different things every time

–illustrated by Paul Meisel

You Don't Want to Do

by Norm D. Bloom

you're asked. To your civic-minded friend, the three things are your job, your family, and your church. To the deacon who wants you to lead a Bible study group, it's your job, your family, and the volunteer fire department. To your boss or your spouse—well, don't carry this one too far.

OPTION B

Icky Medical Problem

■ A sudden illness is always a good excuse, but don't overdo it or you may never be invited anywhere. The illness should be disabling but brief and, if possible, so intimate a problem as to discourage further inquiries. "Intestinal difficulties" is good, as is any reference to a gynecological crisis or a foot fungus. And as none of them has obvious symptoms, you can show up at work or a different party the next day without embarrassment. Another good trick is to mutter something about needing to "adjust my dosage."

OPTION C

I'm Busy

■ Pleading other plans is good, but don't use the old "I have to wash my hair" gag unless you really don't care what the other person thinks. "I have to wash my dog" is more convincing, especially if you toss in a few fragrant details about Fido's water phobia, skin disease, or parasites.

OPTION D

The Secret Agent

■ If you're the type who likes to live dangerously, try being mysterious:

"I'd love to come, really I would, but I can't, and I'm afraid I can't tell you why. I swore never to tell anyone about . . . well, you understand."

"It's in litigation. I can't comment."

"Is a security check required?"

"I can't go anywhere out of range of my ankle bracelet."

OPTION E

That's Not My Department

■ A good bet for anyone who works in a large

corporation or government agency is "I'm not authorized to do that, but if you'll submit your request in writing, I'll pass it along to the proper authorities."

OPTION F

False Humility

■ In Japan, I'm told, magazines turn down unsolicited manuscripts by sending the author a note saying something like "Our humble publication is not worthy of the great honor you do us. Your article is so much better than the miserable work we normally pass off on our ignorant readers that it would be a crime to take advantage of your generosity. Please submit your work to a higher-quality magazine." If you've been invited to a dinner with a lot of stuffed shirts, you could improvise on this theme by saying, "Oh, they're much too smart! I'd feel like an idiot and embarrass us both." Or, if you've been asked to make a speech, you might say, "The last time I made a speech, you could hear the snoring for miles. Better find somebody *really* good."

OPTION G

The Bayonet Charge

■ When Colonel Joshua Lawrence Chamberlain's 20th Maine regiment ran out of ammunition at Gettysburg, he ordered his men to fix bayonets and charge a vastly superior Confederate force—who were so startled that they surrendered! Likewise, if you're caught without a good excuse, go on the attack. If the invitation or request comes from someone you don't know, shoot back, "Who gave you my name?" or "This is supposed to be an unlisted number!" Be sure to make a quick escape, before your opponent comes to his senses. (Some of Chamberlain's men were so excited that they started yelling, "On to Richmond!" The good colonel had to remind them that they were still outnumbered by their prisoners.)

OPTION H

The Slowdown

■ Stalling is often effective, especially when the person asking you to do something is in a hurry. "I'd like to sleep on that," you can say, which is probably perfectly true, and you may never have to reply at all. Or you might

say, "I never accept an invitation without checking my calendar, and I left it at home/at work/at the doctor's office." (If you use the last, you can easily segue into Option B by adding something about how shaken you were by the results of the blood test.)

OPTION I

"X" Won't Let Me

■ When I was a child, I could always say, "My parents won't let me." (And when our children were growing up, we told them we'd always be willing to "not let them" do things they wanted to get out of doing.) It's harder to get away with this one when you're grown up, but there are adult variations on the theme:

"My husband/wife won't let me."

"My pastor won't let me."

"My therapist won't let me."

"My lawyer won't let me."

"My personal trainer won't let me."

"My parole officer won't let me."

Choose the one that best suits the occasion.

OPTION J

The Non Sequitur

■ Just before the last election, a campaign worker for a local candidate called to ask me to stand at the polling place holding a sign. Stunned (I had just passed a sign-holder at a busy intersection and wondered why anyone would do something as silly as that), I spluttered out the first thing that came into my head: "I can't. I'm a teacher!" The caller quickly apologized and hung up. ☐☐

SOLAR POWER

In these times of skyrocketing oil and gas prices and shocking electric bills, many of us are searching for ways to cut down on energy costs. For more and more Americans, the answer is right over our heads.

Since President Carter first installed solar panels on the White House roof in 1979, the technology has come a long way in terms of reliability and affordability. (President Reagan later scrapped Carter's entire program—the panels, the Solar Energy Research Institute, and tax credits for solar homes.) Recent progress stems from private-sector interests, including that of large oil companies such as British Petroleum, investing in solar research and development.

Thanks also to large-scale installations such as those at the 2000 Olympic Games in Sydney, Australia, global public awareness of sustainable energy—energy that can be continuously recycled—has increased. The "Green Games" garnered media attention for the solar-powered SuperDome, the Olympic Boulevard (lit by 19 solar-power towers), and the Olympic Village, the largest solar-powered suburb on Earth, with more than 6,000 solar panels fueling 650 houses.

More good news is that just as technology has progressed, so has the support network. Incentives, tax breaks, and loan programs are available at local, state, and federal levels, depending on where you live. One of the most visible U.S. programs has been former President Clinton's Million Solar Roofs Initiative, led by the Department of Energy. Announced in 1997, the program's goal is to install solar energy systems on 1 million buildings by 2010; by the end of 2000, there were more than 100,000 installations.

Nonetheless, a homeowner's biggest hurdle on the way to installing a domestic solar system is the cost. The average four-person household consumes 1 to 3 kilowatts (kW) of electricity per day. The price of photovoltaic (PV) rooftop panels to produce that much power is between $10,000 and $15,000. To put it another way, it's a choice between remodeling a room or saying good-bye to power bills forever. But many Americans using solar energy today are motivated by more than monetary reasons.

"Most of our customers are concerned about the environment," says Stephen Strong, whose firm, Solar Design Associates, Inc., of Harvard, Massachusetts, drafts architectural plans for solar homes. "They are concerned about the long-term availability and affordability of conventional energy. They are often enamored with cutting-edge technology. Occasionally, they have a dislike for big utility companies. And then there are those who simply want to live where the electricity line doesn't go."

No matter where you live, solar power is available to you. Here are some stories about people who are powered by the Sun.

by Carol Connare

The Perez house in Albany, New York, uses active and passive solar elements.

—Richard Perez

⑤unny Suburbia

Richard Perez's reproduction Colonial home in Albany, New York, has 22 large 12-over-12 windows on the south-facing side. The windows are not an indulgence; they are integral to his home's passive solar design.

(continued)

Perez, an atmospheric sciences research professor specializing in solar radiation and solar-energy applications at the State University of New York at Albany, built the house for himself, his wife, and their two children in 1995, using active and passive solar elements. The active system, a 2-kW PV installation on the roof, provides 40 percent of their electricity.

"The PV system includes the solar panels on the roof plus a small battery bank in the cellar to keep the house running during power outages," explains Perez. "I plan to install an active solar system for domestic hot water on the roof." The passive solar system includes the south-facing windows and thermal mass (heat-absorbing and heat-retaining materials) inside, meeting 60 percent of the family's heating needs. He installed a high-efficiency natural-gas furnace with hot-water baseboards, which provides backup heat.

Perez spent about $14,000 on the PV system. The passive system was much less—"just placing large windows in the right position, maybe $2,000 to $3,000 more than windows in an average house would cost." Because he installed solar components as the house was being built, the total per-square-foot cost of Perez's house was the same or less than that of others in his neighborhood.

The family is satisfied with the outcome. "There is some operational strategy, such as listening to the weather report to find out if it will be cloudy," says Perez. "Living with solar is pleasant; you get a bright house, and there's very little maintenance to perform on the solar systems."

Field of Dreams

Cohousing is a type of communal housing in which the members of the neighborhood come together first, and then the physical setting is developed to suit residents' needs and interests.

In 1999, the Tierra Nueva Co-Housing Project was built for the Grell Co-Housing Group in Oceana, California. Gudrun Grell, an organic farmer who still lives next door, donated five acres of her property, a mature avocado grove a mile from the coast, to Tierra Nueva. She imposed one restriction: The resulting buildings must be at least 75 percent solar-heated as well as passively cooled.

The Grell community was founded by two couples who wanted to create a safe place for their kids to grow up. It now includes 85 people, from young singles to retired couples in their 80s, with varying lifestyles and incomes.

Families and members live in 27 private units, in one of four basic layouts. They share a 3,500-square-foot common house for meals, meetings, and socializing, and as a workshop. The buildings fan out across a south-facing slope, with space for garden and play areas.

Though different in size, all the units face south and use passive solar elements such as south-facing windows and substantial insulation: R-45 in the ceilings

No matter where you

Thoughtful construction in Oceana, California, yields solar energy and avocados.

–Ken Haggard

and R-19 in the walls. A slab floor and two-inch-thick interior stucco walls create the necessary thermal mass. Some residents chose to install solar water-heating systems in their individual units.

The result fully met farmer Grell's wishes. To boot, the buildings cost $59 per square foot—$15 less than average new construction in the region, according to the U.S. Census Bureau. Best of all, half of the avocado grove (about 60 trees) was saved.

Ken Haggard and Polly Cooper led the architectural design team from the San Luis Sustainability Group in Santa Margarita, California. Once Tierra Nueva was fully occupied, Haggard and his colleagues visited it. "We saw that sustainability had created a socially healthy community," he says. "When these people shared more, wasted less, and optimized human resources, there were fewer social problems to interfere with the joys of living."

City of Light

In May 1999, John Berton became the first person in Chicago to live "off the grid"—that is, unplugged from his local utility company. Commonwealth Edison (ComEd), the electric company for the city, became his backup power source. "A huge percentage of ComEd's power is produced by nuclear plants," says Berton. "There is no solution to the

ive, solar power is available to you.

SOLAR POWER

John Berton in Chicago, Illinois, prefers solar panels to nuclear power.

—John Berton

problem of nuclear waste. I don't want to be a part of that."

Berton, a computer consultant, ceramic artist, and wilderness guide, started building his system atop his apartment building in 1991. He tried to follow building codes, but after numerous inquiries to Chicago's building officials about permits for solar power, he recalls that someone finally confessed, "We don't know what you are talking about, and we don't have any codes on that." Except for the National Electrical Code, he was on his own.

He purchased materials as his budget allowed: a small array of panels, an inverter to convert solar power to usable electricity, batteries, cables, and a refrigerator designed to be powered by solar energy. As his system grew, so did his knowledge, enabling him to navigate a sea of problems, from an exploding battery to figuring out how to install the inverter.

"One day during the summer of 1999, I returned to my apartment to see a group of neighbors gathered in the alley behind my garage, chatting with each other. I pushed the button to open my garage door. They were quite surprised," says Berton. "There was a power outage in my neighborhood—the first of many that summer."

New "net metering" laws in 30 states allow solar users to connect to the grid as a backup power source and at the same time be credited for any excess power they produce. Berton is one of many solar-power users who can sell some of his electricity back to the utility company. "I eventually hope to stop selling excess power back to ComEd and instead use it myself, recharging electric vehicle batteries." □□

VISIT ANOTHER SOLAR SYSTEM
Read about a family in Kennebunkport, Maine, who built their solar dream house, and learn more about solar power by clicking on **Article Links 2002** at **www.almanac.com.**

Black Listed Cancer Treatment Could Save Your Life

Baltimore, MD— As unbelievable as it seems the key to stopping many cancers has been around for over 30 years. Yet it has been banned. Blocked. And kept out of your medicine cabinet by the very agency designed to protect your health—the FDA.

In 1966, the senior oncologist at St. Vincent's Hospital in New York rocked the medical world when he developed a serum that **"shrank cancer tumors in 45 minutes!"** 90 minutes later they were gone... Headlines hit every major paper around the world. Time and again this life saving treatment worked miracles, but the FDA ignored the research and hope he brought and shut him down.

You read that right. He was not only shut down—but also forced out of the country where others benefited from his discovery. How many other treatments have they been allowed to hide?

Decades ago, European research scientist Dr. Johanna Budwig, a six-time Nobel Award nominee, discovered a totally natural formula that not only protects against the development of cancer, but has helped people all over the world diagnosed with incurable cancer—now lead normal lives.

After 30 years of study, Dr. Budwig discovered that the blood of seriously ill cancer patients was deficient in certain substances and nutrients. Yet, healthy blood always contained these ingredients. It was the lack of these nutrients that allowed cancer cells to grow wild and out of control.

By simply eating a combination of two natural and delicious foods (found on page 134) not only can cancer be prevented—but in case after case it was actually healed! "Symptoms of cancer, liver dysfunction, and diabetes were completely alleviated." Remarkably, what Dr. Budwig discovered was a totally natural way for eradicating cancer.

However, when she went to publish these results so that everyone could benefit—**she was blocked by manufacturers with heavy financial stakes!** For over 10 years now her methods have proved effective—yet she is denied publication—blocked by the giants who don't want you to read her words.

What's more, the world is full of expert minds like Dr. Budwig who have pursued cancer remedies and come up with remarkable natural formulas and diets that work for hundreds and thousands of patients. *How to Fight Cancer and Win* author William Fischer has studied these methods and revealed their secrets for you—so that you or someone you love may be spared the horrors of conventional cancer treatments.

As early as 1947, Virginia Livingston, M.D., isolated a cancer-causing microbe. She noted that every cancer sample analyzed (whether human or other animal) contained it.

This microbe—a bacteria that is actually in each of us from birth to death—multiplies and promotes cancer when the immune system is weakened by disease, stress, or poor nutrition. Worst of all, the microbes secrete a special hormone protector that short-circuits our body's immune system—allowing the microbes to grow undetected for years. No wonder so many patients are riddled with cancer by the time it is detected. But there is hope even for them...

Turn to page 82 of *How to Fight Cancer and Win* for the delicious diet that can help stop the formation of cancer cells and shrink tumors.

They walked away from traditional cancer treatments...and were healed! Throughout the pages of *How to Fight Cancer and Win* you'll meet real people who were diagnosed with cancer—suffered through harsh conventional treatments—turned their backs on so called modern medicine—only to be miraculously healed by natural means! Here is just a sampling of what others have to say about the book.

"We purchased *How to Fight Cancer and Win*, and immediately my husband started following the recommended diet for his just diagnosed colon cancer. He refused the surgery that our doctors advised. Since following the regime recommended in the book he has had no problems at all, cancer-wise. If not cured, we believe the cancer has to be in remission."—*Thelma B.*

"I bought *How to Fight Cancer and Win* and this has to be the greatest book I've ever read. I have had astounding results from the easy to understand knowledge found in this book. My whole life has improved drastically and I have done so much for many others. The information goes far beyond the health thinking of today."—*Hugh M.*

"I can't find adequate words to describe my appreciation of your work in providing *How to Fight Cancer and Win*. You had to do an enormous amount of research to bring this vast and most important knowledge to your readers.

My doctor found two tumors on my prostate with a high P.S.A. He scheduled a time to surgically remove the prostate, but I canceled the appointment. Instead I went on the diet discussed in the book combined with another supplement. Over the months my P.S.A. has lowered until last reading was one point two."—*Duncan M.*

"In my 55 years as a Country Family Physician, I have never read a more 'down to earth,' practical resume of cancer prevention and treatments, than in this book. It needs to be studied worldwide for the prevention of cancer by all researchers who are looking for a cure."—*Edward S.,MD*

"As a cancer patient who has been battling lymphatic cancer on and off for almost three years now, I was very pleased to stumble across *How to fight Cancer and Win*. The book was inspiring, well-written and packed with useful information for any cancer patient looking to maximize his or her chances for recovery."—*Romany S.*

"I've been incorporating Dr. Budgwig's natural remedy into my diet and have told others about it. Your book is very informative and has information I've never heard about before (and I've read many books on the cancer and nutrition link). Thanks for the wonderful information."—*Molly G.*

Don't waste another minute. Claim your book today and you will be one of the lucky few who no longer have to wait for cures that get pushed "underground" by big business and money hungry giants.

To get your copy of *How to Fight Cancer and Win* call **1-888-821-3609 and ask for code 1997** to order by credit card. Or write "Fight Cancer—Dept. FCBK-1997F" on a plain piece of paper with your name, address, phone number (in case we have a question about your order) and a check for $19.95 plus $4.00 shipping and mail to: **Agora Health Books, Dept. FCBK-1997F, P.O. Box 977, Frederick, MD 21705-9838**

If you are not completely satisfied, return the book within one year for a complete and total refund—no questions asked. This will probably be the most important information you and your loved ones receive—so order.

©2001 St. Paul Street Press, L.L.C.

General Weather Forecast

2 0 0 1 - 2 0 0 2

(For detailed regional forecasts, see pages 142–161.)

This year, every month but January will be warmer than normal, on average. December and February will be mild. Summer temperatures will be near normal, but drought may threaten from the Tennessee Valley to the Middle Atlantic states.

November through March will start cold, with many below-normal temperatures. December will be quite mild in most places. January—at least the middle part—will be cold, despite a thaw. February will be the warmest in history. Most of March will be mild. Overall, November through March will be colder than normal in the Pacific Northwest and the Rockies and near normal from northern Oklahoma to southern Missouri, Illinois, and Indiana. Elsewhere it will be milder than normal, especially from Maryland to central Florida and westward to the Pacific.

Precipitation will be above normal in most of Texas, in the central Great Plains, in northern New England, from southeastern Pennsylvania into Virginia, in southern Florida, and from southern West Virginia into the Deep South. It will be near normal in western Texas, Oklahoma, the northern Great Plains, the Great Lakes states, and North Carolina and below normal elsewhere.

Snowfall will be below normal in most places, near normal in the Rockies, and above normal in the Pacific Northwest, New England, the northern Great Lakes region, and the Texas Panhandle, and from Denver to eastern Iowa.

April and May will be cool from the southern Rockies to the western Great Plains, and in the Desert Southwest, northern Texas, and Oklahoma. Temperatures will be near normal in southern Texas and above normal, on average, elsewhere. Precipitation will be above normal in central and southern Florida, in southern California, and from the northern and eastern Rockies through the central Great Plains and across the lower Great Lakes, as well as in most of Texas and Oklahoma through the Tennessee and Ohio Valleys and on North Carolina's coast. It will be near normal in the Pacific Northwest, the southwestern Rockies, and the northern Great Plains and below normal elsewhere.

June through August will be hotter than normal along the California coast, in New Mexico, from Texas and Oklahoma into the central Great Plains, across the Deep South and Tennessee Valley, and from Virginia to southern New England. It will be cooler than normal in the Pacific Northwest, interior California, the Rockies, North Carolina, and northern New England and near normal elsewhere.

Rainfall will be below normal, with drought threats across the Tennessee Valley into the Smokies and Appalachians and from southern New England through Virginia. It will be below normal in the Rockies, the northwestern Great Plains, Iowa, Texas, and Oklahoma and near normal in the West Coast states. It will be well above normal in southwestern Arizona, southern Florida, coastal Georgia, and South Carolina and above normal elsewhere.

September through October will be cool, especially in northern Texas and Oklahoma. The West Coast states, Wisconsin, the Upper Peninsula of Michigan, and New England will be warmer than normal, and New York City will be near normal. Expect below-normal rainfall in the Pacific Northwest, eastern Great Lakes, New England, New York State, Pennsylvania, and Florida. It will be near normal in the Rockies, Great Plains, and western Great Lakes and above normal elsewhere.

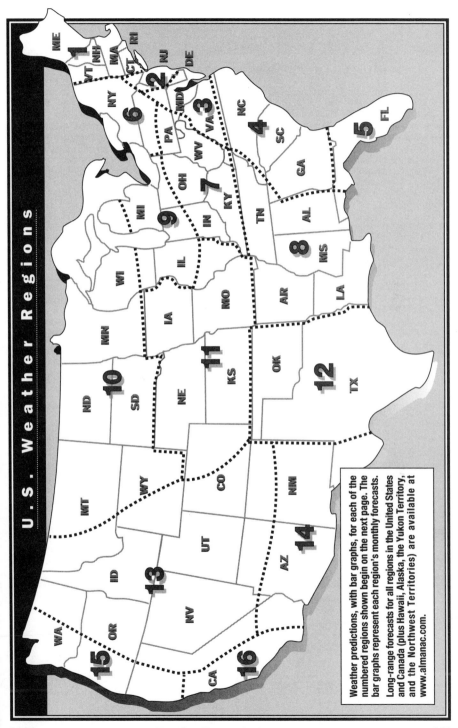

U.S. Weather Regions

Weather predictions, with bar graphs, for each of the numbered regions shown begin on the next page. The bar graphs represent each region's monthly forecasts.

Long-range forecasts for all regions in the United States and Canada (plus Hawaii, Alaska, the Yukon Territory, and the Northwest Territories) are available at www.almanac.com.

New England

SUMMARY: December and February will suggest that global warming is accelerating, but early January will bring back memories of old-fashioned cold winters. Late December, late January, and early February will be cold, but overall, winter will be mild. Expect a mid-January thaw and a mild February. Snowfall throughout the season will be above normal; expect it in mid-November, early and mid-December, early and late January, late February, and early March.

April and May will be pleasant, with above-normal temperatures and below-normal precipitation. Expect seasonable weather in early and late May.

The summer will be cooler and wetter than normal in the north but hot and abnormally dry in the south, threatening a severe drought. Expect occasional heavy rain in the north in June and July. The hottest spells in the south will occur in mid- and late June, and mid- and late July. August will have little rain and no excessive heat.

September and October will be warmer than normal. The south will continue to be dry until heavy rains come in early October.

NOV. 2001: Temp. 42° (1° below avg.); precip. 3.5" (0.5" below avg.). 1-6 Cold, rain; flurries north. 7-10 Warm. 11-14 Cold, snow; rain south. 15-21 Warm, then cold; snow north, rain south. 22-25 Seasonable, dry. 26-30 Cold, snow.

DEC. 2001: Temp. 31.5° (1° below avg. north; 2° above south); precip. 3.5" (avg.; 2" above east). 1-10 Heavy snow and rain. 11-14 Sunny, mild. 15-22 Mild, rain; snow north. 23-26 Heavy snow, cold. 27-31 Cold, dry.

JAN. 2002: Temp. 23° (3° below avg.); precip. 2" (1" below avg.). 1-6 Snow, cold. 7-12 Bitter cold, snow. 13-16 Thaw. 17-23 Cold, flurries. 24-31 Snow, rain, then mild.

FEB. 2002: Temp. 32° (5° above avg.); precip. 2" (1" below avg.; 0.5" above north). 1-2 Sunny, mild. 3-7 Rain, snow, cold. 8-11 Snow north, rain south. 12-15 Sunny, mild. 16-21 Snow north; warm, rain south. 22-28 Cold, snow.

MAR. 2002: Temp. 40° (2° above avg.); precip. 4.5" (1" above avg.; 2" above south). 1-4 Snow north, rain south. 5-9 Snow north; mild, rain south. 10-13 Sunny, seasonable. 14-19 Snow south, then sunny and seasonable. 20-24 Cold north, rain and snow south. 25-26 Sunny. 27-31 Heavy snow, wet snow.

APR. 2002: Temp. 51° (2° above avg.); precip. 1.5" (2" below avg.). 1-4 Windy, rain, snow. 5-9 Sunny days, chilly nights. 10-17 Mild, sunny; showers north. 18-23 Mild, showers. 24-30 Sunny, cool.

MAY 2002: Temp. 58° (1° above avg.); precip. 4.5" (1" above avg.; 0.5" below north). 1-3 Sunny, warm. 4-9 Heavy rain, seasonable. 10-15 Cool, rain. 16-21 Warm, rain. 22-25 Sunny. 26-31 Rain, then pleasant.

JUNE 2002: Temp. 68° (2° above avg. north; 4° above south); precip. 3.5" (2" above avg. northwest; 2" below southeast). 1-6 Showers, then sunny and warm. 7-13 Hot, humid, thunderstorms. 14-16 Sunny, warm. 17-24 Warm, thunderstorms. 25-30 Cool, then hot with thunderstorms.

JULY 2002: Temp. 70.5° (2° below avg. north; 1° above south); precip. 3.5" (2" above avg. north; 2" below south). 1-4 Sunny, warm. 5-9 Thunderstorms north, warm south. 10-12 Sunny, warm. 13-16 Thunderstorms north, hot south. 17-25 Warm, thunderstorms. 26-31 Hot, thunderstorms, then cool.

AUG. 2002: Temp. 68° (2° below avg.); precip. 2" (1.5" below avg.). 1-3 Sunny, warm. 4-9 Showers, cool. 10-18 Sunny. 19-23 Rain, then sunny and cool. 24-31 Warm, showers.

SEPT. 2002: Temp. 64° (1° above avg.); precip. 2" (1" below avg.). 1-6 Seasonable, showers. 7-10 Thunderstorms; hot south. 11-17 Cool, then warm with rain. 18-24 Sunny, cool. 25-30 Cool, dry.

OCT. 2002: Temp. 56.5° (4° above avg. north; 1° above south); precip. 3.5" (avg.; 2" above east). 1-8 Rain, then sunny. 9-14 Sunny, mild, then rain. 15-18 Warm, showers. 19-23 Cold, rain and flurries. 24-31 Rain, mild.

Caribou

Burlington

Boston

Hartford

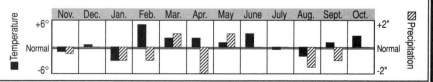

	Nov.	Dec.	Jan.	Feb.	Mar.	Apr.	May	June	July	Aug.	Sept.	Oct.

Temperature: +6°, Normal, -6°
Precipitation: +2", Normal, -2"

Greater New York–New Jersey

SUMMARY: Last winter was near normal in temperature and precipitation, although the heavy snow-storms made it seem like the snow total was above normal. Expect near-normal snowfall again this year, with temperatures one to two degrees warmer, on average. November through March will be milder and drier than normal, with less-than-normal snowfall, and certainly less than last winter. January will be the coldest month, despite a midmonth thaw, and will end with heavy snow. Expect cold spells in late December.

April and May will be dry, threatening drought. Temperatures in both months will be milder than normal.

June through August will be hotter and drier than normal, making drought a serious concern. The hottest temperatures will occur throughout June and July. Showers and thunderstorms will be scattered. A soaking rain in mid- to late August will be too little, too late to affect drought conditions.

September and October will bring heavy rains but, again, not enough. Temperatures will be close to normal as winter approaches.

NOV. 2001: Temp. 44° (1° below avg.); precip. 2.5" (1" below avg.). 1-5 Showers, then cold. 6-10 Sunny, warm. 11-20 Cold, rain; snow north. 21-26 Partly cloudy, chilly. 27-30 Sunny, warm.

DEC. 2001: Temp. 38° (3° above avg.); precip. 4.5" (1" above avg.). 1-4 Cold, showers; flurries north. 5-10 Rain, mild, then cold with heavy snow north. 11-13 Sunny, chilly. 14-18 Mild, rain. 19-24 Cold, rain, snow. 25-31 Sunny, cold, then snow.

JAN. 2002: Temp. 27° (2° below avg.); precip. 2" (1" below avg.). 1-4 Snow, cold. 5-7 Cold, clear. 8-13 Snow, then sunny and cold. 14-17 Warm, rain. 18-20 Cold, snow. 21-24 Seasonable, rain, snow. 25-27 Wet snow; rain southeast. 28-31 Seasonable, sunny, flurries.

FEB. 2002: Temp. 34° (3° above avg.); precip. 2.5" (1" below avg.). 1-4 Mild, rain. 5-10 Seasonable, rain and snow showers. 11-16 Dry, seasonable. 17-19 Mild, sunny. 20-24 Windy, heavy rain, snow. 25-28 Sunny, chilly.

MAR. 2002: Temp. 41.5° (1.5° above avg.); precip. 4.5" (1" above avg.). 1-4 Rain, cold; snow north. 5-8 Sunny, warm. 9-14 Rain, cool. 15-18 Sunny, seasonable. 19-24 Cloudy, chilly, rain; snow west. 25-31 Mild, rain, snow.

APR. 2002: Temp. 52° (2° above avg.); precip. 2" (1.5" below avg.). 1-3 Cold, rain, snow. 4-7 Chilly, rain, flurries. 8-10 Sunny. 11-12 Showers. 13-16 Warm, sunny. 17-23 Warm, showers. 24-30 Sunny, cool.

MAY 2002: Temp. 61° (1° above avg.); precip. 4" (2" above avg. north; 2" below south). 1-4 Sunny, warm. 5-11 Thunderstorms, then sunny and cool. 12-14 Rain, raw. 15-21 Warm, thunderstorms. 22-26 Sunny. 27-31 Seasonable, showers.

JUNE 2002: Temp. 73° (3° above avg.); precip. 1.5" (2" below avg.). 1-5 Sunny, cool. 6-12 Hot, thunderstorms. 13-16 Sunny, warm. 17-24 Warm, humid, thunderstorms. 25-27 Sunny, less humid. 28-30 Hot, humid; thunderstorms north.

JULY 2002: Temp. 76° (1° above avg.); precip. 1.5" (2.5" below avg.). 1-3 Hot, humid, thunderstorms. 4-6 Sunny, mild. 7-12 Showers, then sunny and warm. 13-16 Sunny, hot. 17-21 Showers, then sunny and warm. 22-25 Hazy, humid, thunderstorms. 26-28 Sunny, hot. 29-31 Thunderstorms, then cool.

AUG. 2002: Temp. 72° (1° below avg.); precip. 2.5" (1.5" below avg.). 1-2 Sunny. 3-6 Warm, thunderstorms. 7-8 Pleasant. 9-17 Thunderstorms, then sunny. 18-21 Rain. 22-24 Sunny, cool. 25-31 Warm, thunderstorms, then sunny and cool.

SEPT. 2002: Temp. 66° (avg.); precip. 2" (1.5" below avg.; avg. south). 1-7 Mainly dry. 8-12 Rain, warm. 13-16 Partly cloudy, warm. 17-28 Thunderstorms, then sunny. 29-30 Rain.

OCT. 2002: Temp. 55° (avg.); precip. 3" (0.5" above avg. north; 0.5" below south). 1-7 Rain, then sunny and cool; interior frost. 8-10 Sunny, seasonable. 11-16 Rain, then sunny. 17-22 Rain, then sunny and cold. 23-31 Mild, rain.

New York
Philadelphia
Atlantic City

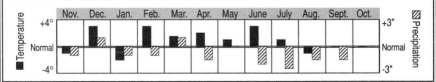

Middle Atlantic Coast

SUMMARY: Expect a mild winter, with above-normal temperatures and rainfall but less snow than average. November will be cool. Mild, sometimes warmer-than-average temperatures will prevail from late November until late December. Expect cold temperatures from late December through mid-January, when Canadian air masses will dominate. Snow flurries will occur during this period, with big snowstorms unlikely. Expect the coldest weather in the second week of January, followed by a brief thaw. Then, but for a few more cold days, winter will essentially be over.

April and May will be mild, despite a chilly spell in mid-April. Overall, temperatures will be warmer than normal. Dry weather now will signal the start of a dry summer.

The summer will be hot, with half the normal rainfall. Expect hot temperatures in early to mid-June, mid-July, and late August. Drought conditions will prevail, as below-normal rainfall continues from April through August.

Expect soaking rains in the first half of September, then dry weather through October. Temperatures will be normal in September. October will be seasonably cool.

NOV. 2001: Temp. 48° (1° below avg.); precip. 2" (1" below avg.). 1-3 Rain, cold. 4-10 Sunny, warm. 11-14 Rain, then sunny. 15-20 Thunderstorms, then cold with flurries. 21-25 Sunny, cold. 26-30 Sunny, warm days; chilly nights.

DEC. 2001: Temp. 44° (5° above avg.); precip. 4" (1" above avg.). 1-5 Dry, warm. 6-10 Rain, mild. 11-15 Warm, showers. 16-18 Rain, warm. 19-21 Cloudy, mild. 22-28 Cold, showers, flurries, then sunny. 29-31 Rain, snow.

JAN. 2002: Temp. 32° (2° below avg.); precip. 4" (1" above avg.). 1-4 Rain, snow. 5-6 Sunny, cold. 7-13 Cold, snow, then sunny. 14-17 Warm, rain. 18-21 Seasonable, dry. 22-29 Snow, then mild with rain. 30-31 Rain, snow.

FEB. 2002: Temp. 39° (2° above avg.); precip. 4" (1" above avg.). 1-4 Mild, rain. 5-9 Seasonable, showers. 10-12 Sunny, seasonable. 13-15 Rain, snow, then sunny and cool. 16-21 Warm, sunny, then rain. 22-26 Rain, snow, then sunny and chilly. 27-28 Cloudy, showers.

MAR. 2002: Temp. 47° (1° above avg.); precip. 4.5" (1" above avg.; avg. south). 1-3 Windy, rain, snow. 4-8 Sunny, warm. 9-13 Rain, cool. 14-21 Seasonable, rain. 22-25 Seasonable, sunny. 26-31 Rain, thunderstorms.

APR. 2002: Temp. 60° (4° above avg.); precip. 1.5" (2" below avg.). 1-5 Rain, then sunny and seasonable. 6-10 Rain, snow, then sunny days and cold nights. 11-17 Warm, showers. 18-25 Sunny, hot, thunderstorms. 26-30 Sunny, cool.

MAY 2002: Temp. 67° (2° above avg.); precip. 3.5" (2" below avg. north; 1" above south). 1-4 Sunny, warm. 5-9 Warm, thunderstorms. 10-16 Cloudy, cool, showers. 17-19 Sunny, warm. 20-26 Thunderstorms, then sunny and cool. 27-31 Cloudy, rain.

JUNE 2002: Temp. 76° (2° above avg.); precip. 2" (2" below avg.). 1-5 Cool, dry. 6-13 Hazy, hot, humid, thunderstorms. 14-16 Sunny, less humid. 17-22 Hot, humid, thunderstorms. 23-27 Thunderstorms, then hot and less humid. 28-30 Sunny, hot, humid.

JULY 2002: Temp. 79° (1° above avg.); precip. 1.5" (3" below avg.). 1-6 Sunny, warm, showers. 7-13 Sunny, warm. 14-16 Hazy, hot, humid. 17-20 Thunderstorms, then sunny and less humid. 21-27 Hot, humid, thunderstorms. 28-31 Thunderstorms, then comfortable.

AUG. 2002: Temp. 76° (avg.); precip. 2.5" (2" below avg.). 1-4 Sunny, warm. 5-10 Sunny, hot. 11-19 Cool, thunderstorms. 20-23 Sunny, seasonable. 24-29 Hot, thunderstorms. 30-31 Sunny.

SEPT. 2002: Temp. 70° (avg.); precip. 5" (avg. north; 3" above south). 1-9 Warm, thunderstorms. 10-14 Heavy thunderstorms, cool. 15-20 Hot, thunderstorms, then seasonable. 21-28 Cool; rain south. 29-30 Rain.

OCT. 2002: Temp. 57° (2° below avg.); precip. 2" (1" below avg.). 1-4 Sunny, mild. 5-10 Sunny, cool. 11-16 Rain, then sunny and seasonable. 17-22 Rain, then sunny and cold. 23-31 Sunny, mild, then rain.

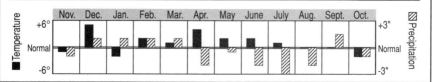

Piedmont and Southeast Coast

SUMMARY: Expect November through March to be mild, with temperatures averaging above normal and with little snow or ice. Rainfall will be near normal in the northwest but below normal in the southeast. Expect cool temperatures through mid-November, then mild temperatures until mid-December. Mid-December through mid-January will be cold, but the coldest period will be in mid-January. Mild weather will arrive in late January and, except for a few chilly days, will continue through February, followed by seasonable temperatures through March.

April and May will be warmer than average, especially in the north. Expect heavy rain in the northeast that will bring localized floods in early and late May. Elsewhere, rainfall will be below normal.

June through August will have near-normal temperatures, with dry weather in the north and heavy rain in the southeast, especially on the Georgia coast. Rainfall in the northwest will be below normal, threatening a drought. The hottest weather will occur from late July through early August, and again in late August, with no prolonged hot spells.

Expect warm temperatures in the first half of September, followed by a quick cooldown. Mid-September through October will be three to five degrees cooler than normal. September will be wetter than normal, followed by a dry October.

NOV. 2001: Temp. 53° (2° below avg.); precip. 1.5" (1.5" below avg.). 1-3 Rain. 4-9 Sunny, warm. 10-15 Cool, rain. 16-17 Sunny, cold. 18-20 Flurries. 21-23 Cool, rain. 24-30 Sunny, warm.

DEC. 2001: Temp. 52° (6° above avg.); precip. 4" (avg.; 1.5" below southeast). 1-3 Sunny, warm. 4-6 Showers, then sunny and warm. 7-9 Rain, warm. 10-15 Sunny, warm. 16-18 Rain, warm. 19-23 Sunny, cool, then showers. 24-28 Sunny, warm, then cold. 29-31 Rain, seasonable.

JAN. 2002: Temp. 45° (1° above avg. north; 5° above south); precip. 3" (0.5" above avg. north; 2" below south). 1-3 Sunny, warm. 4-10 Cool, rain. 11-13 Sunny, cold. 14-17 Mild, rain. 18-20 Chilly; rain north. 21-31 Warm, rain.

FEB. 2002: Temp. 46° (2° above avg.); precip. 3.5" (avg.; 2" below west). 1-4 Warm, rain. 5-9 Sunny, cool. 10-13 Cool, rain. 14-18 Sunny, seasonable. 19-21 Rain, warm. 22-28 Cold, rain.

MAR. 2002: Temp. 54° (avg.); precip. 4.5" (avg.; 3" above west). 1-4 Chilly, rain, then sunny. 5-8 Mild, rain. 9-11 Sunny, warm. 12-19 Rain. 20-25 Sunny, cool. 26-31 Mild, rain.

APR. 2002: Temp. 63° (2° above avg. north; avg. south); precip. 2" (1.5" below avg.). 1-4 Rain, then sunny. 5-8 Cool, rain. 9-12 Mild, rain. 13-17 Warm, thunderstorms. 18-22 Sunny, warm. 23-30 Thunderstorms, then sunny and cool.

MAY 2002: Temp. 72° (2° above avg.); precip. 6.5" (6" above northeast; avg. southwest). 1-3 Sunny, mild. 4-6 Heavy rain. 7-14 Warm, thunderstorms. 15-17 Warm, sunny. 18-21 Warm, thunderstorms. 22-27 Cloudy, mild. 28-31 Warm; heavy thunderstorms.

JUNE 2002: Temp. 75.5° (0.5° below avg.); precip. 4" (2" below avg. northwest; 2" above southeast). 1-5 Rain. 6-14 Hot, thunderstorms. 15-18 Sunny, warm. 19-23 Thunderstorms, seasonable. 24-30 Cloudy north, rain south.

JULY 2002: Temp. 80° (avg.); precip. 1.5" (3" below avg.; 5" above southeast). 1-4 Sunny, hot. 5-10 Hot, thunderstorms. 11-15 Thunderstorms, then sunny. 16-18 Hot, thunderstorms. 19-22 Sunny north, heavy rain south. 23-25 Sunny, warm. 26-31 Thunderstorms.

AUG. 2002: Temp. 78° (1° below avg. north; 1° above south); precip. 3.5" (avg.). 1-5 Sunny, hot. 6-10 Hot, humid, thunderstorms. 11-18 Thunderstorms, then sunny and cool. 19-28 Rain north, then sunny and hot. 29-31 Thunderstorms.

SEPT. 2002: Temp. 72.5° (1.5° below avg.); precip. 6.5" (3" above avg.). 1-4 Rain. 5-8 Sunny, warm. 9-14 Seasonable, thunderstorms. 15-20 Mild, dry. 21-27 Rain, chilly. 28-30 Sunny, cool.

OCT. 2002: Temp. 61° (3° below avg.); precip. 2" (1" below avg.). 1-9 Sunny. 10-12 Rain. 13-15 Sunny, cool. 16-19 Mild, rain. 20-23 Showers, then sunny and cold. 24-26 Chilly, rain. 27-31 Sunny, seasonable.

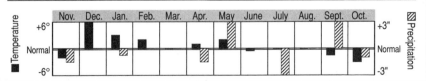

Florida

SUMMARY: November through March will be mild, averaging two degrees above normal. Rainfall will be below normal in the north but above normal midstate and in the south. November will be cooler than normal, with a freeze in the north in the third week. Expect above-normal temperatures from December to March. Rainfall will be below normal through January, with heavy rains in the south in February and in midstate in March.

April and May will be warmer than normal, especially in May in the south. Rainfall will be near normal, but there will be a chance of flooding in the south in the last week of April.

June through August temperatures will be near normal, with thunderstorms. Expect the hottest temperatures in early June, early to mid-July, and early to mid-August. Watch for an early-season tropical storm in the first week of June.

The first and fourth weeks of September will have threats of tropical storms. Otherwise, it will be dry with normal temperatures. October will be cool and dry, especially in the second half.

NOV. 2001: Temp. 64° (4° below avg.); precip. 1" (1" below avg.). 1-3 Cool, rain. 4-7 Sunny days, cool nights. 8-12 Sunny, warm. 13-15 Rain. 16-23 Sunny, chilly. 24-30 Rain, then sunny and warm.

DEC. 2001: Temp. 65.5° (5° above avg. north; avg. south); precip. 1.5" (1" below avg.). 1-6 Sunny, warm. 7-11 Warm, a few showers. 12-17 Sunny, warm. 18-22 Showers, then sunny and chilly. 23-31 Thunderstorms, then sunny and seasonable.

JAN. 2002: Temp. 66° (5° above avg.); precip. 2" (1" below avg.). 1-4 Sunny, warm. 5-8 Seasonable, showers. 9-13 Showers, then cold. 14-16 Rain, then warm. 17-25 Sunny, warm. 26-31 Warm, a few showers.

FEB. 2002: Temp. 65° (2° above avg.); precip. 5" (avg. north; 4" above south). 1-4 Sunny, warm. 5-8 Showers, then sunny and cool. 9-11 Seasonable, sunny. 12-16 Warm, then cool with rain. 17-21 Rain, warm. 22-24 Sunny, seasonable. 25-28 Cool north; rain, warm south.

MAR. 2002: Temp. 67° (avg.); precip. 4.5" (1" above avg.; 3" above central). 1-5 Rain, then sunny and cool. 6-10 Sunny, warm, then thunderstorms. 11-19 Warm, thunderstorms. 20-23 Cool, sunny, then cloudy. 24-31 Rain, warm.

APR. 2002: Temp. 72° (avg.); precip. 6" (0.5" below avg. north; 7" above south). 1-6 Sunny, warm, then thunderstorms. 7-10 Sunny, cool. 11-13 Cloudy, thunderstorms. 14-21 Sunny, warm. 22-25 Heavy thunderstorms. 26-30 Cool, thunderstorms.

MAY 2002: Temp. 75.5° (0.5° above avg.; 2° above north); precip. 4" (avg.). 1-3 Sunny, seasonable. 4-13 Hot north; thunderstorms. 14-20 Sunny, warm. 21-31 Seasonable, thunderstorms.

JUNE 2002: Temp. 80° (avg.); precip. 6" (avg.). 1-4 Tropical storm possible. 5-9 Sunny, warm. 10-15 Sunny, thunderstorms. 16-21 Sunny, daily thunderstorms. 22-30 Warm, thunderstorms.

JULY 2002: Temp. 82° (1° above avg. north; 1° below south); precip. 8" (1" above avg.). 1-4 Hot, thunderstorms. 5-7 Warm, thunderstorms. 8-13 Hot; daily thunderstorms. 14-16 Sunny, dry. 17-21 Hot, thunderstorms. 22-31 Seasonable, partly cloudy, thunderstorms.

AUG. 2002: Temp. 82° (avg.); precip. 8" (1" above avg.; 6" above south). 1-5 Sunny, thunderstorms. 6-10 Hot north; mainly dry. 11-18 Cloudy, thunderstorms. 19-22 Seasonable, thunderstorms south. 23-31 Warm, thunderstorms.

SEPT. 2002: Temp. 80° (avg.); precip. 6" (2" above avg. north; 2" below south). 1-4 Tropical storm possible. 5-17 Sunny, seasonable, thunderstorms. 18-21 Cool, thunderstorms. 22-27 Tropical storm possible. 28-30 Sunny, cool.

OCT. 2002: Temp. 73° (2° below avg.); precip. 3" (3" below avg.). 1-6 Sunny, low humidity north; thunderstorms south. 7-9 Thunderstorms. 10-12 Sunny, warm. 13-15 Cool north, thunderstorms south. 16-18 Warm, thunderstorms. 19-24 Sunny, cool. 25-31 Sunny, warm.

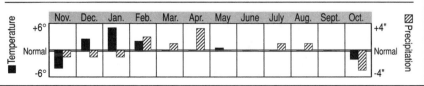

Upstate New York

SUMMARY: Winter will be mild, with temperatures averaging a degree above normal. Snowfall will be near or below normal, except in Buffalo, Watertown, and Albany, where it will be above normal. Expect snow in mid- to late November, late December through early January, early March, and late March to early April. Expect mild temperatures through most of December, with a cold spell from late December to mid-January. Be prepared for record-breaking cold in mid-January. From late January through March, temperatures will be mild, averaging three or four degrees above normal.

April will start chilly with snow but will generally be warmer than normal, followed by a near-normal May. Precipitation will be above normal in the northeast and below normal in the southeast.

Summer will have near-normal temperatures and sunny days. Expect above-normal rainfall in the north and the possibility of drought in the south. Although there will be no prolonged hot spells, record-high temperatures are possible in mid-June and mid-July.

September and October will be cool and dry, possibly intensifying a drought in the south.

NOV. 2001: Temp. 38° (1° below avg.); precip. 2.5" (1" below avg.). 1-4 Cold, showers, then flurries. 5-9 Warm, sunny, then showers. 10-13 Snow east, sunny west. 14-16 Rain, mild. 17-20 Cold, flurries, lake snows. 21-25 Chilly, snow. 26-30 Snow, then warm.

DEC. 2001: Temp. 30° (3° above avg.); precip. 4" (1" above avg.). 1-3 Cold, snow. 4-7 Mild, showers. 8-11 Rain, snow east, then mild. 12-15 Flurries, then mild. 16-18 Mild, rain. 19-24 Cold, flurries, lake snows. 25-31 Flurries, cold.

JAN. 2002: Temp. 18° (3° below avg.); precip. 1.5" (1" below avg.; 1" above west). 1-6 Cold, snow. 7-10 Bitter cold, snow. 11-14 Snow, then mild. 15-17 Thaw, rain. 18-22 Cold, snow. 23-26 Snow, ice, seasonable. 27-31 Mild, sunny.

FEB. 2002: Temp. 27° (4° above avg.); precip. 1.5" (1" below avg.). 1-4 Mild, a few showers. 5-14 Seasonable, flurries, lake snows. 15-19 Sunny, warm. 20-28 Rain, then cold with flurries.

MAR. 2002: Temp. 35° (2° above avg.); precip. 4" (1" above avg.). 1-4 Cold, snow. 5-10 Mild, sunny, showers. 11-18 Cold, snow, then sunny. 19-23 Seasonable, rain, snow. 24-31 Mild, then cold with rain and snow.

APR. 2002: Temp. 48° (3° above avg.); precip. 1.5" (1.5" below avg.; 0.5" above northwest). 1-8 Chilly, rain, snow. 9-12 Mild, showers. 13-17 Warm, dry. 18-21 Warm, sunny, thunderstorms. 22-30 Sunny, cool.

MAY 2002: Temp. 56° (avg.); precip. 5.5" (2" above avg.; 2" below southeast). 1-8 Warm, sunny, then rain. 9-16 Cool, rain. 17-24 Thunderstorms, then sunny. 25-31 Sunny, showers.

JUNE 2002: Temp. 67° (2° above avg.); precip. 3.5" (1" above avg. north; 0.5" below south). 1-4 Sunny. 5-9 Hot, thunderstorms. 10-12 Sunny, hot, humid. 13-16 Thunderstorms, then sunny. 17-22 Warm, thunderstorms. 23-26 Cool, rain, then sunny. 27-30 Thunderstorms.

JULY 2002: Temp. 70° (1° below avg.); precip. 1.5" (2" below avg.; 2" above north). 1-7 Sunny, showers. 8-12 Sunny, warm. 13-15 Sunny, hot. 16-20 Thunderstorms, then sunny. 21-28 Hot, thunderstorms. 29-31 Cool, dry.

AUG. 2002: Temp. 66° (2° below avg.); precip. 2.5" (1.5" below avg.). 1-6 Showers. 7-17 Sunny days, cool nights. 18-23 Thunderstorms, then sunny and cool. 24-31 Warm, showers, then cool.

SEPT. 2002: Temp. 60° (1° below avg.); precip. 2" (1.5" below avg.). 1-3 Sunny days, cool nights. 4-10 Warm, showers. 11-13 Sunny. 14-17 Rain, warm, then cool. 18-30 Sunny, cool.

OCT. 2002: Temp. 49° (1° below avg.); precip. 2" (1" below avg.). 1-7 Showers, then sunny and cool. 8-10 Sunny, mild. 11-15 Showers, then sunny and cool. 16-22 Thunderstorms, warm, then cold with flurries. 23-31 Seasonable, sunny, showers.

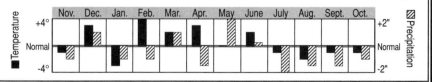

THE ALMANAC.COM COMPANION ▲

A FREE E-NEWSLETTER

from the editors of
The Old Farmer's Almanac and the
Gardener's Companion at

www.almanac.com

☞ SUBSCRIBE TODAY!
Get monthly and special editions
featuring:

- ■ Timely tips for garden and home
- ■ Advance notice of special sales on all Old Farmer's Almanac products
- ■ Recipes for every season
- ■ Astrological and astronomical advice
- ■ Previews of our print publications

Get your FREE subscription today

THE ALMANAC.COM COMPANION

Send e-mail to:
almanac-request@lists.ypi.com

In the Subject field, type:
subscribe yourname@domain.com

for example:
subscribe janesmith@aol.com

THE OLD FARMER'S ALMANAC
www.Almanac.com

After you read this sample, be sure to *sign up for a free subscription!*

THE ALMANAC.COM COMPANION
a newsletter from the publishers of "THE OLD FARMER'S ALMANAC"

January 5, 2001

You are receiving this E-mail message because you subscribed at our Web
site:
www.almanac.com

If you do not wish to receive our regular e-mail newsletter in the future,
please send a message to almanac-request@lists.ypi.com with the word
'unsubscribe' in the subject field.

HAPPY NEW YEAR
from the editors of "The Old Farmer's Almanac" and "The Almanac.com
Companion"

* Thank you for being a valued reader, e-mail subscriber, and customer
the past year.
* We hope to spend the coming year with you.

SENSUAL *Products*

Over 2 MILLION Satisfied Customers!

Exploring your sensuality is as healthy as it is fun. See our new *Xandria Gold Edition Catalogue* and discover a wide array of sexual products for giving and receiving even greater pleasure.

For over 25 years, *Over 2 Million Satisfied Customers* have felt comfortable with us.

Rely on Our Unique, 100%, 3-Way Guarantee:

- • We guarantee your privacy.
- • We guarantee your satisfaction.
- • We guarantee product quality.

We'll mail your catalogue within 24 hours!
Send $4.00 for your catalogue now and we'll include a $4 credit redeemable with your first purchase. Welcome to a new world of enjoyment!

www.xandria.com

The Xandria Collection, Dept. FR0102
P.O. Box 31039, San Francisco, CA 94131-9988

Send me my **Xandria Gold Edition Catalogue** with my $4.00 credit toward my first purchase. Enclosed is a check or money order for $4.00. ($5 Canada, £3 UK)

I am over 21:
Signature required _____

Name _____

Address _____

City _____

State/Zip _____

Xandria, 165 Valley Drive, Brisbane, CA 94005-1340. Void where prohibited by law.

Greater Ohio Valley

SUMMARY: Winter will occur in January—not that there won't be snow or cold the rest of the season, but January will bring the most of both. Expect record cold in mid-January but no other extreme cold spells. Though there will be no big snowstorms, expect frequent flurries in late November, late December, and January. Except for January, November through March will be milder than normal, with below-normal snowfall. Cold in mid- to late November will suggest a severe winter, but it will be followed by record warmth.

Spring will be pleasant, after snow in early April. May will be milder than normal, with near-normal rainfall.

June through August will be great for outdoor activities, with near-normal temperatures and below-normal rainfall, especially in West Virginia, where drought will be a concern. Expect hot spells in mid-June, mid- and late July, and late August but no extreme heat or humidity. Rain will be heavy in June in the north, but throughout the summer, expect below-normal rainfall, especially in the south.

September will start warm but end cool. October will be cool. Rainfall will be near normal.

NOV. 2001: Temp. 45° (avg.); precip. 2" (1.5" below avg.). 1-4 Chilly, showers, flurries. 5-8 Sunny, warm. 9-14 Seasonable, showers. 15-23 Very cold, snow showers. 24-28 Sunny, warm. 29-30 Warm, thunderstorms.

DEC. 2001: Temp. 40° (5° above avg.; 1° below northwest); precip. 3" (avg.; 3" above south). 1-3 Cold, rain, snow. 4-9 Mild, rain. 10-13 Sunny, mild. 14-17 Mild, showers. 18-24 Cold, rain, snow. 25-31 Cold, flurries.

JAN. 2002: Temp. 27° (2° below avg.); precip. 2.5" (avg.; 3" above southeast). 1-3 Mild, rain, snow. 4-12 Cold, snow showers. 13-16 Mild; heavy rain. 17-24 Cold, sunny, snow showers. 25-31 Mild, rain.

FEB. 2002: Temp. 34° (2° above avg.); precip. 2.5" (0.5" below avg.). 1-5 Rain, mild. 6-10 Cold, flurries. 11-15 Dry, seasonable. 16-20 Mild, rain. 21-28 Cold, flurries, sunny.

MAR. 2002: Temp. 44° (1° above avg.); precip. 4.5" (0.5" above avg.). 1-3 Cold, snow; rain south. 4-8 Sunny, mild. 9-16 Cold, rain, snow. 17-23 Chilly, sunny, a few showers. 24-31 Heavy rain.

APR. 2002: Temp. 55° (2° above avg.); precip. 3" (1" below avg.). 1-7 Chilly, rain, snow. 8-12 Mild, rain. 13-16 Warm, showers. 17-21 Hot, thunderstorms. 22-25 Sunny, warm. 26-30 Sunny, chilly.

MAY 2002: Temp. 65° (2° above avg.); precip. 6" (2" above avg.). 1-8 Warm, thunderstorms. 9-11 Cool, sunny. 12-20 Seasonable, sunny, thunderstorms. 21-23 Sunny, seasonable. 24-31 Thunderstorms, then warm and partly cloudy.

JUNE 2002: Temp. 73° (1° above avg.); precip. 3.5" (2" above avg. north; 2" below south). 1-5 Seasonable, dry. 6-12 Hot, humid, thunderstorms. 13-16 Sunny, warm. 17-20 Thunderstorms, then sunny. 21-23 Heavy thunderstorms. 24-27 Sunny, mild. 28-30 Thunderstorms.

JULY 2002: Temp. 76° (avg.); precip. 3" (1" below avg.). 1-7 Sunny, thunderstorms. 8-11 Seasonable, thunderstorms. 12-16 Sunny, hot. 17-20 Thunderstorms, then sunny and mild. 21-28 Sunny, hot, thunderstorms. 29-31 Cool, sunny.

AUG. 2002: Temp. 74° (1° below avg. north; 1° above south;); precip. 2" (1.5" below avg.). 1-3 Sunny, warm. 4-10 Warm, thunderstorms. 11-17 Sunny, seasonable. 18-22 Sunny, showers. 23-26 Sunny, hot. 27-31 Thunderstorms, then cool.

SEPT. 2002: Temp. 67° (1° below avg.); precip. 3" (1" below avg. north; 1" above south). 1-10 Warm, sunny, thunderstorms. 11-13 Sunny, warm. 14-16 Thunderstorms, warm. 17-23 Sunny days, cold nights. 24-30 Sunny, pleasant.

OCT. 2002: Temp. 53° (3° below avg.); precip. 2.5" (avg.). 1-7 Showers, then sunny days and chilly nights. 8-11 Warm, showers. 12-15 Thunderstorms, then sunny and cool. 16-18 Sunny, warm, thunderstorms. 19-22 Cold, flurries. 23-31 Mild, then cold and sunny, a few showers.

Pittsburgh
Indianapolis
Cincinnati
Charleston
Louisville

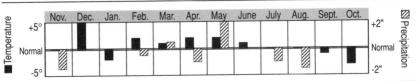

Deep South

SUMMARY: November through March will be milder and wetter than normal, with temperatures averaging one to three degrees above normal. Expect cold temperatures in mid- to late November and the second week of January. Otherwise, temperatures will be mild from December through February and cool in March. Expect snow and ice in the north but no major winter storms. Rainfall will be above normal, with the heaviest in December, January, and March.

April will be near normal in temperature and precipitation, followed by a warm, dry May, especially in the Gulf region. The north will have above-normal rainfall in May.

The summer will be hotter than normal by a degree or so, especially in mid-June, mid- and late July, and early and late August. Rainfall will be near normal, with less than usual in the north and more than usual in the south.

September will be wet, especially in the second week. Expect heavy rain in the south in mid- to late month. October will bring above-normal rainfall to the north, but the south will be dry. Both months will be cool, averaging two to three degrees below normal.

NOV. 2001: Temp. 53° (1° below avg.); precip. 2" (2" below avg.). 1-4 Thunderstorms, then sunny and chilly. 5-8 Sunny, warm. 9-12 Thunderstorms, then sunny and cool. 13-15 Warm, thunderstorms. 16-24 Sunny, cold. 25-28 Sunny, warm. 29-30 Warm, showers.

DEC. 2001: Temp. 50° (5° above avg.); precip. 8" (3" above avg.; 0.5" below northwest). 1-4 Cool, showers. 5-17 Warm, rain. 18-20 Sunny, cool. 21-26 Sunny, mild. 27-31 Showers.

JAN. 2002: Temp. 41.5° (1° below avg. north; 6° above south); precip. 6.5" (3" above avg. north; 1" above south). 1-7 Warm, showers. 8-13 Showers, then very cold, flurries. 14-16 Rain, warm. 17-20 Cool, showers. 21-31 Cool, rain north; warm, thunderstorms south.

FEB. 2002: Temp. 46° (3° above avg.); precip. 4.5" (avg.). 1-4 Rain north; warm, sunny south. 5-8 Showers, cool. 9-16 Thunderstorms, then sunny and cool. 17-20 Rain, mild. 21-28 Sunny, then rain.

MAR. 2002: Temp. 52.5° (0.5° below avg.); precip. 7" (3" above avg.). 1-4 Cold, showers, then sunny. 5-12 Warm, thunderstorms. 13-19 Seasonable, rain. 20-24 Showers north; cool, sunny south. 25-31 Warm; severe thunderstorms.

APR. 2002: Temp. 63° (avg.); precip. 4.5" (avg.). 1-5 Cool, sunny, showers. 6-9 Sunny, cold. 10-17 Warm, showers. 18-23 Warm, thunderstorms north. 24-30 Cool, rain, then sunny.

MAY 2002: Temp. 73° (2° above avg.); precip. 6" (5" above avg. north; 2" below south). 1-3 Mild. 4-8 Warm, rain, then sunny. 9-11 Sunny, warm. 12-20 Warm, sunny, then rain. 21-24 Sunny, warm. 25-31 Warm, rain.

JUNE 2002: Temp. 79° (1° above avg.); precip. 3.5" (avg.). 1-3 Warm, thunderstorms. 4-8 Warm, humid; thunderstorms north. 9-15 Warm, thunderstorms. 16-19 Cool, thunderstorms. 20-23 Thunderstorms. 24-30 Hot, humid, thunderstorms.

JULY 2002: Temp. 81° (1° above avg.); precip. 1.5" (2" below avg.; 2" above south). 1-7 Sunny, hot. 8-13 Hot, thunderstorms. 14-20 Hot, sunny. 21-28 Hot, thunderstorms. 29-31 Mild.

AUG. 2002: Temp. 80° (avg.); precip. 4" (1" below avg.). 1-10 Hot, humid, thunderstorms. 11-17 Thunderstorms, then sunny and less humid. 18-20 Hot south; dry. 21-25 Hot, humid, Gulf thunderstorms. 26-31 Hot, humid, thunderstorms.

SEPT. 2002: Temp. 72° (2° below avg.); precip. 6.5" (3" above avg.). 1-5 Warm, thunderstorms. 6-11 Thunderstorms. 12-16 Warm, thunderstorms. 17-19 Sunny, cool. 20-24 Cool, showers north; rain south. 25-30 Mild, showers.

OCT. 2002: Temp. 61° (3° below avg.); precip. 3" (2" above avg. north; 2" below south). 1-8 Sunny. 9-11 Rain. 12-15 Sunny, cool. 16-18 Rain, warm. 19-23 Sunny, cold. 24-31 Mild, showers, then sunny.

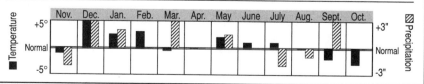

Chicago and Southern Great Lakes

SUMMARY: With the exception of January, November through March will be milder than normal, with record-high warmth in mid-December, late February, and early March. As a result, expect fewer lake snows than usual but above-normal snowfall in some spots. A big snowstorm will hit in early January, but it will also snow in late November, early December, mid-January, early to mid-February, late March, and early April. A chill will blanket the region in mid- to late November, but the coldest spells will occur in the second and third weeks of January, with a thaw in between.

Despite snow in early April, April through May will be milder than normal, with above-normal rainfall, especially in the south.

Summer will be hotter than usual, with above-normal rainfall. Don't expect any long heat waves, but plan on several hot days in mid-June and again in mid-July, late July, and late August. June and July will be wetter than normal, with severe storms in early July.

September and October will be cooler than normal, with near-normal rainfall. Prepare for sharp cold in mid- to late October.

NOV. 2001: Temp. 40.5° (0.5° above avg.); precip. 2" (0.5" below avg.). 1-4 Cool, sunny. 5-9 Mild, showers. 10-11 Cold. 12-14 Mild, rain. 15-25 Cold, occasional flurries. 26-30 Warm, sunny, then thunderstorms.

DEC. 2001: Temp. 31° (3° above avg.); precip. 2" (0.5" below avg.). 1-3 Cold, rain, snow. 4-8 Rain, snow. 9-13 Mild, then cold and dry. 14-17 Mild, showers. 18-23 Seasonable, rain, snow. 24-31 Cold, then seasonable with flurries.

JAN. 2002: Temp. 18° (4° below avg.); precip. 1.5" (avg.). 1-6 Snowstorm, then very cold. 7-12 Bitter cold, flurries. 13-15 Warm. 16-24 Cold, rain, snow. 25-31 Mild, dry.

FEB. 2002: Temp. 28° (3° above avg.); precip. 1.5" (avg.). 1-7 Mild, rain, then cold with snow. 8-12 Snow, seasonable. 13-19 Warm, rain. 20-28 Rain, then cold with flurries.

MAR. 2002: Temp. 38° (1° above avg.); precip. 3.5" (1" above avg.). 1-4 Chilly; snow east. 5-9 Windy, mild, thunderstorms. 10-14 Seasonable, rain, wet snow. 15-18 Sunny, seasonable. 19-23 Cold; wet snow. 24-31 Chilly, rain.

APR. 2002: Temp. 51° (2° above avg.); precip. 4" (1" above avg.). 1-6 Chilly; wet snow. 7-10 Mild, sunny. 11-21 Warm, showers, thunderstorms. 22-30 Mild, then cool and sunny.

MAY 2002: Temp. 59° (avg.); precip. 4.5" (0.5" below avg. north; 2" above south). 1-3 Sunny, warm. 4-7 Cool, thunderstorms. 8-14 Cool, rain.

15-20 Seasonable, showers. 21-24 Warm, sunny. 25-31 Cool, then warm and sunny with rain.

JUNE 2002: Temp. 71° (1° above avg.); precip. 6" (2" above avg.). 1-4 Sunny, chilly, then warm. 5-8 Warm, thunderstorms. 9-12 Hot, humid, thunderstorms. 13-16 Sunny, pleasant, then hot. 17-22 Seasonable, thunderstorms. 23-27 Sunny, warm. 28-30 Showers, thunderstorms.

JULY 2002: Temp. 74° (avg.); precip. 6" (2" above avg.). 1-7 Warm, humid, thunderstorms, some severe. 8-13 Sunny, warm. 14-19 Hot, humid, thunderstorms, then sunny and cool. 20-23 Hot, humid, thunderstorms. 24-27 Sunny, hot, humid. 28-31 Thunderstorms, then cool.

AUG. 2002: Temp. 71.5° (0.5° below avg.); precip. 3.5" (avg.). 1-7 Sunny, warm, dry. 8-16 Thunderstorms, then sunny. 17-23 Warm, sunny, showers. 24-31 Hot, thunderstorms, then sunny and cool.

SEPT. 2002: Temp. 62° (2° below avg.); precip. 2.5" (1" below avg.). 1-3 Sunny, pleasant. 4-9 Seasonable, showers. 10-12 Sunny. 13-16 Warm, then cool with rain. 17-23 Sunny, cool days; chilly nights. 24-30 Sunny, seasonable.

OCT. 2002: Temp. 51° (1° below avg.); precip. 4" (1" above avg.). 1-7 Sunny, cool. 8-11 Warm, rain. 12-15 Sunny, seasonable. 16-21 Heavy rain, then cold with flurries. 22-31 Mild, dry.

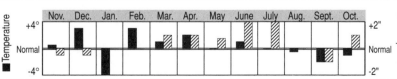

	Nov.	Dec.	Jan.	Feb.	Mar.	Apr.	May	June	July	Aug.	Sept.	Oct.	

Temperature: +4° / Normal / -4°   Precipitation: +2" / Normal / -2"

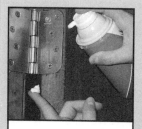

Squeaky hinges? Try shaving cream.

Don't waste money — baking soda plus 2 other "magic" ingredients will unclog that drain!

Brighten your whites by putting a little of this into your wash water?

"Uncommon Uses for Common Household Products"

(By Frank K. Wood)

FC&A, a Peachtree City, Georgia, publisher, announced today the release of a new book for the general public, *"Uncommon Uses for Common Household Products."*

► Grow prettier flowers and yummier vegetables with banana peels.

► Smooth dry, flaky skin with mayonnaise.

► Silence squeaky hardwood floors with baby powder.

► Loosen a rusted lock with Coca-Cola®!

► VCR on the fritz? Get a clear picture once again with aluminum foil. Give this trick a try before calling in a repairman.

► Quick cure for stomach problems costs just pennies. Reach in your kitchen cabinet for a little baking soda and follow the instructions in the book.

► The dings on your car need to be fixed, but you're short on cash. No problem. Take out some crayons.

► Wine stains on your white tablecloth mean a big bill at the cleaners, right? Wrong! The stains come out like magic ... with salt.

► Pantyhose that last for years! Put an end to stocking snags, tears, and runs with nail polish.

► Your carpet's stained badly and company's due in 30 minutes. No sweat. A little ammonia cleans it good as new in just five minutes.

► It takes most folks hours to get messy oil stains off driveways. Not you. You make it disappear in seconds ... with a little cat litter.

► Dread spending an entire afternoon raking up leaves? I don't blame you. But clean up's a snap, if you use an old bedsheet.

► Old wallpaper loosens up and peels off in seconds — almost effortlessly — with this amazing white vinegar tonic.

► Your roses will bloom bigger and prettier this summer without slaving hours in the hot sun. Just toss 'em a "tea bag treat."

► No more scrubbing dull pots and pans. They'll gleam like new if you let apples, rhubarb, or lemons do the cleaning for you.

► Junior leaves filthy handprints and pencil marks on the walls. No big deal. He can clean the walls instantly with a piece of old bread.

► Repel roaches without dangerous pesticides. Instead, grab a cucumber and follow the directions in this book.

► Doggy-do messing up your garden? Mix up a little of this garlic brew, and Fido will never come back into your yard.

► Tired of constantly cleaning bathroom mildew? Take a little tub of car wax and forget about it for a whole year!

► Simple secret that makes frozen fish taste fresher when you serve it. Take a cup of milk, and follow these easy steps.

Learn all these amazing secrets and more. To order a copy, just return this notice with your name and address and a check for $12.99 plus $3.00 shipping and handling to: **FC&A, Dept. COF-02**, 103 Clover Green, Peachtree City, GA 30269. We will send you a copy of *"Uncommon Uses for Common Household Products."*

Sorry, only one copy per customer.

You get a no-time-limit guarantee of satisfaction or your money back.

You must cut out and return this notice with your order. Copies will not be accepted!

**IMPORTANT — FREE GIFT
OFFER EXPIRES IN 30 DAYS**

All orders mailed within 30 days, will receive a free gift, *"Discounts, Discounts, and More Discounts,"* guaranteed. Order right away!

©FC&A 2001

Northern Great Plains–Great Lakes

SUMMARY: November through March will be near normal overall. Temperatures will be below normal in northern Minnesota, northern Wisconsin, and the Upper Peninsula of Michigan, and milder than normal elsewhere. Snowfall will be near or above normal. January will be the coldest month, despite a midmonth thaw. Expect cold also in late November, early December, and mid-February. Plan for snow in mid- to late November, early December, mid-February, March, and early April.

April and May will be cool and wet in the west; the east will be milder than normal, with near-normal rainfall.

Summer overall will be normal, with average temperatures and precipitation. June will be cool; July will be hotter than normal. Expect some hot days in early July and late July into early August. Rainfall will be above normal in Wisconsin and southern Minnesota, below normal in eastern Montana and North Dakota, and near normal elsewhere. Thunderstorms might cause minor flooding, but don't expect widespread flooding or serious drought.

September will be cool. October will be mild in the east and below normal in the west. Precipitation will be near normal.

NOV. 2001: Temp. 32° (avg.); precip. 1.5" (0.5" below avg. east; avg. west). 1-7 Cold, then mild and dry. 8-11 Rain, snow, cold. 12-16 Cold, flurries. 17-21 Flurries east; mild, sunny west. 22-26 Sunny, mild. 27-30 Cold, snow.

DEC. 2001: Temp. 24° (5° above avg.); precip. 1" (avg.). 1-4 Snow east; cold, then mild and sunny west. 5-11 Flurries. 12-15 Sunny, mild. 16-18 Flurries. 19-24 Cloudy, mild. 25-31 Cold, flurries.

JAN. 2002: Temp. 6° (6° below avg.); precip. 0.5" (0.5" below avg.). 1-9 Cold, sunny, flurries. 10-14 Sunny, mild. 15-23 Bitter cold, sunny, flurries. 24-31 Mild, sunny.

FEB. 2002: Temp. 16.5° (3° below avg. east; 4° above west); precip. 1" (0.5" above avg. north; 0.5" below east). 1-9 Flurries east; sunny, mild west. 10-12 Cold. 13-16 Cold, snow. 17-22 Mild, sunny. 23-28 Cold; snow west.

MAR. 2002: Temp. 29° (1° above avg.); precip. 1.5" (0.5" below avg. north; 1" above south). 1-6 Mild, flurries. 7-11 Cold, flurries. 12-15 Sunny, warm. 16-24 Cold, flurries. 25-31 Seasonable, rain, snow east; cold, heavy snow west.

APR. 2002: Temp. 44° (2° above avg. east; 2° below west); precip. 3" (1" above avg.). 1-7 Cold, flurries. 8-10 Dry, seasonable. 11-14 Rain; warm east. 15-21 Thunderstorms, warm east; mild, then cool with showers west. 22-25 Sunny. 26-30 Thunderstorms.

MAY 2002: Temp. 55° (1° below avg.); precip. 3" (1" below avg. east; 4" above west). 1-5 Showers. 6-10 Sunny east; chilly, rain west. 11-19 Cool, thunderstorms. 20-24 Sunny, warm. 25-31 Cool north; hot with thunderstorms south.

JUNE 2002: Temp. 63° (2° below avg. east; 0.5" below west); precip. 5" (2" above avg. east; 0.5" below west). 1-7 Warm, thunderstorms. 8-12 Hot, thunderstorms east; cool, rain west. 13-22 Cool, rain. 23-30 Thunderstorms.

JULY 2002: Temp. 75° (2° above avg.); precip. 3.5" (1" below avg. north; 0.5" above south). 1-2 Warm, thunderstorms. 3-6 Thunderstorms, hot. 7-11 Sunny, hot, thunderstorms. 12-19 Warm, dry. 20-26 Hot, thunderstorms. 27-31 Thunderstorms, cool, then sunny and hot.

AUG. 2002: Temp. 71° (avg.); precip. 3" (0.5" below avg.). 1-3 Warm, thunderstorms. 4-8 Thunderstorms north and east; hot west. 9-14 Sunny. 15-19 Thunderstorms, then sunny. 20-22 Showers, cool. 23-31 Sunny, then showers.

SEPT. 2002: Temp. 58° (1° below avg.); precip. 3" (avg. east; 0.5" below west). 1-6 Warm, sunny, showers. 7-11 Showers east; cool, sunny west. 12-17 Cold, rain. 18-26 Warm, sunny. 27-30 Cool, thunderstorms.

OCT. 2002: Temp. 45° (2° above avg. east; 4° below west); precip. 2.5" (0.5" above avg.). 1-5 Showers, then sunny and chilly. 6-12 Showers east, dry west. 13-16 Showers, cool. 17-20 Showers, then flurries. 21-25 Sunny, mild. 26-31 Seasonable east; cold, flurries, then sunny west.

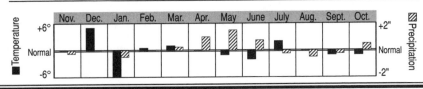

Central Great Plains

SUMMARY: With the exception of January, November through March will be mild. Snowfall will be above normal from Denver to the Tri-Cities but below normal elsewhere. Mid-January will be very cold, followed by a thaw, then a very cold week. Other cold spells will occur in mid-November and early December. Expect snow in mid-November, January, late February, and mid- to late March. Watch for heavy, wet snow in the Colorado foothills in mid-May.

Snowfall from April through May will be near normal. On average, temperatures will be above normal in the east and below normal in the west. Rainfall will be above normal, especially in southern Illinois and southeastern Missouri.

Summer will be hot, with near-normal rainfall. Temperatures will average one to two degrees above normal from June through August. It will be hottest in late June, most of July, and early and late August.

September and October will be cooler than normal, with near-normal rainfall. Expect a widespread freeze in mid-October, with snow in the Colorado foothills and flurries elsewhere.

NOV. 2001: Temp. 42° (1° above avg.); precip. 2.5" (1" below avg. north; 1" above south). 1-3 Cold, flurries, then sunny. 4-7 Sunny, warm. 8-11 Rain, cool. 12-16 Cold, rain, snow. 17-22 Flurries east, sunny west. 23-27 Sunny, mild. 28-30 Rain, cold.

DEC. 2001: Temp. 31° (avg. east; 4° above west); precip. 2" (avg.). 1-3 Cold, rain, snow. 4-11 Mild, then cold with snow. 12-16 Showers. 17-19 Cold, flurries. 20-26 Sunny, mild. 27-31 Flurries.

JAN. 2002: Temp. 20° (4° below avg.); precip. 0.5" (0.5" below avg.). 1-3 Cold, rain, snow. 4-8 Flurries east, mild west. 9-10 Flurries. 11-14 Sunny, warm. 15-24 Flurries. 25-31 Rain, flurries.

FEB. 2002: Temp. 33° (4° above avg.); precip. 1.5" (1" below avg. north; 1" above south). 1-7 Rain, then sunny. 8-12 Sunny, then showers. 13-17 Cold, flurries. 18-20 Mild, rain. 21-24 Sunny. 25-28 Cloudy, snow.

MAR. 2002: Temp. 39° (1° below avg.); precip. 4" (2" above avg.). 1-6 Flurries, then sunny. 7-9 Flurries, cold. 10-14 Rain, then sunny. 15-20 Cold, rain, snow. 21-25 Showers, then sunny. 26-31 Rain east, snow west.

APR. 2002: Temp. 53° (1° above avg.; 2° below west); precip. 2" (1" below avg.; 2" above southeast). 1-4 Cold, rain, snow, then mild. 5-8 Cold, snow, then sunny. 9-11 Showers. 12-20 Warm, thunderstorms east; chilly west. 21-23 Showers. 24-27 Sunny, then showers. 28-30 Sunny, cool.

MAY 2002: Temp. 62° (2° above avg. east; 2° below west); precip. 6" (2" above avg.). 1-7 Thunderstorms, mild east; chilly west. 8-11 Rain east, snow west. 12-17 Thunderstorms east, sunny west. 18-21 Thunderstorms, then sunny and cool. 22-25 Mild, thunderstorms. 26-31 Warm, thunderstorms.

JUNE 2002: Temp. 72° (avg.); precip. 5" (1" below avg. northwest; 3" above southeast). 1-4 Thunderstorms east, sunny west. 5-11 Thunderstorms, hot east; cool west. 12-15 Sunny. 16-17 Cool, showers. 18-21 Thunderstorms, then sunny. 22-30 Hot, thunderstorms.

JULY 2002: Temp. 80° (2° above avg.); precip. 3.5" (avg.). 1-4 Hot, thunderstorms. 5-13 Sunny, hot. 14-23 Hot, thunderstorms. 24-27 Sunny, hot. 28-31 Thunderstorms, then sunny and cool.

AUG. 2002: Temp. 77° (2° above avg.); precip. 2" (3" below avg. east; avg. west). 1-6 Sunny, hot. 7-9 Hot, thunderstorms. 10-14 Cool, showers. 15-19 Sunny, then thunderstorms. 20-26 Hot, thunderstorms. 27-31 Cool, showers.

SEPT. 2002: Temp. 64° (2° below avg.; 0.5° above west); precip. 2" (1" below avg.). 1-3 Sunny. 4-8 Showers, cool. 9-12 Sunny, warm. 13-15 Rain. 16-20 Sunny, cool. 21-26 Sunny, warm. 27-30 Sunny, cool.

OCT. 2002: Temp. 51° (4° below avg.); precip. 4" (1" above avg.). 1-6 Cool, rain. 7-9 Rain, mild. 10-14 Sunny east, rain west. 15-17 Rain, mild. 18-21 Cold, snow. 22-25 Sunny. 26-31 Showers, flurries.

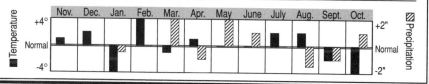

Texas–Oklahoma

SUMMARY: Expect above-normal rainfall from November through March, especially near the Gulf Coast. It will often be cloudy from San Antonio to the Metroplex, with frequent fog, drizzle, and showers. Expect sleet in the Metroplex vicinity during the second half of January. Prepare for flurries in Oklahoma in early December and a snowstorm in the Texas Panhandle in mid-March. Temperatures overall will be near normal in the north and mild in the south. The second week of January will be the coldest period, with a freeze in Houston and the Valley. Mid- to late November, early December, and mid- to late January will also be cold.

April and May will be wet. Temperatures will average near normal in the south but will be cool in the north.

Summer will be hot, with temperatures averaging a degree or two above normal. The hottest spell will be in late July, with other hot periods in late June, early July, and mid-August.

September and October will have rain, with temperatures well below normal. October will be chilly in the north.

NOV. 2001: Temp. 57° (1° above avg.; 2° below south); precip. 0.5" (1.5" below avg.). 1-4 Sunny, cool. 5-8 Sunny, warm. 9-12 Thunderstorms, then sunny and cool. 13-16 Sunny, then thunderstorms and cool. 17-19 Sunny north, showers south. 20-24 Sunny, cool. 25-30 Cloudy, warm.

DEC. 2001: Temp. 51° (2° above avg.); precip. 2" (0.5" above avg.). 1-4 Thunderstorms north, then cool. 5-9 Chilly north, thunderstorms south. 10-16 Warm, thunderstorms. 17-23 Sunny. 24-27 Sunny, mild. 28-31 Warm; showers north and east.

JAN. 2002: Temp. 44.5° (4° below avg. north; 5° above south); precip. 1" (0.5" below avg.; 2" above south). 1-3 Cloudy. 4-9 Flurries north, warm south. 10-13 Cold; snow north. 14-16 Showers, mild. 17-22 Flurries, cold north; rain south. 23-27 Flurries north, showers south. 28-31 Warm, rain north.

FEB. 2002: Temp. 53° (3° above avg.); precip. 2.5" (1" above avg.; 4" above south). 1-7 Sunny, warm. 8-10 Cool, thunderstorms. 11-17 Flurries north, rain south. 18-23 Sunny. 24-28 Mild, showers south; cold, snow north.

MAR. 2002: Temp. 56.5° (2° below avg. north; 1° above south); precip. 3.5" (1" above avg.; 6" above east). 1-7 Mild, showers. 8-16 Sunny north, thunderstorms south. 17-20 Snow north; cold, sunny south. 21-23 Cool, rain. 24-31 Thunderstorms, then sunny and cool.

APR. 2002: Temp. 62° (4° below avg.; 1° below south); precip. 8" (5" above avg.). 1-4 Cloudy, cool. 5-9 Cold, snow north; warm, rain south. 10-13 Warm, dry. 14-19 Mild, thunderstorms. 20-24 Cool. 25-30 Warm, rain, then sunny and cool.

MAY 2002: Temp. 71° (3° below avg. north; 1° above south); precip. 8.5" (4" above avg.). 1-7 Thunderstorms. 8-10 Warm, thunderstorms. 11-13 Cool, dry. 14-19 Warm south, thunderstorms north. 20-23 Warm north, thunderstorms south. 24-31 Cool, thunderstorms.

JUNE 2002: Temp. 81° (1° above avg.); precip. 2.5" (1" below avg.). 1-9 Thunderstorms, then hot. 10-17 Thunderstorms, cool north. 18-20 Sunny, warm. 21-30 Hot.

JULY 2002: Temp. 86° (2° above avg.); precip. 1" (1.5" below avg.). 1-2 Sunny, hot. 3-7 Thunderstorms. 8-12 Sunny, hot. 13-15 Thunderstorms. 16-19 Thunderstorms, cool north. 20-24 Sunny, hot. 25-28 Hot, thunderstorms. 29-31 Thunderstorms.

AUG. 2002: Temp. 83.5° (0.5° above avg.); precip. 3" (avg.). 1-4 Hot, thunderstorms. 5-9 Hot; thunderstorms north. 10-13 Thunderstorms, cool north. 14-19 Sunny. 20-25 Hot, thunderstorms. 26-31 Thunderstorms.

SEPT. 2002: Temp. 73° (3° below avg.); precip. 4" (avg.). 1-4 Thunderstorms, chilly. 5-9 Thunderstorms, mild. 10-13 Sunny, hot. 14-19 Thunderstorms, then cool. 20-30 Sunny, warm.

OCT. 2002: Temp. 61° (6° below avg.; 0.5° above south); precip. 5.5" (2.5" above avg.). 1-4 Showers, cool. 5-9 Rain, seasonable. 10-12 Cool north, thunderstorms south. 13-16 Rain. 17-22 Cold, dry. 23-26 Sunny. 27-31 Seasonable.

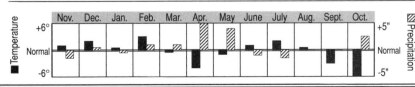

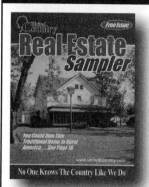

Rocky Mountains

SUMMARY: November through March will average one degree below normal, with near-normal precipitation. Temperatures will be below normal from November through late January but coldest in mid-November, early December, and mid- to late January. From early February to early March, mild air will prevail, with many days warmer than normal. Expect two or three snowstorms in mid- to late January. Snow will also fall in mid-November, late December, mid- to late February, and late March.

April and May will be cooler than normal, with precipitation near or above normal. Watch for a snowstorm in some low elevations the second week of May, then hot weather to close the month.

Overall, June through August will be delightful, averaging one or two degrees cooler than normal, with slightly below-normal rainfall. The hottest spells will occur in mid- to late June, late July, and mid-August.

September will start warm but end cool. Overall, the month will have near-normal temperatures and precipitation. October will be colder than normal, with above-normal precipitation. Expect snow in midmonth, especially in the west, with snow elsewhere toward month's end.

NOV. 2001: Temp. 39° (3° below avg.); precip. 0.5" (0.5" below avg.). 1-6 Sunny, pleasant. 7-12 Cold, rain, snow. 13-21 Sunny, cold; mild east. 22-27 Sunny, seasonable. 28-30 Cold, snow.

DEC. 2001: Temp. 26° (2° below avg.); precip. 0.5" (0.5" below avg.). 1-4 Very cold, flurries. 5-9 Mild, rain, snow. 10-14 Sunny, mild. 15-18 Cold, flurries, then sunny. 19-22 Sunny, seasonable. 23-25 Sunny, cold. 26-31 Flurries.

JAN. 2002: Temp. 23° (3° below avg.); precip. 1" (avg.). 1-5 Snow, then sunny. 6-10 Mild, rain, flurries. 11-13 Sunny, seasonable. 14-19 Cold, flurries. 20-23 Snow east; sunny, very cold west. 24-31 Snow, not as cold.

FEB. 2002: Temp. 37° (5° above avg.); precip. 1.5" (1" above avg. northeast; 0.5" below southwest). 1-5 Flurries, then sunny and mild. 6-12 Sunny, mild. 13-16 Flurries north; mild, rain south. 17-21 Mild, rain. 22-28 Seasonable, rain, flurries.

MAR. 2002: Temp. 39.5° (0.5° above avg.; 0.5° below north); precip. 2" (avg.; 0.5" below southwest). 1-3 Mild, sunny. 4-7 Cold, flurries. 8-13 Seasonable, sunny, dry. 14-18 Cold, rain, flurries, then sunny. 19-22 Mild, rain, then sunny. 23-28 Cold, rain, snow. 29-31 Rain, snow.

APR. 2002: Temp. 47° (1° below avg.); precip. 2" (avg.). 1-6 Snow, then sunny and mild. 7-15 Seasonable, rain, flurries. 16-21 Cold, snow, rain east; sunny west. 22-26 Sunny, warm. 27-30 Cool, showers.

MAY 2002: Temp. 56.5° (2° above avg. north; 3° below south); precip. 3.5" (1.5" above avg.; avg. southwest). 1-6 Cold, rain east; sunny, seasonable west. 7-11 Chilly, rain; snow east. 12-18 Cold, rain. 19-21 Sunny, warm. 22-25 Warm, thunderstorms. 26-31 Sunny, hot.

JUNE 2002: Temp. 65° (1° below avg.); precip. 1" (0.5" below avg.). 1-5 Cool, showers. 6-10 Rain, chilly east; cool west. 11-16 Sunny. 17-19 Sunny, hot. 20-24 Showers, then sunny and hot. 25-30 Dry.

JULY 2002: Temp. 72° (2° below avg.); precip. 1" (avg.). 1-5 Sunny, warm. 6-12 Thunderstorms, cool. 13-17 Sunny, comfortable. 18-22 Thunderstorms, warm. 23-28 Sunny, hot, dry. 29-31 Thunderstorms, cool.

AUG. 2002: Temp. 70.5° (avg. north; 3° below south); precip. 1" (avg.). 1-6 Sunny, pleasant. 7-13 Sunny, hot, thunderstorms. 14-18 Hot, thunderstorms. 19-25 Cool, thunderstorms east. 26-31 Sunny, warm.

SEPT. 2002: Temp. 63° (avg.); precip. 1" (avg.). 1-5 Sunny, warm. 6-10 Sunny, dry. 11-15 Thunderstorms, then sunny and cool. 16-21 Sunny, warm. 22-24 Sunny, hot; cool west. 25-30 Thunderstorms, then sunny and cool.

OCT. 2002: Temp. 51° (2° below avg.); precip. 1.5" (0.5" above avg.). 1-5 Sunny, seasonable. 6-11 Showers, then sunny and cool. 12-15 Cold, rain, flurries. 16-20 Seasonable, sunny, then showers. 21-25 Sunny, seasonable. 26-31 Cold, rain, snow.

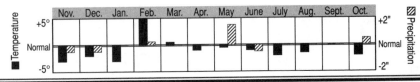

Desert Southwest

SUMMARY: November through March will be mild, averaging three degrees above normal. Expect the coldest spells in mid-November and the first half of December. Warm weather will prevail from late December through early January; the rest of January will be near normal. February will have record warmth, especially in the first half. Average temperatures in March will be similar to those of February, making March near normal. Expect below-normal precipitation from November through March, with rain in early and mid-December, early January, mid- and late February, and mid-March. Plan for snow in the usual places in early December and early and late January.

April and May will be cool, with April about three degrees below normal. Rainfall will be below normal.

June through August will have near- or above-normal temperatures. Rainfall will be near normal in northeastern New Mexico but above normal elsewhere. It will be hottest in late June before the monsoon, and in late July and late August. June will be dry; July and August will have scattered thunderstorms.

September will be drier than normal, with near-normal temperatures. October will be cool and rainy.

NOV. 2001: Temp. 57° (1° below avg. north; 1° above south); precip. 0.2" (0.4" below avg.). 1-7 Sunny, warm. 8-11 Cool, cloudy. 12-15 Sunny, cool. 16-19 Sunny, seasonable. 20-27 Cloudy, then sunny and seasonable. 28-30 Warm, cloudy.

DEC. 2001: Temp. 49° (1° above avg.); precip. 0.6" (0.4" below avg.). 1-5 Cloudy, cool; snow, rain east. 6-11 Sunny, seasonable. 12-16 Rain, snow east; chilly, sunny west. 17-25 Sunny, cool. 26-31 Cloudy, showers.

JAN. 2002: Temp. 51° (4° above avg.); precip. 0.4" (0.2" below avg.; 0.6" above south). 1-7 Warm, rain, snow in the mountains. 8-10 Sunny, mild. 11-14 Sunny, seasonable. 15-17 Showers, cool. 18-21 Mild, showers. 22-25 Cold, rain, snow. 26-31 Warm, cloudy.

FEB. 2002: Temp. 60° (8° above avg.); precip. 0.6" (0.5" above avg. east; 0.5" below west). 1-4 Mild, cloudy. 5-10 Sunny, warm. 11-17 Mild, showers. 18-21 Sunny, mild. 22-28 Thunderstorms, then mild and sunny.

MAR. 2002: Temp. 59° (1° above avg.); precip. 0.4" (0.2" below avg.). 1-3 Sunny, warm. 4-6 Mild, thunderstorms. 7-12 Sunny, warm east; cool west. 13-15 Seasonable, thunderstorms. 16-19 Sunny, cool. 20-23 Seasonable, cloudy. 24-28 Cloudy, showers. 29-31 Sunny, warm.

APR. 2002: Temp. 65.5° (0.5° below avg.); precip. 0.2" (0.2" below avg.). 1-4 Sunny, seasonable.

5-9 Sunny, warm. 10-17 Cool, thunderstorms. 18-21 Sunny, cool. 22-30 Sunny, warm.

MAY 2002: Temp. 71° (3° below avg.); precip. 0.2" (0.1" below avg.). 1-3 Seasonable, thunderstorms. 4-7 Cool, thunderstorms. 8-12 Sunny, mild. 13-18 Sunny, cool; showers west. 19-21 Sunny, warm. 22-31 Thunderstorms, then sunny and hot.

JUNE 2002: Temp. 86° (2° above avg.); precip. 0.1" (0.2" below avg.; 0.2" above south). 1-5 Cool, thunderstorms. 6-11 Mild, cloudy. 12-17 Sunny, hot. 18-22 Sunny; record heat. 23-30 Hot, thunderstorms.

JULY 2002: Temp. 88° (avg.); precip. 2.5" (3" above avg. east; avg. west). 1-5 Warm, thunderstorms. 6-10 Hot, dry. 11-20 Warm, thunderstorms. 21-31 Sunny, hot; thunderstorms east.

AUG. 2002: Temp. 86.5° (1° above avg. east; 2° below west); precip. 1.7" (0.2" above avg.). 1-5 Cloudy, warm, thunderstorms. 6-12 Hot, thunderstorms. 13-16 Warm, thunderstorms; cool west. 17-22 Hot, thunderstorms. 23-26 Cool, thunderstorms. 27-31 Sunny, hot.

SEPT. 2002: Temp. 81° (avg.); precip. 0.5" (0.5" below avg.). 1-4 Hot, thunderstorms. 5-10 Sunny, cool. 11-17 Sunny, cool. 18-26 Seasonable east; sunny, hot west. 27-30 Cool, thunderstorms.

OCT. 2002: Temp. 68° (3° below avg.); precip. 2.8" (2" above avg.). 1-4 Sunny, warm. 5-9 Cool, thunderstorms. 10-13 Mild, thunderstorms. 14-17 Thunderstorms, cool. 18-20 Sunny, cool. 21-26 Warm, thunderstorms. 27-31 Cool, showers.

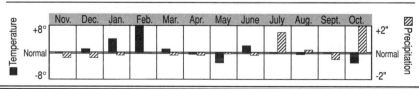

Pacific Northwest

SUMMARY: Overall, temperatures will average two degrees below normal from November through March, with below-normal rainfall. Expect less rain and storminess than usual for the first half of winter, but plan for a few snowstorms. The second half of winter will have above-normal rainfall, with near-normal temperatures. Expect snowstorms in late November, mid-January, and mid-February. Cold spells will come with the snow in late November, mid- to late January, and mid-February.

April and May will be two to three degrees above normal, with less rain than normal.

Summer will be pleasant, with temperatures averaging one to two degrees cooler than normal and near-normal rainfall. The hottest days will be in late June, mid-July, and mid- to late August (the warmest month, on average), but don't expect any very hot weather. Plan for rain in early to mid-June, mid- and late July, and early August.

September will be warmer than usual, with many spots seeing the hottest temperatures of the year in early to mid-September. Rain during September will occur mainly from Oregon southward. October will be cooler and drier than normal, despite rain early in the month.

NOV. 2001: Temp. 42° (4° below avg.); precip. 3" (3" below avg.). 1-4 Cloudy, mild. 5-12 Rain, cool. 13-18 Cool, sunny. 19-25 Sunny, cold. 26-30 Rain, mild, then cold with snow.

DEC. 2001: Temp. 43° (1° above avg.); precip. 4" (2" below avg.). 1-4 Stormy, rain, cool. 5-12 Rain, mild. 13-17 Seasonable, rain. 18-23 Sunny, then cloudy and cold. 24-31 Chilly, rain, drizzle.

JAN. 2002: Temp. 36° (5° below avg.); precip. 4" (2" below avg.). 1-3 Cold, rain, snow. 4-9 Mild, rain. 10-12 Sunny, cold. 13-19 Snowstorm, cold. 20-22 Sunny, cold. 23-27 Cold, rain, snow. 28-31 Mild, rain.

FEB. 2002: Temp. 44° (avg.); precip. 6.5" (2" above avg.). 1-5 Rain, snow north. 6-12 Sunny, seasonable. 13-16 Cold, snow, rain. 17-20 Stormy, warm; heavy rain. 21-23 Mild, sunny. 24-28 Rain, seasonable.

MAR. 2002: Temp. 46.5° (0.5° below avg.); precip. 5.5" (2" above avg.). 1-5 Rain, mild. 6-10 Rain, chilly. 11-18 Seasonable, rain, sunny. 19-21 Sunny, seasonable. 22-31 Rain, mild, then cool.

APR. 2002: Temp. 51.5° (1.5° above avg.); precip. 2" (0.5" below avg.). 1-4 Sunny, pleasant. 5-9 Rain, mild. 10-18 Cool, rain, drizzle. 19-23 Sunny, warm. 24-27 Thunderstorms, then sunny and cool. 28-30 Sunny, warm.

MAY 2002: Temp. 58° (2° above avg.); precip. 2" (avg.). 1-8 Seasonable, sunny, showers. 9-12 Warm, rain. 13-16 Cool, rain. 17-29 Sunny, warm. 30-31 Thunderstorms, cool.

JUNE 2002: Temp. 62° (1° below avg.); precip. 1" (0.5" below avg.). 1-8 Cool, thunderstorms. 9-13 Sunny, pleasant. 14-18 Showers, then sunny. 19-25 Cool, showers. 26-30 Sunny, pleasant.

JULY 2002: Temp. 65.5° (2.5° below avg.); precip. 1.5" (0.5" above avg.). 1-4 Showers north, then sunny. 5-6 Partly cloudy, comfortable. 7-10 Cool, rain. 11-15 Sunny, warm. 16-21 Cool, showers, then sunny. 22-27 Cloudy, seasonable. 28-31 Seasonable, rain.

AUG. 2002: Temp. 68° (1° below avg.); precip. 1" (avg.). 1-4 Rain, cool. 5-9 Sunny, pleasant. 10-13 Cloudy, seasonable. 14-17 Sunny, warm. 18-22 Cloudy, cool. 23-29 Sunny, warm. 30-31 Warm, showers north.

SEPT. 2002: Temp. 66° (2° above avg.); precip. 2" (0.5" below avg. north; 1" above south). 1-8 Sunny, hot. 9-12 Cool, showers. 13-17 Sunny, hot. 18-24 Warm, rain. 25-30 Cloudy, cool, rain.

OCT. 2002: Temp. 55° (1° below avg.); precip. 3" (0.5" below avg.). 1-4 Rain, warm. 5-9 Cool, rain. 10-15 Sunny, pleasant. 16-20 Rain. 21-25 Mild, rain. 26-31 Sunny, cool.

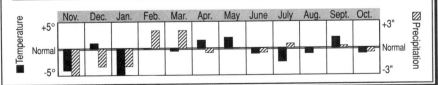

California

SUMMARY: November through March will be drier and warmer than normal, with temperatures averaging one degree above normal in the north and up to three degrees above normal in the south. November will start hot, and early February will be warm. Cold spells will occur in early and mid-December and mid- to late January. November and December will have below-normal rainfall, despite storms late in both months. January and February will have above-normal rainfall. March will be drier than normal, even with rain in the first half.

April and May will be warmer than normal near the coast but cool in the Valley. Expect above-normal rainfall, especially in mid-May, which will have heavy thunderstorms.

June through August will be nearly three degrees warmer than normal near the coast, but the Valley will average one or two degrees cooler than normal. It will be hot in mid- to late June, late July, and mid-August. Expect rain in early June, early to mid-July, and mid-August.

September and October will be warmer than normal near the coast (September will start hot) and cooler than normal in the Valley. Expect above-normal rainfall, especially in the north.

NOV. 2001: Temp. 59° (1° above avg. north; 5° above south); precip. 1.8" (0.7" below avg.). 1-5 Sunny, warm. 6-9 Cloudy, cool. 10-14 Sunny, seasonable. 15-19 Sunny, warm south. 20-26 Cloudy, then sunny; warm south. 27-30 Rain.

DEC. 2001: Temp. 49° (1° below avg.; 3° above south); precip. 0.5" (2" below avg.). 1-4 Cool, showers north. 5-8 Cloudy, mild. 9-15 Cool, showers. 16-22 Sunny, seasonable north; warm south. 23-28 Morning fog, sunny. 29-31 Rain.

JAN. 2002: Temp. 47° (2° below avg.); precip. 3.5" (avg.; 1" above south). 1-7 Rain. 8-12 Sunny, fog in the Valley. 13-19 Rain, seasonable. 20-23 Cold, rain, flurries. 24-31 Sunny, cool.

FEB. 2002: Temp. 56° (4° above avg.); precip. 3.3" (1" above avg. north; 0.5" below south). 1-3 Rain. 4-8 Rain, mild north; warm south. 9-13 Cloudy, mild. 14-18 Stormy. 19-23 Showers. 24-28 Rain north, warm south.

MAR. 2002: Temp. 56° (1° above avg.); precip. 1.5" (1" below avg.). 1-3 Rain. 4-8 Rain north, sunny south. 9-13 Rain. 14-18 Sunny, pleasant. 19-22 Cloudy, warm. 23-25 Cool, showers north. 26-31 Sunny, warm.

APR. 2002: Temp. 58° (1° below avg. east; 1° above west); precip. 1.9" (0.4" above avg.). 1-5 Seasonable, sunny. 6-10 Cloudy, showers. 11-15 Rain, cool, thunderstorms. 16-20 Sunny, mild. 21-23 Sunny, hot. 24-26 Cool, showers north. 27-30 Sunny, warm.

MAY 2002: Temp. 62.5° (2° below avg. east; 1° above west); precip. 2.1" (3" above avg. north; avg. south). 1-8 Cloudy, showers, drizzle. 9-10 Sunny. 11-15 Stormy. 16-19 Cloudy north, sunny south. 20-23 Cloudy, thunderstorms. 24-29 Sunny, hot. 30-31 Sunny, cool.

JUNE 2002: Temp. 69.5° (1° above avg. east; 4° above west); precip. 0.1" (avg.). 1-4 Cloudy, showers. 5-9 Sunny, pleasant; cloudy on the coast. 10-13 Sunny, very hot. 14-19 Sunny, hot. 20-26 Sunny, warm. 27-30 Sunny, hot.

JULY 2002: Temp. 70° (3° below avg. east; 3° above west); precip. 0" (avg.). 1-3 Sunny, warm. 4-9 Sunny, warm, thunderstorms. 10-17 Sunny. 18-25 Sunny, hot. 26-31 Sunny, hot, then cool.

AUG. 2002: Temp. 70° (2° below avg. east; 2° above west); precip. 0" (avg.). 1-5 Sunny, warm. 6-13 Sunny, hot. 14-15 Thunderstorms. 16-22 Sunny, seasonable. 23-31 Sunny, warm.

SEPT. 2002: Temp. 67° (2° below avg. east; 2° above west); precip. 0.8" (1" above avg. north; avg. south). 1-4 Sunny, hot. 5-8 Sunny, warm. 9-12 Thunderstorms. 13-19 Sunny, warm. 20-23 Thunderstorms north. 24-27 Sunny, mild. 28-30 Showers.

OCT. 2002: Temp. 62° (1° below avg. east; 1° above west); precip. 1.8" (1" above avg.). 1-2 Sunny. 3-7 Rain. 8-13 Sunny, pleasant. 14-19 Cloudy, thunderstorms. 20-23 Sunny, mild. 24-31 Sunny north, rain south.

San Francisco

Fresno

Los Angeles

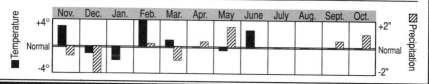

ABSOLUTELY, POSITIVELY

EVERYETHING

YOU NEED TO KNOW ABOUT

MAKING

COMPOST

BY
Adrienne Cook
¬illustrated by Sara Mintz Zwicker

DECAY of once-living

material is the simple definition of composting, a garden practice about which much has been made in recent years. The most familiar example of this occurs in the fall, when billions of leaves hit the ground and are silently transformed into a mushroom-scented, crumbly, dark-brown substance more often—inaccurately—called dirt.

You can re-create this decaying process easily and, in fact, hasten the end result. Why would you? Compost is an extraordinary source of plant nutrients and is remarkable in its ability to chemically balance and build soil. Your plants will love you for it—yielding larger flowers, abundant produce (with, some say, improved flavor), and insect and disease resistance. Here is all you need to know to get started.

The absolute and most basic compost-making is what I call my "passive" system. I stockpile my shredded leaves every fall in a corner of the yard. The pile is big, typically ten feet or more in diameter and four feet high. Then I turn my back on the pile and ignore it.

A year later, I thrust my pitchfork into the steamy center of the pile and pull out compost that is sufficiently decomposed to add to my garden soil. Still a little rough and textured, this compost is not yet at the crumbly "humus" stage that will support a seed-starting project. That comes with time, if I do not use it all the first year.

But I also like to recycle the endless supply of weeds and prunings from the garden, vegetables that rotted or grew too large to eat, kitchen scraps, dead-headed flowers, and even the wonderful mix of manure and hay or sawdust that I get from a neighboring horse farm. This needs to decompose before it goes onto the garden. Uncomposted manure is high in acids that can "burn" plants, especially seedlings. For these, I use an "active" compost system, a method that generates usable compost faster and doesn't take up as much space.

(continued)

WHAT ABOUT A BIN?

WITHOUT a

structure to contain the ingredients, an active compost system will work fine. But it is easier and tidier, and less space is needed to make compost in a bin.

The simplest container is a three-sided pen. The open front allows you to add ingredients and remove compost. An inexpensive one can be fashioned

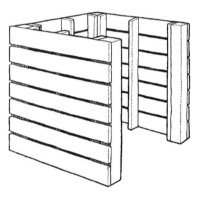

of three discarded shipping pallets (usually available for free) fastened with wire. Another simple structure is a box frame with wire mesh stretched across the frames. You can keep down the cost of this by using scrap lumber for the frame. Wire mesh runs about $10 for a 4x25-foot roll.

One container will suffice, but you may find it difficult to turn the compost within one bin. Turning the ingredients speeds up the process. To make turning easier, build two of these low-cost bins side by side. Start the compost in one bin, and a few weeks later, fork the pile into the other bin. Repeat this periodically.

There are many styles of factory-made bins, and they can be expensive. They are generally made of plastic and range from oversize garbage bins per-

Simple compost bins: one made with shipping pallets (above) and one made with wire mesh stretched across a wooden frame (right).

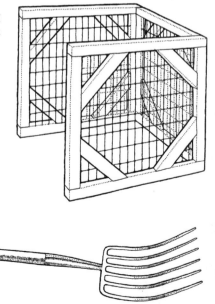

forated to allow air circulation to elaborate drums mounted on a frame that allows you to rotate the entire mechanism to speed decomposition. If you go for a prefab bin, look for a model made from recycled materials, and expect to pay from $100 to $250 for one.

You might see plans in garden books for bins with three ports. These are designed so that you can have a continuous supply of compost. You begin by putting your raw material in the first bin. After a couple of months, fork that into the second bin and start another load of compost in the first. Transfer the material in the second bin to the third bin after a few more weeks. Let it sit there until it's ready to use.

BACK TO THE BASICS

BEFORE you

start building your pile, there are a couple of basic considerations:

■ **SIZE.** The active pile/bin should be between three feet square and as tall (27 cubic feet) and five feet square and at least four feet tall (100 cubic feet). This, according to many studies, generates the optimum heat (145° to $160^\circ F$) for steady decomposition. Although it's handy to have a compost or soil thermometer that tells you how hot your pile is, you don't need one. You can tell there's heat when you pull aside the outer layers of the compost pile and see steam rising from inside. Be careful about feeling it with bare hands; it can burn your skin.

■ **LOCATION.** Most gardeners appreciate having the compost pile near their gardens. You'll be hauling material to and from the pile, so put it in a place that is easy to reach with a wheelbarrow or garden cart. Place it in a level, well-drained location near a water source. Also, consider wintertime disposal of kitchen scraps.

■ **TIME.** It doesn't matter when you start your compost. If you haven't stockpiled your fall leaves (which can be added to the active compost pile at any time, shredded or whole), there are plenty of other organic materials around to start with. In late winter, these might include tree prunings, wood ashes, vegetable scraps—even the Christmas tree, if it's broken up. In the spring, toss in newly pulled weeds that haven't gone to seed, soil from repotted plants, dead houseplants, eggshells, and coffee grounds. Come summer, there's plenty of discarded organic matter—dead flowers, lots of weeds, the debris from cutting back overgrown plants and shrubs, and overgrown zucchinis. (For a more complete list, see page 167.)

(continued)

LAYERS are key to

composting. An active compost pile is built from the ground up, like a layer cake on a cake stand. The cake stand is rough stuff—sticks, twigs, roots, corncobs, woody stems—that permits air to circulate and so speeds up decomposition. Next comes soft stuff, the

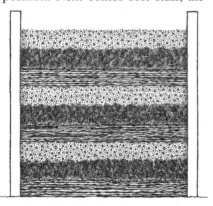

cake: grass clippings, flowers, plants, and vegetables that are still green; shredded leaves; sawdust and wood shavings; and the aforementioned kitchen scraps (but no meats, milk, fat, or bones; use fish and seafood sparingly, and be sure to put these potentially smelly ingredients deep into the middle). The frosting layer in compost includes garden soil, animal manure mixed with hay or sawdust, leaf mold (decomposing, shredded leaves), coffee grounds, discarded potting or germinating soil, and peat moss. The cake and frosting layers can be repeated as often as desired; small twigs, sticks and woody stems, and corncobs also can be added a few at a time, but these are better used as the base for a new or a turned compost pile.

CAN'T WAIT?

WHILE the pas-

sive compost pile is taking a year or more to mature, the active pile can be ready to spread onto a garden in just three months. Adding air, water, and nutrients will speed the process.

Air is provided by building the compost pile on a base. More air can be added by inserting devices—perforated pipes, for example—into the pile. Just as you stir a sauce for even cooking, you can "stir" your compost

to speed it toward its completion. Stirring the compost involves turning it, literally flipping it over, layer by layer, onto a spot next to it, leaving it there for a few weeks, and then flipping it back again. This gets the outside layers into that warm center for even "cooking." How often you do this depends on how much work you want to put into it, how big your compost pile is, and how soon you want your finished product. To have usable compost in three months, flip it at least once, and twice if the pile is large.

Water speeds decomposition. Your compost pile should be thoroughly soaked at its start, and then each month that it doesn't rain, give it another thorough soaking, very slowly oozing water into it for ten minutes and repeating that every couple of hours until it is saturated. Nutrients feed the organisms— worms and microorganisms—that eat away at the raw material and turn it into compost. They'll work faster if they get an energy boost in the form of organic fertilizer or bagged, composted animal manure or, if it's available, barnyard manure. You can use cow, horse, sheep, goat, rabbit, or poultry manure. Among these, the highest in nitrogen also happens to be most fragrant—chicken manure. (Avoid dog, cat, and human waste, which transmit diseases.)

Don't let too much information or too many instructions scare you away from cooking your own compost. There's plenty of room for experimentation, modification, and adjustment. A lot of this depends on what you want to do or can do. In the end, it all will turn to compost. It just takes time.

A RECIPE FOR SUCCESS

Add these ingredients liberally to your active compost pile:

Coffee grounds	Fruit waste	Manure	Seaweed
Corncobs	Grains	Nutshells	Straw
Cornstalks	Grass clippings	Paper	Vegetable scraps
Eggshells	Hair	Peat	Vegetable stalks and
Fish and seafood	Hay	Pine needles	seeds
scraps*	Leaves	Sawdust**	Weeds with no seeds

*Although fish and seafood are excellent compost materials (Native Americans used fish heads as fertilizer), they will attract animals unless they are buried deep in the pile.

**From unpainted, untreated lumber only.

QUICK FIXES FOR A BAD BATCH

■ FOUL ODOR? **Did you add protein foods such as meat and dairy products? You might need more air to penetrate the pile. Turn the compost.**

■ TOO DRY? **Give the pile a good soaking, then water it periodically.**

■ TOO WET? **The pile might be too small. Add woody, dry material—leaves, peat, wood chips—to green organic matter. Make your pile bigger.**

■ NO HEAT OR INSUFFICIENT HEAT? **Not enough nitrogen. Add organic fertilizer and more soft, green ingredients.** □□

DIG DEEPER. Go to www.almanac.com and click on **Article Links 2002** for more information on composting.

Outdoor Planting Table
2 0 0 2

T he best time to plant flowers and vegetables that bear crops above ground is during the *light* of the Moon; that is, from the day the Moon is new to the day it is full. Flowering bulbs and vegetables that bear crops below ground should be planted during the *dark* of the Moon; that is, from the day after it is full to the day before it is new again. The Moon Favorable columns at right give these days, which are based on the Moon's phases for 2002 and the safe periods for planting in areas that receive frost. Consult **page 170** for dates of frosts and lengths of growing seasons. See the **Left-Hand Calendar Pages 64–90** for the exact days of the new and full Moons.

Aboveground Crops Marked (*)

(E) means Early   (L) means Late

Map shading corresponds to shading of date columns.

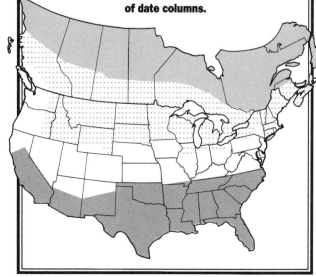

*	Barley	
*	Beans	(E)
		(L)
	Beets	(E)
		(L)
*	Broccoli plants	(E)
		(L)
*	Brussels sprouts	
*	Cabbage plants	
	Carrots	(E)
		(L)
*	Cauliflower plants	(E)
		(L)
*	Celery plants	(E)
		(L)
*	Collards	(E)
		(L)
*	Corn, sweet	(E)
		(L)
*	Cucumbers	
*	Eggplant plants	
*	Endive	(E)
		(L)
*	Flowers	
*	Kale	(E)
		(L)
	Leek plants	
*	Lettuce	
*	Muskmelon	
	Onion sets	
*	Parsley	
	Parsnips	
*	Peas	(E)
		(L)
*	Pepper plants	
	Potatoes	
*	Pumpkin	
	Radishes	(E)
		(L)
*	Spinach	(E)
		(L)
*	Squash	
	Sweet potatoes	
*	Swiss chard	
*	Tomato plants	
	Turnips	(E)
		(L)
*	Watermelon	
*	Wheat, spring	
*	Wheat, winter	

Planting Dates	Moon Favorable	Planting Dates	Moon Favorable	Planting Dates	Moon Favorable	Planting Dates	Moon Favorable
2/15-3/7	2/15-27	3/15-4/7	3/15-28	5/15-6/21	5/15-26, 6/10-21	6/1-30	6/10-24
3/15-4/7	3/15-28	4/15-30	4/15-26	5/7-6/21	5/12-26, 6/10-21	5/30-6/15	6/10-15
8/7-31	8/8-22	7/1-21	7/10-21	6/15-7/15	6/15-24, 7/10-15	—	—
2/7-28	2/7-11, 2/28	3/15-4/3	3/29-4/3	5/1-15	5/1-11	5/25-6/10	5/27-6/9
9/1-30	9/1-5, 9/22-30	8/15-31	8/23-31	7/15-8/15	7/25-8/7	6/15-7/8	6/25-7/8
2/15-3/15	2/15-27, 3/13-15	3/7-31	3/13-28	5/15-31	5/15-26	6/1-25	6/10-24
9/7-30	9/7-21	8/1-20	8/8-20	6/15-7/7	6/15-24	—	—
2/11-3/20	2/12-27, 3/13-20	3/7-4/15	3/13-28, 4/12-15	5/15-31	5/15-26	6/1-25	6/10-24
2/11-3/20	2/12-27, 3/13-20	3/7-4/15	3/13-28, 4/12-15	5/15-31	5/15-26	6/1-25	6/10-24
2/15-3/7	2/28-3/7	3/7-31	3/7-12, 3/29-31	5/15-31	5/27-31	5/25-6/10	5/27-6/9
8/1-9/7	8/1-7, 8/23-9/5	7/7-31	7/7-9, 7/25-31	6/15-7/21	6/25-7/9	6/15-7/8	6/25-7/8
2/15-3/7	2/15-27	3/15-4/7	3/15-28	5/15-31	5/15-26	6/1-25	6/10-24
8/7-31	8/8-22	7/1-8/7	7/10-24	6/15-7/21	6/15-24, 7/10-21	—	—
2/15-28	2/15-27	3/7-31	3/13-28	5/15-6/30	5/15-26, 6/10-24	6/1-30	6/10-24
9/15-30	9/15-21	8/15-9/7	8/15-22, 9/6-7	7/15-8/15	7/15-24, 8/8-15	—	—
2/11-3/20	2/12-27, 3/13-20	3/7-4/7	3/13-28	5/15-31	5/15-26	6/1-25	6/10-24
9/7-30	9/7-21	8/15-31	8/15-22	7/1-8/7	7/10-24	—	—
3/15-31	3/15-28	4/1-17	4/12-17	5/10-6/15	5/12-26, 6/10-15	5/30-6/20	6/10-20
8/7-31	8/8-22	7/7-21	7/10-21	6/15-30	6/15-24	—	—
3/7-4/15	3/13-28, 4/12-15	4/7-5/15	4/12-26, 5/12-15	5/7-6/20	5/12-26, 6/10-20	5/30-6/15	6/10-15
3/7-4/15	3/13-28, 4/12-15	4/7-5/15	4/12-26, 5/12-15	6/1-30	6/10-24	6/15-30	6/15-24
2/15-3/20	2/15-27, 3/13-20	4/7-5/15	4/12-26, 5/12-15	5/15-31	5/15-26	6/1-25	6/10-24
8/15-9/7	8/15-22, 9/6-7	7/15-8/15	7/15-24, 8/8-15	6/7-30	6/10-24	—	—
3/15-4/7	3/15-28	4/15-30	4/15-26	5/7-6/21	5/12-26, 6/10-21	6/1-30	6/10-24
2/11-3/20	2/12-27, 3/13-20	3/7-4/7	3/13-28	5/15-31	5/15-26	6/1-15	6/10-15
9/7-30	9/7-21	8/15-31	8/15-22	7/1-8/7	7/10-24	6/25-7/15	7/10-15
2/15-4/15	2/28-3/12, 3/29-4/11	3/7-4/7	3/7-12, 3/29-4/7	5/15-31	5/27-31	6/1-25	6/1-9, 6/25
2/15-3/7	2/15-27	3/1-31	3/13-28	5/15-6/30	5/15-26, 6/10-24	6/1-30	6/10-24
3/15-4/7	3/15-28	4/15-5/7	4/15-26	5/15-6/30	5/15-26, 6/10-24	6/1-30	6/10-24
2/1-28	2/1-11, 2/28	3/1-31	3/1-12, 3/29-31	5/15-6/7	5/27-6/7	6/1-25	6/1-9, 6/25
2/20-3/15	2/20-27, 3/13-15	3/1-31	3/13-28	5/15-31	5/15-26	6/1-15	6/10-15
1/15-2/4	1/29-2/4	3/7-31	3/7-12, 3/29-31	4/1-30	4/1-11, 4/27-30	5/10-31	5/10-11, 5/27-31
1/15-2/7	1/15-28	3/7-31	3/13-28	4/15-5/7	4/15-26	5/15-31	5/15-26
9/15-30	9/15-21	8/7-31	8/8-22	7/15-31	7/15-24	7/10-25	7/10-24
3/1-20	3/13-20	4/1-30	4/12-26	5/15-6/30	5/15-26, 6/10-24	6/1-30	6/10-24
2/10-28	2/10-11, 2/28	4/1-30	4/1-11, 4/27-30	5/1-31	5/1-11, 5/27-31	6/1-25	6/1-9, 6/25
3/7-20	3/13-20	4/23-5/15	4/23-26, 5/12-15	5/15-31	5/15-26	6/1-30	6/10-24
1/21-3/1	1/29-2/11, 2/28-3/1	3/7-31	3/7-12, 3/29-31	4/15-30	4/27-30	5/15-6/5	5/27-6/5
10/1-21	10/1-5	9/7-30	9/22-30	8/15-31	8/23-31	7/10-31	7/25-31
2/7-3/15	2/12-27, 3/13-15	3/15-4/20	3/15-28, 4/12-20	5/15-31	5/15-26	6/1-25	6/10-24
10/1-21	10/6-21	8/1-9/15	8/8-22, 9/6-15	7/17-9/7	7/17-24, 8/8-22, 9/6-7	7/20-8/5	7/20-24
3/15-4/15	3/15-28, 4/12-15	4/15-30	4/15-26	5/15-6/15	5/15-26, 6/10-15	6/1-30	6/10-24
3/23-4/6	3/29-4/6	4/21-5/2	4/27-5/2	5/15-6/15	5/27-6/9	6/1-30	6/1-9, 6/25-30
2/7-3/15	2/12-27, 3/13-15	3/15-4/15	3/15-28, 4/12-15	5/1-31	5/12-26	5/15-31	5/15-26
3/7-20	3/13-20	4/7-30	4/12-26	5/15-31	5/15-26	6/1-15	6/10-15
1/20-2/15	1/29-2/11	3/15-31	3/29-31	4/7-30	4/7-11, 4/27-30	5/10-31	5/10-11, 5/27-31
9/1-10/5	9/1-5, 9/22-10/5	8/1-20	8/1-7	7/1-8/15	7/1-9, 7/25-8/7	—	—
3/15-4/7	3/15-28	4/15-5/7	4/15-26	5/15-6/30	5/15-26, 6/10-24	6/1-30	6/10-24
2/15-28	2/15-27	3/1-20	3/13-20	4/7-30	4/12-26	5/15-6/10	5/15-26, 6/10
10/15-12/7	10/15-21, 11/4-19, 12/4-7	9/15-10/20	9/15-21, 10/6-20	8/11-9/15	8/11-22, 9/6-15	8/5-30	8/8-22

Frosts and Growing Seasons

Courtesy of National Climatic Center

■ Dates given are normal averages for a light freeze (32°F); local weather and topography may cause considerable variations. The possibility of frost occurring after the spring dates and before the fall dates is 50 percent. The classification of freeze temperatures is usually based on their effect on plants, with the following commonly accepted categories: **Light freeze:** 29° to 32°F—tender plants killed; little destructive effect on other vegetation. **Moderate freeze:** 25° to 28°F—widely destructive effect on most vegetation; heavy damage to fruit blossoms and tender and semihardy plants. **Severe freeze:** 24°F and colder—heavy damage to most plants.

City	State	Growing Season (days)	Last Spring Frost	First Fall Frost	City	State	Growing Season (days)	Last Spring Frost	First Fall Frost
Mobile	AL	272	Feb. 27	Nov. 26	North Platte	NE	136	May 11	Sept. 24
Juneau	AK	133	May 16	Sept. 26	Las Vegas	NV	259	Mar. 7	Nov. 21
Phoenix	AZ	308	Feb. 5	Dec. 15	Concord	NH	121	May 23	Sept. 22
Tucson	AZ	273	Feb. 28	Nov. 29	Newark	NJ	219	Apr. 4	Nov. 10
Pine Bluff	AR	234	Mar. 19	Nov. 8	Carlsbad	NM	223	Mar. 29	Nov. 7
Eureka	CA	324	Jan. 30	Dec. 15	Los Alamos	NM	157	May 8	Oct. 13
Sacramento	CA	289	Feb. 14	Dec. 1	Albany	NY	144	May 7	Sept. 29
San Francisco	CA	*	*	*	Syracuse	NY	170	Apr. 28	Oct. 16
Denver	CO	157	May 3	Oct. 8	Fayetteville	NC	212	Apr. 2	Oct. 31
Hartford	CT	167	Apr. 25	Oct. 10	Bismarck	ND	129	May 14	Sept. 20
Wilmington	DE	198	Apr. 13	Oct. 29	Akron	OH	168	May 3	Oct. 18
Miami	FL	*	*	*	Cincinnati	OH	195	Apr. 14	Oct. 27
Tampa	FL	338	Jan. 28	Jan. 3	Lawton	OK	217	Apr. 1	Nov. 5
Athens	GA	224	Mar. 28	Nov. 8	Tulsa	OK	218	Mar. 30	Nov. 4
Savannah	GA	250	Mar. 10	Nov. 15	Pendleton	OR	188	Apr. 15	Oct. 21
Boise	ID	153	May 8	Oct. 9	Portland	OR	217	Apr. 3	Nov. 7
Chicago	IL	187	Apr. 22	Oct. 26	Carlisle	PA	182	Apr. 20	Oct. 20
Springfield	IL	185	Apr. 17	Oct. 19	Williamsport	PA	168	Apr. 29	Oct. 15
Indianapolis	IN	180	Apr. 22	Oct. 20	Kingston	RI	144	May 8	Sept. 30
South Bend	IN	169	May 1	Oct. 18	Charleston	SC	253	Mar. 11	Nov. 20
Atlantic	IA	141	May 9	Sept. 28	Columbia	SC	211	Apr. 4	Nov. 2
Cedar Rapids	IA	161	Apr. 29	Oct. 7	Rapid City	SD	145	May 7	Sept. 29
Topeka	KS	175	Apr. 21	Oct. 14	Memphis	TN	228	Mar. 23	Nov. 7
Lexington	KY	190	Apr. 17	Oct. 25	Nashville	TN	207	Apr. 5	Oct. 29
Monroe	LA	242	Mar. 9	Nov. 7	Amarillo	TX	197	Apr. 14	Oct. 29
New Orleans	LA	288	Feb. 20	Dec. 5	Denton	TX	231	Mar. 25	Nov. 12
Portland	ME	143	May 10	Sept. 30	San Antonio	TX	265	Mar. 3	Nov. 24
Baltimore	MD	231	Mar. 26	Nov. 13	Cedar City	UT	134	May 20	Oct. 2
Worcester	MA	172	Apr. 27	Oct. 17	Spanish Fork	UT	156	May 8	Oct. 12
Lansing	MI	140	May 13	Sept. 30	Burlington	VT	142	May 11	Oct. 1
Marquette	MI	159	May 12	Oct. 19	Norfolk	VA	239	Mar. 23	Nov. 17
Duluth	MN	122	May 21	Sept. 21	Richmond	VA	198	Apr. 10	Oct. 26
Willmar	MN	152	May 4	Oct. 4	Seattle	WA	232	Mar. 24	Nov. 11
Columbus	MS	215	Mar. 27	Oct. 29	Spokane	WA	153	May 4	Oct. 5
Vicksburg	MS	250	Mar. 13	Nov. 18	Parkersburg	WV	175	Apr. 25	Oct. 18
Jefferson City	MO	173	Apr. 26	Oct. 16	Green Bay	WI	143	May 12	Oct. 2
Fort Peck	MT	146	May 5	Sept. 28	Janesville	WI	164	Apr. 28	Oct. 10
Helena	MT	122	May 18	Sept. 18	Casper	WY	123	May 22	Sept. 22
Blair	NE	165	Apr. 27	Oct. 10	*Frosts do not occur every year.				

OKRA

OUT OF AFRICA AND INTO
THE KITCHEN

"You can have strip pokra,

Give me a girl and a dish of okra."

–Roy Blount Jr., novelist and humorist (b. 1941)

O kra has an image problem to some people's way of thinking. It's slimy. Real slimy. Fresh or frozen, okra pods ooze with slime. Once it's stewed, long mucilaginous strands of chopped okra cling to your fork, your plate, your mouth—or all three. Even southern cooks who are accustomed to okra's sticky personality are split over what to do about it. Some use stewing or deep-frying to nullify the gummy stuff. Others embrace and celebrate the slime as part of okra's subtly scented, delicious charm.

In spite of its public relations issues, okra holds a unique and hallowed spot in America's culinary history, binding our country together since Colonial times. Okra's slippery goo has been used as a kind of natural "food glue" and thickener

BY KRISTA REESE

–illustration, opposite page: courtesy Hunt Institute for Botanical Documentation, Carnegie Mellon University, Pittsburgh, Pa.; from Antonio José Cavanilles' *Monadelphia classics dissertations decem*, 1785–1790.

from its earliest uses in soups and stews to today's bottled ketchup.

A native of Africa, okra was probably first cultivated in Ethiopia or West Africa, according to Alan Davidson, author of *The Oxford Companion to Food* (Oxford University Press, 1999). Later, it spread to North Africa, the Mediterranean region, and India. Early Egyptians recorded its presence beside the Nile River as early as the 13th century.

The slave trade brought okra to the Americas, reaching Brazil and Dutch Guyana by the mid-1600s, and Louisiana by the early 1700s. Thomas Jefferson recorded its Virginia cultivation in 1781, but this annual native of tropical and subtropical climates found a happier home in the hotter fields of the Deep South.

Okra's name is derived from its West African roots, from the Ashanti *nkruma* or *nkru,* which also gave Ghana's capital, Accra, its name. In southern Africa's Bantu tongue, okra was called *quingombo,* which gave us the word *gumbo.* In some southern coastal areas, gumbo means okra stew or the vegetable itself.

Cookbook author Karen Hess, editor of *The Carolina Rice Kitchen: The African Connection* (University of South Carolina Press, 1998), has studied the plant's history extensively. Along with rice, Hess calls okra "the signature dish of the African diaspora."

Currently, Hess is working on a book of "receipts" from Thomas Jefferson's oldest daughter, Martha Jefferson Randolph, and her cousin, Mary Randolph. Their kitchens bore the undeniable imprint of slavery and African cooking. In Hess's manuscript (tentatively titled *Mr. Jefferson's Table: The Culinary Legacy of Monticello,* for the University of South Carolina Press), she notes that Martha Randolph's first recipe was for okra soup, although Martha called it simply "soup." The dish was a sign that the aristocracy had accepted the slaves' influence, Hess says. Other writers have called it the "creolization" of American cooking. In all, there are six recipes for okra or gumbo among the collected family papers.

Today, the South's melting pot bubbles over with okra recipes, and southern cooks and food writers can get pretty bristly about okra. "I don't think it's slimy at all," says cookbook author Damon Fowler (*Beans, Greens, and Sweet Georgia Peaches,* Broadway Books, 1998). "I think it's really wonderful." He says that his recipe, in which small whole, trimmed pods are lightly boiled for just three to four minutes in ¼ cup of water with a dash of butter or olive oil in a heavy-bottomed saucepan, does not produce slime but a succulent sauce. *(continued)*

POD PLANTER

Okra *(Abelmoschus esculentus)* grows quickly, taking only about two months from seed to harvest. Each round, BB-pellet-size seed grows into a tall, generally single-trunked plant, usually around six feet tall. Its flowers are teacup-size, pale yellow, and quickly followed by finger-shaped, short pods. They're not just good eating; dried seedpods make good decorations in dried arrangements.

A member of the mallow family, related to hibiscus, cotton, and hollyhocks, okra is the only one of its kin to have its seedpods harvested as food. Four good cultivars for production are 'Blondy' (dwarf with pale green pods), 'Clemson Spineless' (a tasty, traditional favorite), 'Cajun Queen' (short and stocky, tender even when overmature), and 'Burgundy' (with deep-red foliage and burgundy pods).

Okra seeds have a hard shell and are best soaked for a few hours before sowing. An old-time trick is to soak the seeds in a cup of chlorine bleach for exactly five minutes and then rinse with fresh water. This will help them sprout in a couple of days.

Okra must have warm soil. In the South, the traditional planting time for summer vegetables is early April, when all danger of frost is past. Northerners should wait until Memorial Day or the end of May. Heat- and drought-tolerant, okra will produce all summer if picked regularly. The more you pick, the more flowers will appear. Plants can be tip-pruned to encourage branching and bushier growth. Beware: Okra's large, hairy leaves can cause skin irritation.

Seedpods that are a day or two old (two to four inches long) are softest and most digestible. Pods can reach six to ten inches, becoming woody, unpalatable, and seedy. Thomas Jefferson used to determine okra's freshness by bending the pod. If it gave, it was too old. If it broke, it was just right.

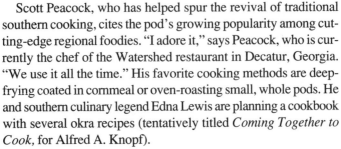

Okra is great for a child's garden: The big seeds are easy for kids to handle, sprout uniformly, and grow all summer with little or no care (no pesticides, no fertilizing, no watering). The plants will still be in production when kids return to school in late summer and fall. Children can also learn to save seeds for next spring's planting.

After the harvest, the seedpods can be dried to make clever holiday decorations. For example, kids can paint each pod to look like a long-bearded Santa Claus.

Scott Peacock, who has helped spur the revival of traditional southern cooking, cites the pod's growing popularity among cutting-edge regional foodies. "I adore it," says Peacock, who is currently the chef of the Watershed restaurant in Decatur, Georgia. "We use it all the time." His favorite cooking methods are deep-frying coated in cornmeal or oven-roasting small, whole pods. He and southern culinary legend Edna Lewis are planning a cookbook with several okra recipes (tentatively titled *Coming Together to Cook,* for Alfred A. Knopf).

Peacock notes that okra is a frequent offering at nationally recognized Atlanta restaurants like Bacchanalia and the Japanese Soto (where it is sliced paper-thin, seasoned, and stirred for a long time to macerate it and lessen its viscosity—then served uncooked but highly flavored).

"Today, you can find okra in many markets where you never used to see it," says Peacock. African and Asian immigrants have helped drive this new demand for okra, a standard ingredient in Indian cooking.

As far as John T. Edge is concerned, bring it on, goop and all: "I like it any way I can get it," he says, "stewed, boiled, fried—whatever. I don't find it off-putting." The director of the Southern Foodways Alliance at the University of Mississippi, Edge also wrote the introduction to *Mrs. Wilkes' Boardinghouse Cookbook* (Ten Speed Press, 2001). At that venerable Savannah institution, locals and tourists line up around the block to savor Mrs. Wilkes' Old South delicacies, served family-style. "What's interesting about Mrs. Wilkes is that she's often serving people who are on their first sojourn into the South," says Edge. "If you're willing to take okra on Mrs. Wilkes' terms, you're in for a long and passionate love affair."

RECIPES

TOMATO-AND-OKRA GUMBO

"People are always asking me how to make this," says Mrs. Wilkes. "It's a good accompaniment to most anything on your plate."

8 medium tomatoes, chopped;
   or 1 can (28 ounces) tomatoes
2 pounds baby okra, fresh or
   frozen, cut into 1/2-inch pieces
1/2 teaspoon salt
1 tablespoon butter or margarine
3 slices bacon, cooked and
   crumbled

Put chopped tomatoes into a saucepan, and add okra, salt, and butter or margarine. Cover and cook on medium heat for 20 minutes or until tender. Sprinkle with crumbled bacon. **Serves 8.**

Reprinted by permission from Mrs. Wilkes' Boardinghouse Cookbook *(Ten Speed Press, 2001).*

BUTTERMILK-FRIED OKRA

1 pound fresh okra
1/2 teaspoon salt
1-1/2 cups buttermilk
2 cups self-rising flour
vegetable oil to depth of 1 inch,
   heated in skillet

Wash and drain okra. Remove tip and stem ends. Cut into ¾-inch pieces. Put into a bowl, sprinkle with salt, add buttermilk, and stir until well coated. Let stand for 15 minutes. Drain well and dredge in flour. In a medium saucepan, deep-fry in hot oil at 375°F until golden brown. Drain on paper towels. **Serves 6.**

Reprinted by permission from the Lake Murray-Irmo Women's Club Cookbook *(1997).*

THE WORLD'S BIGGEST POD PARTY

Okra has been celebrated each year since 1974 at the Okra Strut Festival in the tiny town of Irmo, South Carolina. Inspired by a local radio personality who claimed that the "ancient Irmese" subsisted entirely on okra, the Okra Strut now draws some 90,000 visitors. The Women's Club sells more than 1,600 pounds of fried okra each year. A hardy few brave the okra-eating contest, won by the first to consume two pounds of the cold, boiled vegetable. The Okra Strut Festival is held on the last Friday and Saturday in September. Call 803-407-6440 for information. □□

Find more okra recipes at www.almanac.com.

Mr. Smith's MADDENING Mind-Manglers

Test your math and logic skills with these puzzles, compiled for *The Old Farmer's Almanac* by RAYNOR R. SMITH SR., mathematics teacher at Keene High School, Keene, New Hampshire.

Answers appear on page 225.

1 Claire's grandmother made her famous giant chocolate chip cookies for the school fair. She told the fair director that because they were so big, she made fewer than a dozen. She said that Claire would bring the cookies to school in a box *and* that she would write the number of cookies she made on the box in such a way that Claire couldn't sneak any cookies. Claire overheard her grandmother. Still, she was able to eat three cookies before delivering them, and the fair director never knew she ate them. How did she keep her secret? (There are at least two answers.)

2 Place the digits 1 through 8 each in a separate box in the figure below, such that no two consecutive digits are in boxes that touch each other in any way (corner to corner or side by side).

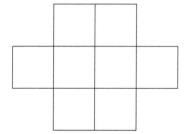

3 The Fungwald City Parking Garage has exactly 400 parking pods for vehicles. A motorcycle uses one pod and is charged $1.50; a car uses two pods and is charged $2.25; and a truck uses three pods at a cost of $3.00. What is the greatest amount of money that the garage can make on a given day if the exact same number of each type of vehicle parks there?

4 Jordan invented a new, stronger, more durable brick—but no one knows how much the brick weighs except Jordan. Instead of simply telling the weight, Jordan came up with a Brick Riddle. See if you can solve it:

If a brick weighs nine ounces plus half a brick, how much does a brick and a half weigh?

5 Substitute a different digit for each letter below to make the statement mathematically correct. (Where the letters are the same, the digits must be the same.)

H A L F
+ H A L F
W H O L E

6 Rocky's boss at the nursery told him to plant 20 rosebushes at the Maxwell Mansion and make sure he did five rows of four bushes each. When Rocky got to the mansion, there were only 10 bushes. "Oh, well," he sighed, and planted the bushes. When he got back to the nursery, the boss asked him if he had planted the bushes in five rows of four each, and he said, "Yes!" How did he do it with only 10 bushes? (Your answer should be a drawing of his garden.)

7 Mr. Hacker, a heavy smoker, decided to give up his unhealthy habit forever. "I'll smoke only these cigarettes I have left, and I'll never smoke again!" he declared. Each time Mr. Hacker smoked one of his smelly cigarettes, he would smoke exactly two-thirds of it and then put it out. He realized that the habit was harder to break than he expected, so with the help of some cellophane tape, he put the remaining pieces together to get more "smokes." If he started with 27 cigarettes, how many "smokes" did he get before he quit?

8 Rob and Ray were discussing the investments they had made. Rob said, "I invested $1,000 two years ago in the stock market. The first year, I made an astounding 80% return on my investment. This year, I went down only 40%, so I did well." Ray answered, "Well, I did better. I invested $1,000 at 4% per year, and for the two years, I made more than you!" Who is right? □□

12 WAYS TO MAKE A CHAMPION

BY MEL ALLEN

You don't have to send your kids to specialized sports camps or get a professional trainer to help them succeed in sports. You need ingenuity, caring, and just maybe some chickens to chase around, as you'll see from these famous athletes, who share stories of the games, amusements, and chance events that helped them.

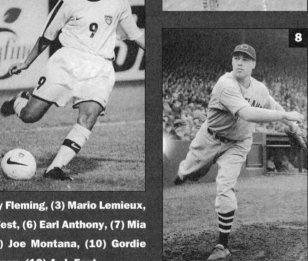

(1) Davis Love III, (2) Peggy Fleming, (3) Mario Lemieux, (4) Doug Flutie, (5) Jerry West, (6) Earl Anthony, (7) Mia Hamm, (8) Bob Feller, (9) Joe Montana, (10) Gordie Howe, (11) Rickey Henderson, (12) A. J. Foyt

1 COME OUT SWINGING

DAVIS LOVE III

GOLFER

Hometown: Sea Island, Georgia

■ **Career Highlights:** Since turning pro in 1985, won 14 Professional Golfers' Association tournaments, including the 1997 PGA championship.

■ **Basic Training:** Davis's father was the teaching pro at the Cloisters resort on Sea Island, Georgia. "The most fun we had was practicing the height of our pitch shots. Dad would park a golf cart near the edge of a practice green and have me hit balls over the roof, under the roof, over the back rack, past the front wheel— anything we could think of. It's very important to learn to hit pitches different heights, because the height of a pitch shot will determine how much the shot rolls."

2 GET UP EARLY

PEGGY FLEMING

FIGURE SKATER

Hometown: Pasadena, California

■ **Career Highlights:** Won the Olympic

gold medal in women's figure skating at Grenoble, France, in 1968.

■ **Basic Training:** Peggy practiced ice skating at the local arena from 5:00 to 7:00 every morning. At that hour, the ice was chewed up from the previous night's skaters. Her father convinced the arena to let him run the Zamboni, the machine that smoothes the ice. "We would arrive at the arena in pitch-blackness, and Dad would make his way across the building to the light switch. It was big and empty, dark and scary in there for the first few moments. Dad would resurface the ice, and I would start skating on the first ice of the day."

3 ICE UP

MARIO LEMIEUX

HOCKEY CENTER

Hometown: Montreal, Quebec

■ **Career Highlights:** One of the most gifted hockey players in history. Joined the Pittsburgh Penguins, 1984. Named to nine all-star games. Named National Hockey League Most Valuable Player (MVP) four times. In 1987, scored the winning goal to lead Team Canada to victory over the U.S.S.R. in the three-game Canada Cup

series. In 1991 and 1992, led the Penguins to Stanley Cup championships. Retired after the 1996-97 season, when he led the NHL in scoring for the sixth time. Inducted into the Hockey Hall of Fame, 1997. Became part-owner of the Penguins and, in December 2000, returned to the ice as a player.

■ **Basic Training:** When Mario and his two brothers were young—too young to play alone in the streets or be left alone at the local ice arena—his mother got an idea. She and his father hauled snow into the house and covered her living room rug. She packed it down tight and opened all the doors and windows, giving her family its own indoor ice rink. Soon the three toddlers were in their skates and laughing. By the time Mario was four years old, people were talking about his hockey skills.

4 GRAB THE SPOON

DOUG FLUTIE

FOOTBALL QUARTERBACK

Hometown: Natick, Massachusetts

■ **Career Highlights:** Won the Heisman Trophy while attending Boston College, 1984. Named MVP in the Canadian Football League six times, 1990 to 1997. Passed for a record 48 touchdowns  in 1994. Joined the NFL's Buffalo Bills in 1998 and was named to the Pro Bowl. Signed a six-year contract with the San Diego Chargers in 2001.

■ **Basic Training:** Dick Flutie, Doug's father, taught his three sons a game called spoons: "You have a card table. You put one spoon in the middle. A person says, 'Ready, go!' The first person who can grab the spoon and bring it back wins. It's a good way to improve hand speed."

5 DRIBBLE ON DIRT

JERRY WEST

BASKETBALL GUARD

Hometown: Cheylan, West Virginia

■ **Career Highlights:** Played for the Los Angeles Lakers, 1961 to 1974. Named to the National Basketball Association all-star team every season. The third player in league history  to score more than 25,000 points. Inducted into the Basketball Hall of Fame, 1979.

■ **Basic Training:** Small and slight in junior high school, Jerry failed to make the football, baseball, or track teams. So he turned to basketball, practicing shots alone, sometimes until his hands bled, no matter what the weather, shooting at a hoop nailed to a shed in his family's yard. His signature shot in the NBA was his quick release off a single hard dribble, a shot he perfected on his dirt "court."

6 HAVE A BALL

EARL ANTHONY

BOWLER

Hometown: Tacoma, Washington

■ **Career Highlights:** First bowler to reach $1 million in career earnings. Between 1974 and 1983, won the Professional Bowlers Association Player of the Year award six times. Widely considered to be the greatest bowler of all time.

■ **Basic Training:** Earl perfected his timing and footwork by shadow bowling: "Shadow bowling is the practice of bowling at imaginary pins; that is, rolling the ball down an empty lane. I found that by shadow bowling, I could concentrate more completely on the bowling problem I was having at that time. I would sometimes shadow bowl 25 to 30 games a day. It was much less expensive, of course, and really it proved to be most effective in improving my bowling style. Sometimes I would trade the alley owner a cleanup job on his pins for letting me shadow bowl on an otherwise unused lane." **(continued)**

7 PLAY THE BOYS

MIA HAMM

SOCCER FORWARD

Hometown: Chapel Hill, North Carolina

■ **Career Highlights:**  All-time leading goal scorer for U.S. National Women's Soccer Team. Named U.S. soccer's Female Athlete of the Year five times, 1994 to 1998. First-ever three-time U.S. Soccer Athlete of the Year, 1994 to 1996. At age 15, was youngest woman ever to play for the U.S. National Women's Soccer Team. Considered the best all-around woman soccer player in the world.

■ **Basic Training:** "Playing with boys helped me develop that combative spirit I have today." Because the teenage boys were stronger and faster, Mia says, "I had to start beating them tactically and technically, not just physically. That brought an entirely different dimension to my game, and having to make decisions at high speed helped me even more."

8 FIELD A TEAM

BOB FELLER

BASEBALL PITCHER

Hometown: Van Meter, Iowa

■ **Career Highlights:** Signed to a major-league contract at age 16. Struck out 17 Philadelphia Athletics players at age 17, establishing a new American League record. Star pitcher for the Cleveland Indians, 1936 to 1956. Won 20 or more games per season six times, including three no-hitters and 12 one-hitters (three of these before the age of 21). Elected to the Baseball Hall of Fame, 1962. One of the fastest-throwing pitchers of all time.

■ **Basic Training:** Growing up in rural Iowa, top baseball competition was scarce, so Bob's father built a baseball field "complete with bleachers, scoreboard, and refreshments right there on the farm." Beginning at age 13, Bob played summer-week-end doubleheaders there against semipro players in their 20s who came from all over Iowa to test themselves against him.

9 HIT THE HOLE

JOE MONTANA

FOOTBALL QUARTERBACK

Hometown: Monongahela, Pennsylvania

■ **Career Highlights:** Led the San Francisco 49ers to four Super Bowl championships. Named All-Pro seven times. Named National Football League MVP twice. Inducted into the Football Hall of Fame, 2000.

■ **Basic Training:** When Joe's father came home from work, he and Joe went to the neighbor's yard, where a tire swing hung from a tree. Joe's dad would push the tire back and forth, and Joe would try to throw a football through its  center. Other times, his father ran pass patterns.

🔟 HORSE AROUND

GORDIE HOWE

HOCKEY RIGHT WING

Hometown: Saskatoon, Saskatchewan

■ **Career Highlights:** Canada's "Mr. Hockey." From 1946 to 1972, played 25 seasons with the Detroit Red Wings, one season with the Hartford Whalers. Selected to the National Hockey League all-star team a record 21 times. Set records for

most regular-season games, most career goals in regular-season play, and most career points by a right wing. Inducted into the Hockey Hall of Fame, 1972.

■ **Basic Training:** Gordie grew up poor in the midst of the Depression, and hockey equipment was scarce. His mother told the Toronto *Globe and Mail* about Gordie's first skates: "There were a lot of people on social aid. A neighbor lady, whose husband was sick, came to the door with a grain sack filled with things and asked me if I would buy it to help her feed her baby. I reached into my milk money and gave her a dollar and a half. We dumped the contents of the sack on the floor. Out fell a pair of skates. Gord pounced on them." Later Gordie trailed after milk wagons collecting the round horse droppings, what he called "road apples," to use as pucks.

🔟 CHASE CHICKENS

RICKEY HENDERSON

BASEBALL OUTFIELDER

Hometown: Pine Bluff, Arkansas

■ **Career Highlights:** Called the "man of steal." Holds the major-league records for stolen bases in a season (130) and career (1,339). Named American League MVP in 1990 while with the Oakland Athletics.

■ **Basic Training:** Rickey chased chickens on his grandmother's farm: "Put dozens of chickens together in one coop, and they run every which way. I had to be fast to keep up with them, but there wasn't a chicken on that entire farm that could outrun me. I think that's when Momma realized I was going to be faster than most kids."

🔟 TAKE THE WHEEL

A. J. FOYT

RACE CAR DRIVER

Hometown: Houston, Texas

■ **Career Highlights:** First four-time winner of the Indianapolis 500, winning in 1961, 1964, 1967, and 1977.

■ **Basic Training:** When A. J. was five years old, his father built him a race car: "A blue and white midget-type race car, with a number 8 painted on it. Powered

by a three-horsepower lawnmower motor, it could go maybe 50 miles an hour. [He] took me and that race car out to the Houston Speed Bowl. . . . I was supposed to drive the midget around the track, sort of a prerace show for the fans." But A. J. had other plans. He challenged a top midget-racer named Doc Cossey to a race. A. J. won. "From that moment on, my only thoughts were of race cars." □□

Fly Rod Crosby?

A tale of one of America's most accomplished—but least known—anglers.

A CENTURY AGO, every fly fisherman worth his fanwing (that's a dry fly) knew the name and admired the skill of a six-foot-tall angler from the backwoods of Maine. "Fly Rod Crosby was absolutely formidable with a fishing rod," says Gary Tanner, executive director of the American Museum of Fly Fishing in Manchester, Vermont. "We're talking about someone who could cast farther than just about anyone, catch more than a fish a minute, and reel in hundreds of trout in an afternoon." These accomplishments were all the more remarkable given the fact that Fly Rod was a prim and thoroughly proper Victorian lady.

Cornelia Crosby, or "Fly Rod," as she came to be known, was born in 1854 in Phillips, a small, pristine town nestled among the mountains and lakes of western

A FORMIDABLE FIGURE. *So deft was her skill and so available the fish in Maine's Rangeley region that Fly Rod could catch more than a fish a minute—taking 31 trout in 30 minutes one day.*

b y   V i c t o r i a   D o u d e r a

Maine. Her father died of tuberculosis when she was a toddler, and shortly thereafter, Fly Rod herself was diagnosed with the disease. Advised to spend as much time as possible in the great outdoors, she grew up roaming the woods and streams of the neighboring countryside, testing what she described as "the healing power of nature." Her earliest experience with a rod and reel came during one such excursion: "A brook full of trout came laughingly dashing down the mountainside, and from there I took my first trout, with an alder pole."

When she and a friend visited the Rangeley region of Maine's North Woods in 1881, Fly Rod was smitten with the sporting life of rustic hotels and sprawling fishing camps. An articulate writer, she began describing her hunting and fishing experiences for her hometown newspaper, the *Phillips Phonograph*. In her column, called "Fly Rod's Notebook," she shared fishing secrets, anecdotes, and even a bit of backwoods society gossip about the famous politicians and businessmen who frequented the camps. So entertaining were her "scribblings" that several national newspapers throughout the East soon carried her column as well.

Despite occasional relapses of tuberculosis, Fly Rod juggled several careers. She was a journalist, a bank clerk, a telegrapher, a guide, and a publicist for the Central Maine Railroad. In the course of her colorful life, she also ac-complished legendary feats: She was the woman who shot the last caribou legally in Maine; she held the first registered guide license in that state; she was a champion marketer who coined the phrase "The Nation's Playground"; and she was a crack shot who competed against her friend Annie Oakley in a sharpshooting contest. "She was a pro athlete 80 years before professional women's sports were taken seriously in North America," says historian Julia Hunter, coauthor of *Fly Rod Crosby: The Woman Who Marketed Maine* (Tilbury House, 2000).

Yet she always made time to do what she loved best—fishing. "I would rather fish any day than go to heaven," she once confessed to an interviewer. As soon as the ice left Maine's inland lakes, Fly Rod and her split-bamboo rods were there, tempting the wary brook trout she called "speckled beauties." Sporting a dark-colored long skirt and knee-high button boots, Fly Rod often outfished her male companions and encouraged other women to do the same. "Why should not a woman do her fair share of tramping, hunting, and fishing, and ask no odds of the men?" Fly Rod once mused in her column. "Thank kind Providence the time is past when it was unladylike for a woman to be a good shot or a skillful angler."

Meanwhile, her fame as a Maine woods expert grew. She tracked bear, moose, and caribou; paddled canoes

HOOKED FOR LIFE. *Fly Rod with a companion at the foot of Mt. Keneo on Moosehead Lake in Maine. "I would rather fish any day than go to heaven," she once said.*   –photo: Maine State Museum

down rushing rivers; and shot partridge and duck on the wing. "Her prowess as a huntress and as a fisherwoman has been heralded all over the country," boasted a newspaper clipping saved by her friend Kathleen Toothacker. "She thinks nothing of taking a forty-mile tramp, and has gone into the woods with the snow two feet deep on the ground. She can follow a trail with the sagacity of an old woodsman."

Fly Rod became a bona fide celebrity at the first Sportsmen's Exposition at New York's Madison Square Garden in 1895. On one peak day of attendance, 15,000 people admired her daring display of a Maine log cabin she had built herself, as well as several stuffed deer, moose, fish, and birds. The next year's show featured a tank full of live trout and

salmon (shipped by train from Bangor) into which she demonstrated her casting abilities. Though some folks were shocked by the 42-year-old's new green leather suit, tanned in Paris, with its scandalously short knee-length skirt, most were thrilled to see the "Queen of Anglers" in action. Newspapers up and down the eastern seaboard reported her exploits, with the *New York Journal* calling her "an athletic country girl, born in the state of Maine . . . as proud of her $1,000 collection of fishing tackle as most girls are of souvenir spoons or blue and white china."

Politically, Fly Rod was active in legislation to protect fish and game—although not so much for the animals as for the sportsmen. She was a vocal supporter of the technique now called "catch and

🐟 Dame Julianna Berners was such a fly-fishing fan that in 1496, she penned the first treatise ever written on the sport.

🐟 Four centuries later, Mary Orvis Marbury wrote *My Favorite Flies*, the first book containing fly patterns from around the world.

🐟 More recently, Joan Wulff of Lew Beach, New York, won the national fly-casting distance title in 1951, besting all the men who had entered. In her 70s, Ms. Wulff is still sought out by anglers who want to learn her techniques.

🐟 Nearly one-fifth of fly fishermen are women, estimates the International Game Fishing Association, and that number is growing.

release," at a time when hauls of more than a hundred fish a day were common. "There is no one who enjoys fishing more than I," she wrote, "and yet we don't want to have to give it up for many years because the trout have all been put on ice and given a ride over the narrow gauge railroad."

"Fly Rod Crosby was a real pioneer, able not just to succeed but to excel in what was a bastion of maleness," says Tanner. "I don't think she was seen as a curiosity; she was taken seriously by serious fishermen. They listened, for instance, when she urged preservation of wildlife."

Despite being ahead of her time in fish and game matters, Fly Rod held on to some old-fashioned values. "She was the only female member of the Maine Sportsmen's Fish and Game Association, and yet she was completely against the idea of women voting," says Hunter. As Fly Rod herself once explained: "I am a very strong anti-suffrage woman. I have too much faith in the men of these United States to want to vote."

"She was a woman of contradictions," says Hunter. "She was a proper Victorian lady who held tea parties, taught Sunday school, and amassed a collection of more than 200 china pitchers. She'd been to a finishing school as a girl and was always ladylike. She kept her feelings to herself and was determinedly cheerful, even when dealing with a severe illness that plagued her all her life."

Despite poor health, Fly Rod lived to age 93. When she died in 1946, the *Rangeley Record* ran her obituary on page 1, ending with: "Rangeley has lost one of its most famous people, and America has lost its most famous woman sportsman. May her soul rest in peace." □□

GO FISH! For a list of U.S. fly-fishing spots and what you can expect to catch there, as well as 20 fly-fishing terms and information on a special fly-fishing program for women with breast cancer, click on **Article Links 2002** at www.almanac.com.

Best Fishing Days, 2002

Probably the best fishing times are when the ocean tides are restless before their turn and in the first hour of ebbing. All fish in all waters, salt and fresh, feed most heavily at those times.

The best temperatures for different fish species vary widely, of course, and are important mainly if you are going to have your own fishpond. The best temperatures for brook trout are 45° to 65°F. Brown trout and rainbow trout are more tolerant of higher temperatures. Smallmouth black bass do best in cool water. Horned pout take what they find.

Most of us go fishing when we can get time off, not because it is the best time. But there *are* best times, according to fishing lore:

■ One hour before and one hour after high tides, and one hour before and one hour after low tides. (The times of high tides for Boston are given on pages 64–90 and corrected for your locality on pages 234–235. Inland, the times for high tides correspond with the times the Moon is due south. Low tides are halfway between high tides.)

■ During "the morning rise" (after sunup for a spell) and "the evening rise" (just before sundown and the hour or so after).

■ When the barometer is steady or on the rise. (But, of course, even in a three-day driving northeaster, the fish aren't going to give up feeding. Their hunger clock keeps right on working, and the smart fisherman will find just the right bait.)

■ When there is a hatch of flies—caddis flies or mayflies, commonly. (The fisherman will have to match the hatching flies with *his* fly or go fishless.)

■ When the breeze is from a westerly quarter rather than from the north or east.

■ When the water is still or rippled, rather than during a wind.

■ Starting on the day the Moon is new and continuing through the day it is full.

Moon Between New & Full, 2002

- January 13–28
- February 12–27
- March 13–28
- April 12–26
- May 12–26
- June 10–24
- July 10–24
- August 8–22
- September 6–21
- October 6–21
- November 4–19
- December 4–19

What People Fish for Most (freshwater)

Bass	35%
Trout	18%
Catfish	11%
All species	9%
Bream	6%
Crappie	6%
Carp/muskie/panfish/ pike/shad/steelhead/ striper	5%
Walleye	5%
Perch	3%
Salmon	2%

–courtesy American Sportfishing Association

MOCKINGBIRDS

LOVE 'EM OR LOATHE 'EM, BUT AT LEAST GIVE 'EM A LISTEN

by Mike Handley

The words below, first published in 1960 by novelist Harper Lee, of Monroeville, Alabama, explain southerners' affection for the drab-colored mockingbird, as common in the region as pinecones.

> *"Mockingbirds don't do one thing but make music for us to enjoy. . . . They don't do one thing but sing their hearts out for us. That's why it's a sin to kill a mockingbird."*
>
> –To Kill a Mockingbird

Lee wasn't alone in singing the mockingbird's praises. Many years earlier, in 1870, John J. Audubon, writing in *The Birds of America*, described the mocker's appeal: "There is probably no bird in the world that possesses all the musical qualifications of this king of song, who has derived all from Nature's self."

Of course, not everyone thinks so kindly of these birds. Curiosity-seekers have their heads dive-bombed as this winged creature protects its nest from onlookers. Light sleepers in suburbia often curse the incessant serenade. And birdwatchers rarely pay them much attention.

But what this feisty gray bird lacks in plumage and tact, it more than compensates for with a songbook that is unrivaled among North American birds. In a voice that some believe is sweeter than that of the nightingale, mockingbirds typically sing the same tune three or more times before going on to the next melody, singing this way sometimes for hours on end, including at night when there is a full Moon or artificial lighting.

Their repertoires might include the songs of other

THE MOST BOOKISH OF BIRDS

Few birds have been as honored in literature as the temperamental mockingbird has. It has appeared in numerous novels and plays and has figured prominently in other works, including the following:

■

Walt Whitman's poem "Out of the Cradle Endlessly Rocking"

■

The sonnet "To the Mocking-Bird" by Richard Henry Wilde

■

Richard Milburn's familiar song, "Listen to the Mockingbird," which he wrote in 1855.

MASTERFUL SONGBIRD
In addition to being a great mimic, the northern mockingbird has a sweet voice.

birds, as well as their attempts to mimic sounds in their everyday environment. They've been known to imitate barking dogs, squeaky gates, pianos, sirens, and even the sound of a cackling hen. The greatest number of imitations by one mockingbird has been noted as 32. Other sources have found that number to be over 100—but whatever the number, the birds' abilities are remarkable. Their mimicry is so precise that even electronic analysis can't tell the imitation from the original.

> *Mockingbirds have been known to imitate barking dogs, squeaky gates, pianos, sirens, and even the sound of a cackling hen.*

In the spring, the males sing in an effort to attract a mate. After attracting a female, the male takes the lead in building the nest. Although some believe that the female does not sing during this mating time, she does; her song is much quieter and occurs mostly when the male is away from the nest.

The female lays three to five pale-greenish-blue speckled eggs sometime between March and May. After the last one is laid, she sits on the eggs until they hatch, about 12 days later. During the next 12 days, both parents feed the youngsters. In the fall, males and females all sing, proclaiming their winter territory, which is usually a food source such as a fruit-bearing tree or bush.

There are about ten different species of mockingbirds, ranging from southern Canada to Chile and Argentina. The most common one in the United States is the northern mockingbird, particularly prevalent below the Mason-Dixon line.

To date, five southern states—Texas, Florida, Arkansas, Tennessee, and Mississippi (in that order)—have claimed it as their state bird. In Texas, it wasn't the bird's vocal talent, however, that impressed lawmakers in 1927. Despite a push by *The Dallas Morning News* to declare the wild turkey the state bird, legislators there sided with the Federation of Women's Clubs in choosing the mockingbird. Their unanimous resolution praised the bird's prowess as a "fighter for the protection of his home, falling, if need be, in its defense, like any true Texan."

No encroacher, including snakes, cats, dogs, hawks, or humans, is too large or too fierce for the 9- to 11-inch bird to attack if one strays too close to its nest or favorite food source. In fact, in 1986, Houston mail carriers received *Texas Monthly* magazine's Bum Steer Award for refusing to deliver mail because of threatening mockingbirds.

With such a clever and spunky personality, the mockingbird has become a natural icon for its native region. From 18th-century naturalist William Bartram, who identified the bird's call with an idyllic, agrarian South, to Harper Lee, who used the bird as a symbol of contemporary racial injustice, the mockingbird continues to inspire and move southern hearts. □□

MORE ON MOCKINGBIRDS
Go to **www.almanac.com** and click on **Article Links 2002** to learn more about the legend and lore of mockingbirds.

The
HOLLAND TUNNEL

A Story of Tragedy and Triumph

One of the greatest engineering feats of modern times is virtually invisible. Tourists rarely, if ever, pose in front of it, it has inspired no movies, and only one meager technical book has been written about it. Soon after it was completed, in 1927, most people mistakenly thought it was named after a European country.

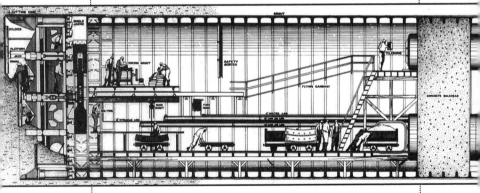

THE VISION. *A longitudinal view of the tunneling operations: The shield is at the far left; dollies carry away mud and deliver the cast-iron sections used for the walls.*

One hundred years ago, New York City was becoming a sprawling metropolis, and the island of Manhattan was a burgeoning borough. The streets were clogged with thousands of workers and all means of transportation—horses and buggies, omnibuses and wagons—with drivers shouting and cursing. Then all of a sudden, there were cars—lots of them, with horns honking and engines cranking. The traffic was especially bad for vehicles traveling between Manhattan and New Jersey from the island's Canal Street area. Every day, mornings and nights, 20,000 vehicles laden with people and freight waited hours for ferries to take them across the mile-wide Hudson River.

In 1906, the Bridge and Tunnel Commissions from New York and New Jersey formed a coalition to address the problem of getting people and vehicles across the Hudson River. Eventually, in 1913, they decided to build a tunnel. It would be the first in the world designed specifically for motor traffic, would double the traffic load across the river, and would cut the 20-minute ferry ride in half. The skeptics howled. It couldn't be done, they said. **(continued)**

THE VISIONARY. *Clifford Holland, chief engineer of the tunnel, worked obsessively to accomplish what many people thought was impossible.*

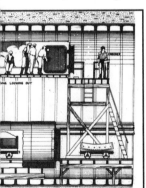

by Jamie Kageleiry

–photos and illustrations: The Port Authority of New York and New Jersey

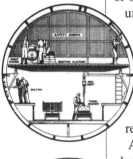

THE RENDERING.

Cross-sectional views of erecting the cast-iron wall (top), bolting and grouting the wall (middle), and four locks, or pressure chambers (bottom).

I n fact, the project was daunting. The tunnel would be 1¾ miles long, and a mile of that would be under water, 16 feet beneath the river bottom. Engineers had no idea what they would encounter—silt or solid rock. In addition, they would have to design metal joints so the tunnel could move fractions of an inch in response to shifting tides and temperatures. To accommodate several lanes of traffic, the tunnel would demand a vastly larger diameter than any railroad or subway tube ever had, and it would require a solution to a unique 20th-century problem: how to eliminate the auto exhaust that would accumulate. Without ventilation, drivers and their passengers would pass out from the poisonous carbon monoxide before reaching the other side.

After finally winning public and legislative approval in 1919, the commission named 36-year-old Clifford Holland as chief engineer. Holland had designed several of the city's subway tunnels; he knew he could design a ventilation system.

Holland called his design "vertical transverse flow." It involved 42 blowing fans and 42 exhaust fans housed in four ten-story ventilation buildings (two at each end of the tunnel), as well as a system of air shafts along the length of the tubes. The fans would circulate clean air through the length of tunnel; the air would be completely changed every 90 seconds.

Work on the new tunnel began on October 13, 1920. Every morning, Holland left his wife, Anna, and four daughters in Brooklyn and

went to work on the tunnel. He was among America's first generation of commuters, driving to a job from a home in the suburbs.

Holland's design called for "twin" tubes—each measuring 20 feet wide and 12½ feet high and having two lanes—that would run together within one large tube. The tunnel was built from both ends, with a team of workers, or sandhogs, in each of the two tubes coming from the New Jersey side, and another two teams coming from the Manhattan side. Each team followed an enormous 240-ton hydraulically powered shield, a tube-shaped metal box through which the men in the front dug, drilled, and blasted forward. Those in the rear erected the cast-iron ribs, or lining, of

THE REALITY.

Occasionally, a void in the silt caused the compressed air in the tunnel to rush out through the shield, allowing water and mud to flow back in.

The job was fraught with hazards. . . . Dynamite blasts stirred up fumes and deadly dust. "Blowouts" sent men scrambling for the exit.

the tunnel. Later, the walls and ceiling would be tiled. The shield was pushed ahead through the earth after every few feet of digging. On a good day, the shield moved about 40 feet; on bad days, not at all. Most of the digging was through silt, but near the New York shore, the workers ran into 1,000 feet of solid rock, which they had to blast through. Progress slowed to less than a foot a day.

Troubles Above and Below

Above ground, political walls of resistance proved just as formidable. Shortly after work had begun in Manhattan, sandhogs prepared to start digging in New Jersey. But disgruntled members of the joint commission there halted them. They resented the smaller entry plaza designed for their side and even complained about the size of the desks in their offices. Some threatened lawsuits.

Finally, Holland took a small crew to Jersey City, and under the cover of darkness, they broke ground for the tunnel themselves. The commission considered this a "mean trick," and police were summoned every time work began. After several months, Holland presented the New Jersey commission with a revised plaza design. The logjam broke and the work was able to continue. However, a groundbreaking celebration was canceled because the two sides were disgusted with each other.

Work went on every day of the week, every hour of the day. Holland would go home for dinner after a full day on the job,

TIGHT SPACES. *The method used in tightening the 1¾-inch-by-6½-inch tunnel bolts required three men and a five-foot wrench.*

then return in the evening. Above and below ground, his enthusiasm and dedication to the project spread. Several newspapers affectionately dubbed him "Head Mole," and he earned respect from the normally crusty sandhogs. "That bird could come down here blindfolded in the dark and tell us if we was going wrong," one of them remarked.

The job was fraught with hazards. Working in the compressed air of the tunnel, which was used to counter the incredible pressure bearing down from the water and riverbed above, sometimes caused the men to suffer from "the bends"—an affliction caused by a rapid decrease in pressure when they left at the day's end. Dynamite blasts stirred up fumes and deadly dust. "Blowouts"— trickles, then sudden gushes of water through the tunnel roof— sent men scrambling for the exit. And it was oppressively hot.

During one blowout, 35 men barely escaped. As water forced its way through the tunnel roof, compressed air in the tube was driven up through the silt, blasting a 50-foot geyser in the Hudson. A small boat was struck, causing it to tumble about like a toy. Of the 1,000 feet that had been dug, 300 feet were flooded.

Death hissed and grumbled from all sides. Ultimately, 13 sandhogs died during the construction of the tunnel. But the men never refused to go on. "Ten minutes to Jersey by wheel" was their cry.

CUTTING EDGES. *Sandhogs pause on the edge and hood of the New York shield the day before the junction was made with the New Jersey shield (visible on the right).*

Hoping to "Hole Through"

As the summer of 1924 wore on, the newspapers reported that the tunnel was "nearing its zero hour," the moment when the tunneling teams from each side would meet in the middle, or "hole through." The two sides had to meet exactly in the middle, or the project would be a failure. Holland would accept a variance of only an inch or less. He constantly monitored the instrument men so that they held the shields precisely to the specified line and grade.

When it appeared that the holing through would happen in late October, a huge celebration was planned. A telegraph wire was run to the White House, where President Calvin Coolidge would push a button, sending a signal to ignite a charge and blast the last hole through. **(continued)**

Holland worked obsessively, going in and out of pressurized chambers, day and night, with an already-weak heart. By early October, it was clear he needed a rest. The board voted to give

him a month off with pay, and he retreated to a sanitarium in Battle Creek, Michigan.

Holland's wife later said in a *New York Times* interview that she knew his workload and working conditions were not good for him, "but he was so completely wrapped up . . . I really do not know if my pleadings would have had any effect."

THE CEREMONY. *New York Governor A. E. Smith (above, center) shakes hands with New Jersey Governor A. H. Moore at the state line marker, with tunnel commissioners in attendence.*

THE CELEBRATION. *The New York Plaza on the opening day of the Holland Tunnel (right), November 13, 1927.*

As the north tunnel neared completion, Holland kept up with the news. Days before the holing through, a friend visited, and Holland expressed regret at not being able to witness the event he had worked toward for so long. He vowed, however, to see the tunnel through to completion.

But he did not. That night, after seeing his friend off at the station, Clifford Holland had a heart attack and died.

The next day, October 28, 1924, the north tunnel was holed through. Two brothers, the chiefs of sandhog teams from each side, cast the final shovelfuls

aside. Out of respect for Holland, the celebration had been canceled, and the sandhogs remained silent as the governors of each state shook hands through the new hole. The sides had met with only a ¾-inch variance. Holland had succeeded.

Soon after that, officials voted to name the project the Holland Tunnel. Milton Freeman, Holland's second-in-command, took over as chief engineer. Ironically, he died five months later of pneumonia. His deputy and third in charge, Ole Singstad, took the reins and finished the tunnel.

Today, a bronze bust of Clifford Holland presides over the New Jersey entrance to the Holland Tunnel with a plaque that reads: "The underground highway which joins a continent to a city." It honors the man who once remarked to a friend, "I am going into tunnel work, and I am going to put a lot more into it than I'll ever be paid for."

HOW TO LIVE WELL

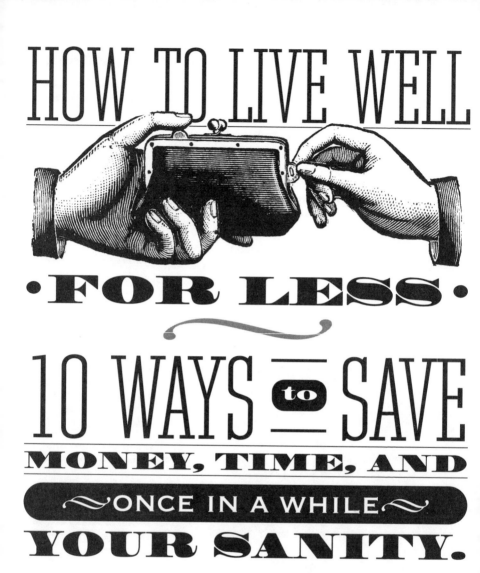

·FOR LESS·

10 WAYS to SAVE

MONEY, TIME, AND

~ONCE IN A WHILE~

YOUR SANITY.

*T*he Yankee frugality that, for centuries, has defined the economic habits of many New Englanders has been praised, criticized, mocked, and satirized. But the fact is, many of those money-sav-ing ideas are practical, easy, and effective. (Some also may seem odd, but Yankees are used to that.) What's more, Yankee-style frugality can be prac-ticed by anyone any-where. It's not about being cheap, stingy, or tight-fisted; it's about being clever, creative, and mind-ful, and living within your means. Simply put, it's about living well for less.

 **HERE'S HOW:**

1 **Put a Freeze on Impulse Purchases.** Freeze your credit card(s) in a block of ice: Place the card(s) in the bottom of an empty ice-cream carton and fill it with ice cubes (to keep the cards from floating to the top). Then fill the carton with water and freeze it. You'll have to wait for it to defrost before you can use the card(s), and because microwaving will melt them, you'll have to let the carton thaw at room temperature.

2 **Hand Over a Portion of Your Harvest.** Has it been a banner year for produce from your garden? Call the manager of a homeless shelter or soup kitchen and offer your surplus—a donation that, for you, could be a noncash charitable contribution in the eyes of the IRS. You can consider the fair market value of your donation to be the grocery store price for comparable produce.

3 **Organize a Vintage Year.** Don't buy a fancy file cabinet to organize the receipts you need to do your taxes. Get a 12-bottle wine box from a restaurant or a liquor store. Write the months' names onto index cards, and staple the cards inside the opening of each square compartment. Drop in that month's utility bills, receipts, mileage accounts, and other paperwork.

4 **Nip Burglaries in the Bud.** Don't buy new locks, alarms, and security systems to make your house safer. Here are two landscaping ideas that will enhance your security: 1) Trim the bushes to allow a clear view of your house. Tall hedges that cover doors and ground-floor windows may look decorative, but they provide cover for anyone trying to break in.

2) Buy plants or bushes with long thorns, and plant them under windows and near doors.

5 **Keep Your Furniture's Finish Fresh.** Need a trivet or coaster so you won't take the finish off your table or leave a ring with a pot or coffee mug? A tile square, just like those on a bathroom or kitchen wall, will work perfectly, look good, and be inexpensive. You'll find tile squares in a hardware store or a home-remodeling center, and probably in many colors. Before using a tile, glue some small felt pads onto the bottom so you won't scratch your table. Cut pads from felt fabric or buy the self-adhesive type that are used for the bottom of chair legs.

6 **Drape to Distraction.**

You're ready to paint and you realize that one of your walls needs work. Rather than repairing the wall, hide it with a curtain or drape—a beautiful and interesting room accent. First, using the color for your room, paint the corners of the bad wall to a distance of at least one foot in. When the paint is dry, hang a curtain rod near the ceiling. (For an extra-long rod, buy a long dowel at a your local home-improvement store.) Choose a fabric that matches your décor, and put fancy finials at the ends of the rod.

(c o n t i n u e d)

7 Gather Ye Rosebuds. Are you aware that when funeral services end, many of the floral arrangements stay behind, and by law in most states, funeral homes can't resell or reuse them? We're not suggesting that you root through the trash, but you might ask if you could stop by occasionally to pick out a bunch of flowers before they are tossed away. (You may come away with a free vase and floral arrangement forms, too.) If all this seems morbid, consider what one old Yankee we know, who was in the funeral business, optimistically observed: "Flowers are for the living."

8 EXPRESS YOUR APPRECIATION.

If you really love a product,

∽ WRITE TO THE MANUFACTURER ∽

EXPRESSING YOUR DEVOTION AND BRAND LOYALTY.

You may receive a reply—along with a bunch of coupons for savings or free samples!

9 Scale Down on Postage. Ever wonder if you have enough first-class postage on a piece of mail? You could add another first-class stamp, but why waste the extra postage? Check the weight this way: Place a pencil onto a flat surface. (A six-sided wooden pencil is best because it won't roll.) Next, lay a 12-inch ruler on the pencil, so that it crosses the pencil at the six-inch mark. At one end of the ruler, stack five quarters (which weigh one ounce). At the other end, lay the envelope. If it lifts the quarters, it needs more postage.

10 Find Pencils and Pens in a Flash! Do you pay your bills or write your grocery lists near the refrigerator? If so, here's a neat way to keep writing implements instantly available. Buy a flashlight with a built-in magnet. Remove the top, the bulb housing, and the batteries, and put them together in a nearby drawer. Then hang the body of the empty flashlight onto the fridge, and place your pens and pencils into it.

☐☐

Ringing In The EARS?

The ANSWER To Your Prayers!

If you ever experience ringing in the ears, buzzing, hissing or any other annoying sounds that may be interfering with your life, you should know about *Dr. John's Special Ear Drops™*.

The drops are truly remarkable; for example: 79-year-old Gloria Gains of Richmond, VA writes: "I tried everything available and my doctor told me I would have to live with my trouble. I had trouble sleeping at night and the sounds were driving me out of my mind. Thank God, I seen your advertisement. I hardly notice anything at all anymore and I'm sleeping like a baby. Your drops have been a God-Send."

Thousands of users like Gloria have written to us regarding *Dr. John's Special Ear Drops™*. If your doctor has not been able to help you, I strongly urge you to give *Dr. John's Special Ear Drops™* a try. You won't be sorry!

The drops are guaranteed to be better for you than anything you have ever tried or you will get every cent of your money back, no questions asked. You can't beat that!

Send $16.95 plus $3.00 S&H (only $19.95) for 1 ounce bottle. Or better yet save $10.00 by ordering 2 full ounces for only $26.95 plus $3.00 S&H (a total of $29.95). Write ear drops on a sheet of paper and send payment with name and address to:

Dr. John's Research, Dept. FA-R2002, Box 667, Taylor, MI 48180

PSORIASIS?

If you suffer from *Psoriasis* like I do, you should know about a wonderful new cream that's guaranteed to work better than anything you have ever used before!

My name is Tom Randles and I have suffered with Psoriasis for more than 20 years and found very little relief with other products. **Then I discovered the gentle, rub-on** *Burdock Folate Lotion™*. Before I knew it my *Psoriasis* disappeared. **All my scaly, itchy skin disappeared; in its place was new natural skin—soft and normal looking. The redness and irritation was gone and I never felt or looked better.**

I swear by it and highly recommend it to anyone with Psoriasis, eczema, contact allergies or other skin disorders. **It works very fast, almost overnight, and provides long lasting, soothing relief. Stop suffering! Order** *Burdock Folate Lotion™* **right now.** It's guaranteed to work for you or you will get every penny of your money back. ***Send $16.95 plus $3.00 S&H (total of $19.95) for 120ml bottle; or better yet save nearly $10.00 by sending $26.95 plus $3.00 S&H (total of $29.95) for a 240ml bottle*** to:

Total Research, Inc., Dept. P2002-FA, Box 667, Taylor, MI 48180

ALSO *Burdock Folate Shampoo™* (for scalp trouble) ONLY $15.95 plus $2.00 S&H
NEW *Burdock Folate Tonic™* (for internal use) $16.95 plus $3.00 S&H or better yet 2 bottles at nearly a $10.00 savings only $26.95 plus $3.00 S&H (send $29.95 for 2 bottles)

Dr. John's Research and Total Research, Inc. is celebrating its 23rd anniversary this rear providing only the best products to its customers. A testimonial reflects the opinion of that individual. Individual results may vary. The Food and Drug Administration does not review claims made on herbal products. Dr. John's & Total Research do not diagnose. These items do not treat, cure or prevent any disease. Don't suffer a moment longer. You have nothing to lose and so very much to gain.

INTO THE DEEP

BY ALAN BEHR

The first nuclear-powered submarine changed the world and the ways of warfare.

On June 14, 1952, as had happened often before at the Electric Boat Company in Groton, Connecticut, the keel was laid for a new submarine. The fact that President Harry S. Truman did the job himself, however, was a signal to the world of how unique this new boat would be. As it took shape, the USS *Nautilus* outwardly looked like other subs of its time, with a streamlined conning tower (called a sail) atop a standard submarine hull. But just over two-and-a-half years later, when the *Nautilus* was

MAKING WAVES. The *Nautilus* under way with decks awash, entering New York Harbor after making the first-ever voyage under the ice cap of the North Pole (inset).

Not since the advance from sail to steam had a new method of propulsion been so profound.

first put to sea, it sent perhaps the most famous signal in peacetime naval history: "Underway on nuclear power."

Not since the advance from sail to steam had a new method of propulsion been so profound. Since 1900, when the USS *Holland* (named after designer John P. Holland) was commissioned as the U.S. Navy's first submarine, all subs had used internal combustion (usually by diesel engines) for operating on the surface. Because diesels "breathed" air, they were unusable below the surface. Electric motors were therefore used for underwater operation, but they were typically slow, and battery power was limited. A dived sub would lack either the speed or the range to overtake and destroy a fast-moving ship. Until nuclear power, a submarine was little more than a submersible torpedo boat, operating largely on the surface and diving mainly for attack or escape.

At first, that hardly mattered. Etiquette for submarine attack in the early part of World War I required a submarine to surface and

DECADES OF DIFFERENCE. Technology limited the time that WWI sub crews could stay submerged (above); *Nautilus* crews spent months in cramped quarters (left).

wait for the crew and passengers of a target merchant ship to take to their lifeboats. Only then could the submarine launch a torpedo or fire a deck gun to destroy the ship. The problem for German submariners was that such courtesy opened them to counterattack, especially if the target was a Q-ship—a British sub hunter disguised as an unarmed merchantman. So Germany sometimes conducted unrestricted submarine warfare: Its submarines, the famous U-boats (for the German word for submarine, *Unterseeboot*), would torpedo unarmed ships from below the surface without warning. That policy, shown most dramatically in the 1915 sinking of the British passenger ship SS *Lusitania,* in which about 1,200 lives were lost, brought an angry United States into the conflict against Germany and its allies.

During World War II, both sides (the Allies and the Axis nations) practiced unrestricted submarine warfare, the Germans taking a toll on Allied shipping, and the Americans doing the same to the Japanese. Although the diesel-electric subs were now free to attack from under water, they still couldn't stay submerged for long periods at high speed either to stalk or to flee. Though warfare was now unrestricted, the subs were still restricted by technology.

Late in the war, the Germans came up with an interim solution—the snorkel—which brought in fresh air and sent out diesel exhaust. A U-boat could now ride at periscope depth while on its diesels, and at the same time recharge its batteries. But a sub that close to the surface could often be seen from the air, and radar and sonar devices made it easier to detect the metal structure of the submarine and the heat of its diesels. A nuclear power source, requiring neither air nor batteries, would allow a sub to stay deep under water until the crew's food—or patience—ran out. The problem was that, in 1952, no one had yet tried to power anything, moving or stationary, with this new technology.

The man who promoted the development of the nuclear submarine was a Navy officer and engineer named Hyman G. Rickover. A 1922 graduate of the U.S. Naval Academy, Rickover was a controversial figure, admired by many who worked for him, yet outspoken in his criticism of naval dogma. Due to an act of Congress that exempted him from ordinary retirement rules, Rickover served in the U.S. Navy for 63 years; he died in 1986.

THE DRIVING FORCE. Admiral Hyman G. Rickover developed the *Nautilus* and, later, the U.S. nuclear fleet.

What the Navy got in the *Nautilus* was a 319-foot submarine that displaced 4,092 tons of water on the surface—about twice the displacement of the World War II models that still made up most of the U.S. submarine fleet. Because the *Nautilus* required more manpower, its 111 officers and enlisted men lived in the cramped conditions submariners had

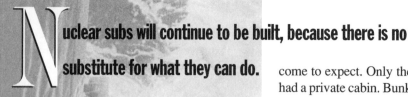

Nuclear subs will continue to be built, because there is no substitute for what they can do.

THE *NAUTILUS* BY THE NUMBERS

NORMAL CREW CAPACITY: 11 officers, 100 sailors

■

LENGTH: 319 feet

■

NUMBER OF TONS DISPLACED: 4,092

■

DEPTH TO WHICH IT COULD SUBMERGE: 700 feet

■

SPEED THAT IT COULD MAINTAIN INDEFINITELY: 24 knots

■

DISTANCE/TIME OF FIRST VOYAGE: 1,381 miles in 89.9 hours

■

DURATION OF ONBOARD FOOD SUPPLY: 60–90 days. Cans of food were stacked right on the decks and covered with plywood, becoming a new floor.

■

YEAR COMMISSIONED: 1954

■

YEAR DECOMMISSIONED: 1980

■

YEAR NAMED A NATIONAL HISTORIC LANDMARK: 1982

■

NUMBER OF VISITORS PER YEAR TO THE SUBMARINE FORCE MUSEUM: 275,000

come to expect. Only the captain had a private cabin. Bunks for enlisted men were stacked three high, with a small curtain for privacy. Not only were the men of the *Nautilus* expected to go about their business just steps away from a live nuclear reactor (to say nothing of 24 torpedoes tipped with high explosive), but they could be called upon to spend weeks or even months under water.

The *Nautilus* operated for over two years, covering 62,562 miles, before its first refueling. In 1958, it made the first polar voyage in history, running submerged under the ice cap of the North Pole on August 3. It then sent another famous signal: *"Nautilus* 90 North," signifying its accomplishment.

By the 1960s, with more-advanced submarines in commission, the *Nautilus* was no longer considered a "first-line" boat. It was decommissioned on March 30, 1980; in 1985, it was put on permanent exhibit in Groton, the town where it was built.

By then, many of the world's major navies were using nuclear submarines. A British boat, the *Conqueror,* made the first nuclear-sub "kill," sinking the Argentine cruiser *General Belgrano* (with more than 320 officers and crewmen) during the Falklands War of 1982. The *General Belgrano* had

THE ULTIMATE WEAPON. The USS *Ohio,* equipped with 24 Trident missiles.

survived Pearl Harbor without damage, but it was an easy target for the *Conqueror,* which sent it to the bottom with two torpedoes.

Nuclear submarines can also be dangerous to their own crews, even in peacetime. The U.S. Navy has lost two subs in accidents, each with all crew members on board: the *Thresher* in 1963 (129 dead) and the *Scorpion* in 1968 (99 dead). Because of worldwide media coverage, the most dramatic loss has been that of the Russian *Kursk,* in 2000, with its crew of 118.

Nonetheless, nuclear subs will continue to be built, because there is no substitute for what they can do. Within a few years after the start of construction of the *Nautilus,* a highly specialized derivation of it joined the U.S. fleet: the nuclear-powered fleet ballistic missile submarine, or SSBN. It is not intended

for control and protection on the sea, which most earlier warships had been built for. The mission of the SSBN is nuclear deterrence—protection of nations and international alliances rather than ships.

The first was the USS *George Washington,* which entered service in 1959. The newest SSBNs in the American fleet, the subs of the Ohio class, displace 16,764 tons on the surface—more than four times the displacement of the *Nautilus.* Each submarine's 24 ballistic-missile tubes holds a Trident missile with multiple warheads. Together, the ability of the Trident to strike thousands of miles inland and the ability of its submerged launch vehicle to hide in all the world's oceans make the SSBN the ultimate weapon of war—one that therefore must never be used.

It is rare, but sometimes a single advance in technology immediately changes a method of war. For submarines, it occurred with the laying of the keel for the *Nautilus.*

DIVE! DIVE!
Go to **www.almanac.com** and click on **Article Links 2002** for Web sites related to this article.

THE SHELL NAME GAME

■ **Despite the complex engineering needed to build the world's first nuclear submarine—or any sub—one aspect of construction is inspired by a simple design from nature. The nautilus, a saltwater mollusk, which scientists think has been around for 200 million years, lives within a spiral, chambered shell. The shell serves not only as protection but also as a flotation device. It contains a tube through which the nautilus can introduce or remove gases, just as buoyancy-control tanks in a submarine operate to allow it to ascend or descend in the water.**

A cross section of a nautilus shell (above); a diagram of Fulton's *Nautilus* (below).

Creators of submarines both real and imaginary have honored the nautilus by naming their vessels after it. The first submarine ever launched (by inventor Robert Fulton in 1801) was named the *Nautilus.* The historic nuclear-powered *Nautilus* is the sixth vessel to be christened as such by the U.S. Navy. Science-fiction enthusiasts will recall that it was also the name given by Jules Verne to the submarine in his novel *20,000 Leagues Under the Sea.* □ □

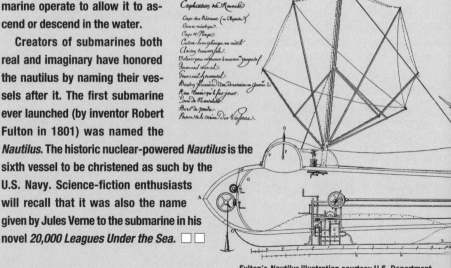

–Fulton's *Nautilus* illustration courtesy U.S. Department of the Navy Submarine Force Museum

Winning Essays

in the 2001 Essay Contest

My Most Memorable Family Car Trip

FIRST PRIZE

It was the summer of '59. The family—Mom, Dad, my four sisters, one brother, two cats, and one dog—were leaving at 5 A.M. for the Thousand Islands [in the St. Lawrence River, between southern Ontario and northern New York state]. We had a nine-passenger station wagon and trailed a Boston Whaler. With all the wisdom of a 13-year-old, I'd chosen for my travel clothes a sugar-starched, three-layered, pink crinoline with my fullest skirt.

Fifteen minutes into the seven-hour trip, I knew I'd made a serious mistake. It was s o - o - o - o scratchy, and the sugar was starting to melt. By the time we stopped to eat, I was miserable. I ran to the Ladies' Room and ripped it off. I washed my sticky legs, balled up the crinoline, and jammed it down into the boat. As we got back on the road, I saw my crinoline start to wave up out of the boat, the wind pulling it out more and more. Finally, it let go, but it wrapped itself around Dad's 60-hp Mercury outboard motor. As we pulled up to the cabin, the owner came out to greet us and said,

"That's a real unusual motor cover you folks got there."

–*Eileen Engels Bayersdorfer, Toms River, New Jersey*

SECOND PRIZE

This preschool experience of some 60 years ago is etched in my mind because it is also my earliest recollection of going to church. We lived in a rural area of northern Minnesota, and when the weather and roads were agreeable, we attended a rural "church," which was really a Sunday school for all ages except for when a traveling missionary came to preach occasionally. Our family car, like a lot of family cars of that time, was a Model A Ford, but ours had four doors when most Model As had two. Our family consisted of my parents, my sister, two brothers, and my grandmother. Now, a group of seven was quite a load for a little car like that, but somehow we all fit into it. Mother and Dad and my physically handicapped 8-year-old brother sitting on Mother's lap were in the front seat. In the backseat were my 16-year-old sister, my 12-year-old brother, and my grandmother holding me. Naturally, we all had our Sunday school books and Bibles, and I had two pennies for the offering tied in the corner of my hanky. Added to the cargo was the music for the church service, which was my father's violin (not fiddle) in the front seat and my sister's large, auditorium-size guitar in a case in the backseat. The little Ford never complained, and if occasionally we came upon people walking to church, we would stop and roll down the windows, and they would stand on the running boards to hitch a ride. Mother didn't like the wind blowing on her from the window, and to her dismay, a rider would sometimes stick his head inside the car to converse during the trip. If the new passengers were carrying a baby, it would be placed inside the car, of course, but don't ask me who held it. Looking back, we didn't complain. We were glad to have wheels when some people had horses. They are laughable but good memories.

–Leona Muzzy, Thief River Falls, Minnesota

While traveling through the rolling hills of Riverside County, California, with my wife, three of our young sons, and my wife's sister and her three young children, the close quarters and time spent in the car became boring to the children. Although they were good, they began to get at each other, and stress was beginning to set in. We had viewed a cow or two here and there in the hills but always ones that were brown and white. To stimulate interest in the drive, and to relieve tension, I offered a nickel for every black-and-white cow that someone could spot. This created some peace to the drive and generated new interest for the children—until we went up a slight hill and around a corner, when all of a sudden the hillside was covered with black-and-white cows belonging to a dairy farm. While the children counted as fast as they could and I drove out of the area as quickly as possible, the amount of nickels due got bigger and bigger. That day cost me many rows of nickels, and the family long remembers the sudden appearance of black-and-white dairy cows.

–G. Robert Young, Surprise, Arizona

Announcing the 2002 Essay Contest

My Brush with Fame

■ **Have you ever won an award, captured a prize, or met a famous person? Please describe your experience in 200 words or less. See page 219 for prizes, rules, and submission information.**

Winning Recipes
in the 2001 Recipe Contest

Soups and Chowders

Thank you to all the readers of The Old Farmer's Almanac *who sent recipes. To see some of the other submissions, go to* **www.almanac.com**.

SWEET-POTATO CHOWDER

4 slices bacon, chopped
1/2 cup chopped onion
1/4 cup chopped green pepper
1/4 cup chopped red pepper
2 cloves garlic, minced
3 cups chicken broth
1 can (15 ounces) diced sweet potatoes, drained
1 large baking potato, peeled and diced
1 can (14.5 ounces) stewed tomatoes
2 cups milk
1 teaspoon curry powder
1/4 teaspoon freshly ground pepper

Sauté bacon, onion, peppers, and garlic in large soup pot. Add chicken broth and continue heating. Puree sweet potatoes in food processor or blender. Whisk into broth mixture. Stir in potatoes and tomatoes. Cover and simmer for 45 minutes, until potatoes are tender. Whisk in milk, curry powder, and pepper; heat, but do not boil. Serve. **Serves 6.**

–Liz Barclay, Annapolis, Maryland

JAMBALAYA BOWL

4 slices bacon, halved, for garnish
6 spicy sausage links, cut into 1-inch slices
2 chicken breast halves, boned, skinned, and
    cut into 1/2-inch pieces
3 teaspoons Cajun seasoning, divided
1 cup cubed, cooked ham (1/2-inch cubes)
1 medium onion, peeled and diced
1 large green bell pepper, seeded and diced
4 stalks celery, diced
1/2 cup long-grain rice
1 can (14.5 ounces) chicken broth
1 can (14.5 ounces) tomato sauce or seasoned,
    diced tomatoes for soup and stew
3 to 4 cups tomato juice
6 to 8 drops hot sauce, to taste
8 ounces small raw shrimp, shelled, deveined
salt and pepper, to taste
fresh basil sprigs, for garnish

Place bacon into a large Dutch oven over medium heat, and cook for 5 to 6 minutes, turning, until browned and crisp. Drain on paper towels; crumble pieces and reserve. Remove and reserve all but 2 tablespoons pan drippings. Add sausage slices; sauté for 3 to 4 minutes, stirring, until lightly browned. Remove to plate lined with paper towels. Meanwhile, toss chicken pieces with 1 teaspoon Cajun seasoning; add to pan along with ham cubes; sauté until golden, for 3 to 4 minutes. Remove to plate with sausage slices. Add reserved bacon drippings to pan as needed. Stir onion, peppers, celery, and 1 teaspoon Cajun seasoning into pan; cook until vegetables are soft, for 3 to 4 minutes. Add rice and remaining 1 teaspoon Cajun seasoning; cook, stirring, until rice is translucent, for 3 to 4 minutes. Pour in broth, cover pan,

and raise heat to medium-high. Cook until rice is soft, for 10 to 12 minutes. Stir in tomato sauce, 3 cups tomato juice, and hot sauce to taste; lower heat and simmer, uncovered, for 5 minutes. Add more tomato juice, if necessary; soup should be the consistency of heavy cream. Return cooked meats to pan and add shrimp. Cook, uncovered, just until meats are hot and shrimp is pink, for 4 to 5 minutes. Taste and adjust seasoning. Ladle into heated bowls. Serve garnished with reserved bacon crumbles and basil sprigs. **Serves 8.**

–Marilou Robinson, Portland, Oregon

SPICY PUMPKIN-AND-POTATO SOUP

3 tablespoons olive oil, divided
1 onion, chopped
2 cloves garlic, minced
2 medium potatoes, peeled and diced
1/2 teaspoon chili powder
1/2 teaspoon ground cumin
6 cups chicken or vegetable broth
1/4 cup chopped cilantro
1 jalapeño pepper, seeded and minced
1 cup solid-pack canned pumpkin
1/4 cup half-and-half or light cream, heated
fresh cilantro sprigs, for garnish

In a large Dutch oven, heat 2 tablespoons oil. Add the onion, garlic, potatoes, chili powder, and cumin. Sauté over medium heat for 5 minutes. Add the broth and cook until the potatoes are tender, about 15 minutes. Process the soup in a blender, along with the cilantro and jalapeño. In a separate bowl, combine the pumpkin, half-and-half, and the rest of the oil, mixing until well combined. Ladle the potato soup into 6 bowls. Swirl the pumpkin mixture into the soup, creating a marbling effect. Garnish and serve. **Serves 6.**

–Roxanne E. Chan, Albany, California

Beautiful Beet Soup That's To Die For

8 medium beets
2 turnips, peeled
1 potato
2 carrots
2 cups shredded cabbage
2 cups chopped onion
2 tablespoons margarine or butter
1 teaspoon caraway seeds
2 to 3 quarts stock or water
1 teaspoon dried dill, or 2 tablespoons fresh
1/2 cup cider vinegar
1 tablespoon honey
1 cup tomato puree
1/2 cup orange juice
1/4 teaspoon paprika
salt, to taste
sour cream or fresh dill sprigs, for garnish

Scrub the beets, trim the ends, and grate. Chop or slice the turnips, potato, and carrots. Beets can be messy to prepare, so grate them last (and don't wear white!). In a large stockpot, sauté the onion in margarine or butter for a few minutes, then add the caraway and the rest of the vegetables. Add the stock and the remaining ingredients. If you use fresh dill, add it at the end. Cover and simmer for 40 to 45 minutes, testing occasionally for doneness. Once cooked, you can puree this soup in a blender or food processor for a more delicate texture. Serve hot, garnished with a dollop of sour cream or a sprig of dill. **Serves 8.**

–Fred Race, Strongsville, Ohio

Chocolate-Hazelnut Soup

4 cups light cream
6 ounces sweet chocolate
1/3 cup sugar
4 egg yolks
1/3 cup crème de cacao
3 tablespoons Frangelico liqueur
1/2 cup heavy cream, whipped, for topping
1/2 cup flaked, toasted hazelnuts, for topping

Combine cream, chocolate, and sugar in saucepan over medium heat, stirring until chocolate melts. Thoroughly beat egg yolks. Stir in ½ cup of chocolate soup mixture into egg yolks, then whisk egg yolk mixture into soup. Simmer, stirring for 5 minutes. Remove from heat and stir in liqueurs. Serve hot or cold, garnished with whipped cream and nuts. **Serves 6.**

For nonalcoholic version, substitute:
1/2 cup Nutella (chocolate-hazelnut spread) for the liqueurs

Add the Nutella with the cream, chocolate, and sugar, and heat slowly until the chocolate and Nutella have melted.

–S.D. Milholland, Lindbergh, Alberta, Canada

Special thanks to recipe judge Sylvia Wright.

Announcing the 2002 Recipe Contest

Casseroles

■ Send us your favorite one-dish recipe. It will be reviewed—and perhaps tested —by the cooks at *Cook's Illustrated* magazine, home of "America's Test Kitchen" show on public television.

Recipe and Essay Contest Rules

Cash prizes (first prize, $100; second prize, $75; third prize, $50) will be awarded for the best original essays on the subject "My Brush with Fame" and the best recipes for casseroles. All entries become the property of Yankee Publishing Inc., which reserves all rights to the material. Winners will be announced in the 2003 edition of *The Old Farmer's Almanac* and posted on our Web site: www.almanac.com. Deadline is February 1, 2002. Please type all essays and recipes. Label "Essay Contest" or "Recipe Contest" and send to: The Old Farmer's Almanac, P.O. Box 520, Dublin, NH 03444. E-mail (subject: Essay Contest or Recipe Contest) to almanac@yankeepub.com. ☐ ☐

Fannie, Our First Foodie

A century ago, Fannie Farmer changed the way we cook. Thank goodness!

by Alice Cary

*W*hen Mr. and Mrs. Charles Shaw of Cambridge, Massachusetts, decided to take in a mother's helper back in the 1880s, they had no idea their decision would forever change the way families cook and eat. Little did they realize that their shy helper, a young woman named Fannie Merritt Farmer, would become a founder of modern culinary arts.

Born in Boston in 1857 to John Farmer, a printer, and his wife, Mary, Fannie was the oldest of four girls. Devout Unitarians, the Farmers strongly believed in education. Even though their income was modest, they planned to send their girls to college—an uncommon idea for the time.

But illness dashed Fannie's hopes of college. She fell sick during her high school years, most likely with polio, and she never graduated. For several years, she remained an invalid, confined to her bed. When she finally walked, she had a permanent limp. She made herself useful by helping her family with household chores.

The time came when John Farmer had trouble making ends meet, so wealthy friends, the Shaws, hired Fannie. She hadn't done much cooking, but she showed interest and talent, so Mrs. Shaw encouraged her.

Legend has it that the Shaws' daughter, Marcia, asked Fannie about measuring terms. In those days, recipes often called for such inexact amounts as smidgens, pinches, and "butter the size of an egg." Measuring cups and spoons weren't widely used until the 1880s; before then, cooks used anything handy—teacups, kitchen spoons, and the like—so amounts often varied. Marcia supposedly spurred Fannie into a lifelong mission of encouraging accurate measuring.

In 1887, Fannie enrolled in the Boston Cooking-School. In class, the instructors insisted, but with inconsistent direction, that all students use measuring cups and spoons. The students sometimes heaped flour, sugar, and other ingredients into rounded mounds of varying heights. Later, in her classes, writings, and demonstrations, Fannie so stressed the importance of level measurements that she is often called the "Mother of Level Measurements."

When she started going to the Boston Cooking-School, Fannie had hoped to become a teacher there. She more than met her goal. Upon graduation in 1889, she became assistant director, and in 1894 was named director.

Two years later, Fannie wrote *The Boston Cooking-School Cook Book.* The project evolved out of a text used at the school, *Mrs. Lincoln's Boston Cook Book,* to which Fannie added her own recipes as well as cooking and nutrition philosophy. She wasn't the only one stressing these ideals, but she was the only one to explain them in a simple and straightforward style.

Regardless, Fannie's publisher, the revered Little, Brown and Company, wasn't convinced that her cookbook would be a success. In fact, the company was so worried that it made Fannie pay for the initial costs. But the first printing soon sold out, and so did many other orders. Before long, people all over the country had heard of Fannie Farmer and her book. Soon they simply called it by her name rather than the school's name.

Income from cookbooks she wrote allowed Fannie to open her own school, Miss Farmer's School of Cookery, in 1902. As a result, the Boston Cooking-School soon closed. Everyone wanted to learn from Fannie. No matter that this plump woman with a "plain" face had no interest in fashion; her recipes turned meals into occasions—to a degree of detail almost unheard of at the time. (For instance, she suggested dyeing St. Patrick's Day food green and dressing up a Christmas dessert with a wooden

doll wearing a festive outfit.) Her red hair and blue eyes shone as she lectured, dressed in a white chef's hat and a long white apron. Her demonstrations drew crowds, including newspaper reporters. To satisfy the public's appetite for more, her sister Cora helped her write a monthly cooking page for the *Woman's Home Companion.*

Fannie not only had a healthy appetite (she has been described as "one of the few cooking teachers who really liked to eat"), but she had nonstop enthusiasm for all matters culinary. When she and her parents dined in fine restaurants, for instance, Fannie often quizzed chefs about recipes and ingredients. If a chef was not forthcoming, she sneaked a sample back to her kitchen for analysis.

As the years passed, Fannie increasingly turned her attention to food for the ill, perhaps as a result of her own years as an invalid. She lectured at Harvard University Medical School and taught nurses and hospital dietitians. She met Dr. Elliott P. Joslin, a pioneer in the field of diabetes, who credits her as his inspiration for beginning to write about the subject. In 1904, Fannie published *Food and Cookery for the Sick and Convalescent,* which she considered her most important book.

Eventually, Fannie's health worsened. A series of strokes confined her to a wheelchair, although she continued to lecture. By 1915, the year she died, her first cookbook had sold more than 360,000 copies. Now called *The Fan-* *nie Farmer Cookbook,* it has remained a classic for more than 100 years, having sold over 4 million copies.

One of Fannie's Favorites

BREAD PUDDING
(as it appears in the original
Boston Cooking-School Cook Book*)*

2 cups stale bread crumbs
1 quart scalded milk
1/3 cup sugar
2 tablespoons melted butter
2 eggs
1/2 teaspoon salt
1 teaspoon vanilla or 1/4 teaspoon spice

Soak bread crumbs in milk, set aside until cool; add sugar, butter, eggs slightly beaten, salt, and flavoring; bake one hour in a buttered pudding-dish in slow oven [*Editor's note:* 300°F]; serve with Vanilla Sauce. In preparing bread crumbs for puddings, avoid using outside crusts. With a coarse grater there need be but little waste.

Vanilla Sauce

3/4 cup sugar
1/4 cup water
2 teaspoons butter
1 teaspoon vanilla

■ Make a syrup by boiling sugar and water eight minutes; remove from fire; add butter and vanilla. □□

COOKBOOKS & BITES
For more information on books by or about Fannie Farmer, click on **Article Links 2002** at **www.almanac.com.**

Table of Measures

Apothecaries'

1 scruple = 20 grains
1 dram = 3 scruples
1 ounce = 8 drams
1 pound = 12 ounces

Avoirdupois

1 ounce = 16 drams
1 pound = 16 ounces
1 hundredweight = 100 pounds
1 ton = 2,000 pounds
1 long ton = 2,240 pounds

Cubic

1 cubic foot = 1,728 cubic inches
1 cubic yard = 27 cubic feet
1 cord = 128 cubic feet
1 U.S. liquid gallon = 4 quarts = 231 cubic inches
1 Imperial gallon = 1.20 U.S. gallons = 0.16 cubic foot
1 board foot = 144 cubic inches

Dry

2 pints = 1 quart
4 quarts = 1 gallon
2 gallons = 1 peck
4 pecks = 1 bushel

Liquid

4 gills = 1 pint
2 pints = 1 quart
4 quarts = 1 gallon
63 gallons = 1 hogshead
2 hogsheads = 1 pipe or butt
2 pipes = 1 tun

Linear

1 foot = 12 inches
1 yard = 3 feet
1 rod = 5½ yards
1 mile = 320 rods = 1,760 yards = 5,280 feet
1 Int. nautical mile = 6,076.1155 feet
1 knot = 1 nautical mile per hour

1 furlong = ⅛ mile = 660 feet = 220 yards
1 league = 3 miles = 24 furlongs
1 fathom = 2 yards = 6 feet
1 chain = 100 links = 22 yards
1 link = 7.92 inches
1 hand = 4 inches
1 span = 9 inches

Square

1 square foot = 144 square inches
1 square yard = 9 square feet
1 square rod = 30¼ square yards = 272¼ square feet
1 acre = 160 square rods = 43,560 square feet
1 square mile = 640 acres = 102,400 square rods
1 square rod = 625 square links
1 square chain = 16 square rods
1 acre = 10 square chains

Household

120 drops of water = 1 teaspoon
60 drops thick fluid = 1 teaspoon
2 teaspoons = 1 dessertspoon
3 teaspoons = 1 tablespoon
16 tablespoons = 1 cup
1 cup = 8 ounces
2 cups = 1 pint
2 pints = 1 quart
4 quarts = 1 gallon
3 tablespoons flour = 1 ounce
2 tablespoons butter = 1 ounce
2 cups granulated sugar = 1 pound

3¾ cups confectioners' sugar = 1 pound
3½ cups wheat flour = 1 pound
5⅓ cups dry coffee = 1 pound
6½ cups dry tea = 1 pound
2 cups shortening = 1 pound
1 stick butter = ½ cup
2 cups cornmeal = 1 pound
2¾ cups brown sugar = 1 pound
2⅜ cups raisins = 1 pound
9 eggs = 1 pound
1 ounce yeast = 1 scant tablespoon

Metric

1 inch = 2.54 centimeters
1 centimeter = 0.39 inch
1 meter = 39.37 inches
1 yard = 0.914 meter
1 mile = 1,609.344 meters = 1.61 kilometers
1 kilometer = 0.62 mile
1 square inch = 6.45 square centimeters
1 square yard = 0.84 square meter
1 square mile = 2.59 square kilometers
1 square kilometer = 0.386 square mile
1 acre = 0.40 hectare
1 hectare = 2.47 acres
1 cubic yard = 0.76 cubic meter
1 cubic meter = 1.31 cubic yards
1 liter = 1.057 U.S. liquid quarts
1 U.S. liquid quart = 0.946 liter
1 U.S. liquid gallon = 3.78 liters
1 gram = 0.035 ounce
1 ounce = 28.349 grams
1 kilogram = 2.2 pounds
1 pound avoirdupois = 0.45 kilogram

Gestation and Mating Table

	Proper Age for First Mating	Period of Fertility (years)	Number of Females for One Male	Period of Gestation (days) AVERAGE	RANGE
Ewe	90 lb. or 1 yr.	6		147 / 151[8]	142–154
Ram	12–14 mo., well matured	7	50–75[2] / 35–40[3]		
Mare	3 yr.	10–12		336	310–370
Stallion	3 yr.	12–15	40–45[4] / Record 252[5]		
Cow	15–18 mo.[1]	10–14		283	279–290[6] 262–300[7]
Bull	1 yr., well matured	10–12	50[4] / Thousands[5]		
Sow	5–6 mo. or 250 lb.	6		115	110–120
Boar	250–300 lb.	6	50[2] / 35–40[3]		
Doe goat	10 mo. or 85–90 lb.	6		150	145–155
Buck goat	Well matured	5	30		
Bitch	16–18 mo.	8		63	58–67
Male dog	12–16 mo.	8			
She cat	12 mo.	6		63	60–68
Doe rabbit	6 mo.	5–6		31	30–32
Buck rabbit	6 mo.	5–6	30		

[1]Holstein and beef: 750 lb.; Jersey: 500 lb. [2]Hand-mated. [3]Pasture. [4]Natural. [5]Artificial. [6]Beef; 8–10 days shorter for Angus. [7]Dairy. [8]For fine wool breeds.

Maximum Life Spans of Animals in Captivity (years)

Ant (queen) ...... 18+
Badger 26
Beaver .... 15+
Box turtle (Eastern) 138
Camel........... 35+
Cat (domestic) 34
Chicken (domestic).. 25
Chimpanzee 51
Coyote .... 21+
Dog (domestic) 29
Dolphin.......... 25
Duck (domestic)... 23
Eagle............ 55
Elephant 75
Giraffe 36
Goat (domestic) 20
Goldfish 41
Goose (domestic)... 20
Gorilla .... 50+
Horse 62
Housefly...... 17 days
Kangaroo 30
Lion............ 29
Monarch butterfly .. 1+
Mouse (house) 6
Mussel
  (freshwater)... 70–80
Octopus 2–3
Quahog.......... 150
Rabbit........... 18+
Squirrel, gray 23
Tiger............ 26
Toad 40
Tortoise (Marion's)152+
Turkey (domestic)... 16

Incubation Periods of Birds and Poultry (days)

Canary.....14–15
Chicken 21
Duck 26–32
Goose......30–34
Guinea.....26–28
Parakeet....18–20
Pheasant....22–24
Swan 42
Turkey........28

Gestation Periods of Wild Animals (days)

Black bear 210
Hippo....225–250
Moose ...240–250
Otter.....270–300
Reindeer .210–240
Seal 330
Squirrel, gray...44
Whale, sperm.. 480
Wolf.......60–63

	Estral (estrous) Cycle Including Heat Period AVERAGE	RANGE	Length of Heat (estrus) AVERAGE	RANGE	Usual Time of Ovulation	When Cycle Recurs if Not Bred
Mare	21 days	10–37 days	5–6 days	2–11 days	24–48 hours before end of estrus	21 days
Sow	21 days	18–24 days	2–3 days	1–5 days	30–36 hours after start of estrus	21 days
Ewe	16½ days	14–19 days	30 hours	24–32 hours	12–24 hours before end of estrus	16½ days
Goat	21 days	18–24 days	2–3 days	1–4 days	Near end of estrus	21 days
Cow	21 days	18–24 days	18 hours	10–24 hours	10–12 hours after end of estrus	21 days
Bitch	24 days		7 days	5–9 days	1–3 days after first acceptance	Pseudo-pregnancy
Cat		15–21 days	3–4 days, if mated	9–10 days, in absence of male	24–56 hours after coitus	Pseudo-pregnancy

Mr. Smith's MADDENING Mind-Manglers

From page 178.

1 Claire's grandmother could have indicated the number of cookies on the box with the capital letters IX, which is also the number 9 in Roman numerals. Claire could have put an S in front of the IX so that she could eat three cookies. Or her grandmother could have written the digit 9 on the box, and Claire would only have had to turn the box upside-down for it to read as 6.

2 Place the digits 8 and 1 in the two middle boxes, since they each only have one digit next to them. Then place 2 and 7 on opposite ends, away from 8 and 1. Place the others accordingly.

	6	4	
2	8	1	7
	5	3	

3 If you allow *n* to represent the number of spaces each vehicle uses, then you need 1*n* for each motorcycle, 2*n* for each car, and 3*n* for each truck. For the combination of one of each type of vehicle, you need 6 spaces ($1n + 2n + 3n = 6n$). From $6n = 400$, solve for *n* by dividing the total number of spaces (400) by 6 (spaces) to get 66.67. Because you can't have part of a vehicle in a pod, round that off and you have 66 of each type of vehicle. Now calculate the fees:
66 motorcycles @ $1.50 = $99.00
66 cars @ $2.25 = $148.50
66 trucks @ $3.00 = $198.00
Add those, and the total is $445.50.

4 The answer is 27 ounces. If a brick weighs 9 ounces plus half a brick, then each half-brick is 9 ounces. So a whole brick weighs 18 ounces (2 halves @ 9 ounces each = 18 ounces), and a brick and a half weighs 27 ounces.

5 Zero is the only number that, when added to itself, equals itself. So L must be 0, and the sum of two Fs must be less than 10, so you do not carry a 1. The two As have to be the same number and be greater than 10 when added together, so that you can increase H + H by 1. H must be 9. With that in mind, there are several solutions. HALF can equal 9703, 9604, or 9802.

6

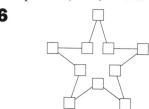

7 He had 40 smokes. Here's why: He started with 27 cigarettes and always smoked only two-thirds of each. He made 9 more cigarettes by taping the 27 leftover thirds ($27 \div 3 = 9$); he made 3 more cigarettes by taping the 9 leftover thirds ($9 \div 3 = 3$); he made 1 more cigarette by taping the last 3 leftover thirds. $27 + 9 + 3 + 1 = 40$.

8 Ray is. He made $81.60 for the two years, while Rob made $80. Here's why:
In Ray's first year, his $1,000 @ 4% made him $40. Add this interest to his total. In his second year, his $1,040 @ 4% made him $41.60. Now, add this interest to his first-year interest ($40). Ray's total gain is $81.60.
In Rob's first year, his $1,000 @ 80% made him $800. Add this return to his total. In his second year, his $1,800 @ –40% lost him $720. Rob's total gain is $80. □□

Secrets of the Zodiac

Ancient astrologers associated each of the signs with a part of the body over which they felt the sign held some influence. The first sign of the zodiac—Aries—was attributed to the head, with the rest of the signs moving down the body, ending with Pisces at the feet.

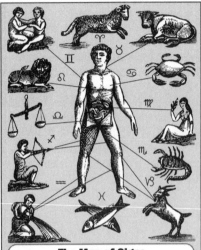

The Man of Signs

♈	Aries, head.	**ARI**	*Mar. 21–Apr. 20*
♉	Taurus, neck	**TAU**	*Apr. 21–May 20*
♊	Gemini, arms	**GEM**	*May 21–June 20*
♋	Cancer, breast.	**CAN**	*June 21–July 22*
♌	Leo, heart	**LEO**	*July 23–Aug. 22*
♍	Virgo, belly	**VIR**	*Aug. 23–Sept. 22*
♎	Libra, reins.	**LIB**	*Sept. 23–Oct. 22*
♏	Scorpio, secrets	**SCO**	*Oct. 23–Nov. 22*
♐	Sagittarius, thighs . . .	**SAG**	*Nov. 23–Dec. 21*
♑	Capricorn, knees	**CAP**	*Dec. 22–Jan. 19*
♒	Aquarius, legs	**AQU**	*Jan. 20–Feb. 19*
♓	Pisces, feet	**PSC**	*Feb. 20–Mar. 20*

Astrology and Astronomy

■ Astrology is a tool we use to time events according to the *astrological* placement of the two luminaries (the Sun and the Moon) and eight planets in the 12 signs of the zodiac. Astronomy, on the other hand, is the charting of the *actual* placement of the known planets and constellations, taking into account precession of the equinoxes. As a result, *the placement of the planets in the signs of the zodiac is not the same astrologically and astronomically.* (The Moon's astronomical place is given in the **Left-Hand Calendar Pages 64–90,** and its astrological place is given in **Gardening by the Moon's Sign, page 227.**)

Modern astrology is a study of synchronicities. The planetary movements do not cause events. Rather, they explain the "flow," or trajectory, that events tend to follow. Because of free will, you can choose to plan a schedule in harmony with the flow, or you can choose to swim against the current.

The dates given in the **Astrological Timetable (page 228)** have been chosen with particular care to the astrological passage of the Moon. However, because other planets also influence us, it's best to take a look at all indicators before seeking advice on major life decisions. An astrologer can study the current relationship of the planets and your own personal birth chart to assist you in the best possible timing for carrying out your plans.

When Mercury Is Retrograde

■ Sometimes when we look out from our perspective here on Earth, the other planets appear to be traveling backward through the zodiac. (All heavenly bodies move forward. An optical illusion makes them seem as if they are moving backward.) We call this *retrograde motion.*

Mercury's retrograde periods, which occur three or four times a year, can cause travel delays and misconstrued communications. Plans have a way of unraveling, too. However, this is an excellent time to research or look into the past. Intuition is high during these periods, and coincidences can be extraordinary.

When Mercury is retrograde, astrologers advise us to keep plans flexible, allow extra time for travel, and avoid signing contracts. It's OK and even useful to look over projects and plans, because we may see them with different eyes at these times. However, our normal system of checks and balances might not be active, so it's best to wait until Mercury is direct again to make any final decisions. In 2002, Mercury will be retrograde from January 18 to February 8, May 15 to June 8, and September 14 to October 6. *—Celeste Longacre*

Gardening by the Moon's Sign

■ It is important to note that *the placement of the planets through the signs of the zodiac is not the same in astronomy and astrology.* The *astrological* placement of the Moon, by sign, is given in the table below. (The *astronomical,* or actual, placement is given in the **Left-Hand Calendar Pages 64–90.**)

For planting, the most fertile signs are the three water signs: Cancer, Scorpio, and Pisces. Good second choices are Taurus, Virgo, and Capricorn.

Weeding and plowing are best done when the Moon occupies the sign of Aries, Gemini, Leo, Sagittarius, or Aquarius. Insect pests can also be handled at these times. Transplanting and grafting are best done under a Cancer, Scorpio, or Pisces Moon. Pruning is best done under an Aries, Leo, or Sagittarius Moon, with growth encouraged during waxing (from the day of new to the day of full Moon) and discouraged during waning (from the day after full to the day before new Moon). (The dates of the Moon's phases can be found **on pages 64–90.**) Clean out the garden shed when the Moon occupies Virgo so that the work will flow smoothly. Fences and permanent beds can be built or mended when Capricorn predominates. Avoid indecision when under the Libra Moon.

Moon's Place in the Astrological Zodiac

	NOV. 2001	DEC. 2001	JAN. 2002	FEB. 2002	MAR. 2002	APR. 2002	MAY 2002	JUNE 2002	JULY 2002	AUG. 2002	SEPT. 2002	OCT. 2002	NOV. 2002	DEC. 2002
1	TAU	GEM	LEO	VIR	LIB	SAG	CAP	AQU	PSC	TAU	GEM	LEO	VIR	SCO
2	TAU	CAN	LEO	LIB	LIB	SAG	CAP	PSC	ARI	TAU	CAN	LEO	LIB	SCO
3	GEM	CAN	VIR	LIB	SCO	CAP	AQU	PSC	ARI	GEM	CAN	VIR	LIB	SAG
4	GEM	LEO	VIR	SCO	SCO	CAP	AQU	ARI	TAU	GEM	LEO	VIR	SCO	SAG
5	CAN	LEO	LIB	SCO	SAG	CAP	PSC	ARI	TAU	CAN	LEO	LIB	SCO	CAP
6	CAN	LEO	LIB	SAG	SAG	AQU	PSC	ARI	TAU	CAN	VIR	LIB	SAG	CAP
7	LEO	VIR	SCO	SAG	CAP	AQU	PSC	TAU	GEM	LEO	VIR	SCO	SAG	CAP
8	LEO	VIR	SCO	CAP	CAP	PSC	ARI	TAU	GEM	LEO	LIB	SCO	CAP	AQU
9	VIR	LIB	SCO	CAP	AQU	PSC	ARI	GEM	CAN	LEO	LIB	SAG	CAP	AQU
10	VIR	LIB	SAG	CAP	AQU	PSC	TAU	GEM	CAN	VIR	SCO	SAG	AQU	PSC
11	LIB	SCO	SAG	AQU	AQU	ARI	TAU	GEM	LEO	VIR	SCO	SAG	AQU	PSC
12	LIB	SCO	CAP	AQU	PSC	ARI	TAU	CAN	LEO	LIB	SAG	CAP	PSC	ARI
13	SCO	SAG	CAP	PSC	PSC	TAU	GEM	CAN	VIR	LIB	SAG	CAP	PSC	ARI
14	SCO	SAG	AQU	PSC	ARI	TAU	GEM	LEO	VIR	SCO	CAP	AQU	PSC	ARI
15	SCO	CAP	AQU	PSC	ARI	TAU	CAN	LEO	LIB	SCO	CAP	AQU	ARI	TAU
16	SAG	CAP	AQU	ARI	ARI	GEM	CAN	VIR	LIB	SAG	CAP	PSC	ARI	TAU
17	SAG	CAP	PSC	ARI	TAU	GEM	CAN	VIR	SCO	SAG	AQU	PSC	ARI	GEM
18	CAP	AQU	PSC	TAU	TAU	CAN	LEO	LIB	SCO	CAP	AQU	PSC	TAU	GEM
19	CAP	AQU	ARI	TAU	GEM	CAN	LEO	LIB	SCO	CAP	PSC	ARI	TAU	GEM
20	AQU	PSC	ARI	TAU	GEM	LEO	VIR	SCO	SAG	AQU	PSC	ARI	GEM	CAN
21	AQU	PSC	ARI	GEM	GEM	LEO	VIR	SCO	SAG	AQU	ARI	TAU	GEM	CAN
22	AQU	PSC	TAU	GEM	CAN	VIR	LIB	SAG	CAP	AQU	ARI	TAU	CAN	LEO
23	PSC	ARI	TAU	CAN	CAN	VIR	LIB	SAG	CAP	PSC	ARI	TAU	CAN	LEO
24	PSC	ARI	GEM	CAN	LEO	LIB	SCO	CAP	AQU	PSC	TAU	GEM	CAN	VIR
25	ARI	TAU	GEM	LEO	LEO	LIB	SCO	CAP	AQU	ARI	TAU	GEM	LEO	VIR
26	ARI	TAU	GEM	LEO	VIR	SCO	SAG	CAP	PSC	ARI	TAU	CAN	LEO	LIB
27	ARI	GEM	CAN	VIR	VIR	SCO	SAG	AQU	PSC	ARI	GEM	CAN	VIR	LIB
28	TAU	GEM	CAN	VIR	LIB	SCO	CAP	AQU	PSC	TAU	GEM	CAN	VIR	LIB
29	TAU	GEM	LEO	—	LIB	SAG	CAP	PSC	ARI	TAU	CAN	LEO	LIB	SCO
30	GEM	CAN	LEO	—	SCO	SAG	AQU	PSC	ARI	GEM	CAN	LEO	LIB	SCO
31	—	CAN	VIR	—	SCO	—	AQU	—	TAU	GEM	—	VIR	—	SAG

Astrological Timetable, 2002

■ The following month-by-month chart is based on the Moon's sign and shows the most favorable times each month for certain activities. –*Celeste Longacre*

	JAN.	FEB.	MAR.	APR.	MAY	JUNE	JULY	AUG.	SEPT.	OCT.	NOV.	DEC.
Give up smoking	2, 6, 29	2, 11	1, 10, 29	6, 7, 11	4, 5, 9, 31	5, 27, 28	2, 3, 29, 30	25, 26	4, 5, 22, 23	1, 2, 29, 30	2, 3, 25, 26	22, 23, 26, 27
Begin diet to lose weight	2, 6, 29	2, 11	1, 10, 29	6, 7, 11	4, 5, 9, 31	5, 27, 28	2, 3, 29, 30	25, 26	4, 5, 22, 23	1, 2, 29, 30	2, 3, 25, 26	22, 23, 26, 27
Begin diet to gain weight	15, 20	16, 25	15, 25	15, 16, 24, 25	18, 21, 22	14, 15, 18, 19	15, 16	12, 13, 21	8, 9, 17, 18	14, 15, 19, 20	10, 11, 15, 16	8, 9, 13, 14
Cut hair to encourage growth	17, 18, 22, 23	18, 19, 25, 26	17, 18, 24, 25	17, 18, 24, 25	22, 23	14, 15, 18, 19	15, 16	12, 13	8, 9, 19, 20	7, 17, 18	13, 14, 18, 19	10, 11, 15, 16
Cut hair to discourage growth	1, 5, 6, 29	1, 2	1, 2, 29	1, 2, 28, 29	6, 7, 11	2, 3, 7, 8	4, 5, 6, 28	1, 2, 28, 29	4, 5	1, 2, 29, 30	2, 3, 29, 30	22, 23, 26, 27
Have dental care	3, 4, 30, 31	27, 28	26, 27	22, 23	19, 20	16, 17	13, 14	10, 11	6, 7	3, 4	1, 27, 28	24, 25
End old projects	11, 12	10, 11	12, 13	10, 11	10, 11	8, 9	8, 9	6, 7	5, 6	4, 5	2, 3	2, 3
Start new projects	14, 15	13, 14	15, 16	13, 14	13, 14	11, 12	11, 12	9, 10	8, 9	7, 8	5, 6	5, 6
Entertain	1, 2, 28, 29	25, 26	24, 25	20, 21	17, 18, 19	14, 15	11, 12	8, 9	4, 5	2, 3, 29, 30	25, 26	22, 23
Go camping	9, 10	6, 7	5, 6	1, 2, 29, 30	26, 27	22, 23	20, 21	16, 17	12, 13	9, 10, 11	6, 7	3, 4, 31
Plant aboveground crops	17, 18, 23, 27	13, 14, 23, 24	17, 18, 22, 23	15, 22, 23	15, 16, 17	12, 13, 20, 21	10, 18, 19	10, 14, 15	10, 11, 19, 20	16, 17, 18	13, 14, 18, 19	10, 11, 15, 16
Plant belowground crops	8, 9, 31	4, 5, 28	3, 4, 8, 12	8, 9, 28	5, 6, 7, 29	2, 3, 29, 30	1, 27, 28	5, 6, 23, 24	2, 3, 29, 30	26, 27, 28	23, 24	1, 2, 29, 30
Destroy pests and weeds	20, 21	7, 16, 17	15, 16	11, 12	8, 9	4, 5, 6	2, 3, 29, 30	25, 26, 27	21, 22, 23	19, 20	15, 16	13, 14
Graft or pollinate	27, 28	23, 24	22, 23	18, 19	15, 16, 17	12, 13	9, 10	5, 6	2, 3, 29, 30	27, 28	23, 24	20, 21
Prune to encourage growth	19, 20	7, 16, 25, 26	15, 16, 24, 25	20, 21	18, 19	14, 15, 23	20, 21	16, 17	12, 13	19, 20	6, 7, 15, 16	13, 14
Prune to discourage growth	1, 2, 29, 30	6, 7	5, 6	1, 2, 29, 30	8, 9, 27	4, 5	2, 3, 29, 30	25, 26, 27	4, 5, 22, 23	1, 2, 29, 30	25, 26	22, 23, 31
Harvest above-ground crops	12, 13, 22, 23	18, 19	17, 18, 26, 27	13, 14, 15, 23	20, 21	16, 17	22, 23	10, 11	14, 15, 16	12, 13	8, 9, 18, 19	6, 7
Harvest below-ground crops	3, 4, 30, 31	8, 9, 28	7, 8	3, 4	1, 2, 28, 29	7, 8, 25, 26	4, 5, 9	1, 2, 28, 29	6, 24, 25	3, 4, 31	1, 27, 28	24, 25
Cut hay	20, 21	15, 16, 17	15, 16	11, 12	8, 9	4, 5, 6	2, 3, 29, 30	25, 26, 27	21, 22, 23	19, 20	15, 16	13, 14
Begin logging	12, 13	8, 9	7, 8	3, 4, 5	1, 2, 28, 29	25, 26	22, 23	18, 19	14, 15, 16	12, 13	8, 9	5, 6, 7
Set posts or pour concrete	12, 13	8, 9	7, 8	3, 4, 5	1, 2, 28, 29	25, 26	22, 23	18, 19	14, 15, 16	12, 13	8, 9	5, 6, 7
Breed	7, 8	3, 4	3, 4, 30, 31	26, 27, 28	24, 25	20, 21	17, 18, 19	14, 15	10, 11	7, 8	3, 4	1, 2, 29, 30
Wean	2, 6, 29	2, 11	1, 10, 29	6, 7, 11	4, 5, 9, 31	5, 27, 28	2, 3, 29, 30	25, 26	4, 5, 22, 23	1, 2, 29, 30	2, 3, 25, 26	22, 23, 26, 27
Castrate animals	14, 15	10, 11, 12	10, 11	6, 7	3, 4, 30, 31	1, 27, 28	24, 25	21, 22	17, 18	14, 15	10, 11	8, 9
Slaughter	7, 8	3, 4	3, 4, 30, 31	27, 28	24, 25	20, 21	18, 19	14, 15	10, 11	8, 9	4, 5	1, 2, 29, 30

Time Corrections

■ Times of sunrise/sunset and moonrise/moonset, selected times for observing the visible planets, and transit times of the bright stars are given for Boston **on pages 64–90, 54–55, and 58.** Use the Key Letter shown to the right of each time on those pages with this table to find the number of minutes, already adjusted for different time zones, that you must add to or subtract from Boston time to get the correct time for your city. (Because of complex calculations for different locales, times may not be precise to the minute.) If your city is not listed, find the city closest to you in latitude and longitude and use those figures. Boston's latitude is 42° 22' and its longitude is 71° 03'. Canadian cities appear at the end of the table. For further information on the use of Key Letters and this table, see **How to Use This Almanac, page 39.**

Time Zone Code: Codes represent *standard time.* Atlantic is –1, Eastern is 0, Central is 1, Mountain is 2, Pacific is 3, Alaska is 4, and Hawaii-Aleutian is 5.

City	North Latitude ° '		West Longitude ° '		Time Zone Code	A (min.)	B (min.)	C (min.)	D (min.)	E (min.)
Aberdeen, SD 45		28	98	29	1	+37	+44	+49	+54	+59
Akron, OH.............. 41		5	81	31	0	+46	+43	+41	+39	+37
Albany, NY 42		39	73	45	0	+ 9	+10	+10	+11	+11
Albert Lea, MN.......... 43		39	93	22	1	+24	+26	+28	+31	+33
Albuquerque, NM........ 35		5	106	39	2	+45	+32	+22	+11	+ 2
Alexandria, LA 31		18	92	27	1	+58	+40	+26	+ 9	– 3
Allentown–Bethlehem, PA.. 40		36	75	28	0	+23	+20	+17	+14	+12
Amarillo, TX............. 35		12	101	50	1	+85	+73	+63	+52	+43
Anchorage, AK 61		10	149	59	4	–46	+27	+71	+122	+171
Asheville, NC 35		36	82	33	0	+67	+55	+46	+35	+27
Atlanta, GA 33		45	84	24	0	+79	+65	+53	+40	+30
Atlantic City, NJ 39		22	74	26	0	+23	+17	+13	+ 8	+ 4
Augusta, GA 33		28	81	58	0	+70	+55	+44	+30	+19
Augusta, ME 44		19	69	46	0	–12	– 8	– 5	– 1	0
Austin, TX............... 30		16	97	45	1	+82	+62	+47	+29	+15
Bakersfield, CA.......... 35		23	119	1	3	+33	+21	+12	+ 1	– 7
Baltimore, MD 39		17	76	37	0	+32	+26	+22	+17	+13
Bangor, ME.............. 44		48	68	46	0	–18	–13	– 9	– 5	– 1
Barstow, CA 34		54	117	1	3	+27	+14	+ 4	– 7	–16
Baton Rouge, LA 30		27	91	11	1	+55	+36	+21	+ 3	–10
Beaumont, TX............ 30		5	94	6	1	+67	+48	+32	+14	0
Bellingham, WA......... 48		45	122	29	3	0	+13	+24	+37	+47
Bemidji, MN 47		28	94	53	1	+14	+26	+34	+44	+52
Berlin, NH 44		28	71	11	0	– 7	– 3	0	+ 3	+ 7
Billings, MT 45		47	108	30	2	+16	+23	+29	+35	+40
Biloxi, MS 30		24	88	53	1	+46	+27	+11	– 5	–19
Binghamton, NY......... 42		6	75	55	0	+20	+19	+19	+18	+18
Birmingham, AL......... 33		31	86	49	1	+30	+15	+ 3	–10	–20
Bismarck, ND 46		48	100	47	1	+41	+50	+58	+66	+73
Boise, ID 43		37	116	12	2	+55	+58	+60	+62	+64
Brattleboro, VT.......... 42		51	72	34	0	+ 4	+ 5	+ 5	+ 6	+ 7
Bridgeport, CT 41		11	73	11	0	+12	+10	+ 8	+ 6	+ 4
Brockton, MA 42		5	71	1	0	0	0	0	0	– 1
Brownsville, TX.......... 25		54	97	30	1	+91	+66	+46	+23	+ 5
Buffalo, NY.............. 42		53	78	52	0	+29	+30	+30	+31	+32
Burlington, VT 44		29	73	13	0	0	+ 4	+ 8	+12	+15
Butte, MT 46		1	112	32	2	+31	+39	+45	+52	+57
Cairo, IL 37		0	89	11	1	+29	+20	+12	+ 4	– 2
Camden, NJ 39		57	75	7	0	+24	+19	+16	+12	+ 9
Canton, OH 40		48	81	23	0	+46	+43	+41	+38	+36
Cape May, NJ 38		56	74	56	0	+26	+20	+15	+ 9	+ 5
Carson City–Reno, NV..... 39		10	119	46	3	+25	+19	+14	+ 9	+ 5

City	North Latitude °	'	West Longitude °	'	Time Zone Code	A (min.)	B (min.)	C (min.)	D (min.)	E (min.)
Casper, WY	42	51	106	19	2	+19	+19	+20	+21	+22
Charleston, SC	32	47	79	56	0	+64	+48	+36	+21	+10
Charleston, WV	38	21	81	38	0	+55	+48	+42	+35	+30
Charlotte, NC	35	14	80	51	0	+61	+49	+39	+28	+19
Charlottesville, VA	38	2	78	30	0	+43	+35	+29	+22	+17
Chattanooga, TN	35	3	85	19	0	+79	+67	+57	+45	+36
Cheboygan, MI	45	39	84	29	0	+40	+47	+53	+59	+64
Cheyenne, WY	41	8	104	49	2	+19	+16	+14	+12	+11
Chicago–Oak Park, IL	41	52	87	38	1	+ 7	+ 6	+ 6	+ 5	+ 4
Cincinnati–Hamilton, OH	39	6	84	31	0	+64	+58	+53	+48	+44
Cleveland–Lakewood, OH	41	30	81	42	0	+45	+43	+42	+40	+39
Columbia, SC	34	0	81	2	0	+65	+51	+40	+27	+17
Columbus, OH	39	57	83	1	0	+55	+51	+47	+43	+40
Cordova, AK	60	33	145	45	4	−55	+13	+55	+103	+149
Corpus Christi, TX	27	48	97	24	1	+86	+64	+46	+25	+ 9
Craig, CO	40	31	107	33	2	+32	+28	+25	+22	+20
Dallas–Fort Worth, TX	32	47	96	48	1	+71	+55	+43	+28	+17
Danville, IL	40	8	87	37	1	+13	+ 9	+ 6	+ 2	0
Danville, VA	36	36	79	23	0	+51	+41	+33	+24	+17
Davenport, IA	41	32	90	35	1	+20	+19	+17	+16	+15
Dayton, OH	39	45	84	10	0	+61	+56	+52	+48	+44
Decatur, AL	34	36	86	59	1	+27	+14	+ 4	− 7	−17
Decatur, IL	39	51	88	57	1	+19	+15	+11	+ 7	+ 4
Denver–Boulder, CO	39	44	104	59	2	+24	+19	+15	+11	+ 7
Des Moines, IA	41	35	93	37	1	+32	+31	+30	+28	+27
Detroit–Dearborn, MI	42	20	83	3	0	+47	+47	+47	+47	+47
Dubuque, IA	42	30	90	41	1	+17	+18	+18	+18	+18
Duluth, MN	46	47	92	6	1	+ 6	+16	+23	+31	+38
Durham, NC	36	0	78	55	0	+51	+40	+31	+21	+13
Eastport, ME	44	54	67	0	0	−26	−20	−16	−11	− 8
Eau Claire, WI	44	49	91	30	1	+12	+17	+21	+25	+29
Elko, NV	40	50	115	46	3	+ 3	0	− 1	− 3	− 5
Ellsworth, ME	44	33	68	25	0	−18	−14	−10	− 6	− 3
El Paso, TX	31	45	106	29	2	+53	+35	+22	+ 6	− 6
Erie, PA	42	7	80	5	0	+36	+36	+35	+35	+35
Eugene, OR	44	3	123	6	3	+21	+24	+27	+30	+33
Fairbanks, AK	64	48	147	51	4	−127	+ 2	+61	+131	+205
Fall River–New Bedford, MA	41	42	71	9	0	+ 2	+ 1	0	0	− 1
Fargo, ND	46	53	96	47	1	+24	+34	+42	+50	+57
Flagstaff, AZ	35	12	111	39	2	+64	+52	+42	+31	+22
Flint, MI	43	1	83	41	0	+47	+49	+50	+51	+52
Fort Myers, FL	26	38	81	52	0	+87	+63	+44	+21	+ 4
Fort Scott, KS	37	50	94	42	1	+49	+41	+34	+27	+21
Fort Smith, AR	35	23	94	25	1	+55	+43	+33	+22	+14
Fort Wayne, IN	41	4	85	9	0	+60	+58	+56	+54	+52
Fresno, CA	36	44	119	47	3	+32	+22	+15	+ 6	0
Gallup, NM	35	32	108	45	2	+52	+40	+31	+20	+11
Galveston, TX	29	18	94	48	1	+72	+52	+35	+16	+ 1
Gary, IN	41	36	87	20	1	+ 7	+ 6	+ 4	+ 3	+ 2
Glasgow, MT	48	12	106	38	2	− 1	+11	+21	+32	+42
Grand Forks, ND	47	55	97	3	1	+21	+33	+43	+53	+62
Grand Island, NE	40	55	98	21	1	+53	+51	+49	+46	+44
Grand Junction, CO	39	4	108	33	2	+40	+34	+29	+24	+20
Great Falls, MT	47	30	111	17	2	+20	+31	+39	+49	+58
Green Bay, WI	44	31	88	0	1	0	+ 3	+ 7	+11	+14
Greensboro, NC	36	4	79	47	0	+54	+43	+35	+25	+17

City	North Latitude ° '		West Longitude ° '		Time Zone Code	A (min.)	B (min.)	C (min.)	D (min.)	E (min.)
Hagerstown, MD	39	39	77	43	0	+35	+30	+26	+22	+18
Harrisburg, PA	40	16	76	53	0	+30	+26	+23	+19	+16
Hartford–New Britain, CT	41	46	72	41	0	+ 8	+ 7	+ 6	+ 5	+ 4
Helena, MT	46	36	112	2	2	+27	+36	+43	+51	+57
Hilo, HI	19	44	155	5	5	+94	+62	+37	+ 7	−15
Honolulu, HI	21	18	157	52	5	+102	+72	+48	+19	− 1
Houston, TX	29	45	95	22	1	+73	+53	+37	+19	+ 5
Indianapolis, IN	39	46	86	10	0	+69	+64	+60	+56	+52
Ironwood, MI	46	27	90	9	1	0	+ 9	+15	+23	+29
Jackson, MI	42	15	84	24	0	+53	+53	+53	+52	+52
Jackson, MS	32	18	90	11	1	+46	+30	+17	+ 1	−10
Jacksonville, FL	30	20	81	40	0	+77	+58	+43	+25	+11
Jefferson City, MO	38	34	92	10	1	+36	+29	+24	+18	+13
Joplin, MO	37	6	94	30	1	+50	+41	+33	+25	+18
Juneau, AK	58	18	134	25	4	−76	−23	+10	+49	+86
Kalamazoo, MI	42	17	85	35	0	+58	+57	+57	+57	+57
Kanab, UT	37	3	112	32	2	+62	+53	+46	+37	+30
Kansas City, MO	39	1	94	20	1	+44	+37	+33	+27	+23
Keene, NH	42	56	72	17	0	+ 2	+ 3	+ 4	+ 5	+ 6
Ketchikan, AK	55	21	131	39	4	−62	−25	0	+29	+56
Knoxville, TN	35	58	83	55	0	+71	+60	+51	+41	+33
Kodiak, AK	57	47	152	24	4	0	+49	+82	+120	+154
LaCrosse, WI	43	48	91	15	1	+15	+18	+20	+22	+25
Lake Charles, LA	30	14	93	13	1	+64	+44	+29	+11	− 2
Lanai City, HI	20	50	156	55	5	+99	+69	+44	+15	− 6
Lancaster, PA	40	2	76	18	0	+28	+24	+20	+17	+13
Lansing, MI	42	44	84	33	0	+52	+53	+53	+54	+54
Las Cruces, NM	32	19	106	47	2	+53	+36	+23	+ 8	− 3
Las Vegas, NV	36	10	115	9	3	+16	+ 4	− 3	−13	−20
Lawrence–Lowell, MA	42	42	71	10	0	0	0	0	0	+ 1
Lewiston, ID	46	25	117	1	3	−12	− 3	+ 2	+10	+17
Lexington–Frankfort, KY	38	3	84	30	0	+67	+59	+53	+46	+41
Liberal, KS	37	3	100	55	1	+76	+66	+59	+51	+44
Lihue, HI	21	59	159	23	5	+107	+77	+54	+26	+ 5
Lincoln, NE	40	49	96	41	1	+47	+44	+42	+39	+37
Little Rock, AR	34	45	92	17	1	+48	+35	+25	+13	+ 4
Los Angeles–Pasadena–Santa Monica, CA	34	3	118	14	3	+34	+20	+ 9	− 3	−13
Louisville, KY	38	15	85	46	0	+72	+64	+58	+52	+46
Macon, GA	32	50	83	38	0	+79	+63	+50	+36	+24
Madison, WI	43	4	89	23	1	+10	+11	+12	+14	+15
Manchester–Concord, NH	42	59	71	28	0	0	0	+ 1	+ 2	+ 3
McAllen, TX	26	12	98	14	1	+93	+69	+49	+26	+ 9
Memphis, TN	35	9	90	3	1	+38	+26	+16	+ 5	− 3
Meridian, MS	32	22	88	42	1	+40	+24	+11	− 4	−15
Miami, FL	25	47	80	12	0	+88	+57	+37	+14	− 3
Miles City, MT	46	25	105	51	2	+ 3	+11	+18	+26	+32
Milwaukee, WI	43	2	87	54	1	+ 4	+ 6	+ 7	+ 8	+ 9
Minneapolis–St. Paul, MN	44	59	93	16	1	+18	+24	+28	+33	+37
Minot, ND	48	14	101	18	1	+36	+50	+59	+71	+81
Moab, UT	38	35	109	33	2	+46	+39	+33	+27	+22
Mobile, AL	30	42	88	3	1	+42	+23	+ 8	− 8	−22
Monroe, LA	32	30	92	7	1	+53	+37	+24	+ 9	− 1
Montgomery, AL	32	23	86	19	1	+31	+14	+ 1	−13	−25
Muncie, IN	40	12	85	23	0	+64	+60	+57	+53	+50
Nashville, TN	36	10	86	47	1	+22	+11	+ 3	− 6	−14
Newark–East Orange, NJ	40	44	74	10	0	+17	+14	+12	+ 9	+ 7

City	North Latitude °	′	West Longitude °	′	Time Zone Code	A (min.)	B (min.)	C (min.)	D (min.)	E (min.)
New Haven, CT	41	18	72	56	0	+11	+ 8	+ 7	+ 5	+ 4
New London, CT	41	22	72	6	0	+ 7	+ 5	+ 4	+ 2	+ 1
New Orleans, LA	29	57	90	4	1	+52	+32	+16	− 1	−15
New York, NY	40	45	74	0	0	+17	+14	+11	+ 9	+ 6
Norfolk, VA	36	51	76	17	0	+38	+28	+21	+12	+ 5
North Platte, NE	41	8	100	46	1	+62	+60	+58	+56	+54
Norwalk–Stamford, CT	41	7	73	22	0	+13	+10	+ 9	+ 7	+ 5
Oakley, KS	39	8	100	51	1	+69	+63	+59	+53	+49
Ogden, UT	41	13	111	58	2	+47	+45	+43	+41	+40
Ogdensburg, NY	44	42	75	30	0	+ 8	+13	+17	+21	+25
Oklahoma City, OK	35	28	97	31	1	+67	+55	+46	+35	+26
Omaha, NE	41	16	95	56	1	+43	+40	+39	+37	+36
Orlando, FL	28	32	81	22	0	+80	+59	+42	+22	+ 6
Ortonville, MN	45	19	96	27	1	+30	+36	+40	+46	+51
Oshkosh, WI	44	1	88	33	1	+ 3	+ 6	+ 9	+12	+15
Palm Springs, CA	33	49	116	32	3	+28	+13	+ 1	−12	−22
Parkersburg, WV	39	16	81	34	0	+52	+46	+42	+36	+32
Paterson, NJ	40	55	74	10	0	+17	+14	+12	+ 9	+ 7
Pendleton, OR	45	40	118	47	3	− 1	+ 4	+10	+16	+21
Pensacola, FL	30	25	87	13	1	+39	+20	+ 5	−12	−26
Peoria, IL	40	42	89	36	1	+19	+16	+14	+11	+ 9
Philadelphia–Chester, PA	39	57	75	9	0	+24	+19	+16	+12	+ 9
Phoenix, AZ	33	27	112	4	2	+71	+56	+44	+30	+20
Pierre, SD	44	22	100	21	1	+49	+53	+56	+60	+63
Pittsburgh–McKeesport, PA	40	26	80	0	0	+42	+38	+35	+32	+29
Pittsfield, MA	42	27	73	15	0	+ 8	+ 8	+ 8	+ 8	+ 8
Pocatello, ID	42	52	112	27	2	+43	+44	+45	+46	+46
Poplar Bluff, MO	36	46	90	24	1	+35	+25	+17	+ 8	+ 1
Portland, ME	43	40	70	15	0	− 8	− 5	− 3	− 1	0
Portland, OR	45	31	122	41	3	+14	+20	+25	+31	+36
Portsmouth, NH	43	5	70	45	0	− 4	− 2	− 1	0	0
Presque Isle, ME	46	41	68	1	0	−29	−19	−12	− 4	+ 2
Providence, RI	41	50	71	25	0	+ 3	+ 2	+ 1	0	0
Pueblo, CO	38	16	104	37	2	+27	+20	+14	+ 7	+ 2
Raleigh, NC	35	47	78	38	0	+51	+39	+30	+20	+12
Rapid City, SD	44	5	103	14	2	+ 2	+ 5	+ 8	+11	+13
Reading, PA	40	20	75	56	0	+26	+22	+19	+16	+13
Redding, CA	40	35	122	24	3	+31	+27	+25	+22	+19
Richmond, VA	37	32	77	26	0	+41	+32	+25	+17	+11
Roanoke, VA	37	16	79	57	0	+51	+42	+35	+27	+21
Roswell, NM	33	24	104	32	2	+41	+26	+14	0	−10
Rutland, VT	43	37	72	58	0	+ 2	+ 5	+ 7	+ 9	+11
Sacramento, CA	38	35	121	30	3	+34	+27	+21	+15	+10
St. Johnsbury, VT	44	25	72	1	0	− 4	0	+ 3	+ 7	+10
St. Joseph, MI	42	5	86	26	0	+61	+61	+60	+60	+59
St. Joseph, MO	39	46	94	50	1	+43	+38	+35	+30	+27
St. Louis, MO	38	37	90	12	1	+28	+21	+16	+10	+ 5
St. Petersburg, FL	27	46	82	39	0	+87	+65	+47	+26	+10
Salem, OR	44	57	123	1	3	+17	+23	+27	+31	+35
Salina, KS	38	50	97	37	1	+57	+51	+46	+40	+35
Salisbury, MD	38	22	75	36	0	+31	+23	+18	+11	+ 6
Salt Lake City, UT	40	45	111	53	2	+48	+45	+43	+40	+38
San Antonio, TX	29	25	98	30	1	+87	+66	+50	+31	+16
San Diego, CA	32	43	117	9	3	+33	+17	+ 4	− 9	−21
San Francisco–Oakland– San Jose, CA	37	47	122	25	3	+40	+31	+25	+18	+12
Santa Fe, NM	35	41	105	56	2	+40	+28	+19	+ 9	0

City	North Latitude °	'	West Longitude °	'	Time Zone Code	A (min.)	B (min.)	C (min.)	D (min.)	E (min.)
Savannah, GA	32	5	81	6	0	+70	+54	+40	+25	+13
Scranton–Wilkes-Barre, PA	41	25	75	40	0	+21	+19	+18	+16	+15
Seattle–Tacoma– Olympia, WA	47	37	122	20	3	+ 3	+15	+24	+34	+42
Sheridan, WY	44	48	106	58	2	+14	+19	+23	+27	+31
Shreveport, LA	32	31	93	45	1	+60	+44	+31	+16	+ 4
Sioux Falls, SD	43	33	96	44	1	+38	+40	+42	+44	+46
South Bend, IN	41	41	86	15	0	+62	+61	+60	+59	+58
Spartanburg, SC	34	56	81	57	0	+66	+53	+43	+32	+23
Spokane, WA	47	40	117	24	3	−16	− 4	+ 4	+14	+23
Springfield, IL	39	48	89	39	1	+22	+18	+14	+10	+ 6
Springfield–Holyoke, MA	42	6	72	36	0	+ 6	+ 6	+ 6	+ 5	+ 5
Springfield, MO	37	13	93	18	1	+45	+36	+29	+20	+14
Syracuse, NY	43	3	76	9	0	+17	+19	+20	+21	+22
Tallahassee, FL	30	27	84	17	0	+87	+68	+53	+35	+22
Tampa, FL	27	57	82	27	0	+86	+64	+46	+25	+ 9
Terre Haute, IN	39	28	87	24	0	+74	+69	+65	+60	+56
Texarkana, AR	33	26	94	3	1	+59	+44	+32	+18	+ 8
Toledo, OH	41	39	83	33	0	+52	+50	+49	+48	+47
Topeka, KS	39	3	95	40	1	+49	+43	+38	+32	+28
Traverse City, MI	44	46	85	38	0	+49	+54	+57	+62	+65
Trenton, NJ	40	13	74	46	0	+21	+17	+14	+11	+ 8
Trinidad, CO	37	10	104	31	2	+30	+21	+13	+ 5	0
Tucson, AZ	32	13	110	58	2	+70	+53	+40	+24	+12
Tulsa, OK	36	9	95	60	1	+59	+48	+40	+30	+22
Tupelo, MS	34	16	88	34	1	+35	+21	+10	− 2	−11
Vernal, UT	40	27	109	32	2	+40	+36	+33	+30	+28
Walla Walla, WA	46	4	118	20	3	− 5	+ 2	+ 8	+15	+21
Washington, DC	38	54	77	1	0	+35	+28	+23	+18	+13
Waterbury–Meriden, CT	41	33	73	3	0	+10	+ 9	+ 7	+ 6	+ 5
Waterloo, IA	42	30	92	20	1	+24	+24	+24	+25	+25
Wausau, WI	44	58	89	38	1	+ 4	+ 9	+13	+18	+22
West Palm Beach, FL	26	43	80	3	0	+79	+55	+36	+14	− 2
Wichita, KS	37	42	97	20	1	+60	+51	+45	+37	+31
Williston, ND	48	9	103	37	1	+46	+59	+69	+80	+90
Wilmington, DE	39	45	75	33	0	+26	+21	+18	+13	+10
Wilmington, NC	34	14	77	55	0	+52	+38	+27	+15	+ 5
Winchester, VA	39	11	78	10	0	+38	+33	+28	+23	+19
Worcester, MA	42	16	71	48	0	+ 3	+ 2	+ 2	+ 2	+ 2
York, PA	39	58	76	43	0	+30	+26	+22	+18	+15
Youngstown, OH	41	6	80	39	0	+42	40	+38	+36	+34
Yuma, AZ	32	43	114	37	2	+83	+67	+54	+40	+28
CANADA										
Calgary, AB	51	5	114	5	2	+13	+35	+50	+68	+84
Edmonton, AB	53	34	113	25	2	− 3	+26	+47	+72	+93
Halifax, NS	44	38	63	35	−1	+21	+26	+29	+33	+37
Montreal, QC	45	28	73	39	0	− 1	+ 4	+ 9	+15	+20
Ottawa, ON	45	25	75	43	0	+ 6	+13	+18	+23	+28
Peterborough, ON	44	18	78	19	0	+21	+25	+28	+32	+35
Saint John, NB	45	16	66	3	−1	+28	+34	+39	+44	+49
Saskatoon, SK	52	10	106	40	1	+37	+63	+80	+101	+119
Sydney, NS	46	10	60	10	−1	+ 1	+ 9	+15	+23	+28
Thunder Bay, ON	48	27	89	12	0	+47	+61	+71	+83	+93
Toronto, ON	43	39	79	23	0	+28	+30	+32	+35	+37
Vancouver, BC	49	13	123	6	3	0	+15	+26	+40	+52
Winnipeg, MB	49	53	97	10	1	+12	+30	+43	+58	+71

Tide Corrections

■ Many factors affect the times and heights of the tides: the coastal configuration, the time of the Moon's southing (crossing the meridian), and the Moon's phase. The High Tide column on the **Left-Hand Calendar Pages 64–90** lists the times of high tide at Commonwealth Pier in Boston Harbor. The heights of some of these tides, reckoned from Mean Lower Low Water, are given on the **Right-Hand Calendar Pages 65–91**. Use this table to calculate the approximate times and heights of high water at the places shown. Apply the time difference to the times of high tide at Boston **(pages 64–90)** and the height difference to the heights at Boston **(pages 65–91)**.

Estimations derived from this table are *not* meant to be used for navigation. *The Old Farmer's Almanac* accepts no responsibility for errors or any consequences ensuing from the use of this table.

Predictions for many other stations can be found at the National Ocean Service Web site, http://co-ops.nos. noaa.gov, and at Canada's Department of Fisheries and Oceans Web site, www.dfo-mpo.gc.ca/ home-accueil_e.htm.

Coastal Site	Difference: Time (h. m.)	Height (ft.)
Canada		
Alberton, PE	−5 45**	−7.5
Charlottetown, PE	−0 45**	−3.5
Halifax, NS	−3 23	−4.5
North Sydney, NS	−3 15	−6.5
Saint John, NB	+0 30	+15.0
St. John's, NF	−4 00	−6.5
Yarmouth, NS	−0 40	+3.0
Maine		
Bar Harbor	−0 34	+0.9
Belfast	−0 20	+0.4
Boothbay Harbor	−0 18	−0.8
Chebeague Island	−0 16	−0.6
Eastport	−0 28	+8.4
Kennebunkport	+0 04	−1.0
Machias	−0 28	+2.8
Monhegan Island	−0 25	−0.8
Old Orchard	0 00	−0.8
Portland	−0 12	−0.6
Rockland	−0 28	+0.1
Stonington	−0 30	+0.1

Coastal Site	Difference: Time (h. m.)	Height (ft.)
York	−0 09	−1.0
New Hampshire		
Hampton	+0 02	−1.3
Portsmouth	+0 11	−1.5
Rye Beach	−0 09	−0.9
Massachusetts		
Annisquam	−0 02	−1.1
Beverly Farms	0 00	−0.5
Boston	0 00	0.0
Cape Cod Canal		
East Entrance	−0 01	−0.8
West Entrance	−2 16	−5.9
Chatham Outer Coast	+0 30	−2.8
Inside	+1 54	*0.4
Cohasset	+0 02	−0.07
Cotuit Highlands	+1 15	*0.3
Dennis Port	+1 01	*0.4
Duxbury–Gurnet Point	+0 02	−0.3
Fall River	−3 03	−5.0
Gloucester	−0 03	−0.8
Hingham	+0 07	0.0
Hull	+0 03	−0.2
Hyannis Port	+1 01	*0.3
Magnolia–Manchester	−0 02	−0.7
Marblehead	−0 02	−0.4
Marion	−3 22	−5.4
Monument Beach	−3 08	−5.4
Nahant	−0 01	−0.5
Nantasket	+0 04	−0.1
Nantucket	+0 56	*0.3
Nauset Beach	+0 30	*0.6
New Bedford	−3 24	−5.7
Newburyport	+0 19	−1.8
Oak Bluffs	+0 30	*0.2
Onset–R.R. Bridge	−2 16	−5.9
Plymouth	+0 05	0.0
Provincetown	+0 14	−0.4
Revere Beach	−0 01	−0.3
Rockport	−0 08	−1.0
Salem	0 00	−0.5
Scituate	−0 05	−0.7
Wareham	−3 09	−5.3
Wellfleet	+0 12	+0.5
West Falmouth	−3 10	−5.4
Westport Harbor	−3 22	−6.4
Woods Hole		
Little Harbor	−2 50	*0.2
Oceanographic Inst.	−3 07	*0.2
Rhode Island		
Bristol	−3 24	−5.3
Narragansett Pier	−3 42	−6.2
Newport	−3 34	−5.9
Point Judith	−3 41	−6.3

Coastal Site	Difference:	Time (h. m.)	Height (ft.)	Coastal Site	Difference:	Time (h. m.)	Height (ft.)
Providence		−3 20	−4.8	Yorktown		−2 13	−7.0
Sakonnet		−3 44	−5.6	**North Carolina**			
Watch Hill		−2 50	−6.8	Cape Fear		−3 55	−5.0
Connecticut				Cape Lookout		−4 28	−5.7
Bridgeport		+0 01	−2.6	Currituck		−4 10	−5.8
Madison		−0 22	−2.3	Hatteras			
New Haven		−0 11	−3.2	Inlet		−4 03	−7.4
New London		−1 54	−6.7	Kitty Hawk		−4 14	−6.2
Norwalk		+0 01	−2.2	Ocean		−4 26	−6.0
Old Lyme				**South Carolina**			
Highway Bridge		−0 30	−6.2	Charleston		−3 22	−4.3
Stamford		+0 01	−2.2	Georgetown		−1 48	*0.36
Stonington		−2 27	−6.6	Hilton Head		−3 22	−2.9
New York				Myrtle Beach		−3 49	−4.4
Coney Island		−3 33	−4.9	St. Helena			
Fire Island Light		−2 43	*0.1	Harbor Entrance		−3 15	−3.4
Long Beach		−3 11	−5.7	**Georgia**			
Montauk Harbor		−2 19	−7.4	Jekyll Island		−3 46	−2.9
New York City–Battery		−2 43	−5.0	St. Simon's Island		−2 50	−2.9
Oyster Bay		+0 04	−1.8	Savannah Beach			
Port Chester		−0 09	−2.2	River Entrance		−3 14	−5.5
Port Washington		−0 01	−2.1	Tybee Light		−3 22	−2.7
Sag Harbor		−0 55	−6.8	**Florida**			
Southampton				Cape Canaveral		−3 59	−6.0
Shinnecock Inlet		−4 20	*0.2	Daytona Beach		−3 28	−5.3
Willets Point		0 00	−2.3	Fort Lauderdale		−2 50	−7.2
New Jersey				Fort Pierce Inlet		−3 32	−6.9
Asbury Park		−4 04	−5.3	Jacksonville			
Atlantic City		−3 56	−5.5	Railroad Bridge		−6 55	*0.1
Bay Head–Sea Girt		−4 04	−5.3	Miami Harbor Entrance		−3 18	−7.0
Beach Haven		−1 43	*0.24	St. Augustine		−2 55	−4.9
Cape May		−3 28	−5.3				
Ocean City		−3 06	−5.9				
Sandy Hook		−3 30	−5.0				
Seaside Park		−4 03	−5.4				
Pennsylvania							
Philadelphia		+2 40	−3.5				
Delaware							
Cape Henlopen		−2 48	−5.3				
Rehoboth Beach		−3 37	−5.7				
Wilmington		+1 56	−3.8				
Maryland							
Annapolis		+6 23	−8.5				
Baltimore		+7 59	−8.3				
Cambridge		+5 05	−7.8				
Havre de Grace		+11 21	−7.7				
Point No Point		+2 28	−8.1				
Prince Frederick							
Plum Point		+4 25	−8.5				
Virginia							
Cape Charles		−2 20	−7.0				
Hampton Roads		−2 02	−6.9				
Norfolk		−2 06	−6.6				
Virginia Beach		−4 00	−6.0				

*Where the difference in the Height column is so marked, height at Boston should be multiplied by this ratio.

**Varies widely; accurate only within 1½ hours. Consult local tide tables for precise times and heights.

Example: The conversion of the times and heights of the tides at Boston to those of Cape Fear, North Carolina, is given below:

Sample tide calculation July 4, 2002:

High tide Boston (p. 80)	7:00 A.M. EDT
Correction for Cape Fear	−3:55 hrs.
High tide Cape Fear	3:05 A.M. EDT
Tide height Boston (p. 81)	8.5 ft.
Correction for Cape Fear	−5.0 ft.
Tide height Cape Fear	3.5 ft.

The Twilight Zone

How to determine the length of twilight and the times of dawn and dark.

■ Twilight is the period of time between dawn and sunrise, and again between sunset and dark. Both dawn and dark are defined as moments when the Sun is 18 degrees below the horizon. The latitude of a place and the time of year determine the length of twilight. To find the latitude of your city or the city nearest you, consult the **Time Corrections table, page 229.** Use that figure in the chart below with the appropriate date, and you will have the length of twilight in your area.

Latitude	Length of Twilight (hours and minutes)								
	Jan. 1 to Apr. 10	Apr. 11 to May 2	May 3 to May 14	May 15 to May 25	May 26 to July 22	July 23 to Aug. 3	Aug. 4 to Aug. 14	Aug. 15 to Sept. 5	Sept. 6 to Dec. 31
25° N to 30° N	1 20	1 23	1 26	1 29	1 32	1 29	1 26	1 23	1 20
31° N to 36° N	1 26	1 28	1 34	1 38	1 43	1 38	1 34	1 28	1 26
37° N to 42° N	1 33	1 39	1 47	1 52	1 59	1 52	1 47	1 39	1 33
43° N to 47° N	1 42	1 51	2 02	2 13	2 27	2 13	2 02	1 51	1 42
48° N to 49° N	1 50	2 04	2 22	2 42	—	2 42	2 22	2 04	1 50

■ To determine when dawn will break and when dark will descend, apply the length of twilight to the times of sunrise and sunset. Follow the instructions given in **How to Use This Almanac, page 39,** to determine sunrise/sunset times for your locality. Subtract the length of twilight from the time of sunrise for dawn. Add the length of twilight to the time of sunset for dark. (See examples at right.)

	Boston, Mass. (latitude 42° 22')	Oshkosh, Wis. (latitude 44° 1')
Sunrise, August 1	5:37 A.M.	5:40 A.M.
Length of twilight	−1:52	−2:13
Dawn breaks	3:45 A.M. EDT	3:27 A.M. CDT
Sunset, August 1	8:04 P.M.	8:16 P.M.
Length of twilight	+1:52	+2:13
Dark descends	9:56 P.M. EDT	10:29 P.M. CDT

Tidal Glossary

Apogean Tide: A monthly tide of decreased range that occurs when the Moon is at apogee (farthest from Earth).

Diurnal Tide: A tide with one high water and one low water in a tidal day of approximately 24 hours.

Mean Lower Low Water: The arithmetic mean of the lesser of a daily pair of low waters, observed over a specific 19-year cycle called the National Tidal Datum Epoch.

Neap Tide: A tide of decreased range that occurs twice a month, when the Moon is in quadrature (during its first and last quarters, when the Sun and the Moon are at right angles to each other relative to Earth).

Perigean Tide: A monthly tide of increased range that occurs when the Moon is at perigee (closest to Earth).

Semidiurnal Tide: A tide with one high water and one low water every half day. East Coast tides, for example, are semidiurnal, with two highs and two lows during a tidal day of approximately 24 hours.

Spring Tide: A tide of increased range that occurs at times of syzygy each month. Named not for the season of spring but from the German *springen* ("to leap up"), a spring tide also brings a lower low water.

Syzygy: The nearly straight-line configuration that occurs twice a month, when the Sun and the Moon are in conjunction (on the same side of Earth at the new Moon) and when they are in opposition (on opposite sides of Earth at the full Moon). In both cases, the gravitational effects of the Sun and the Moon reinforce each other, and tidal range is increased.

Vanishing Tide: A mixed tide of considerable inequality in the two highs and two lows, so that the lower high (or higher low) may become indistinct or appear to vanish.

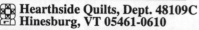

The Old Farmer's
The **Old Farmer's**

General Store

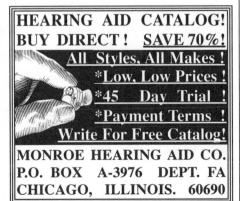

The **Old Farmer's**
General Store

Classified Advertising

ALTERNATIVE ENERGY

YOUR OWN ELECTRICITY COSTS LESS! Generators. Imperial-OF, 8569 Ward North, Kinsman OH 44428. 888-830-0498.www.imperialsource.com.

GO SOLAR! REDUCE UTILITY BILLS! Solar water heating and electricity. South Carolina Solar. 803-802-5522. www.scsolar.com.

ART & COLLECTIBLES

NORMAN ROCKWELL prints, posters. $4. Refundable. Rockwell Gallery Collection, Box 1260F, Huntingdon Valley PA 19006. 215-969-5619. Web site: www.rockwellsite.com. E-mail: rockwellsite@snip.net.

ASTROLOGY/OCCULT

GIFTED LIVE PSYCHICS. 24 hours daily. Guaranteed 100% satisfaction or money back. Over 50,000 happy clients. Psychic Source . . . We know . . . 877-236-9718. www.psychicsource.com.

FREE MINI READINGS. Psychic Diana has the ability to solve all problems. Removes spells and reunites loved ones. Toronto, Ontario; 416-226-5418.

POWERFUL SPELLS performed by Gabrielle. Specializing in reuniting lovers. Guaranteed in two hours. 504-471-2693.

DO YOU NEED HELP? God-gifted spiritual healer can help in all problems in life. Free reading. Sister Star. 304-525-9400.

FREE! ONE BLACK OR WHITE MAGIC SPELL! Tell me what you need! Eskes, PO Box 9315(B), San Bernardino CA 92427-9315.

ASTROLOGY—FREE CATALOG: books, tapes, tarot, spirituality. 800-500-0453 or 714-255-9218. Church of Light at www.light.org.

DEVELOP AWESOME OCCULT AND PSYCHIC POWERS. Train by correspondence course to be a psychic, spiritual advisor, counselor, healer, or teacher. Become a recognized professional, earning unlimited income, with our Ph.D. doctoral degree program. No previous education required. Metaphysical University, 2110 Artesia Blvd., Admissions #B-264, Redondo Beach CA 90278-3014. 310-398-1638. E-mail: mysticadamad@mediaone.net.

DO YOU NEED HELP finding and returning a loved one? Get all the answers to better your life. Miss Hart, 2146 Celanese Rd., Rock Hill SC 29732. 803-981-7680.

OCCULT POWER CATALOG: Large selection herbs, oils, incense, books, etc. $3. Power Products, PO Box 442, Mars Hill NC 28754.

MISS LISA, astrology reader and advisor. Extraordinary powers. Call for help with all problems. Waycross GA 31501. 912-283-3206.

MRS. JANE, Louisiana bayou power! Reunites lovers. Solves problems. Readings. White Magic spells/packages. 318-356-9419.

NUMEROLOGIST translates your full name into Lucky Numbers. $10. Farrar, PO Box 23725, Normandy MO 63121.

FREE READINGS. Sister Jones. God-gifted psychic. Solves all problems, reunites lovers. 110% successful. Phone 512-845-2053.

FREE PROTECTIVE PENTACLE! Come home to the old ways. Wicca Nature Religion, PO Box 297-OP, Hinton WV 25951.

WITCH WORKS™. Empowered Moon-cultivated herbal potions, essences. Box 1839, Royal Oak MI 48068-1839. 248-542-3113. www.witchworks.com.

MRS. KING, spiritual reader and advisor, will help in all matters of life where all others have failed. Call 912-283-0635.

FREE LUCKY NUMBERS. Send birth date, self-addressed stamped envelope. Mystic, Box 2009-R, Jamestown NC 27282.

AUCTIONS

ATTENTION! Wholesale auction 24 hours a day on eBay. Search by seller code: mwire. Or go to www.whsl.net.

BED & BREAKFASTS/COUNTRY INNS

THE DINOSAUR CAPITAL OF TEXAS, just a short drive from Dallas–Ft. Worth. Stay at the new Best Western Hotel in Glen Rose, Texas. Dinosaur Valley Inn and Suites, 1311 Northeast Big Bend Trail, directly adjacent to Somervell County Exposition Center. Visit us at our Web site: www.dinosaurvalleyinn.com for a virtual tour, or call 800-280-2055 for reservations.

BEE-KEEPING EQUIPMENT

YOU NEED BEES. Pollinate your garden, produce honey, and more. Everything to start. Free 80-page catalog. 800-233-7929. Web site: www.beeequipment.com.

COOKBOOKS

NEBRASKA CHILDREN'S Home Society cookbook. 800 family recipes. *Recipes Made with Love.* Mail $17 check. NCHS, 4700 Valley Rd., Lincoln NE 68510.

CRAFTS

ANGELICALLY illuminated, recycled angel group or single angel plans $5. Charming garden angel plans $5. LSASE to Angel Works, PO Box 422, Rutherford NJ 07070.

DATE LINE

IT'S FREE! Ladies talk to local guys. It's new, fun, and exciting! Call 800-485-4047. 18+.

DEER CONTROL

DEER PROBLEMS? We can help! Free catalog. Call Deerbusters, 888-422-3337. Web site: www.deerbusters.com.

DOLLHOUSES

DOLLHOUSES FOR BARBIE. Beautiful, sturdy! A lifetime of enjoyment. Plans, kits, or finished wooden dollhouses. www.woodendollhouses.com.

EDUCATION/INSTRUCTION

LEARN TO RESOLVE YOUR IRS PROBLEMS (liens, garnishments, returns). SASE. Preferred $ervices, 203 Argonne B209, Long Beach CA 90803. www.preferredservices.org.

BECOME A HOME INSPECTOR. Approved home study. Free literature. P.C.D.I., Atlanta, Georgia. 800-362-7070, Dept. PPK554.

BECOME A MEDICAL BILLING/CLAIMS SPECIALIST. Home study. P.C.D.I., Atlanta, Georgia. Free career literature. Call 800-362-7070, Dept. MCK554.

BECOME A MEDICAL TRANSCRIPTIONIST. Home study. Free career literature. P.C.D.I., Atlanta, Georgia. 800-362-7070, Dept.YYK554.

STUDY AT HOME. Certification in health information counseling. View free catalog and videos at www.wholehealtheducation.com.

COMPLETE HIGH SCHOOL AT HOME. Diploma awarded. Low tuition. Est. 1897. Accredited. Telephone 800-531-9268 for free information, or write to American School, Dept. #348, 2200 E. 170th St., Lansing IL 60438.

LEARN LANDSCAPING at home. Free brochure. Call 800-326-9221, or write Lifetime Career Schools, Dept: OB0191, 101 Harrison St., Archbald PA 18403.

FARM SUPPLIES

BELOW RETAIL! Incubators, supplies, chicks. www.dblrsupply.com or 321-768-1912.

FARM SUPPLIES WANTED

WANTED MILLSTONE(S). Will pay reasonable price/shipping. Send photos: Henry Hine, 2706 Harvest Dr., SE Conyers GA 30013-2410. Days 404-897-7566.

FINANCIAL

LET THE GOVERNMENT START your business. Free internet service—free grants and loans—free incorporation—free merchant account—free credit card processing software. 800-306-0873. www.capitalpublications.com.

FLAGS

BETSY ROSS FLAG, 3'x5', sewn cotton, appliquéd stars. $46 ppd. FCTC, PO Box 822, Kimberton PA 19442. Visa/MC. www.usflagshop.com.

FUND-RAISING

MAKE GOOD MONEY for your school, group, or organization selling The Old Farmer's Almanac publications and calendars to friends and neighbors. Great products sell themselves! Great prices! Great opportunity! Call today 800-424-6906. The Old Farmer's Almanac Fund-Raising, 220 South St., Bernardston MA 01337. www.gbimarketing.com.

GARDENING

FRAGRANCE. Seeds for fragrant, rare, and old-fashioned plants. Catalog $2. The Fragrant Path, PO Box 328F, Ft. Calhoun NE 68023.

GARDENING SUPPLIES

NEW! Raised-bed modular frames made of 100% recycled plastic! Never rot! Snap together! Maintenance free! 770-513-1372. Web site: ecologicalsusa@hotmail.com.

CANNING SUPPLIES. Extensive selection. Canners, dryers, jars, ingredients, tools, books. Free catalog. 800-776-0575. www.kitchenkrafts.com.

GENEALOGY

GENEALOGIES FOR SALE. Over 12,000 rare family and local history books for sale. Catalogs $5. Higginson Books, 148-FA Washington St., Salem MA 01970. MC/Visa. 978-745-7170. Web site: www.higginsonbooks.com.

GIFTS

FINE GIFTS FOR ALL OCCASIONS! Unique assortment of unusual items. Free shipping on orders over $50. www.gloriagifts.com.

BE LUCKY, BE HAPPY at theluckshop.com. Curios, treasures for your joy, comfort, and fun.

BEAUTIFUL HAND-PAINTED MAILBOXES. Great gifts! Florals, birds, baskets, more. Web site: www.countrymailboxes.com. 603-899-2146.

UNIQUE GIFTS for weddings, anniversaries, and birthdays. Traditional and commemorative coins. Details $2. R. A. Rogers, PO Box 1122, Cowpen SC 29330.

GINSENG

GINSENG. First-year roots. $20/100. Seed $12/oz. Information $1. Ginseng, OFA, Flag Pond TN 37657.

GOURDS

DRIED GOURDS, seeds, books, international folk art gourds, and more. Free catalog. The Gourd Garden and Curiosity, 4808 E. County Rd. 30-A, Santa Rosa Beach FL 32459. 850-231-2007. Web site: www.gourdgarden.com.

GREENHOUSES

GREENHOUSES! Beautiful, strong, functional, do-it-yourself hobby-/commercial-size kits and accessories. 800-531-GROW (4769). Web site: www.GothicArchGreenhouses.com.

HEALTH/BEAUTY/NUTRITION

COLLOIDAL MINERAL $5.97 quart/case. Colloidal silver $5.97 pint. CoQ10/90-count 100 mg $20.41. 800-999-9345. www.4cornersminerals.com.

WANTED 29 PEOPLE to lose weight now. We pay you to lose weight. www.e247diet.net. 877-502-9354.

SCIENTIFIC BREAKTHROUGH in skin care. New formula to make skin newer-looking or to repair damaged skin. www.zoneskincare.com/ronc.

BROTHER DAVID, powerful Caribbean remedies will help with all problems. Guaranteed fast results. 334-479-7775. 3229 Springhill Ave., Mobile AL 36607.

THREE FREE TAROT CARD READINGS. Call 781-646-9729. Spiritual healer. Gives advice. Pray to St. Jude. Call 781-367-6897.

NEED A HEALTHIER LIFESTYLE? Visit www.applesforhealth.com, a free Web site with new health information and features added weekly. For great recipes and a healthy slice of life, bookmark this useful site today.

HERBAL SUPPLEMENTS

ANCIENT HERBS unleash giant sex drive. Terminate most illnesses, revive youth energy. Write today: PO Box 1061, West Babylon NY 11704.

HERBS

HERB PLANTS and scented geraniums. Free catalog and newsletter. Possum Creek Herb Farm. www.possumcreekherb.com. 423-332-0347. E-mail: poscreek@bellsouth.net.

INVENTIONS/PATENTS

INVENTIONS, IDEAS, NEW PRODUCTS! Presentation to industry/exhibition at national innovation exposition. Patent services. 888-439-IDEA (4332).

A BETTER IDEA? Full-service marketing firm. Over 20 years' experience patenting services. Free kit. 800-846-8368. www.theconceptnetwork.com.

MAINE RESORTS

BAR HARBOR and Acadia National Park. 153 ocean-view rooms. Atlantic-Oakes-By-The-Sea. Open year-round. 800-33-MAINE (62463). www.barharbor.com.

NURSERY STOCK

EVERGREEN TREE SEEDLINGS direct from grower. Carino Nurseries, Box 538AL, Indiana PA 15701. Free catalog. 800-223-7075. Web site: www.carinonurseries.com.

JOHNSON NURSERY, 1352 Big Creek Rd., Ellijay GA 30540. 888-276-3187 (toll-free). Hardy fruit trees with antique and disease-resistant varieties. Catalog free. www.johnsonnursery.com.

ORGANIZATIONS

UNMARRIED CATHOLICS. Nationwide club. Huge membership. Newsletter. Free information. Sparks, Box 872-FA, Troy NY 12181.

PERSONAL

NICE SINGLES, CHRISTIAN values, 18–90. Free magazine. Singles, Box 310-OFA, Allardt TN 38504. www.nicesingles.com.

SISTER ROGERS, psychic reader and advisor. Can help you with problems, love, business, marriage, and health. 903-454-4406.

ATTENTION: SISTER LIGHT, Spartanburg, South Carolina. One free reading when you call. I will help in all problems. 864-576-9397.

FREE MONEY AVAILABLE! Wealthy foundations unload billions in grants! Blessing, Box 47-44, Springfield MO 65801.

POWERFUL SPELLS PERFORMED. Dominique reunites lovers immediately. Reveals future love, finance. One free reading. 423-472-3035.

RUSSIAN LADIES, truly beautiful, educated, seek relationships. 8,000 selected from 120,000+ ladies. Exciting tours, videos. Free color catalog, 500 photos! 770-458-0909. www.russianladies.com.

MOTHER DOROTHY tells past, present, and future. Gifted healer. 404-755-1301. 1214 Gordon St., Atlanta GA 30310. Write or call.

LIVELINKS®, LOCAL CHAT. Call 888-245-4545 for your local number. Enter free-trial code: 1080. 18+.

MEET LATIN WOMEN! Beautiful Mexican–South American ladies seeking marriage! All ages. Free brochures! TLC, PO Box 924994, Houston TX 77292-4994. 713-896-9224. Web site: www.tlcworldwide.com.

BEAUTIFUL ASIAN LADIES overseas seek love, marriage. Lowest rates! Free brochure: PR, Box 1245FA, Benicia CA 94510. 707-747-6906.

MRS. RUTH, southern-born spiritualist, removes evil, bad luck. Helps in all problems. Free sample reading. 334-616-6363.

SINGLE NONSMOKERS make a date to find your health-minded mate. 603-256-8686. E-mail: sniusa@together.net.

WOMEN WANT YOU FROM AROUND THE WORLD. Thousands of beautiful women desire love and marriage! Free photo magazine! Cherry Blossoms, Box 190/71, Kapaau HI 96755. 800-322-3267 ext. 71, blossoms.com/?adid=71.

LOVERS REUNITED. You deserve to be happy. Write today: Florentine, Box 5387-R, High Point NC 27262.

POULTRY

GOSLINGS, DUCKLINGS, CHICKS, TURKEYS, GUINEAS, books. Picture catalog $1. Pilgrim Goose Hatchery, GC-20, Williamsfield OH 44093.

FREE CATALOG. Baby chicks, ducks, geese, turkeys, game birds, Canadian honkers, wood ducks. Eggs to incubators. Books and supplies. Call 800-720-1134 or www.strombergschickens.com. Stromberg's, Pine River 45, MN 56474-0400.

GOSLINGS, DUCKLINGS, GUINEAS, chicks, turkeys, bantams, quail, pheasants. Books, medications, equipment. Hoffman Hatchery, Gratz PA 17030.

REAL ESTATE

LET THE GOVERNMENT PAY for your new or existing home. Hundreds of programs (Web site: www.usgovermentinformation.com). Free recorded message: 707-448-3210 (8KE1).

GOVERNMENT LAND NOW AVAILABLE for claim. 160 acres per person. (Web site: www.usgovernmentinformation.com). Free recorded message: 707-448-1887 (4KE1).

GEOTHERMAL AREA 160 acres northern Nevada. Approximately one mile from electricity-generating plant. Call Dale 775-423-2362. Broker/owner.

ESCAPE TO THE HILLS OF SOUTH-CENTRAL KENTUCKY. Secluded country properties, inexpensive homes. Call Century 21, Vibbert Realty, 800-267-2800 for free brochure.

RECIPES/FOOD

CENTURY-OLD STRAWBERRY CORDIAL RECIPE. Easy and delicious. $2 U.S. cash + LSASE to Recipe, c/o 421 Hagman Rd., Nordman ID 83848.

MAKE HOMEMADE ICE CREAM AND FROZEN YOGURT without a machine, 30 flavors. Recipes $3. Susan, PO Box 21491, Indianapolis IN 46221.

THE ONLY ORIGINAL Hungarian Gulyas recipe. $5/U.S., $8/Canadian to Gabor's Gourmet, PO Box 561, Stayton OR 97383.

NEED A HEALTHIER LIFESTYLE? Visit www.applesforhealth.com, a free Web site with new health information and features added weekly. For great recipes and a healthy slice of life, bookmark this useful site today.

TOTALLY NUTS brand peanuts, cashews, and other assorted nuts. Call us at 888-489-6887 or e-mail totallynutzz@aol.com.

COLORADO ROCKY ROAD FUDGE. Make, sell. $13 per pound. Send $3 SAE to Svita's, PO Box 6111, Colorado Springs CO 80904.

RELIGION

CHRIST'S RETURN—"THE RAPTURE"—ANTICHRIST. Free booklet. Clearwater Bible Students, PO Box 8216, Clearwater FL 33758.

RESORTS

CAPE COD WATERFRONT RESORT: Orleans Inn. Spectacular lodging, dining, receptions. Historic Victorian mansion. 508-255-2222. Web site: www.orleansinn.com.

SEEDS & PLANTS

CATALOG FREE! Tree seedlings. Wholesale prices. Flickinger's Nursery, Box 245, Sagamore PA 16250. 800-368-7381.

THE ORIGINAL "Grow Your Own" seed company. Tobacco, medicinal plants, tropicals, and more. Free catalog. E.O.N.S., Dept/FA, PO Box 4604, Hallandale FL 33008. 954-455-0229. Web site: www.eonseed.com.

FREE CATALOG. Top-quality vegetable, flower, and herb seeds since 1900. Burrell, Box 150-OFA, Rock Ford CO 81067.

RARE HILARIOUS PETER, FEMALE, and squash pepper seeds. $3 per package. Any two $5, all three $8, over 100 others. Seeds, 2119 Hauss Nursery Rd., Atmore AL 36502.

Index to Advertisers

Be one of the first to receive
The Old Farmer's Almanac

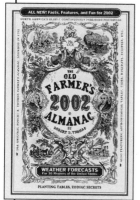

conveniently delivered to your mailbox—
―3 YEARS FOR ONLY $14―

You'll save precious time, conserve on gasoline, lock in the price, and be one of the first to read it each year! Have *The Old Farmer's Almanac* delivered to you each September for three years. Select the regional issue that's adapted to where you live.

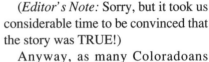

Pleasantries

A sampling from the hundreds of letters, clippings, and e-mails sent to us by Almanac readers from all over the United States and Canada during the past year.

Remembering "Mike," the Headless Wonder Chicken

Courtesy of E. F. of Grand Junction, Colorado, as well as several other Colorado readers.

Everyone around this section of western Colorado is familiar with the town of Fruita's annual "do" the third weekend in May celebrating the life of Mike, the chicken who lived and thrived for 18 months without his head. How come the Almanac hasn't told this story yet?

(*Editor's Note:* Sorry, but it took us considerable time to be convinced that the story was TRUE!)

Anyway, as many Coloradoans know, Mike lost his head on September 10, 1945, when his owner, farmer Lloyd Olsen, chopped it off, intending for Mike to become Sunday dinner. When Mike began running around, Olsen didn't think much of it. Beheaded chickens do that, you know. So he left him for a while. When he returned to the chicken house an hour later, Mike was strutting around normally with all the other chickens, preening his feathers and even attempting to peck for food—unsuccessfully, of course.

The next morning, Olsen found Mike still very much alive, sleeping with what was left of his neck tucked under his wing. That was when Olsen decided he had something pretty remarkable and tried feeding him grain and water with an eyedropper down his esophagus. Worked fine. A week later, he took him over to the University of Utah in Salt Lake City, where scientists determined that Olsen's ax blade had partially missed the jugular vein, that what was left of it had clotted, and that, although most of Mike's

Possibly the Four Worst Jokes of the Year

Courtesy of F. P. of West Caldwell, New Jersey, who included an apology.

1 Evidence has been found that William Tell and his family were avid bowlers. However, all the records of their league were unfortunately destroyed in a fire. Thus we'll never know for whom the Tells bowled.

2 A man rushed into the doctor's office and shouted, "Doctor! I think I'm shrinking!" The doctor calmly responded, "Now, settle down. You'll just have to be a little patient."

3 A marine biologist developed a race of genetically engineered dolphins that could live forever if they were fed a steady diet of seagulls. One day, his supply of the birds ran out, so he had to go out and trap some more. On the way back, he spied two lions asleep on the road. Afraid to wake them, he gingerly stepped over them. Immediately, he was arrested and charged with transporting gulls across sedate lions for immortal porpoises.

4 Back in the 1800s, the Tates Watch Company of Massachusetts wanted to produce other products. Because they already made cases for pocket watches, they decided to market compasses—which would also need cases—for the pioneers traveling west. It turned out that although their watches were of finest quality, their compasses were so bad that people often ended up in Canada or Mexico rather than California. This, of course, is the origin of the expression, "He who has a Tates is lost!"

head was now in a glass jar back at the Olsen farm, part of his brain stem and one ear remained on his body. Apparently, that was enough, they declared, to sustain Mike's life.

Over the next 18 months, during which time Mike gained eight pounds, the Olsens took him on a national tour. People everywhere lined up to pay 25 cents to see him. He seemed so healthy and happy that it was difficult for people to object to his being allowed to live without his head.

However, Mike finally died in a motel one night while on tour in Arizona. When he began choking, the Olsen's couldn't find the eyedropper to clear his throat in time. Too bad, because some people felt that with proper care and without a head to grow old, he might have been able to live on practically forever.

continued

How an Idaho Boy Fooled Almost Everyone

Courtesy of L.M.R. of Pocatello, Idaho.

Because your publication often deals with scientific matters, I thought maybe your readers would be interested in knowing how a freshman at Eagle Rock Junior High won first prize at the Greater Idaho Falls Science Fair. In his project, he urged students to sign a petition demanding strict control or total elimination of the chemical dihydrogen monoxide, and for plenty of good reasons:

- It can cause excessive sweating and vomiting.
- It is a major component in acid rain.
- It can cause severe burns in its gaseous state.
- Accidental inhalation can kill you.
- It contributes to erosion.
- It decreases the effectiveness of automobile brakes.
- It has been found in tumors of terminal cancer patients.

He asked 50 students if they supported a ban of the chemical. Of those, 43 said yes and 6 were undecided.

Only 1 knew that the chemical, dihydrogen monoxide, was water (H_2O).

There's a Lot You Should Know About Selling Cabbage

Courtesy of R.D.S. of Eugene, Oregon, and several others who sent us this item from the Internet. (Note that numbers may be approximate).

- Pythagorean theorem: 24 words
- The Lord's Prayer: 53–70 words
- Archimedes' Principle: 67 words
- The Ten Commandments: 179 words
- The Gettysburg Address: 286 words
- The Declaration of Independence: 1,324 words
- The U.S. government regulations on the sale of cabbage: 26,911 words

What Life Was Like EXACTLY 100 YEARS AGO

Courtesy of B.L.M. of Columbus, Ohio; C.S.V. of Madison, Wisconsin; M.F.B. of Allentown, Pennsylvania; and F.P. of West Caldwell, New Jersey.

- Only 14 percent of homes in the United States had a bathtub.
- Alabama, Mississippi, Iowa, and Tennessee were each more heavily populated than California.

Why You Might Want to Give Your Coworkers an Occasional Nudge

We're not sure if the following item from the Sunday Mercury *of Birmingham, U.K., is true—can it be? It came to us via the Internet courtesy of readers J. M. of Manchester, New Hampshire, as well as R.T.M. of Albany, New York.*

Bosses of a publishing firm are trying to work out why no one noticed that one of their employees had been sitting dead at his desk for *five days* before anyone asked if he was feeling OK.

George Turklebaum, 51, who had been employed as a proofreader at a New York firm for 30 years, had a heart attack in the open-plan office he shared with 23 other workers. He quietly passed away on Monday, but nobody noticed until Saturday morning, when an office cleaner asked why he was still working during the weekend.

His boss, Elliot Wachiaski, said, "George was always the first guy in each morning and the last to leave at night, so no one found it unusual that he was in the same position all that time and didn't say anything. He was always absorbed in his work and kept much to himself."

A postmortem examination revealed that he had been dead for five days after suffering a coronary. Ironically, George was proofreading manuscripts of medical textbooks when he died.

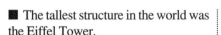

■ The tallest structure in the world was the Eiffel Tower.

■ **Some medical authorities warned that professional seamstresses were apt to become sexually aroused by the steady rhythm, hour after hour, of the sewing machine's foot pedals. They recommended slipping bromide—thought to diminish sexual desire—into the women's drinking water.**

■ There was no Mother's Day or Father's Day.

■ **More than 95 percent of all births in the United States took place at home.**

■ Most women washed their hair only once a month and used borax or egg yolks for shampoo.

■ **Marijuana, heroin, and morphine were all available over the counter at corner drugstores.**

■ Diarrhea was the third leading cause of death in the United States. Pneumonia and influenza were first, and tuberculosis was second.

■ **About 230 murders were reported in the United States annually.**

■ 42 percent of the U.S. workforce was in farming (compared with less than 3 percent today).

continued

Readers Write Us the Darnedest Things

For instance . . .

"It will be a great day when schools have all the money they need and the Air Force will have to hold a bake sale to buy a bomber."

A. Z. (age 7), Chicago, Illinois

"Another cure for headaches is to take a lime, cut it in half, and rub it on your forehead. Works more than half the time."

R.T.L., Jefferson City, Missouri

"It's always darkest before dawn. So if you're going to 'borrow' your neighbor's morning newspaper, that's the time to do it."

F.J.S., Bangor, Maine

"Never test the depth of the water with both feet and never squat with spurs on."

G.L.T., Albuquerque, New Mexico

"If you think nobody cares if you're alive, try missing a couple of car payments."

T. S., Halifax, Nova Scotia

"The sentence 'The quick brown fox jumps over the lazy dog' uses every letter in the alphabet, and the only 15-letter word that can be spelled without repeating a letter is 'uncopyrightable.'"*L. H., Boston, Massachusetts*

"If you lend someone $20 and then never see that person again, it may well be worth it."

J.L.P., Boca Raton, Florida

And the "Kitty-of-the-Year Award" Goes to . . . STORMY!

Courtesy of C. R. of Santa Barbara, California.

Because you occasionally feature cats in your publication, I thought your readers might enjoy this true story:

A few years ago, Wendy Ohmstead and her daughter, Vanessa, moved from their farm in Georgetown, Minnesota, to a southern California town named Solvang. Naturally, they took along their beloved cat, Stormy, whom they'd raised from a kitten after buying him from an animal rescue shelter for $30.

One day, about three months after they'd become settled in their new home, Stormy disappeared. "As the days went by," recalled Wendy, "I was sure that some animal must have gotten him."

About a year later, Wendy and Vanessa returned to Minnesota for a brief visit with relatives. While there, they just happened to read a tiny ad in the local newspaper, placed there by Duane and Bonnie Severson. "Found," the ad said, "all-gray cat."

Well, Stormy had been "all gray," so, on a hunch, they answered the ad. Miracle of miracles, it turned out to be none other than *their* Stormy! The local veterinarian confirmed the identity by matching the "found" cat's teeth to Stormy's old dental records.

So, in about a year's time, Stormy

had walked some 2,000 miles over snowy mountains and desolate plains, from Solvang, California, to his former home in Georgetown, Minnesota.

Was he the worse for wear? Well, yes. He'd lost ten pounds—a lot for a cat—and several of his claws had broken off or were worn down to the roots.

He's now back in California, regaining his health. But these days, Wendy and Vanessa are careful not to let him out of the house unsupervised. They suspect that poor Stormy is still convinced his real home is in Minnesota and that, despite Thomas Wolfe's old saying to the contrary, you can, indeed, go home again.

WHAT THEY SAY ABOUT CATS

■ "Cats are smarter than dogs. You can't get eight cats to pull a sled through snow."
—Jeff Valdez

■ "There are two means of refuge from the miseries of life: music and cats."
—Albert Schweitzer

■ "I got rid of my husband. My cat was allergic." *—Unknown*

The Lady Who Asked to Be Buried with a Fork in Her Hand

Courtesy of K.R.S. of Toronto, Ontario.

A Canadian woman with a terminal illness made sure her pastor knew exactly what hymns she'd like sung at her funeral, her favorite prayers, and so on. Then she told him she'd also like to be buried "with a fork in my hand."

When her incredulous pastor asked why, she said that following the main course at dinner parties throughout her life, when someone told her to "save her fork," it meant dessert was going to be something scrumptious, like chocolate cake or deep-dish apple pie.

In other words, she explained, having a fork in her hand meant that "the best was yet to come."

SHARE YOUR ANECDOTES AND PLEASANTRIES

☞ We'd love to hear from you. Send your contribution for the 2003 edition of *The Old Farmer's Almanac* by February 1, 2002, to: "A & P," The Old Farmer's Almanac, P.O. Box 520, Dublin, NH 03444; or e-mail it to almanac@yankeepub.com (subject: A & P).

□□

2001

January
S	M	T	W	T	F	S
	1	2	3	4	5	6
7	8	9	10	11	12	13
14	15	16	17	18	19	20
21	22	23	24	25	26	27
28	29	30	31			

February
S	M	T	W	T	F	S
				1	2	3
4	5	6	7	8	9	10
11	12	13	14	15	16	17
18	19	20	21	22	23	24
25	26	27	28			

March
S	M	T	W	T	F	S
				1	2	3
4	5	6	7	8	9	10
11	12	13	14	15	16	17
18	19	20	21	22	23	24
25	26	27	28	29	30	31

April
S	M	T	W	T	F	S
1	2	3	4	5	6	7
8	9	10	11	12	13	14
15	16	17	18	19	20	21
22	23	24	25	26	27	28
29	30					

May
S	M	T	W	T	F	S
		1	2	3	4	5
6	7	8	9	10	11	12
13	14	15	16	17	18	19
20	21	22	23	24	25	26
27	28	29	30	31		

June
S	M	T	W	T	F	S
					1	2
3	4	5	6	7	8	9
10	11	12	13	14	15	16
17	18	19	20	21	22	23
24	25	26	27	28	29	30

July
S	M	T	W	T	F	S
1	2	3	4	5	6	7
8	9	10	11	12	13	14
15	16	17	18	19	20	21
22	23	24	25	26	27	28
29	30	31				

August
S	M	T	W	T	F	S
			1	2	3	4
5	6	7	8	9	10	11
12	13	14	15	16	17	18
19	20	21	22	23	24	25
26	27	28	29	30	31	

September
S	M	T	W	T	F	S
						1
2	3	4	5	6	7	8
9	10	11	12	13	14	15
16	17	18	19	20	21	22
23	24	25	26	27	28	29
30						

October
S	M	T	W	T	F	S
	1	2	3	4	5	6
7	8	9	10	11	12	13
14	15	16	17	18	19	20
21	22	23	24	25	26	27
28	29	30	31			

November
S	M	T	W	T	F	S
				1	2	3
4	5	6	7	8	9	10
11	12	13	14	15	16	17
18	19	20	21	22	23	24
25	26	27	28	29	30	

December
S	M	T	W	T	F	S
						1
2	3	4	5	6	7	8
9	10	11	12	13	14	15
16	17	18	19	20	21	22
23	24	25	26	27	28	29
30	31					

2002

January
S	M	T	W	T	F	S
		1	2	3	4	5
6	7	8	9	10	11	12
13	14	15	16	17	18	19
20	21	22	23	24	25	26
27	28	29	30	31		

February
S	M	T	W	T	F	S
					1	2
3	4	5	6	7	8	9
10	11	12	13	14	15	16
17	18	19	20	21	22	23
24	25	26	27	28		

March
S	M	T	W	T	F	S
					1	2
3	4	5	6	7	8	9
10	11	12	13	14	15	16
17	18	19	20	21	22	23
24	25	26	27	28	29	30
31						

April
S	M	T	W	T	F	S
	1	2	3	4	5	6
7	8	9	10	11	12	13
14	15	16	17	18	19	20
21	22	23	24	25	26	27
28	29	30				

May
S	M	T	W	T	F	S
			1	2	3	4
5	6	7	8	9	10	11
12	13	14	15	16	17	18
19	20	21	22	23	24	25
26	27	28	29	30	31	

June
S	M	T	W	T	F	S
						1
2	3	4	5	6	7	8
9	10	11	12	13	14	15
16	17	18	19	20	21	22
23	24	25	26	27	28	29
30						

July
S	M	T	W	T	F	S
	1	2	3	4	5	6
7	8	9	10	11	12	13
14	15	16	17	18	19	20
21	22	23	24	25	26	27
28	29	30	31			

August
S	M	T	W	T	F	S
				1	2	3
4	5	6	7	8	9	10
11	12	13	14	15	16	17
18	19	20	21	22	23	24
25	26	27	28	29	30	31

September
S	M	T	W	T	F	S
1	2	3	4	5	6	7
8	9	10	11	12	13	14
15	16	17	18	19	20	21
22	23	24	25	26	27	28
29	30					

October
S	M	T	W	T	F	S
		1	2	3	4	5
6	7	8	9	10	11	12
13	14	15	16	17	18	19
20	21	22	23	24	25	26
27	28	29	30	31		

November
S	M	T	W	T	F	S
					1	2
3	4	5	6	7	8	9
10	11	12	13	14	15	16
17	18	19	20	21	22	23
24	25	26	27	28	29	30

December
S	M	T	W	T	F	S
1	2	3	4	5	6	7
8	9	10	11	12	13	14
15	16	17	18	19	20	21
22	23	24	25	26	27	28
29	30	31				

2003

January
S	M	T	W	T	F	S
			1	2	3	4
5	6	7	8	9	10	11
12	13	14	15	16	17	18
19	20	21	22	23	24	25
26	27	28	29	30	31	

February
S	M	T	W	T	F	S
						1
2	3	4	5	6	7	8
9	10	11	12	13	14	15
16	17	18	19	20	21	22
23	24	25	26	27	28	

March
S	M	T	W	T	F	S
						1
2	3	4	5	6	7	8
9	10	11	12	13	14	15
16	17	18	19	20	21	22
23	24	25	26	27	28	29
30	31					

April
S	M	T	W	T	F	S
		1	2	3	4	5
6	7	8	9	10	11	12
13	14	15	16	17	18	19
20	21	22	23	24	25	26
27	28	29	30			

May
S	M	T	W	T	F	S
				1	2	3
4	5	6	7	8	9	10
11	12	13	14	15	16	17
18	19	20	21	22	23	24
25	26	27	28	29	30	31

June
S	M	T	W	T	F	S
1	2	3	4	5	6	7
8	9	10	11	12	13	14
15	16	17	18	19	20	21
22	23	24	25	26	27	28
29	30					

July
S	M	T	W	T	F	S
		1	2	3	4	5
6	7	8	9	10	11	12
13	14	15	16	17	18	19
20	21	22	23	24	25	26
27	28	29	30	31		

August
S	M	T	W	T	F	S
					1	2
3	4	5	6	7	8	9
10	11	12	13	14	15	16
17	18	19	20	21	22	23
24	25	26	27	28	29	30
31						

September
S	M	T	W	T	F	S
	1	2	3	4	5	6
7	8	9	10	11	12	13
14	15	16	17	18	19	20
21	22	23	24	25	26	27
28	29	30				

October
S	M	T	W	T	F	S
			1	2	3	4
5	6	7	8	9	10	11
12	13	14	15	16	17	18
19	20	21	22	23	24	25
26	27	28	29	30	31	

November
S	M	T	W	T	F	S
						1
2	3	4	5	6	7	8
9	10	11	12	13	14	15
16	17	18	19	20	21	22
23	24	25	26	27	28	29
30						

December
S	M	T	W	T	F	S
	1	2	3	4	5	6
7	8	9	10	11	12	13
14	15	16	17	18	19	20
21	22	23	24	25	26	27
28	29	30	31			

A Reference Compendium

COMPILED BY MARE-ANNE JARVELA

Total Solar Eclipses (2002–2024)

Date		Regions with Visible Totality
2002	Dec. 4	Indian Ocean, southern Africa, Australia
2003	Nov. 23	Antarctica
2005	Apr. 8	S. Pacific Ocean
2006	Mar. 29	Africa, Turkey, Russia
2008	Aug. 1	Greenland, Siberia, China
2009	July 22	India, China, S. Pacific Ocean
2010	July 11	S. Pacific Ocean, southern South America
2012	Nov. 13	Australia, S. Pacific Ocean
2013	Nov. 3	Atlantic Ocean, Central Africa
2015	Mar. 20	N. Atlantic Ocean, Arctic
2016	Mar. 9	Southeast Asia, N. Pacific Ocean
2017	Aug. 17	United States
2019	July 2	S. Pacific Ocean, South America
2020	Dec. 14	S. Pacific Ocean, South America
2021	Dec. 4	Antarctica
2023	Apr. 20	Indonesia
2024	Apr. 8	Mexico, United States, Canada

Easter (2002–2006)

■ Christian churches that follow the Gregorian calendar (Eastern Orthodox churches follow the Julian calendar) celebrate Easter on the first Sunday after the full Moon that occurs on or just after the vernal equinox.

In	Easter will fall on
2002	March 31
2003	April 20
2004	April 11
2005	March 27
2006	April 16

When Will the Moon Rise Today?

■ A lunar puzzle involves the timing of moonrise. Folks who enjoy the out-of-doors and the wonders of nature may wish to commit to memory the following gem:

**The new Moon always rises at sunrise
And the first quarter at noon.
The full Moon always rises at sunset
And the last quarter at midnight.**

Moonrise occurs about 50 minutes later each day. The new Moon is invisible because its illuminated side faces away from Earth, which occurs when the Moon lines up between Earth and the Sun. One or two days after the date of the new Moon, you can see it in the western sky as a thin crescent setting just after sunset. (See pages 64–90 for exact moonrise times.)

Triskaidekaphobia

Here are a few conclusions on Friday the 13th:

Of the 14 possible configurations for the annual calendar (see any perpetual calendar), the occurrence of Friday the 13th is this:

■ 6 of 14 years have one Friday the 13th.
6 of 14 years have two Fridays the 13th.
2 of 14 years have three Fridays the 13th.

There is no year without one Friday the 13th, and no year with more than three.

■ There are two Fridays the 13th in 2002. The next year to have three Fridays the 13th is 2009.

■ The reason we say "Fridays the 13th" is that no one can pronounce "Friday the 13ths."

Month Names

January
Named for the Roman god Janus, protector of gates and doorways. Janus is depicted with two faces, one looking into the past, the other into the future.

February
From the Latin word *februa*, "to cleanse." The Roman Februalia was a month of purification and atonement.

March
Named for the Roman god of war, Mars. This was the time of year to resume military campaigns that had been interrupted by winter.

April
From the Latin word *aperio*, "to open (bud)," because plants begin to grow in this month.

May
Named for the Roman goddess Maia, who oversaw the growth of plants. Also from the Latin word *maiores*, meaning "elders," who were celebrated during this month.

June
Named for the Roman goddess Juno, patroness of marriage and the well-being of women. Also from the Latin word *juvenis*, "young people."

July
Named to honor Roman dictator Julius Caesar (100 B.C.–44 B.C.). In 46 B.C., Julius Caesar made one of his greatest contributions to history: With the help of Sosigenes, he developed the Julian calendar, the precursor to the Gregorian calendar we use today.

August
Named to honor the first Roman emperor (and grandnephew of Julius Caesar), Augustus Caesar (63 B.C.–A.D. 14).

September
From the Latin word *septem*, "seven," because this had been the seventh month of the early Roman calendar.

October
From the Latin word *octo*, "eight," because this had been the eighth month of the early Roman calendar.

November
From the Latin word *novem*, "nine," because this had been the ninth month of the early Roman calendar.

December
From the Latin word *decem*, "ten," because this had been the tenth month of the early Roman calendar.

Dining by the Calendar

Traditional foods for feasts and fasts.

■ JANUARY

Feast of the Circumcision: Black-eyed peas and pork (United States); oat-husk gruel or oatmeal porridge (Scotland).

Epiphany: Cake with a lucky bean baked in it; the one who finds the bean is the king or queen of the feast, in memory of the Three Wise Men (France).

Robert Burns Day: Haggis—sheep's stomach stuffed with suet, chopped organ meat (heart, lungs, liver), onions, oatmeal, and seasonings (Scotland). Haggis is a traditional Scottish delicacy served on all holidays of national importance.

■ FEBRUARY

Candlemas: Pancakes eaten today will prevent hemorrhoids for a full year (French American).

St. Agatha: Round loaves of bread blessed by a priest (southern Europe).

Shrove Tuesday: Pancakes (England); oatcakes (Scotland); rabbit (Ireland). Rich foods are eaten to usher in the Lenten fast; pancakes use up the last of the eggs and butter.

Lent: Simnel, a large fruitcake baked so hard it has sometimes been mistaken by recipients for a hassock or footstool (Great Britain).

■ MARCH

St. David: Leeks, to be worn (Wales) or eaten raw (England). Recalls a Welsh victory over the Saxons in A.D. 640; the Welsh wore leeks in their hats to distinguish them from the enemy.

St. Benedict: Nettle soup (ancient monastic practice). Picking nettles, which irritate the skin, was a penance in keeping with the spirit of the monastic rule of St. Benedict.

Purim: Strong drink and three-cornered cookies flavored with poppy seeds (Jewish). These cookies, called hamantaschen, are said to represent the three-cornered hat of Haman, the enemy of the Jewish people, whose downfall is celebrated on this holiday.

Maundy Thursday: Green foods or foods colored green (southern Europe). The medieval liturgical observance called for green vestments; in some parts of Europe, it is still called Green Thursday.

Good Friday: Hot cross buns. If made properly on this day, they will never get moldy (England).

Easter: Lamb as symbol of sacrifice; also ham.

■ APRIL

Beltane, May Day Eve: Strong ale (England); oatcakes with nine knobs to be broken off one by one and offered to each of nine supernatural protectors of domestic animals (Scotland).

■ MAY

Ascension Day: Fowl, or pastries molded into the shape of birds, to commemorate the taking of Jesus into the skies (medieval Europe).

Whitsunday (Pentecost): Dove or pigeon in honor of the Holy Spirit (southern Europe); strong ale (England).

St. Dunstan: Beer. Cider pressed today will go bad (England).

Corpus Christi: Orange peel dipped in chocolate, chicken stuffed with sauerkraut (Basque Provinces).

■ JUNE

St. Anthony of Padua: Liver, possibly based on the pre-Christian custom of eating liver on the summer solstice.

Feast of St. John the Baptist: First fruits of spring harvest.

■ JULY

St. Swithin: Eggs, because the saint miraculously restored intact a basket of eggs that had been broken by a poor woman taking them to market; he also looks after apples (medieval England).

St. James: Oysters, because James was a fisherman (England).

■ AUGUST

Lammas Day: Oatcakes (Scotland); loaves made from new grain of the season (England); toffee; seaweed pudding. Blueberries in baskets as an offering to a sweetheart are the last vestige of this holiday as a pagan fertility festival (Ireland).

St. Lawrence of Rome: Because the saint was roasted to death on a gridiron, it is courteous to serve only cold meat today (southern Europe).

Feast of the Assumption: Onions, possibly because they have always been considered wholesome and potent against evil (Polish American).

■ SEPTEMBER
St. Giles: Tea loaf with raisins (Scotland).

Rosh Hashanah: Sweet foods; honey; foods colored orange or yellow to represent a bright, joyous, and sweet new year (Jewish).

Nativity of Mary: Blackberries, possibly because the color is reminiscent of the depiction of the Virgin's blue cloak (Brittany).

Yom Kippur: Fast day; the day before, eat kreplach (filled noodles), considered by generations of mothers to be good and filling (Jewish).

Michaelmas Day: New wine (Europe); goose, originally a sacrifice to the saint (Great Britain); cake of oats, barley, and rye (Scotland); carrots (Ireland).

■ OCTOBER
St. Luke: Oatcakes flavored with anise and cinnamon (Scotland).

Sts. Simon and Jude: Dirge cakes, simple fried buns made for distribution to the poor. Also apples or potatoes, for divination (Scotland and England). Divination with apples is accomplished by peeling the fruit in one long strip and tossing the peel over one's shoulder. The letter formed by the peel is then interpreted.

All Hallows Eve: Apples and nuts for divination (England); buttered oat-husk gruel (Scotland); bosty, a mixture of potatoes, cabbage, and onions (Ireland).

■ NOVEMBER
All Saints' Day: Chestnuts (Italy); ginger-bread and oatcakes (Scotland); milk (central Europe); doughnuts, whose round shape indicates eternity (Austria).

All Souls' Day: Skull-shaped candy (Mexico); beans, peas, and lentils, considered food of the poor, as penance for souls in purgatory (southern Europe).

St. Martin: Last religious feast day before the beginning of the Advent fast. Goose, last of fresh-killed meat before winter; blood pudding (Great Britain).

St. Andrew: Haggis—stuffed sheep's stomach (Scotland; see Robert Burns Day, January).

Chanukah: Latkes—potato pancakes (Jewish).

■ DECEMBER
St. Nicholas: Fruit, nuts, candy for children (Germany). Commemorates, in part, the miracle by which the saint restored to life three young boys who had been murdered by a greedy innkeeper.

St. Lucy: Headcheese; cakes flavored with saffron or cardamom, raisins, and almonds (Sweden). The saffron imparts a yellow color to the cakes, representing sunlight, whose return is celebrated at the solstice.

Christmas Day: Boar's head or goose, plum pudding, nuts, oranges (England); turkey (United States); spiced beef (Ireland).

St. John the Evangelist: Small loaves of bread made with blessed wine (medieval Europe). On this feast, wine is ritually blessed in memory of the saint, who drank poisoned wine and miraculously survived.

Holy Innocents Day: Baby food, pablum, farina, in honor of the children killed by King Herod of Judea (monastic observance).

St. Sylvester: Strong drink (United States); haggis, oatcakes and cheese, oat-husk gruel or porridge (Scotland).   –E. Brady

How to Find the Day of the Week for Any Given Date

To compute the day of the week for any given date as far back as the mid-18th century, proceed as follows:

■ Add the last two digits of the year to one-quarter of the last two digits (discard any remainder if it doesn't come out even), the given date, and the month key from the key box below. Divide the sum by 7; the number left over is the day of the week (1 is Sunday, 2 is Monday, and so on). If it comes out even, the day is Saturday. If you go back before 1900, add 2 to the sum before dividing; before 1800, add 4. Don't go back before 1753. From 2000 to 2099, subtract 1 from the sum before dividing.

Example: **The Dayton Flood was on Tuesday, March 25, 1913.**

Last two digits of year:	13
One-quarter of these two digits:	3
Given day of month:	25
Key number for March:	4
Sum:	45

45 ÷ 7 = 6, with a remainder of 3. The flood took place on Tuesday, the third day of the week.

KEY	
January	1
leap year	0
February	4
leap year	3
March	4
April	0
May	2
June	5
July	0
August	3
September	6
October	1
November	4
December	6

Day Names

■ The Romans named the days of the week after the Sun, the Moon, and the five known planets. These names have survived in European languages, but English names also reflect an Anglo-Saxon influence.

LATIN	FRENCH	ITALIAN	SPANISH	SAXON	ENGLISH
Solis (Sun)	dimanche	domenica	domingo	Sun	Sunday
Lunae (Moon)	lundi	lunedì	lunes	Moon	Monday
Martis (Mars)	mardi	martedì	martes	Tiw (the Anglo-Saxon god of war, the equivalent of the Norse Tyr or the Roman Mars)	Tuesday
Mercurii (Mercury)	mercredi	mercoledì	miércoles	Woden (the Anglo-Saxon equivalent of the Norse Odin or the Roman Mercury)	Wednesday
Jovis (Jupiter)	jeudi	giovedì	jueves	Thor (the Norse god of thunder, the equivalent of the Roman Jupiter)	Thursday
Veneris (Venus)	vendredi	venerdì	viernes	Frigg (the Norse god of love and fertility, the equivalent of the Roman Venus)	Friday
Saturni (Saturn)	samedi	sabato	sábado	Saterne (Saturn, the Roman god of agriculture)	Saturday

Chinese Zodiac

■ The animal designations of the Chinese zodiac follow a 12-year cycle and are always used in the same sequence. The Chinese year of 354 days begins three to seven weeks into the western 365-day year, so the animal designation changes at that time, rather than on January 1. See page 42 for exact date.

Rat
Ambitious and sincere, you can be generous with your money. Compatible with the dragon and the monkey. Your opposite is the horse.

1900	1960
1912	1972
1924	1984
1936	1996
1948	2008

Rabbit (Hare)
Talented and affectionate, you are a seeker of tranquility. Compatible with the sheep and the pig. Your opposite is the rooster.

1903	1963
1915	1975
1927	1987
1939	1999
1951	2011

Horse
Physically attractive and popular, you like the company of others. Compatible with the tiger and the dog. Your opposite is the rat.

1906	1966
1918	1978
1930	1990
1942	2002
1954	2014

Rooster (Cock)
Seeking wisdom and truth, you have a pioneering spirit. Compatible with the snake and the ox. Your opposite is the rabbit.

1909	1969
1921	1981
1933	1993
1945	2005
1957	2017

Ox (Buffalo)
A leader, you are bright and cheerful. Compatible with the snake and the rooster. Your opposite is the sheep.

1901	1961
1913	1973
1925	1985
1937	1997
1949	2009

Dragon
Robust and passionate, your life is filled with complexity. Compatible with the monkey and the rat. Your opposite is the dog.

1904	1964
1916	1976
1928	1988
1940	2000
1952	2012

Sheep (Goat)
Aesthetic and stylish, you enjoy being a private person. Compatible with the pig and the rabbit. Your opposite is the ox.

1907	1967
1919	1979
1931	1991
1943	2003
1955	2015

Dog
Generous and loyal, you have the ability to work well with others. Compatible with the horse and the tiger. Your opposite is the dragon.

1910	1970
1922	1982
1934	1994
1946	2006
1958	2018

Tiger
Forthright and sensitive, you possess great courage. Compatible with the horse and the dog. Your opposite is the monkey.

1902	1962
1914	1974
1926	1986
1938	1998
1950	2010

Snake
Strong-willed and intense, you display great wisdom. Compatible with the rooster and the ox. Your opposite is the pig.

1905	1965
1917	1977
1929	1989
1941	2001
1953	2013

Monkey
Persuasive and intelligent, you strive to excel. Compatible with the dragon and the rat. Your opposite is the tiger.

1908	1968
1920	1980
1932	1992
1944	2004
1956	2016

Pig (Boar)
Gallant and noble, your friends will remain at your side. Compatible with the rabbit and the sheep. Your opposite is the snake.

1911	1971
1923	1983
1935	1995
1947	2007
1959	2019

Phases of the Moon

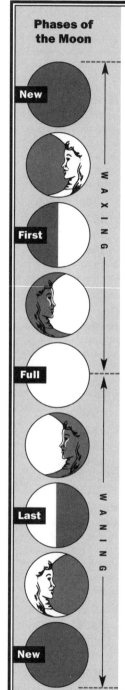

New

WAXING

First

Full

Last

WANING

New

Full-Moon Names

■ Historically, the Native Americans of what are now the northern and eastern United States kept track of the seasons by giving a distinctive name to each recurring full Moon, this name being applied to the entire month in which it occurred. With some variations, these names were used by the Algonquin tribes from New England to Lake Superior.

NAME	MONTH	OTHER NAMES USED
Full Wolf Moon	**January**	Full Old Moon
Full Snow Moon	**February**	Full Hunger Moon
Full Worm Moon	**March**	Full Crow Moon Full Crust Moon Full Sugar Moon Full Sap Moon
Full Pink Moon	**April**	Full Sprouting Grass Moon Full Egg Moon Full Fish Moon
Full Flower Moon	**May**	Full Corn Planting Moon Full Milk Moon
Full Strawberry Moon	**June**	Full Rose Moon Full Hot Moon
Full Buck Moon	**July**	Full Thunder Moon Full Hay Moon
Full Sturgeon Moon	**August**	Full Red Moon Full Green Corn Moon
Full Harvest Moon*	**September**	Full Corn Moon Full Barley Moon
Full Hunter's Moon	**October**	Full Travel Moon Full Dying Grass Moon
Full Beaver Moon	**November**	Full Frost Moon
Full Cold Moon	**December**	Full Long Nights Moon

*The Harvest Moon is always the full Moon closest to the autumnal equinox. If the Harvest Moon occurs in October, the September full Moon is usually called the Corn Moon.

Recipes for Your Garden

A little of this, a little of that.

SOIL MIX FOR CONTAINERS

1 part peat moss or substitute
1 part rich garden soil or potting soil
1 part sand

■ With a hoe or trowel, mix ingredients in a bucket, tub, or wheelbarrow until well blended. Use for outdoor potted vegetables and flowers.

CORNELL MIX

2 gallons vermiculite
2 gallons peat moss or substitute
2 tablespoons superphosphate
2 tablespoons ground limestone
1/2 cup bonemeal (or dried cow manure)

■ Combine all ingredients and use for outdoor potted plants.

KITCHEN COMPOST TEA

■ Fill your blender with water to within a few inches of the top. Add about 1 cup of compostable kitchen garbage (vegetable peelings, coffee grounds, etc.). Mix at high speed until the organic matter is very fine and suspended in the water. Immediately use on container gardens or potted plants.

MANURE TEA

■ Fill a large trash can ⅔ full with water. Add 2 large buckets of chicken manure and let steep for several hours. Stir with a hoe until thoroughly murky. Ladle around vegetables and flowers. Old-timers claim this concoction will keep tomato blight away.

FERMENTED COMPOST TEA

Barbara Pleasant offers this recipe in The Gardener's Guide to Plant Diseases *(Storey Communications, 1994). She says* the beneficial bacteria in the tea can give plants a boost and help them fight botrytis mold, tomato blight, and downy and powdery mildew.

1 part mature compost (including some
    rotted horse, cow, or chicken manure)
5 parts water

■ Mix ingredients in a plastic milk jug and let the mixture sit in a shady place for 2 weeks. Strain to remove large particles. (Warning: This can stink; work outdoors.) If necessary, dilute with more water. Spray or dribble it onto plants with a watering can, coating both sides of leaves. Reapply after 2 to 3 weeks.

MOSS FRAPPÉ

1/2 cup garden moss
1 cup buttermilk

■ Combine ingredients in a blender and mix at medium speed until smooth. Sprinkle mixture over a prepared soil bed, and moss will grow there.

ALCOHOL BUG SPRAY

2 parts rubbing alcohol
5 parts water
1 tablespoon liquid soap

■ Combine all ingredients and spray to deter whiteflies, aphids, and destructive beetles.

TRANSPLANTING JUICE

1 package dry yeast
2 gallons warm water

■ Combine ingredients in a watering can or bucket and stir until yeast dissolves. Use to water newly transplanted vegetable and flower seedlings.

A Beginner Garden

■ A good size for a beginner vegetable garden is 10x16 feet and features crops that are easy to grow. A plot this size, planted as suggested below, can feed a family of four for one summer, with a little extra for canning and freezing (or giving away).

Make your garden 11 rows of ten feet each of the following:

ROW	
1	**Zucchini (4 plants)**
2	**Tomatoes (5 plants, staked)**
3	**Peppers (6 plants)**
4	**Cabbage**
5	**Bush beans**
6	**Lettuce**
7	**Beets**
8	**Carrots**
9	**Chard**
10	**Radishes**
11	**Marigolds (to discourage rabbits!)**

Ideally the rows should run north and south to take full advantage of the Sun.

Plants with Interesting Foliage

■ **Airy/fine foliage**
Barrenwort, *Epimedium* spp.
Maidenhair fern, *Adiantum pedatum*
Meadow rue, *Thalictrum* spp.
Silver mound, *Artemisia schmidtiana*

■ **Linear foliage**
Blazing star, *Liatris* spp.
Daylily, *Hemerocallis* spp.
Iris, *Iris* spp.
Yucca, *Yucca* spp.

■ **Textured foliage**
Lamb's ears, *Stachys byzantina*
Sea holly, *Eryngium* spp.
Silver sage, *Salvia argentea*
Woolly thyme, *Thymus pseudolanuginosus*

■ **Foliage with attractive shapes**
Cranesbill, *Geranium* spp.
Foam flower, *Tiarella cordifolia*
Hybrid lupine, *Lupinus* x *rus selianus*
Lady's mantle, *Alchemilla vulgaris*

Perennials for Cutting Gardens

Aster *(Aster)*

Baby's breath *(Gypsophila)*

Bellflower *(Campanula)*

Black-eyed Susan
  (Rudbeckia)

Blanket flower *(Gaillardia)*

Chrysanthemum
  (Chrysanthemum)

Delphinium *(Delphinium)*

False sunflower *(Heliopsis)*

Flowering onion *(Allium)*

Foxglove *(Digitalis)*

Gayfeather *(Liatris)*

Globe thistle *(Echinops)*

Goldenrod *(Solidago)*

Iris *(Iris)*

Lavender *(Lavandula)*

Meadow rue *(Thalictrum)*

Peony *(Paeonia)*

Phlox *(Phlox)*

Purple coneflower
  (Echinacea purpurea)

Sea holly *(Eryngium)*

Speedwell *(Veronica)*

Tickseed *(Coreopsis)*

Yarrow *(Achillea)*

Herb Gardening

Name	Height (inches)	Part Used	Name	Height (inches)	Part Used
Anise	18	Seeds	Hyssop	14	Leaves
Basil	20	Leaves	Lemon balm	20	Leaves
Borage	18	Leaves, flowers	Marjoram	18	Leaves
Caraway	18	Seeds	Mint	24	Leaves
Catnip	24	Leaves	Parsley	20	Leaves
Chamomile	10	Flowers	Rosemary	18	Leaves
Chevril	15	Leaves	Sage	16	Leaves
Chive	12	Leaves	Savory	16	Leaves
Coriander	20	Leaves, seeds	Tarragon	20	Leaves
Dill	36	Leaves, seeds	Thyme	7	Leaves

Herbs to Plant in Lawns

■ Choose plants that suit your soil and your climate. All these can withstand mowing and considerable foot traffic.

- ❀ Ajuga or bugleweed *(Ajuga reptans)*
- ❀ Corsican mint *(Mentha requienii)*
- ❀ Dwarf cinquefoil *(Potentilla tabernaemontani)*
- ❀ English pennyroyal *(Mentha pulegium)*
- ❀ Green Irish moss *(Sagiona subulata)*
- ❀ Pearly everlasting *(Anaphalis margaritacea)*
- ❀ Roman chamomile *(Chamaemelum nobile)*
- ❀ Rupturewort *(Herniaria glabra)*
- ❀ Speedwell *(Veronica officinalis)*
- ❀ Stonecrop *(Sedum ternatum)*
- ❀ Sweet violets *(Viola odorata* or *tricolor)*
- ❀ Thyme *(Thymus serpyllum)*
- ❀ White clover *(Trifolium repens)*
- ❀ Wild strawberries *(Fragaria virginiana)*
- ❀ Wintergreen or partridgeberry *(Mitchella repens)*

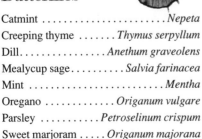

Herbs That Attract Butterflies

Catmint	*Nepeta*
Creeping thyme	*Thymus serpyllum*
Dill	*Anethum graveolens*
Mealycup sage	*Salvia farinacea*
Mint	*Mentha*
Oregano	*Origanum vulgare*
Parsley	*Petroselinum crispum*
Sweet marjoram	*Origanum majorana*

Heat-Loving Wildflowers

Bee balm *(Monarda)*

Black-eyed Susan *(Rudbeckia)*

Blazing star *(Liatris)*

Butterfly weed *(Asclepias tuberosa)*

Four-o'clocks *(Mirabilis)*

Prairie coneflower *(Ratibida pinnata)*

Purple coneflower *(Echinacea purpurea)*

Wild indigo *(Baptisia)*

Flowers That Attract Butterflies

Allium . . . . *Allium*	Helen's flower . . *Helenium*	Purple coneflower
Aster . . . . *Aster*	Hollyhock . . . . *Alcea*	. . . . *Echinacea purpurea*
Bee balm . . . . . . *Monarda*	Honeysuckle . . . . *Lonicera*	Purple loosestrife . . *Lythrum*
Butterfly bush . . . *Buddleia*	Lavender . . . . . *Lavendula*	Rock cress . . . . *Arabis*
Clove pink . . . . . *Dianthus*	Lilac . . . . *Syringa*	Sea holly . . . . *Eryngium*
Cornflower . . . . *Centaurea*	Lupine . . . . *Lupinus*	Shasta daisy *Chrysanthemum*
Daylily . . . . *Hemerocallis*	Lychnis . . . . *Lychnis*	Snapdragon . . *Antirrhinum*
False indigo . . . . . *Baptisia*	Mallow . . . . *Malva*	Stonecrop . . . . *Sedum*
Fleabane . . . . *Erigeron*	Milkweed . . . . . . *Asclepias*	Sweet alyssum . . *Lobularia*
Floss flower . . . *Ageratum*	Pansy . . . . *Viola*	Sweet rocket . . . . . *Hesperis*
Globe thistle . . . . *Echinops*	Phlox . . . . *Phlox*	Tickseed . . . . . . *Coreopsis*
Goldenrod . . . . . . *Solidago*	Privet . . . . *Ligustrum*	Zinnia . . . . *Zinnia*

Flowers That Attract Hummingbirds

Beard tongue . . . . *Penstemon*	Lily . . . . *Lilium*
Bee balm . . . . *Monarda*	Lupine . . . . *Lupinus*
Butterfly bush . . . . *Buddleia*	Petunia . . . . *Petunia*
Catmint . . . . *Nepeta*	Pincushion flower . . . . *Scabiosa*
Clove pink . . . . *Dianthus*	Red-hot poker . . . . *Kniphofia*
Columbine . . . . *Aquilegia*	Scarlet sage . . . . *Salvia splendens*
Coral bells . . . . *Heuchera*	Soapwort . . . . *Saponaria*
Daylily . . . . *Hemerocallis*	Summer phlox . . . . *Phlox paniculata*
Desert candle . . . . *Yucca*	Trumpet honeysuckle . . . . *Lonicera*
Flag iris . . . . *Iris*	*sempervirens*
Flowering tobacco . . . . . . *Nicotiana alata*	Verbena . . . . *Verbena*
Foxglove . . . . *Digitalis*	Weigela . . . . *Weigela*
Larkspur . . . . *Delphinium*	**Note: Choose varieties in red and orange shades.**

Forcing Blooms Indoors

■ Here is a list of some shrubs and trees that can be forced to flower indoors. (The trees tend to be stubborn and their blossoms may not be as rewarding as those of the shrubs.) The numbers indicate the approximate number of weeks they will take to flower.

Buckeye 5	**Flowering quince** . . . 4	**Red maple** 2
Cherry 4	**Forsythia** 1	**Redbud** 2
Cornelian dogwood . . 2	**Honeysuckle** 3	**Red-twig dogwood** . . . 5
Crab apple 4	**Horse chestnut** 5	**Spicebush** 2
Deutzia 3	**Lilac** 4	**Spirea** 4
Flowering almond . . . 3	**Magnolia** 3	**Wisteria** 3
Flowering dogwood . . 5	**Pussy willow** 2	–courtesy Purdue University Cooperative Extension Service

Fall-Planted Bulbs

	Planting Depth (inches)	Spacing (inches)	Flower Height (inches)
Early-Spring Blooms			
Crocus	3	2-3	4-6
Glory of the snow	3	2-3	6-10
Grape hyacinth	3-4	3	8-10
Snowdrop	4	2-3	6
Mid-Spring Blooms			
Daffodil	7	3-4	6-18
Squill	2	4-6	8
Tulip	8	3-6	6-28
Windflower	2	3-4	3-18
Late-Spring Blooms			
Dutch iris	4	3-6	15-24
Hyacinth	6	6-8	4-12
Ornamental onion	6	4-6	6-24
Spanish bluebell	3	3-6	15-20

Spring-Planted Bulbs

	Planting Depth (inches)	Spacing (inches)	Flower Height (inches)
Summer Blooms			
Begonia	2	12	8-18
Blazing star	3-4	6	18
Caladium	2	8-12	12-24
Canna lily	5	16	18-72
Dahlia	4-6	16	12-60
Freesia	2	2-4	12-24
Gladiolus	5	4	24-34
Gloxinia	4	15	12-24
Lily	6-8	12	24-72

Forcing Bulbs Indoors

■ The technique is simple. Plant bulbs in pots of rich soil so tips are just even with pot rims. Store in a cold frame, cellar, or refrigerator at a cold temperature for two to several months. Water bulbs just enough to keep them from drying out. When roots can be seen poking out through bottoms of pots, bring them into a lighted room to flower.

The table below shows estimated times for rooting and ideal temperatures for flowering for some of the most common spring bulbs.

Name of Bulb	Time for Rooting	Temperature for Flowering
Crocus (Crocus)	8-12 weeks	55-60°F
Daffodil (Narcissus)	10-12 weeks	50-60°F
Freesia (Freesia)	8-12 weeks	50-55°F
Glory of the snow (Chionodoxa)	10-14 weeks	55-60°F
Grape hyacinth (Muscari)	10-12 weeks	55-60°F
Hyacinth (Hyacinthus)	8-10 weeks	55-60°F
Lily-of-the-valley (Convallaria)	10-12 weeks	60-65°F
Netted iris (Iris reticulata)	10-14 weeks	55-60°F
Snowdrop (Galanthus)	9-12 weeks	55-60°F
Squill (Scilla)	12-16 weeks	55-60°F
Striped squill (Puschkinia)	8-12 weeks	50-55°F
Tulip (Tulipa)	12-16 weeks	55-60°F

Planning Your Garden

Sow or plant in cool weather	Beets/chard, broccoli, Brussels sprouts, cabbage, lettuce, onions, parsley, peas, radishes, spinach, turnips
Sow or plant in warm weather	Beans, carrots, corn, cucumbers, eggplant, melons, okra, peppers, squash, tomatoes
One crop per season	Corn, eggplant, leeks, melons, peppers, potatoes, spinach (New Zealand), squash, tomatoes
Resow for additional crops	Beans, beets, cabbage family, carrots, kohlrabi, lettuce, radishes, rutabagas, spinach, turnips

Vegetable Seeds Best Sown in the Ground

Beans, bush and pole
Beets
Carrots
Collards
Corn
Cucumbers
Endive
Kale
Kohlrabi
Mustard greens
Parsnips
Peas
Potatoes
Radishes
Spinach
Squash, summer and
winter
Swiss chard
Turnips

Vegetables and Herbs Best Started Indoors

Seeds	Weeks Before Last Frost in Spring
Basil	6
Broccoli	6-8
Brussels sprouts	4-8
Cabbage	6-8
Cauliflower	6-8
Celeriac	6-8
Celery	6-8
Chives	8-12
Eggplant	8-10
Leeks	8-12
Lettuce	4-6
Onions	10-12
Parsley	8
Peppers	8-10
Sweet marjoram	8
Tomatoes	6-8

Minimum Soil Temperature for Seeds to Germinate

Vegetable	Minimum Soil Temperature (°F)
Beans	48-50
Beets	39-41
Cabbage	38-40
Carrots	39-41
Corn	46-50
Melons	55-60
Onions	34-36
Peas	34-36
Radishes	39-41
Squash	55-60
Tomatoes	50-55

The Healthiest Vegetables

■ These results come from adding up the percent of the USRDA for six nutrients (vitamin A, vitamin C, folate, iron, copper, calcium) plus fiber for each vegetable.

1	Sweet potatoes	6	Kale
2	Carrots	7	Dandelion greens
3	Spinach	8	Broccoli
4	Collard greens	9	Brussels sprouts
5	Red peppers	10	Potatoes

Critical Low Temperatures for Frost Damage to Vegetables

Vegetable	Temperature (°F)
Artichokes	31-32
Asparagus	30-31
Beans	31-32
Beets (roots)	29-30
Beets (tops)	31-32
Broccoli	29-30
Cabbage	26-28
Carrots	28-30
Cauliflower	27-29
Celery	31-32
Cucumbers	30-32
Kale	27-29
Muskmelon	33-34
Okra	29-30
Peas	28-30
Potato tubers	28-30
Pumpkins	31-32
Radishes	30-32
Spinach	30-32
Squash (summer)	31-33
Squash (winter)	30-32
Sweet corn	32-33
Sweet potatoes	32-33
Tomatoes	32-34
Watermelon	32-33

When Is a Good Time to Fertilize Your Vegetables?

Crop	Time of Application
Asparagus....	Before growth starts in spring.
Beans	After heavy blossom and set of pods.
Broccoli.....	Three weeks after transplanting.
Cabbage	Three weeks after transplanting.
Cauliflower ...	Three weeks after transplanting.
Corn......	When eight to ten inches tall and again when silk first appears.
Cucumbers ...	One week after blossoming and again three weeks later.
Eggplant	After first fruit-set.
Kale......	When plants are one-third grown.
Lettuce, head ..	Two to three weeks after transplanting.
Muskmelon ...	One week after blossoming and again three weeks later.
Onions	When bulbs begin to swell and again when plants are one foot tall.
Peas......	After heavy bloom and set of pods.
Peppers.....	After first fruit-set.
Potatoes	At blossom time or time of second hilling.
Spinach.....	When plants are one-third grown.
Squash	Just before vines start to run, when plants are about one foot tall.
Tomatoes	One to two weeks before first picking and again two weeks after first picking.
Watermelon ...	Just before vines start to run, when plants are about one foot tall.

Fertilizer Formulas

■ Fertilizers are labeled to show the percentages by weight of nitrogen (N), phosphorus (P), and potassium (K). Nitrogen is needed for leaf growth. Phosphorus is associated with root growth and fruit production. Potassium helps the plant fight off diseases. A 100-pound bag of 10-5-10 contains 10 pounds of nitrogen, 5 pounds of phosphorus, and 10 pounds of potassium. The rest is filler.

Lawn Fertilizing Tips

■ Test your soil: The pH balance should be 7.0 or more—6.2 to 6.7 puts your lawn at risk for fungal diseases. If the pH is too low, correct it with liming, best done in the fall.

■ Control weeds by promoting healthy lawn growth with natural fertilizers in spring and early fall.

■ If you put lime and fertilizer on your lawn, spread half of it as you walk north to south, the other half as you walk east to west to cut down on missed areas.

Manure Guide

TYPE OF MANURE	WATER CONTENT	Primary Nutrients (pounds per ton)		
		NITROGEN	PHOSPHATE	POTASH
Cow, horse	60%–80%	12–14	5–9	9–12
Sheep, pig, goat	65%–75%	10–21	7	13–19
Chicken:				
Wet, sticky, and caked	75%	30	20	10
Moist, crumbly to sticky	50%	40	40	20
Crumbly	30%	60	55	30
Dry	15%	90	70	40
Ashed	None	None	135	100

TYPE OF GARDEN	BEST TYPE OF MANURE	BEST TIME TO APPLY
Flowers	Cow, horse	Early spring
Vegetables	Chicken, cow, horse	Fall, spring
Potatoes or root crops	Cow, horse	Fall
Acid-loving plants (blueberries, azaleas, mountain laurels, rhododendrons)	Cow, horse	Early fall or not at all

Soil Fixes

■ **CLAY SOIL:** Add coarse sand (not beach sand) and compost.

■ **SILT SOIL:** Add coarse sand (not beach sand) or gravel and compost, or well-rotted horse manure mixed with fresh straw.

■ **SANDY SOIL:** Add humus or aged manure, or sawdust with some extra nitrogen. Heavy, clay-rich soil can also be added.

Soil Amendments

■ **BARK, GROUND:** Made from various tree barks. Improves soil structure.

■ **COMPOST:** Excellent conditioner.

■ **LEAF MOLD:** Decomposed leaves. Adds nutrients and structure to soil.

■ **LIME:** Raises the pH of acidic soil and helps loosen clay soil.

■ **MANURE:** Best if composted. Good conditioner.

■ **SAND:** Improves drainage in clay soil.

■ **TOPSOIL:** Usually used with another amendment. Replaces existing soil.

Container Gardening

- Feed container plants at least twice a month with liquid fertilizer, following the instructions on the label.

- Clay pots are usually more attractive than plastic ones, but plastic pots retain moisture better. To get the best of both, slip a plastic pot into a slightly larger clay pot.

- Best suited for containers are vegetables which may be easily transplanted. Transplants can be purchased from local nurseries or can be grown at home.

- Avoid small containers. They often can't store enough water to get through hot days.

- Add about one inch of coarse gravel in the bottom of the container to improve drainage.

- An occasional application of fish emulsion or compost will add trace elements to container soil.

- Watch for and control plant insect pests. Place containers where they will receive maximum sunlight and good ventilation.

VEGETABLE GARDENING IN CONTAINERS

■ Lack of yard space is no excuse for not gardening, because many vegetables can be readily grown in containers. In addition to providing five hours or more of full sun, you must give attention to choosing the proper container, using a good soil mix, planting and spacing requirements, fertilizing, watering, and variety selection.

VEGETABLE	TYPE OF CONTAINER	RECOMMENDED VARIETIES
Beans, snap	5-gallon window box	Bush 'Blue Lake', Bush 'Romano', 'Tender Crop'
Broccoli	1 plant/5-gallon pot 3 plants/15-gallon tub	'DeCicco', 'Green Comet'
Carrots	5-gallon window box at least 12 inches deep	'Danvers Half Long', 'Short 'n Sweet', 'Tiny Sweet'
Cucumbers	1 plant/1-gallon pot	'Patio Pik', 'Pot Luck', 'Spacemaster'
Eggplant	5-gallon pot	'Black Beauty', 'Ichiban', 'Slim Jim'
Lettuce	5-gallon window box	'Ruby', 'Salad Bowl'
Onions	5-gallon window box	'White Sweet Spanish', 'Yellow Sweet Spanish'
Peppers	1 plant/2-gallon pot 5 plants/15-gallon tub	'Cayenne', 'Long Red', 'Sweet Banana', 'Wonder', 'Yolo'
Radishes	5-gallon window box	'Cherry Belle', 'Icicle'
Tomatoes	Bushel basket	'Early Girl', 'Patio', 'Small Fry', 'Sweet 100', 'Tiny Tim'

–courtesy North Carolina Cooperative Extension Service

pH Preferences of Selected Garden Crops, Trees, Shrubs, and Flowers

Common Name/Optimum pH Range

TREES AND SHRUBS

Apple 5.0–6.5
Ash 6.0–7.5
Azalea 4.5–6.0
Basswood 6.0–7.5
Beautybush 6.0–7.5
Beech 5.0–6.7
Birch 5.0–6.5
Blackberry 5.0–6.0
Blueberry 4.0–6.0
Boxwood 6.0–7.5
Cherry, sour 6.0–7.0
Chestnut 5.0–6.5
Crab apple 6.0–7.5
Currant, black 6.0–7.5
Currant, red 5.5–7.0
Dogwood 5.0–7.0
Elder, box 6.0–8.0
Fir, balsam 5.0–6.0
Fir, Douglas 6.0–7.0
Gooseberry 5.0–6.5
Hazelnut 6.0–7.0
Hemlock 5.0–6.0
Hickory 6.0–7.0
Hydrangea, blue-
flowered 4.0–5.0
Hydrangea, pink-
flowered 6.0–7.0
Juniper 5.0–6.0
Laurel, mountain . . 4.5–6.0
Lemon 6.0–7.5
Lilac 6.0–7.5
Maple, sugar 6.0–7.5
Oak, white 5.0–6.5
Orange 6.0–7.5
Peach 6.0–7.0
Pear 6.0–7.5
Pecan 6.4–8.0
Pine, red 5.0–6.0

Common Name/Optimum pH Range

Pine, white 4.5–6.0
Plum 6.0–8.0
Raspberry, red 5.5–7.0
Rhododendron 4.5–6.0
Spruce 5.0–6.0
Walnut, black 6.0–8.0
Willow 6.0–8.0

VEGETABLES

Asparagus 6.0–8.0
Bean, pole 6.0–7.5
Beet 6.0–7.5
Broccoli 6.0–7.0
Brussels sprout 6.0–7.5
Carrot 5.5–7.0
Cauliflower 5.5–7.5
Celery 5.8–7.0
Chive 6.0–7.0
Cucumber 5.5–7.0
Garlic 5.5–8.0
Kale 6.0–7.5
Lettuce 6.0–7.0
Pea, sweet 6.0–7.5
Pepper, sweet 5.5–7.0
Potato 4.8–6.5
Pumpkin 5.5–7.5
Radish 6.0–7.0
Spinach 6.0–7.5
Squash, crookneck . . 6.0–7.5
Squash, Hubbard . . 5.5–7.0
Tomato 5.5–7.5

FLOWERS

Alyssum 6.0–7.5
Aster, New England 6.0–8.0
Baby's breath 6.0–7.0
Bachelor's button . . 6.0–7.5
Balloon flower 5.0–6.0
Bee balm 6.0–7.5
Begonia 5.5–7.0

Common Name/Optimum pH Range

Black-eyed Susan . . 5.5–7.0
Bleeding heart 6.0–7.5
Canna 6.0–8.0
Carnation 6.0–7.0
Chrysanthemum . . . 6.0–7.5
Clematis 5.5–7.0
Coleus 6.0–7.0
Coneflower, purple . 5.0–7.5
Cosmos 5.0–8.0
Crocus 6.0–8.0
Daffodil 6.0–6.5
Dahlia 6.0–7.5
Daisy, Shasta 6.0–8.0
Daylily 6.0–8.0
Delphinium 6.0–7.5
Foxglove 6.0–7.5
Geranium 6.0–8.0
Gladiolus 5.0–7.0
Hibiscus 6.0–8.0
Hollyhock 6.0–8.0
Hyacinth 6.5–7.5
Iris, blue flag 5.0–7.5
Lily-of-the-valley . . 4.5–6.0
Lupine 5.0–6.5
Marigold 5.5–7.5
Morning glory 6.0–7.5
Narcissus, trumpet 5.5–6.5
Nasturtium 5.5–7.5
Pansy 5.5–6.5
Peony 6.0–7.5
Petunia 6.0–7.5
Phlox, summer 6.0–8.0
Poppy, oriental 6.0–7.5
Rose, hybrid tea . . . 5.5–7.0
Rose, rugosa 6.0–7.0
Snapdragon 5.5–7.0
Sunflower 6.0–7.5
Tulip 6.0–7.0
Zinnia 5.5–7.0

How Much Water Is Enough?

■ When confronted with a dry garden and the end of a hose, many gardeners admit to a certain insecurity about just how much water those plants really need. Here's a guide to help you estimate when and how much to water, assuming rich, well-balanced soil. Increase frequency during hot, dry periods.

Vegetable	Critical time(s) to water for a 5-foot row
● **Beans**	When flowers form and during pod-forming and picking.
■ **Beets**	Before soil gets bone-dry.
■ **Broccoli**	Don't let soil dry out for 4 weeks after transplanting.
■ **Brussels sprouts**	Don't let soil dry out for 4 weeks after transplanting.
▲ **Cabbage**	Water frequently in dry weather for best crop.
■ **Carrots**	Before soil gets bone-dry.
▲ **Cauliflower**	Water frequently for best crop.
▲ **Celery**	Water frequently for best crop.
● **Corn**	When tassels form and when cobs swell.
▲ **Cucumbers**	Water frequently for best crop.
▲ **Lettuce/ Spinach**	Water frequently for best crop.
■ **Onions**	In dry weather, water in early stage to get plants going.
■ **Parsnips**	Before soil gets bone-dry.
● **Peas**	When flowers form and during pod-forming and picking.
● **Potatoes**	When the size of marbles.
▲ **Squash (all types)**	Water frequently for best crop.
● **Tomatoes**	For 3 to 4 weeks after transplanting and when flowers and fruit form.

▲ Needs a lot of water during dry spells.   ● Needs water at critical stages of development

Number of gallons of water needed	Comments
2 per week depending on rainfall	Dry soil when pods are forming will adversely affect quantity and quality.
1 at early stage; 2 every 2 weeks	Water sparingly during early stages to prevent foliage from becoming too lush at the expense of the roots; increase water when round roots form.
1 to 1½ per week	Best crop will result with no water shortage.
1 to 1½ per week	Plants can endure dry conditions once they are established. Give 2 gallons the last 2 weeks before harvest for most succulent crop.
2 per week	If crop suffers some dry weather, focus efforts on providing 2 gallons 2 weeks before harvest. (Too much water will cause heads to crack.)
1 at early stage; 2 every 2 weeks as roots mature	Roots may split if crop is watered after soil has become too dry.
2 per week	Give 2 gallons before harvest for best crop.
2 per week	If conditions are very dry, water daily.
2 at important stages (see critical time, left)	Cob size will be smaller if plants do not receive water when ears are forming.
1 per week	Water diligently when fruits form and throughout growth; give highest watering priority.
2 per week	Best crop will result with no water shortage.
½ to 1 per week if soil is very dry	Withhold water from bulb onions at later growth stages to improve storage qualities; water salad onions anytime soil is very dry.
1 per week in early stages	Water when dry to keep plants growing steadily. Too much water will encourage lush foliage and small roots.
2 per week	To reduce excess foliage and stem growth, do not water young seedlings unless wilting.
2 per week	In dry weather, give 2 gallons throughout the growing season every 10 days. Swings from very dry to very wet produce oddly shaped and cracked tubers.
1 per week	Water diligently when fruits form and throughout their growth; give highest watering priority.
1 twice a week or more	Frequent watering may increase yield but adversely affect flavor.

■ Does not need frequent watering.

Plant Resources

BULBS

American Daffodil Society
4126 Winfield Rd.
Columbus, OH
43220-4606
www.daffodilusa.org

Netherlands Flower Bulb Information Center
30 Midwood St.
Brooklyn, NY 11225
718-693-5400
www.bulb.com

FERNS

American Fern Society
326 West St. NW
Vienna, VA 22180-4151
http://amerfernsoc.org

The Hardy Fern Foundation
P.O. Box 166
Medina, WA 98036-0166
www.hardyferns.org

FLOWERS

Hardy Plant Society
Mid-Atlantic Group
801 Concord Rd.
Glen Mills, PA 19342

National Wildflower Research Center
4801 La Crosse Ave.
Austin, TX 78739
512-292-4200
www.wildflower.org

Perennial Plant Association
3383 Schirtzinger Rd.
Hilliard, OH 43026
614-771-8431

FRUITS

California Rare Fruit Growers
The Fullerton Arboretum-CSUF
P.O. Box 6850
Fullerton, CA 92834-6850
www.crfg.org

Home Orchard Society
P.O. Box 230192
Tigard, OR 97281-0192

North American Fruit Explorers
1716 Apples Rd.
Chapin, IL 62628
www.nafex.org

HERBS

American Herb Association
P.O. Box 1673
Nevada City, CA
95959-1673
530-265-9552
fax 530-274-3140

The Flower and Herb Exchange
3076 North Winn Rd.
Decorah, IA 52101
319-382-5990

Herb Research Foundation
1007 Pearl St., Ste. 200
Boulder, CO 80302
303-449-2265
800-748-2617
www.herbs.org

Herb Society of America
9019 Kirtland Chardon Road
Kirtland, OH 44094
440-256-0514
www.herbsociety.org

VEGETABLES

National Hot Pepper Association
Betty Payton
400 Northwest 20th St.
Ft. Lauderdale, FL
33311-3818
954-565-4972
http://inter-linked.com/org/nhpa

Seeds of Change
P.O. Box 15700
Santa Fe, NM 87506
888-762-7333
www.seedsofchange.com

Southern Exposure Seed Exchange
P.O. Box 460
Mineral, VA 23117
www.southernexposure.com

Tomato Growers Supply Company
P.O. Box 2237
Fort Myers, FL 33902
888-478-7333
www.tomatogrowers.com

Seed Savers Exchange
3076 North Winn Rd.
Decorah, IA 52101
319-382-5990
www.seedsavers.org

GENERAL RESOURCES

Biological Urban Gardening Services (BUGS)
P.O. Box 76
Citrus Heights, CA 95611-0076
916-726-5377
www.organiclandscape.com
Devoted to reducing pesticide use, particularly in urban landscape environments.

Internet Gardening Links
http://learning.lib.vt.edu/garden.html

The Lawn Institute
www.lawninstitute .com

Lists of Gardening Catalogs
http://pbmfaq.dvol.com/list
www.cog.brown.edu/gardening

The Official Seedstarting Home Page
www.chestnut-sw.com/seedhp.htm

The U.S. National Arboretum "Web Version" of the USDA Plant Hardiness Zone Map
www.ars-grin.gov/ars/ Beltsville/na/ hardzone/ushzmap.html?

Water-Wise Gardening
http://smartgardening.com/waterwise_ gardening.htm

IN CANADA

Calgary Horticultural Society
208-50 Avenue SW, Calgary,
AB T2S 2S1; 403-287-3469
www.calhort.org

Canadian Iris Society
RR 9, Bains Rd., Dunnville, ON
N1A 2W8
http://members.attcanada.ca/~cris/cis.html

Canadian Organic Growers
Box 6408, Station J, Ottawa, ON
K2A 3Y6
www.cog.ca

Canadian Rose Society
10 Fairfax Crescent, Scarborough, ON
M1L 1Z8
www.mirror.org/groups/crs

Environment Canada
www.msc-smc.ec.gc.ca

Family Gardening
www.familygardening.com

Get Set! To Garden!
www.gardeningbc.com

I Can Garden
http://icangarden.com

North American Native Plant Society
Box 336, Station F, Toronto, ON
M4Y2L7

Seeds of Diversity Canada
P.O. Box 36, Station Q, Toronto, ON
M4T 2L7; 905-623-0353
www.seeds.ca

Cooperative Extension Services

ALABAMA
www.acenet.auburn.edu

ALASKA
zorba.uafadm.alaska
.edu/coop-ext/index.html

ARIZONA
ag.arizona.edu/extension

ARKANSAS
www.uaex.edu

CALIFORNIA
danr.ulop.edu/regional.htm
www.uckac.edu/danrscr

COLORADO
www.arapcsuext.org/horti/
indxhort.html

CONNECTICUT
www.lib.uconn.edu/canr/ces/
index.html

DELAWARE
http://bluehen.ags.udel
.edu/deces

FLORIDA
www.ifas.ufl.edu/www/
agator/htm/ces.htm

GEORGIA
www.ces.uga.edu

HAWAII
www2.ctahr.hawaii.edu

IDAHO
www.uidaho.edu/ag/
extension

ILLINOIS
www.ag.uiuc.edu/~robsond/
solutions/hort.html

INDIANA
www.agriculture.purdue.edu/
arp/agreswww.html

IOWA
www.exnet.iastate.edu

KANSAS
www.oznet.ksu.edu

KENTUCKY
www.ca.uky.edu

LOUISIANA
www.agctr.lsu.edu/wwwac/
lces.html

MAINE
www.umext.maine.edu

MARYLAND
www.agnr.umd.edu/ces

MASSACHUSETTS
www.umass.edu/umext

MICHIGAN
www.msue.msu.edu/msue

MINNESOTA
www.extension.umn.edu

MISSISSIPPI
ext.msstate.edu

MISSOURI
extension.missouri.edu

MONTANA
extn.msu.montana.edu

NEBRASKA
www.ianr.unl.edu/ianr/
coopext/coopext.htm

NEVADA
www.nce.unr.edu/nce/
extnhome.htm

NEW HAMPSHIRE
ceinfo.unh.edu

NEW JERSEY
www.rce.rutgers.edu

NEW MEXICO
www.cahe.nmsu.edu/ces

NEW YORK
www.cce.cornell.edu

NORTH CAROLINA
www.ces.ncsu.edu

NORTH DAKOTA
www.ext.nodak.edu

OHIO
www.ag.ohio-state.edu

OKLAHOMA
www.okstate.edu/OSU_
Ag/oces

OREGON
wwwagcomm.ads
.orst.edu/AgComWebFile/
extser/index.html

PENNSYLVANIA
www.cas.psu.edu/docs/
coext/coopext.html

RHODE ISLAND
www.edc.uri.edu

SOUTH CAROLINA
virtual.clemson.edu/
groups/extension

SOUTH DAKOTA
www.abs.sdstate.edu/ces

TENNESSEE
www.utextension.utk.edu

TEXAS
agextension.tamu.edu

UTAH
ext.usu.edu/

VERMONT
ctr.uvm.edu/ext

VIRGINIA
www.ext.vt.edu

WASHINGTON
ext.wsu.edu

WEST VIRGINIA
www.wvu.edu/~exten

WISCONSIN
www.uwex.edu/ces

WYOMING
www.uwyo.edu/ag/ces/
ceshome.htm

Clouds

1. High clouds (bases starting at an average of 20,000 feet)

Cirrus: thin feather-like crystal clouds.
Cirrostratus: thin white clouds that resemble veils.
Cirrocumulus: thin clouds that appear as small "cotton patches."

2. Middle clouds (bases starting at about 10,000 feet)

Altostratus: grayish or bluish layer of clouds that can obscure the Sun.
Altocumulus: gray or white layer or patches of solid clouds with rounded shapes.

3. Low clouds (bases starting near Earth's surface to 6,500 feet)

Stratus: thin, gray sheet-like clouds with low base; may bring drizzle and snow.
Stratocumulus: rounded cloud masses that form on top of a layer.
Nimbostratus: dark, gray shapeless cloud layers containing rain, snow, and ice pellets.

4. Clouds with vertical development (high clouds that form at almost any altitude and that reach up to 14,000 feet)

Cumulus: fair-weather clouds with flat bases and domeshaped tops.
Cumulonimbus: large, dark, vertical clouds with bulging tops that bring showers, thunder, and lightning.

Snowflakes

■ Snowflakes are made up of six-sided crystals. If you look carefully at the snowflakes during the next snowstorm, you might be able to find some of the crystal types below. The temperature at which a crystal forms mainly determines the basic shape. Sometimes a snowflake is a combination of more than one type of crystal.

Capped columns (also called tsuzumi crystals) occur when colder than 12°F.	**Columns** (dense crystals, act like prisms) occur when colder than 12°F.	**Needles** (long and thin but still six-sided) occur at warmer temperatures, 21° to 25°F.
Plates (mirror-like crystals) occur under special weather conditions.	**Spatial dendrites** (irregular and feathery) occur in high-moisture clouds, 3° to 10°F.	**Stellar crystals** (beautiful, delicate crystals) occur under special weather conditions.

Windchill Table

■ As wind speed increases, the air temperature against your body falls. The combination of cold temperature and high wind creates a cooling effect so severe that exposed flesh can freeze. (Inanimate objects, such as cars, do not experience windchill.)

To gauge wind speed: At 10 miles per hour, you can feel wind on your face; at 20, small branches move and dust or snow is raised; at 30, large branches move and wires whistle; at 40, whole trees bend.

–courtesy Mount Washington Observatory

Wind Velocity (mph)	Temperature (°F)												
	50	41	32	23	14	5	–4	–13	–22	–31	–40	–49	–58
	Equivalent Temperature (°F)												
	(Equivalent in cooling power on exposed flesh under calm conditions)												
5	48	39	28	19	10	1	–9	–18	–27	–36	–51	–56	–65
10	41	30	18	7	–4	–15	–26	–36	–49	–60	–71	–81	–92
20	32	19	7	–6	–18	–31	–44	–58	–71	–83	–96	–108	–121
30	28	14	1	–13	–27	–40	–54	–69	–81	–96	–108	–123	–137
40	27	12	–2	–17	–31	–45	–60	–74	–89	–103	–116	–130	–144
50	25	10	–4	–18	–33	–47	–62	–76	–90	–105	–119	–134	–148

Little Danger*	Increasing Danger*	Great Danger*

*from freezing of exposed flesh (for properly clothed person)

Heat Index

■ As humidity increases, the air temperature feels hotter to your skin. The combination of hot temperature and high humidity reduces your body's ability to cool itself. For example, the heat you feel when the actual temperature is 90°F with a relative humidity of 70 percent is 106°.

Humidity (%)	Temperature (°F)										
	70	75	80	85	90	95	100	105	110	115	120
	Equivalent Temperature (°F)										
0	64	69	73	78	83	87	91	95	99	103	107
10	65	70	75	80	85	90	95	100	105	111	116
20	66	72	77	82	87	93	99	105	112	120	130
30	67	73	78	84	90	96	104	113	123	135	148
40	68	74	79	86	93	101	110	123	137	152	
50	69	75	81	88	96	107	120	135	150		
60	70	76	82	90	100	114	132	149			
70	70	77	85	93	106	124	144				
80	71	78	86	97	113	136					
90	71	79	88	102	122						
100	72	80	91	108							

Visit www.almanac.com *for more wit, wisdom, and weather.*

Is It Raining, Drizzling, or Misting?

	Drops (per sq. ft. per sec.)	Diameter of Drops (mm)	Intensity (in. per hr.)
Cloudburst	113	2.85	4.00
Excessive rain	76	2.40	1.60
Heavy rain	46	2.05	.60
Moderate rain	46	1.60	.15
Light rain	26	1.24	.04
Drizzle	14	.96	.01
Mist	2,510	.10	.002
Fog	6,264,000	.01	.005

A Table Foretelling the Weather Through All the Lunations of Each Year (Forever)

■ This table is the result of many years of actual observation and shows what sort of weather will probably follow the Moon's entrance into any of its quarters. For example, the table shows that the week following February 12, 2002, will be stormy with snow, because the Moon becomes new that day at 2:41 A.M. EST. (See Left-Hand Calendar Pages 64-90 for 2002 Moon phases.)

Editor's note: Although the data in this table is taken into consideration in the yearlong process of compiling the annual long-range weather forecasts for *The Old Farmer's Almanac*, we rely far more on our projections of solar activity.

Time of Change	Summer	Winter
Midnight to 2 A.M.	Fair	Hard frost, unless wind is south or west
2 A.M. to 4 A.M.	Cold, with frequent showers	Snow and stormy
4 A.M. to 6 A.M.	Rain	Rain
6 A.M. to 8 A.M.	Wind and rain	Stormy
8 A.M. to 10 A.M.	Changeable	Cold rain if wind is west; snow if east
10 A.M. to noon	Frequent showers	Cold with high winds
Noon to 2 P.M.	Very rainy	Snow or rain
2 P.M. to 4 P.M.	Changeable	Fair and mild
4 P.M. to 6 P.M.	Fair	Fair
6 P.M. to 10 P.M.	Fair if wind is northwest; rain if wind is south or southwest	Fair and frosty if wind is north or northeast; rain or snow if wind is south or southwest
10 P.M. to midnight	Fair	Fair and frosty

This table was created more than 160 years ago by Dr. Herschell for the Boston Courier; *it first appeared in* The (Old) Farmer's Almanac *in 1834.*

Beaufort Wind Force Scale

"Used Mostly at Sea but of Help to All Who Are Interested in the Weather"

■ A scale of wind velocity was devised by Admiral Sir Francis Beaufort of the British Navy in 1805. The numbers 0 to 12 were arranged by Beaufort to indicate the strength of the wind from a calm, force 0, to a hurricane, force 12. Here's a scale adapted to land.

Beaufort Force	Description	When You See This	Wind Speed mph	km/h
0	Calm	Smoke goes straight up. No wind.	less than 1	less than 2
1	Light air	Direction of wind is shown by smoke drift but not by wind vane.	1-3	2-5
2	Light breeze	Wind felt on face. Leaves rustle. Wind vane moves.	4-7	6-11
3	Gentle breeze	Leaves and small twigs move steadily. Wind extends small flag straight out.	8-12	12-19
4	Moderate breeze	Wind raises dust and loose paper. Small branches move.	13-18	20-29
5	Fresh breeze	Small trees sway. Waves form on lakes.	19-24	30-39
6	Strong breeze	Large branches move. Wires whistle. Umbrellas are hard to use.	25-31	40-50
7	Moderate gale	Whole trees are in motion. Hard to walk against the wind.	32-38	51-61
8	Fresh gale	Twigs break from trees. Very hard to walk against wind.	39-46	62-74
9	Strong gale	Small damage to buildings. Roof shingles are removed.	47-54	75-87
10	Whole gale	Trees are uprooted.	55-63	88-101
11	Violent storm	Widespread damage from wind.	64-72	102-116
12	Hurricane	Widespread destruction from wind.	73+	117+

Atlantic Hurricane Names for 2002

Arthur	Edouard	Josephine	Nana	Teddy
Bertha	Fay	Kyle	Omar	Vicky
Cristobal	Gustav	Lili	Paloma	Wilfred
Dolly	Hanna	Marco	Rene	
	Isidore		Sally	

East-Pacific Hurricane Names for 2002

Alma	Fausto	Kenna	Polo	Winnie
Boris	Genevieve	Lowell	Rachel	Xavier
Cristina	Hernan	Marie	Simon	Yolanda
Douglas	Iselle	Norbert	Trudy	Zeke
Elida	Julio	Odile	Vance	

Retired Atlantic Hurricane Names

■ These are some of the most destructive and costly storms whose names have been retired from the six-year rotating hurricane list.

Year Retired	Name	Year Retired	Name	Year Retired	Name
1970	Celia	1980	Allen	1990	Diana
1972	Agnes	1983	Alicia	1990	Klaus
1974	Carmen	1985	Elena	1991	Bob
1975	Eloise	1985	Gloria	1992	Andrew
1977	Anita	1988	Gilbert	1995	Opal
1979	David	1988	Joan	1995	Roxanne
1979	Frederic	1989	Hugo	1998	Mitch

Fujita Scale (or F Scale) for Measuring Tornadoes

■ This is a system developed by Dr. Theodore Fujita to classify tornadoes based on wind damage. All tornadoes, and most other severe local windstorms, are assigned a single number from this scale according to the most intense damage caused by the storm.

F0 (weak) ...... 40-72 mph, light damage
F1 (weak).. 73-112 mph, moderate damage
F2 (strong) .... 113-157 mph, considerable damage
F3 (strong) .. 158-206 mph, severe damage
F4 (violent) .... 207-260 mph, devastating damage
F5 (violent) .... 261-318 mph (rare), incredible damage

Richter Scale for Measuring Earthquakes

Magnitude	Possible Effects
1	Detectable only by instruments
2	Barely detectable, even near the epicenter
3	Felt indoors
4	Felt by most people; slight damage
5	Felt by all; minor to moderate damage
6	Moderately destructive
7	Major damage
8	Total and major damage

–devised by American geologist Charles W. Richter in 1935 to measure the magnitude of an earthquake

Winter Weather Terms

Winter Storm Watch
■ Possibility of a winter storm. Be alert to changing weather conditions. Avoid unnecessary travel.

Winter Storm Warning
■ A severe winter storm has started or is about to begin in the forecast area. You should stay indoors during the storm. If you must go outdoors, wear several layers of lightweight clothing, which will keep you warmer than a single heavy coat. In addition, wear gloves or mittens and a hat to prevent loss of body heat. Cover your mouth to protect your lungs.

Heavy Snow Warning
■ Snow accumulations are expected to approach or exceed six inches in 12 hours but will not be accompanied by significant wind. This warning could also be issued if eight inches or more of snow accumulation is expected in a 24-hour period. During a heavy snow warning, freezing rain and sleet are not expected.

Blizzard Warning
■ Sustained winds or frequent gusts of 35 miles per hour or greater will occur in combination with considerable falling and/or blowing snow for a period of at least three hours. Visibility will often be reduced to less than ¼ mile in a blizzard.

Ice Storm Warning
■ A significant coating of ice, ½ inch thick or more, is expected.

Windchill Warning
■ Windchills reach life-threatening levels of -50°F or lower.

Windchill Advisory
■ Windchill factors fall between -35° and -50°F.

Sleet
■ Frozen or partially frozen rain in the form of ice pellets hit the ground so fast they bounce off with a sharp click.

Freezing Rain
■ Rain falls as a liquid but turns to ice on contact with a frozen surface to form a smooth ice coating called glaze.

Safe Ice Thickness*

Ice Thickness	Permissible Load
2 inches	One person on foot
3 inches	Group in single file
7-1/2 inches	Passenger car (2-ton gross)
8 inches	Light truck (2-1/2-ton gross)
10 inches	Medium truck (3-1/2-ton gross)
12 inches	Heavy truck (8-ton gross)
15 inches	10 tons
20 inches	25 tons
30 inches	70 tons
36 inches	110 tons

*Solid clear blue/black pond and lake ice

■ Slush ice has only half the strength of blue ice.

■ Strength value of river ice is 15 percent less.

–courtesy American Pulpwood Association

Proper Canning Practices

- Carefully select and wash fresh food.
- Peel some fresh foods.
- Hot-pack many foods.
- Add acids (lemon juice or vinegar) to some foods.
- Use acceptable jars and self-sealing lids.
- Process jars in a boiling-water or pressure canner for the correct amount of time.

Quantities Needed for Canning

	Quantity per Quart Canned (pounds)		Quantity per Quart Canned (pounds)		Quantity per Quart Canned (pounds)

Fruits
Apples .... 2½ to 3
Blackberries .... 1½ to 3½
Blueberries....... 1½ to 3
Cherries .... 2 to 2½
Grapes 4
Peaches .... 2 to 3

Pears .... 2 to 3
Raspberries ...... 1½ to 3
Strawberries...... 1½ to 3

Vegetables
Asparagus ...... 2½ to 4½
Beans.......... 1½ to 2½
Beets........... 2 to 3½

Cauliflower 3
Corn .... 3 to 6
Peas.............. 3 to 6
Peppers............. 3
Spinach .... 2 to 3
Tomatoes....... 2½ to 3½

How to Order Two Bun Halves Filled with Cheese, Meat, Onions, Peppers, and Other Stuff

Place	Name	Place	Name
Norfolk, VA	Submarine	Norristown, PA	Zeppelin
Akron, OH	"	Mobile, AL	Poor boy
Jacksonville, FL	"	Sacramento, CA	"
Los Angeles, CA	"	Houston, TX	"
Philadelphia, PA	Hoagie	Montgomery, AL	"
Ann Arbor, MI	"	New Orleans, LA	Poor boy or muffuletta
Knoxville, TN	"	Gary, IN	Submarine or torpedo
Newark, NJ	"	Allentown, PA	Hoagie or Italian sandwich
Providence, RI	"	Cheyenne, WY	Hoagie, submarine, or rocket
Des Moines, IA	Grinder	Cincinnati, OH	Hoagie, submarine, or rocket
Hartford, CT	"	Buffalo, NY	Hoagie, submarine, or bomber
Chester, PA	"	Dublin, NH	Two bun halves filled with cheese, meat, onions, peppers, and other stuff
Cleveland, OH	"		
Madison, WI	Garibaldi		

Pan Sizes and Equivalents

■ In the midst of cooking but without the right pan? You can substitute one size for another, keeping in mind that when you change the pan size, you must sometimes change the cooking time. For example, if a recipe calls for using an 8-inch round cake pan and baking for 25 minutes, and you substitute a 9-inch pan, the cake may bake in only 20 minutes, because the batter forms a thinner layer in the larger pan. (Use a toothpick inserted into the center of the cake to test for doneness. If it comes out clean, the cake has finished baking.) Also, specialty pans such as tube and Bundt pans distribute heat differently; you may not get the same results if you substitute a regular cake pan for a specialty one, even if the volume is the same.

Pan Size	Volume	Substitute
9-inch pie pan	4 cups	■ 8-inch round cake pan
8x4x2-1/2-inch loaf pan	6 cups	■ Three 5x2-inch loaf pans ■ Two 3x1-1/4-inch muffin tins ■ 12x8x2-inch cake pan
9x5x3-inch loaf pan	8 cups	■ 8x8-inch cake pan ■ 9-inch round cake pan
15x10x1-inch jelly roll pan	10 cups	■ 9x9-inch cake pan ■ Two 8-inch round cake pans ■ 8x3-inch springform pan
10x3-inch Bundt pan	12 cups	■ Two 8x4x2-1/2-inch loaf pans ■ 9x3-inch angel food cake pan ■ 9x3-inch springform pan
13x9x2-inch cake pan	14-15 cups	■ Two 9-inch round cake pans ■ Two 8x8-inch cake pans

■ If you are cooking a casserole and don't have the correct size dish, here are some baking-pan substitutions. Again, think about the depth of the ingredients in the dish and lengthen or shorten the baking time accordingly.

CASSEROLE SIZE	BAKING-PAN SUBSTITUTE
1-1/2 quarts	9x5x3-inch loaf pan
2 quarts	8x8-inch cake pan
2-1/2 quarts	9x9-inch cake pan
3 quarts	13x9x2-inch cake pan
4 quarts	14x10x2-inch cake pan

Food for Thought

FOOD	CALORIES
Piece of pecan pie	580
Grilled cheese sandwich	440
Chocolate shake	364
Bagel with cream cheese	361
20 potato chips	228
10 french fries	214
Half a cantaloupe	94
Corn on the cob (no butter)	70
Carrot	30

Don't Freeze These

Bananas
Canned hams
Cooked eggs
Cooked potatoes
Cream fillings and puddings
Custards
Fried foods
Gelatin dishes
Mayonnaise
Raw vegetables, such as cabbage, celery, green onions, radishes, and salad greens
Soft cheeses, cottage cheese
Sour cream
Yogurt

Appetizer Amounts

Occasion	Number of Bites per Person
Hors d'oeuvres (with meal following)	4
Cocktail party	10
Grand affair, no dinner following (e.g., wedding reception)	10-15

The Party Planner

How much do you need when you're cooking for a crowd?

■ If you're planning a big meal, these estimates can help you determine how much food you should buy. They're based on "average" servings; adjust quantities upward for extra-big eaters and downward if children are included.

Food	To Serve 25	To Serve 50	To Serve 100
MEATS			
Chicken or turkey breast	12-1/2 pounds	25 pounds	50 pounds
Fish (fillets or steaks)	7-1/2 pounds	15 pounds	30 pounds
Hamburgers	8 to 9 pounds	15 to 18 pounds	30 to 36 pounds
Ham or roast beef	10 pounds	20 pounds	40 pounds
Hot dogs	6 pounds	12-1/2 pounds	25 pounds
Meat loaf	6 pounds	12 pounds	24 pounds
Oysters	1 gallon	2 gallons	4 gallons
Pork	10 pounds	20 pounds	40 pounds
MISCELLANEOUS			
Bread (loaves)	3	5	10
Butter	3/4 pound	1-1/2 pounds	3 pounds
Cheese	3/4 pound	1-1/2 pounds	3 pounds
Coffee	3/4 pound	1-1/2 pounds	3 pounds
Milk	1-1/2 gallons	3 gallons	6 gallons
Nuts	3/4 pound	1-1/2 pounds	3 pounds
Olives	1/2 pound	1 pound	2 pounds
Pickles	1/2 quart	1 quart	2 quarts
Rolls	50	100	200
Soup	5 quarts	2-1/2 gallons	5 gallons
SIDE DISHES			
Baked beans	5 quarts	2-1/2 gallons	5 gallons
Beets	7-1/2 pounds	15 pounds	30 pounds
Cabbage for cole slaw	5 pounds	10 pounds	20 pounds
Carrots	7-1/2 pounds	15 pounds	30 pounds
Lettuce for salad (heads)	5	10	20
Peas (fresh)	12 pounds	25 pounds	50 pounds
Potatoes	9 pounds	18 pounds	36 pounds
Potato salad	3 quarts	1-1/2 gallons	3 gallons
Salad dressing	3 cups	1-1/2 quarts	3 quarts
DESSERTS			
Cakes	2	4	8
Ice cream	1 gallon	2 gallons	4 gallons
Pies	4	9	18
Whipping cream	1 pint	2 pints	4 pints

Substitutions for Common Ingredients

ITEM	QUANTITY	SUBSTITUTION
Allspice	1 teaspoon	½ teaspoon cinnamon plus ⅛ teaspoon ground cloves
Arrowroot, as thickener	1½ teaspoons	1 tablespoon flour
Baking powder	1 teaspoon	¼ teaspoon baking soda plus ⅝ teaspoon cream of tartar
Bread crumbs, dry	¼ cup	1 slice bread
Bread crumbs, soft	½ cup	1 slice bread
Buttermilk	1 cup	1 cup plain yogurt
Chocolate, unsweetened	1 ounce	3 tablespoons cocoa plus 1 tablespoon butter or fat
Cracker crumbs	¾ cup	1 cup dry bread crumbs
Cream, heavy	1 cup	¾ cup milk plus ⅓ cup melted butter (this will not whip)
Cream, light	1 cup	⅞ cup milk plus 3 tablespoons melted butter
Cream, sour	1 cup	⅞ cup buttermilk or plain yogurt plus 3 tablespoons melted butter
Cream, whipping	1 cup	⅔ cup well-chilled evaporated milk, whipped; **or** 1 cup nonfat dry milk powder whipped with 1 cup ice water
Egg	1 whole	2 yolks
Flour, all-purpose	1 cup	1⅛ cups cake flour; **or** ⅝ cup potato flour; **or** 1¼ cups rye or coarsely ground whole grain flour; **or** 1 cup cornmeal
Flour, cake	1 cup	1 cup minus 2 tablespoons sifted all-purpose flour
Flour, self-rising	1 cup	1 cup all-purpose flour plus 1¼ teaspoons baking powder plus ¼ teaspoon salt
Garlic	1 small clove	⅛ teaspoon garlic powder; **or** ½ teaspoon instant minced garlic
Herbs, dried	½ to 1 teaspoon	1 tablespoon fresh, minced and packed
Honey	1 cup	1¼ cups sugar plus ½ cup liquid

Measuring Vegetables

Asparagus: 1 pound = 3 cups chopped

Beans (string): 1 pound = 4 cups chopped

Beets: 1 pound (5 medium) = 2-1/2 cups chopped

Broccoli: 1/2 pound = 6 cups chopped

Cabbage: 1 pound = 4-1/2 cups shredded

Carrots: 1 pound = 3-1/2 cups sliced or grated

Celery: 1 pound = 4 cups chopped

Cucumbers: 1 pound (2 medium) = 4 cups sliced

Eggplant: 1 pound = 4 cups chopped (6 cups raw, cubed = 3 cups cooked)

Garlic: 1 clove = 1 teaspoon chopped

Leeks: 1 pound = 4 cups chopped (2 cups cooked)

Mushrooms: 1 pound = 5 to 6 cups sliced = 2 cups cooked

Onions: 1 pound = 4 cups sliced = 2 cups cooked

Parsnips: 1 pound unpeeled = 1-1/2 cups cooked, pureed

Peas: 1 pound whole = 1 to 1-1/2 cups shelled

Potatoes: 1 pound (3 medium) sliced = 2 cups mashed

Pumpkin: 1 pound = 4 cups chopped = 2 cups cooked and drained

Spinach: 1 pound = 3/4 to 1 cup cooked

ITEM	QUANTITY	SUBSTITUTION
Lemon	1	1 to 3 tablespoons juice, 1 to 1½ teaspoons grated rind
Lemon juice	1 teaspoon	½ teaspoon vinegar
Lemon rind, grated	1 teaspoon	½ teaspoon lemon extract
Milk, skim	1 cup	⅓ cup instant nonfat dry milk plus about ¾ cup water
Milk, to sour	1 cup	Add 1 tablespoon vinegar or lemon juice to 1 cup milk minus 1 tablespoon. Stir and let stand 5 minutes.
Milk, whole	1 cup	½ cup evaporated milk plus ½ cup water; **or** 1 cup skim milk plus 2 teaspoons melted butter
Molasses	1 cup	1 cup honey
Mustard, prepared	1 tablespoon	1 teaspoon dry or powdered mustard
Onion, chopped	1 small	1 tablespoon instant minced onion; **or** 1 teaspoon onion powder; **or** ¼ cup frozen chopped onion
Sugar, granulated	1 cup	1 cup firmly packed brown sugar; **or** 1¾ cups confectioners' sugar (do not substitute in baking); **or** 2 cups corn syrup; **or** 1 cup superfine sugar
Tomatoes, canned	1 cup	½ cup tomato sauce plus ½ cup water; **or** 1⅓ cups chopped fresh tomatoes, simmered
Tomato juice	1 cup	½ cup tomato sauce plus ½ cup water plus dash each salt and sugar; **or** ¼ cup tomato paste plus ¾ cup water plus salt and sugar
Tomato ketchup	½ cup	½ cup tomato sauce plus 2 tablespoons sugar, 1 tablespoon vinegar, and ⅛ teaspoon ground cloves
Tomato puree	1 cup	½ cup tomato paste plus ½ cup water
Tomato soup	1 can (10¾ oz.)	1 cup tomato sauce plus ¼ cup water
Vanilla	1-inch bean	1 teaspoon vanilla extract
Yeast	1 cake (⅗ oz.)	1 package active dried yeast (1 scant tablespoon)
Yogurt, plain	1 cup	1 cup buttermilk

Squash (summer): 1 pound = 4 cups grated = 2 cups salted and drained

Squash (winter): 2 pounds = 2-1/2 cups cooked, pureed

Sweet potatoes: 1 pound = 4 cups grated = 1 cup cooked, pureed

Swiss chard: 1 pound = 5 to 6 cups packed leaves = 1 to 1-1/2 cups cooked

Tomatoes: 1 pound (3 or 4 medium) = 1-1/2 cups seeded pulp

Turnips: 1 pound = 4 cups chopped = 2 cups cooked, mashed

Measuring Fruits

Apples: 1 pound (3 or 4 medium) = 3 cups sliced

Bananas: 1 pound (3 or 4 medium) = 1-3/4 cups mashed

Berries: 1 quart = 3-1/2 cups

Dates: 1 pound = 2-1/2 cups pitted

Lemon: 1 whole = 1 to 3 tablespoons juice; 1 to 1-1/2 teaspoons grated rind

Lime: 1 whole = 1-1/2 to 2 tablespoons juice

Orange: 1 medium = 6 to 8 tablespoons juice; 2 to 3 tablespoons grated rind

Peaches: 1 pound (4 medium) = 3 cups sliced

Pears: 1 pound (4 medium) = 2 cups sliced

Rhubarb: 1 pound = 2 cups cooked

Strawberries: 1 quart = 3 cups sliced

Substitutions for Uncommon Ingredients

Cooking an ethnic dish but can't find a special ingredient?
Here are a few ideas for alternatives.

ITEM	SUBSTITUTION
Balsamic vinegar, 1 tablespoon	1 tablespoon red wine vinegar plus ½ teaspoon sugar
Bamboo shoots	Asparagus (in fried dishes)
Bergamot	Mint
Chayotes	Yellow summer squash **or** zucchini
Cilantro	Parsley (for color only; flavor cannot be duplicated)
Coconut milk	2½ cups water plus 2 cups shredded, unsweetened coconut. Combine and bring to a boil. Remove from heat; cool. Mix in a blender for 2 minutes; strain. Makes about 2 cups.
Delicata squash	Butternut squash **or** sweet potato
Green mangoes	Sour, green cooking apples
Habanero peppers	5 jalapeño peppers **or** serrano peppers
Italian seasoning	Equal parts basil, marjoram, oregano, rosemary, sage, and thyme
Lemon grass	Lemon zest (zest from 1 lemon equals 2 stalks lemon grass)
Limes or lime juice	Lemons or lemon juice
Lo Mein noodles	Egg noodles
Mascarpone, 1 cup	3 tablespoons heavy cream plus ¾ cup cream cheese plus 4 tablespoons butter
Neufchâtel	Cream cheese **or** Boursin
Palm sugar	Light brown sugar
Rice wine	Pale, dry sherry **or** white vermouth
Red peppers	Equal amount pimientos
Romano cheese	Parmesan cheese
Saffron	Turmeric (for color; flavor is different)
Shallots	Red onions **or** Spanish onions
Shrimp paste	Anchovy paste
Tamarind juice	5 parts ketchup to 1 part vinegar

Knots

overhand knot   figure-eight knot   granny knot   square knot

common whipping   cow hitch   clove hitch   fisherman's knot

sheet bend   double sheet bend   running bowline   bowline

bowline on a bight   sheepshank   heaving line knot

INCHES		1		2		3		4
CENTIMETERS	1 2	3	4 5	6	7 8	9	10	

Makeshift Measurers

■ When you don't have a measuring stick or tape, use what is at hand. To this list, add any other items that you always (or nearly always) have handy.

Credit card: 3-3/8" x 2-1/8"
Business card (standard): 3-1/2" x 2"
Floor tile: 12" square
Dollar bill: 6-1/8" x 2-5/8"
Quarter (diameter): 1"
Penny (diameter): 3/4"
Sheet of paper: 8-1/2" x 11"
   (legal size: 8-1/2" x 14")

Your foot/shoe: _____

Your outstretched arms, fingertip to fingertip:

_____

Your shoelace: _____

Your necktie: _____

Your belt: _____

Hand Thermometer for Outdoor Cooking

■ Hold your palm close to where the food will be cooking: over the coals or in front of a reflector oven. Count "one-and-one, two-and-two," and so on, for as many seconds as you can hold your hand still.

Seconds Counted	Heat	Temperature
6-8	Slow	250°-350°F
4-5	Moderate	350°-400°F
2-3	Hot	400°-450°F
1 or less	Very hot	450°-500°F

Life Expectancy by Current Age

If your age now is . . .   **You can expect to live to age . . .**

	Men	Women
0	72	79
20	74	80
25	74	80
30	75	80
35	75	81
40	76	81
45	76	81
50	77	82
55	78	82
60	79	83
65	80	84
70	82	86
75	85	87
80	87	89
85	90	92

–courtesy U.S. Department of Health and Human Services, 1995

Is It a Cold or the Flu?

Symptoms	Flu	Cold	Allergy	Sinusitis
Headache	Always	Occasionally	Occasionally	Always
Muscle aches	Always	Usually	Rarely	Rarely
Fatigue, weakness	Always	Usually	Rarely	Rarely
Fever	Always	Occasionally	Never	Occasionally
Cough	Usually	Occasionally	Occasionally	Usually
Runny, stuffy nose	Occasionally	Usually	Usually	Always
Nasal discharge	Occasionally	Usually	Usually	Always
Sneezing	Rarely	Occasionally	Usually	Rarely
Sore throat	Rarely	Usually	Occasionally	Rarely
Itchy eyes, nose, throat	Rarely	Rarely	Usually	Never

Are You Skinny, Just Right, or Overweight?

■ Here's an easy formula to figure your Body Mass Index (BMI), now thought to be a more accurate indicator of relative body size than the old insurance charts. **W** is your weight in pounds and **H** is your height in inches.

$$BMI = \frac{(W \times 705) \div H}{H}$$

■ If the result is 25 or less, you are within a healthy weight range.

■ If it's 19 or below, you are too skinny.

■ Between 25 and 27, you are as much as 8 percent over your healthy weight.

■ Between 27 and 30, you are at increased risk for health problems.

■ Above 30, you are more than 20 percent over your healthy weight. It puts you at a dramatically increased risk for serious health problems.

There are a couple of exceptions to the above. Very muscular people with a high BMI generally have nothing to worry about, and extreme skinniness is generally a symptom of some other health problem, not the cause.

Here's another way to see if you are dangerously overweight. Measure your waistline. A waist measurement of 35 inches or more in women and 41 inches or more in men, regardless of height, suggests a serious risk of weight-related health problems.

Calorie Burning

■ If you hustle through your chores to get to the fitness center, relax. You're getting a great workout already. The left-hand column lists "chore" exercises, the middle column shows number of calories you burn per minute per pound of your body weight, the right-hand column lists comparable "recreational" exercises. For example, a 150-pound person forking straw bales burns 9.45 calories per minute, the same workout he/she would get playing basketball.

Chore	Calories	Recreational
Chopping with an ax, fast.	0.135	Skiing, cross country, uphill
Climbing hills, with 44-pound load	0.066	Swimming, crawl, fast
Digging trenches	0.065	Skiing, cross country, steady walk
Forking straw bales	0.063	Basketball
Chopping down trees	0.060	Football
Climbing hills, with 9-pound load	0.058	Swimming, crawl, slow
Sawing by hand	0.055	Skiing, cross country, moderate
Mowing lawns	0.051	Horseback riding, trotting
Scrubbing floors	0.049	Tennis
Shoveling coal	0.049	Aerobic dance, medium
Hoeing	0.041	Weight training, circuit training
Stacking firewood	0.040	Weight lifting, free weights
Shoveling grain	0.038	Golf
Painting houses	0.035	Walking, normal pace, asphalt road
Weeding	0.033	Table tennis
Shopping for food	0.028	Cycling, 5.5 mph
Mopping floors	0.028	Fishing
Washing windows	0.026	Croquet
Raking	0.025	Dancing, ballroom
Driving a tractor	0.016	Drawing, standing position

How Much Paint Will You Need?

■ Estimate your room size and paint needs before you go to the store. Running out of a custom color halfway through the job could mean disaster. For the sake of the following exercise, assume you have a 10x15-foot room with an 8-foot ceiling. The room has two doors and two windows.

For Walls

■ Measure the total distance (perimeter) around the room:
(10 ft. + 15 ft.) x 2 = 50 ft.

■ Multiply the perimeter by the ceiling height to get the total wall area:
50 ft. x 8 ft. = 400 sq. ft.

■ Doors are usually 21 square feet (there are two in this exercise):
21 sq. ft. x 2 = 42 sq. ft.

■ Windows average 15 square feet (there are two in this exercise):
15 sq. ft. x 2 = 30 sq. ft.

■ Take the total wall area and subtract the area for the doors and windows to get the wall surface to be painted:
400 sq. ft. (wall area)
– 42 sq. ft. (doors)
– 30 sq. ft. (windows)
_____
328 sq. ft.

■ As a rule of thumb, one gallon of quality paint will usually cover 400 square feet. One quart will cover 100 square feet. Since you need to cover 328 square feet in this example, one gallon will be adequate to give one coat of paint to the walls. (Coverage will be affected by the porosity and texture of the surface. In addition, bright colors may require a minimum of two coats.)

For Ceilings

■ Using the rule of thumb for coverage above, you can calculate the quantity of paint needed for the ceiling by multiplying the width by the length:
10 ft. x 15 ft. = 150 sq. ft.

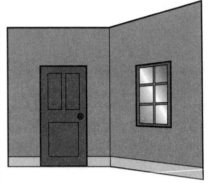

This ceiling will require approximately two quarts of paint. (A flat finish is recommended to minimize surface imperfections.)

For Doors, Windows, and Trim

■ The area for the doors and windows has been calculated above. Determine the baseboard trim by taking the perimeter of the room, less 3 feet per door (3 ft. x 2 = 6 ft.), and multiplying this by the average trim width of your baseboard, which in this example is 6 inches (or 0.5 feet).

50 ft. (perimeter) - 6 ft. = 44 ft.
44 ft. x 0.5 ft. = 22 sq. ft.

■ Add the area for doors, windows, and baseboard trim.
42 sq. ft. (doors)
+30 sq. ft. (windows)
+22 sq. ft. (baseboard trim)
_____
94 sq. ft.

One quart will probably be sufficient to cover the doors, windows, and trim in this example.

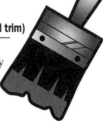

–courtesy M.A.B. Paints

Exterior Paint

■ Here's how to estimate the number of gallons needed for one-coat coverage of a home that is 20 feet wide by 40 feet long, has walls that rise 16 feet to the eaves on the 40-foot sides, and has full-width gables on the 20-foot sides rising 10 feet to the peaks.

■ First, find the area of the walls. Add the width to the length:

20 ft. + 40 ft. = 60 ft.

Double it for four sides:

60 ft. x 2 = 120 ft.

Multiply that by the height of the walls:

120 ft. x 16 ft. = 1,920 sq. ft.

The area of the walls is 1,920 square feet.

■ Next, find the area of the gables. Take half the width of one gable at its base:

20 ft. ÷ 2 = 10 ft.

Multiply that by the height of the gable:

10 ft. x 10 ft. = 100 sq. ft.

Multiply that by the number of gables:

100 sq. ft. x 2 = 200 sq. ft.

The area of the gables is 200 square feet.

■ Add the two figures together for the total area:

1,920 sq. ft. + 200 sq. ft. = 2,120 sq. ft.

■ Finally, divide the total area by the area covered by a gallon of paint (400 square feet) to find the number of gallons needed:

2,120 sq. ft. ÷ 400 sq. ft./gal. = 5.3 gal.

Buy five gallons of paint to start with. The sixth gallon might not be necessary.

How Much Wallpaper Will You Need?

■ Measure the length of each wall, add these figures together, and multiply by the height of the walls to get the area (square footage) of the room.

■ Calculate the square footage of each door, window, or other opening in the room. Add these figures together and subtract the total from the area of the room.

■ Take that figure and multiply by 1.15, to account for a waste rate of about 15 percent in your wallpaper project.

■ Wallpaper is sold in single, double, and triple rolls. (Average coverage for a double roll, for example, is 56 square feet.) Divide the coverage figure (from the label) into the total square footage of the room you're papering. Round the answer up to the nearest whole number. This is the number of rolls you need to buy.

■ Save leftover wallpaper rolls, carefully wrapped to keep them clean.

Guide to Lumber and Nails

Lumber Width and Thickness (in inches)

NOMINAL SIZE	ACTUAL SIZE Dry or Seasoned
1 x 3	¾ x 2½
1 x 4	¾ x 3½
1 x 6	¾ x 5½
1 x 8	¾ x 7¼
1 x 10	¾ x 9¼
1 x 12	¾ x 11¼
2 x 3	1½ x 2½
2 x 4	1½ x 3½
2 x 6	1½ x 5½
2 x 8	1½ x 7¼
2 x 10	1½ x 9¼
2 x 12	1½ x 11¼

Nail Sizes

The nail on the left is a 5d (penny) finish nail; on the right, 20d common. The numerals below the nail sizes indicate the approximate number of common nails per pound.

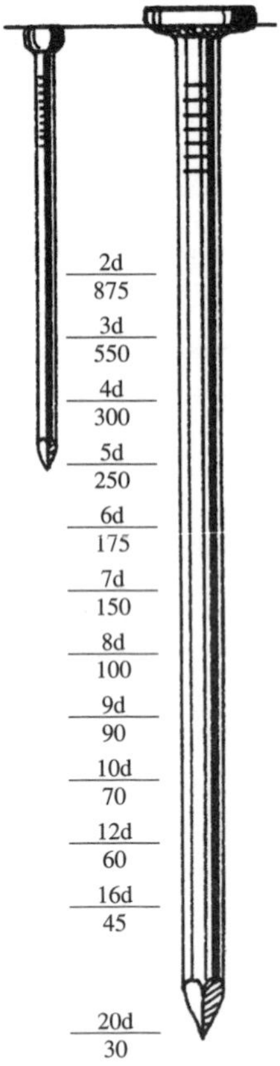

2d	875
3d	550
4d	300
5d	250
6d	175
7d	150
8d	100
9d	90
10d	70
12d	60
16d	45
20d	30

Lumber Measure in Board Feet

Size in Inches	12 ft.	14 ft.	16 ft.	18 ft.	20 ft.
1 x 4	4	4⅔	5⅓	6	6⅔
1 x 6	6	7	8	9	10
1 x 8	8	9⅓	10⅔	12	13⅓
1 x 10	10	11⅔	13⅓	15	16⅔
1 x 12	12	14	16	18	20
2 x 3	6	7	8	9	10
2 x 4	8	9⅓	10⅔	12	13⅓
2 x 6	12	14	16	18	20
2 x 8	16	18⅔	21⅓	24	26⅔
2 x 10	20	23⅓	26⅔	30	33⅓
2 x 12	24	28	32	36	40
4 x 4	16	18⅔	21⅓	24	26⅔
6 x 6	36	42	48	54	60
8 x 8	64	74⅔	85⅓	96	106⅔
10 x 10	100	116⅔	133⅓	150	166⅔
12 x 12	144	168	192	216	240

Firewood Heat Values

High Heat Value

1 CORD = 200-250 GALLONS OF FUEL OIL

American beech
Apple
Ironwood
Red oak
Shagbark hickory
Sugar maple
White ash
White oak
Yellow birch

Medium Heat Value

1 CORD = 150-200 GALLONS OF FUEL OIL

American elm
Black cherry
Douglas fir
Red maple
Silver maple
Tamarack
White birch

Low Heat Value

1 CORD = 100-150 GALLONS OF FUEL OIL

Aspen
Cottonwood
Hemlock
Lodgepole pine
Red alder
Redwood
Sitka spruce
Western red cedar
White pine

How Many Trees in a Cord of Wood?

Diameter of Tree (breast high, in inches)	Number of Trees (per cord)
4	50
6	20
8	10
10	6
12	4
14	3

Heat Values of Fuels
(approximate)

Fuel	BTU	Unit of Measure
Oil	141,000	Gallon
Coal	31,000	Pound
Natural gas	1,000	Cubic foot
Steam	1,000	Cubic foot
Electricity	3,413	Kilowatt-hour
Gasoline	124,000	Gallon

How to Find the Number of Bricks in a Wall or Building

(Or how to estimate how many nonmodular standard bricks will be needed for a project.)

Rule

■ Multiply the length of the wall in feet by its height in feet, and that by its thickness in feet, and then multiply that result by 20. The answer will be the number of bricks in the wall.

Example

■ 30 feet (length) x 20 feet (height) x 1 foot (thickness) = 600 x 20 = 12,000 bricks

Animal Terminology

Animal	Male	Female	Young
Ant	Male ant (reproductive)	Queen (reproductive), worker (nonreproductive)	Antling
Antelope	Ram	Ewe	Calf, fawn, kid, yearling
Ass	Jack, jackass	Jenny	Foal
Bear	Boar, he-bear	Sow, she-bear	Cub
Beaver	Boar	Sow	Kit, kitten
Bee	Drone	Queen or queen bee, worker (nonreproductive)	Larva
Buffalo	Bull	Cow	Calf, yearling, spike-bull
Camel	Bull	Cow	Calf, colt
Caribou	Bull, stag, hart	Cow, doe	Calf, fawn
Cat	Tom, tomcat, gib, gibcat, boarcat, ramcat	Tabby, grimalkin, malkin, pussy, queen	Kitten, kit, kitling, kitty, pussy
Cattle	Bull	Cow	Calf, stot, yearling, bullcalf, heifer
Chicken	Rooster, cock, stag, chanticleer	Hen, partlet, biddy	Chick, chicken, poult, cockerel, pullet
Deer	Buck, stag	Doe	Fawn
Dog	Dog	Bitch	Whelp
Duck	Drake, stag	Duck	Duckling, flapper
Elephant	Bull	Cow	Calf
Fox	Dog	Vixen	Kit, pup, cub
Giraffe	Bull	Cow	Calf
Goat	Buck, billy, billie, billy goat, he-goat	She-goat, nanny, nannie, nanny goat	Kid
Goose	Gander, stag	Goose, dame	Gosling
Horse	Stallion, stag, horse, stud	Mare, dam	Colt, foal, stot, stag, filly, hog-colt, hogget
Kangaroo	Buck	Doe	Joey
Leopard	Leopard	Leopardess	Cub
Lion	Lion, tom	Lioness, she-lion	Shelp, cub, lionet
Moose	Bull	Cow	Calf
Partridge	Cock	Hen	Cheeper
Quail	Cock	Hen	Cheeper, chick, squealer
Reindeer	Buck	Doe	Fawn
Seal	Bull	Cow	Whelp, pup, cub, bachelor
Sheep	Buck, ram, male sheep, mutton	Ewe, dam	Lamb, lambkin, shearling, yearling, cosset, hog
Swan	Cob	Pen	Cygnet
Swine	Boar	Sow	Shoat, trotter, pig, piglet, farrow, suckling
Termite	King	Queen	Nymph
Walrus	Bull	Cow	Cub
Whale	Bull	Cow	Calf
Zebra	Stallion	Mare	Colt, foal

Collective
Colony, nest, army, state, swarm
Herd
Pace, drove, herd
Sleuth, sloth
Family, colony
Swarm, grist, cluster, nest, hive, erst
Troop, herd, gang
Flock, train, caravan
Herd
Clowder, clutter (kindle or kendle of kittens)
Drove, herd
Flock, run, brood, clutch, peep
Herd, leash
Pack (cry or mute of hounds, leash of greyhounds)
Brace, team, paddling, raft, bed, flock, flight
Herd
Leash, skulk, cloud, troop
Herd, corps, troop
Tribe, trip, flock, herd
Flock (on land), gaggle, skein (in flight), gaggle or plump (on water)
Haras, stable, remuda, herd, string, field, set, pair, team
Mob, troop, herd
Leap
Pride, troop, flock, sawt, souse
Herd
Covey
Bevy, covey
Herd
Pod, herd, trip, rookery, harem
Flock, drove, hirsel, trip, pack
Herd, team, bank, wege, bevy
Drift, sounder, herd, trip (litter of pigs)
Colony, nest, swarm, brood
Pod, herd
Gam, pod, school, herd
Herd

More Animal Collectives

army of caterpillars, frogs
bale of turtles
band of gorillas
bed of clams, oysters
brood of jellyfish
business of flies
cartload of monkeys
cast of hawks
cete of badgers
charm of goldfinches
chatter of budgerigars
cloud of gnats, flies, grasshoppers, locusts
colony of penguins
congregation of plovers
convocation of eagles
crash of rhinoceri
descent of woodpeckers
dole of turtles
down of hares
dray of squirrels
dule of turtle doves
exaltation of larks
family of sardines
flight of birds
flock of lice
gang of elks
hatch of flies
horde of gnats
host of sparrows

hover of trout
husk of hares
knab of toads
knot of toads, snakes
murder of crows
murmuration of starlings
mustering of storks
nest of vipers
nest or nide of pheasants
pack of weasels
pladge of wasps
plague of locusts
scattering of herons
sedge or siege of cranes
smuck of jellyfish
span of mules
spring of teals
steam of minnows
tittering of magpies
troop of monkeys
troubling of goldfish
volery of birds
watch of nightingales
wing of plovers
yoke of oxen

All About Dogs

Smartest Breeds	Most Popular Breeds	Top Dog Names (U.S.)	Top Dog Names (Can.)
Border collie	Labrador retriever	Lady	Buddy
Poodle	Rottweiler	King	Lady
German shepherd	Cocker spaniel	Duke	Brandy
(Alsatian)	German shepherd	Peppy	Bear
Golden retriever	Poodle	Prince	Max
Doberman pinscher	Golden retriever	Pepper	Shadow
Shetland sheepdog	Beagle	Snoopy	Misty
Labrador retriever	Dachshund	Princess	Bailey
Papillon	Shetland sheepdog	Heidi	Sandy
Rottweiler	Chow chow	Sam/Coco	Sheba
Australian cattle dog			

Don't Poison Your Pussycat!

■ Certain common houseplants are poisonous to cats. They should not be allowed to eat the following:

- Azalea *(Rhododendron)*
- Common or cherry laurel *(Prunus laurocerasus)*
- Dumb cane *(Dieffenbachia)*
- Elephant's ears *(Caladium)*
- Mistletoe *(Ficus deltoidea)*
- Oleander *(Nerium oleander)*
- Philodendron *(Philodendron)*
- True ivy *(Hedera)*
- Winter or false Jerusalem cherry *(Solanum capiscastrum)*

Ten Most Intelligent Animals

(not including humans)

■ According to Edward O. Wilson, behavioral biologist, professor of zoology, Harvard University, they are:

1. Chimpanzee (two species)
2. Gorilla
3. Orangutan
4. Baboon (seven species, including drill and mandrill)
5. Gibbon (seven species)
6. Monkey (many species, especially the macaques, the patas, and the Celebes black ape)
7. Smaller toothed whale (several species, especially killer whale)
8. Dolphin (many of the approximately 80 species)
9. Elephant (two species)
10. Pig

Nutritional Value of Various Insects per 100 Grams

Insect	Protein (g)	Fat (g)	Carbohydrate (g)	Calcium (mg)	Iron (mg)
Giant water beetle	19.8	8.3	2.1	43.5	13.6
Red ant	13.9	3.5	2.9	47.8	5.7
Silkworm pupa	9.6	5.6	2.3	41.7	1.8
Dung beetle	17.2	4.3	0.2	30.9	7.7
Cricket	12.9	5.5	5.1	75.8	9.5
Small grasshopper	20.6	6.1	3.9	35.2	5.0
Large grasshopper	14.3	3.3	2.2	27.5	3.0
June beetle	13.4	1.4	2.9	22.6	6.0
Termite	14.2	—		—	35.5
Weevil	6.7	—		—	13.1
Compared with:					
Beef (lean ground)	27.4	—	—	—	3.5
Fish (broiled cod)	28.5	—	—	—	1.0

–courtesy Department of Entomology, Iowa State University

Food for Birds

	Sunflower seeds	Millet (white proso)	Niger (thistle seeds)	Safflower seeds	Corn, cracked	Corn, whole	Peanuts	Peanut butter	Suet	Raisins	Apples	Oranges and grapefruit
Blue jay	■			■	■	■	■			■		
Bunting	■	■	■	■	■							
Cardinal	■	■		■	■					■	■	■
Catbird										■	■	■
Cedar waxwing											■	■
Chickadee	■	■		■	■		■	■	■			
Cowbird		■										
Crossbill	■	■		■				■				
Duck		■			■	■						
Finch	■	■	■	■	■		■	■				■
Flicker							■	■	■			
Goldfinch	■		■									
Goose					■	■						
Grackle	■											
Grosbeak	■	■		■			■			■	■	■
Junco	■	■	■	■	■							
Mockingbird										■	■	
Mourning dove	■	■		■	■	■	■					
Nuthatch	■	■		■			■	■	■			
Oriole												■
Pheasant					■							
Pine siskin	■	■	■	■			■			■		■
Redpoll	■	■	■	■								
Sparrow	■	■		■	■		■					
Starling					■							
Tanager												■
Thrasher					■		■			■	■	
Thrush										■	■	
Titmouse	■	■		■	■		■	■	■			
Towhee		■										
Warbler							■					■
Woodpecker							■	■	■			

Know Your Angels

I. First Group— nearest to God
Seraphim
Cherubim
Thrones

II. Second Group— receives the reflection of Divine Presence from the first group
Dominions
Virtues
Powers

III. Angelic Group— ministers directly to human beings
Principalities
Archangels
Angels

Famous Last Words of Real People

"My exit is the result of too many entrees."
–Richard Monckton Milnes (Victorian politician)

"I'm dying, as I have lived, beyond my means."
–Oscar Wilde (Irish poet)

"I am going to the great perhaps."
–Rabelais (writer, priest, physician)

"Well, if this is dying, there is nothing unpleasant about it."
–Maria Mitchell (professor of astronomy)

"Oh, God, here I go!"
–Max Baer (heavyweight boxing champion of the world, 1934–1935)

"I am about to—or I am going to—die: either expression is used."
–Dominique Bouhours (philosopher and grammarian)

". . . the fog is rising." –Emily Dickinson (American poet)

The Golden Rule
(It's true in all faiths.)

Brahmanism:
This is the sum of duty: Do naught unto others which would cause you pain if done to you.
Mahabharata 5:1517

Buddhism:
Hurt not others in ways that you yourself would find hurtful.
Udana-Varga 5:18

Confucianism:
Surely it is the maxim of loving-kindness: Do not unto others what you would not have them do unto you.
Analects 15:23

Taoism:
Regard your neighbor's gain as your own gain and your neighbor's loss as your own loss.
T'ai Shang Kan Ying P'ien

Zoroastrianism:
That nature alone is good which refrains from doing unto another whatsoever is not good for itself.
Dadistan-i-dinik 94:5

Judaism:
What is hateful to you, do not to your fellowman. That is the entire Law; all the rest is commentary.
Talmud, Shabbat 31a

Christianity:
All things whatsoever ye would that men should do to you, do ye even so to them; for this is the law and the prophets.
Matthew 7:12

Islam:
No one of you is a believer until he desires for his brother that which he desires for himself.
Sunnah
–courtesy Elizabeth Pool